THE
BIG
BASICS
BOOK OF
WORD FOR
WINDOWS® 95

by Sandy Eddy Schnyder, David Haskin,
and Ed Guilford

que®

A Division of Macmillan Computer Publishing
201 West 103rd Street, Indianapolis, Indiana 46290 USA

International Standard Book Number:0-7897-0460-9
Library of Congress Catalog Card Number: 95-72554

97 96 95   8 7 6 5 4 3 2 1

Interpretation of the printing code: the rightmost number of the first series of numbers is the year of the book's printing; the rightmost number of the second series of numbers is the number of the book's printing. For example, a printing code of 95-1 shows that the first printing of the book occurred in 1995.

Screen reproductions in this book were created by means of the program Collage Complete from Inner Media, Inc., Hollis, NH.

Printed in the United States of America

President
Roland Elgey

Vice President and Publisher
Marie Butler-Knight

Editorial Services Director
Elizabeth Keaffaber

Publishing Manager
Barry Pruett

Managing Editor
Michael Cunningham

Development Editor
Heather Stith

Technical Editor
C. Herbert Feltner

Production Editor
Phil Kitchel

Copy Editor
San Dee Phillips

Cover Designer
Jay Corpus

Book Designer
Barbara Kordesh

Indexer
Ginny Bess

Production Team
Claudia Bell
Brian Buschkill
Jason Hand
Bill Hartman
John Hulse
Clint Lahnen
Bob LaRoche
Stephanie Layton
Michelle Lee
Laura Robbins
Bobbi Satterfield
Michael Thomas
Scott Tullis
Kelly Warner
Todd Wente
Suzanne Whitmer

Contents

Part 1 How To...

Format Pages and Paragraphs   141

Enhance a Document   169

Work with Tables   201

Add Graphics to a Document   **239**

Use Mail Merge   **285**

Automate Work with a Macro   **299**

Part 2   Do It Yourself...

Customize Your Workspace   **311**

Part 3   Quick Fixes...

Part 4   Handy References

Handy Reference   535

Introduction

Word processors, such as Word for Windows 95, are perhaps the most useful and most-used applications on computers today. You can use Word for Windows 95 for all your word processing and desktop publishing needs. However, if you are a new user, you may need a little help.

Why This Book?

When you first use Word for Windows 95, you may search for an all-purpose book that shows you, step-by-step, how to use and manage Word features and to create Word documents. With the *Big Basics Book of Word for Windows 95*, your search is over! This book provides *Guided Tours* of Word features, commands, and shortcut keys and *Do It Yourself* steps for many Word projects. By following the illustrations and text, you can learn all the basics you need to know to become proficient—quickly and easily.

Where's the Information I Need?

You can use this book in several ways. Read it from beginning to end to build your knowledge, feature-by-feature. Or, when you need to quickly solve a problem or learn a particular task, just jump to the appropriate topic using the Table of Contents, Index, or both. If you are leafing through the book, just look at the running heads at the top of each page to find an interesting topic or group of tasks you want to learn. The running heads not only name each task but also identify the chapter.

This book consists of four distinct parts so you can quickly find specific information:

Part 1, How To, covers all the skills that a novice Word user needs to know. You learn how to start and exit Word, enter text, edit and manage a document, and format all the parts of a document—from a single character to the entire document. Each task leads you step-by-step, picture-by-picture through the basics. To get the details of each task, read the accompanying explanation.

Part 2, Do It Yourself, shows you how to apply your newly acquired skills to customize Word to fit your needs and to create real-life documents you can adapt or use as is. Using the projects in Part 2, you'll not only learn how to change the appearance of the Word screen and your documents, but you'll also find out how to create documents such as letterheads, résumés, newsletters, and fax cover sheets.

Part 3, Quick Fixes, provides quick answers to your questions and quick solutions to your problems. If you are using a feature and run into a roadblock, you can find a solution here. A Quick Finder table at the beginning of Part 3 helps you zero in on the appropriate solution for a particular problem.

Part 4, Handy References, is a convenient collection of reference information: complete sets of definitions for options in common dialog boxes and a comprehensive table of key combinations, descriptions, and equivalent menu commands.

Conventions, Conventions, Conventions

This book has been designed with the novice user in mind: the titles point you to the appropriate task and the *Guided Tours* under the titles show you step-by-step how to perform the task or complete a project. To the right of each *Guided Tour* is additional text that tells you why you might want to perform the task and provides additional details on what to do. The following figure shows you the format of the book.

The following special conventions make the book easier to use:

Text you type and keys you press are in boldface type. For example, if the step says…

1. Type **Acme Buggywhips** and press **Enter**.

…you type the text "Acme Buggywhips" and press the Enter key on your keyboard.

Menu names and **commands** you need to choose are also bold. When you're told to open a menu and select a command, move the mouse pointer to the menu, click to open it and reveal the commands, then click on the desired command.

Key+Key combinations appear when you have to press two or more keys to enter a command. When you encounter one of these key combinations, hold down the first key and press the second key.

Look for these sidebars for notes, tips, hints, and shortcuts.

Running heads help you find what you want to learn.

Tips provide shortcuts or reference other useful information.

Additional information answers all your questions.

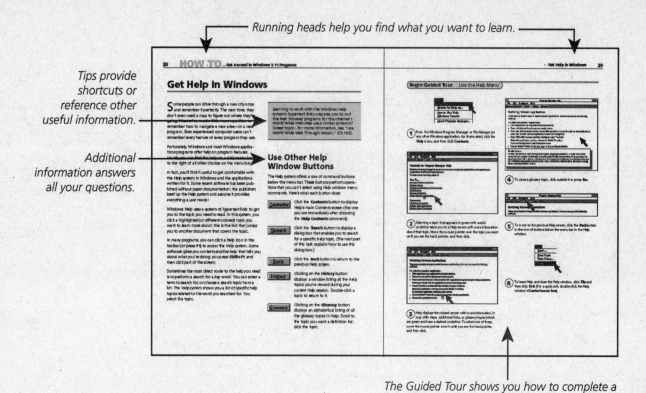

The Guided Tour shows you how to complete a computer task step-by-step.

Trademarks

Terms suspected of being trademarks or service marks have been appropriately capitalized. Que Corporation cannot attest to the accuracy of this information. Use of a term in this book should not be regarded as affecting the validity of any trademark or service mark.

The "Return to Zork" walk-through used in some example screen shots is copyrighted by Diana Griffith and *The Electronic Gamer*™ on CompuServe Information Service. They appear with the permission of the authors, and may not be reproduced. Thanks to the authors for their permission.

PART 1

How To...

Part 1 provides information about Word for Windows 95 features and takes you on guided tours that will help you master Word one step at a time. You'll not only read about what you can do with a feature and learn about its options but also get valuable hands-on experience.

You'll find out how to install Word step-by-step, and you'll learn how to start Word and exit from it. You'll gain an understanding of Word's standard elements: menus, menu commands, dialog boxes, toolbars, scroll bars, and application and document windows.

From there you'll learn how to enter text; add, change, or delete text; copy, cut, and paste; get help; and change the look of an entire document, selected paragraphs, and blocks of text. As you master text processing, you'll also explore the Word commands and dialog boxes that you'll use most often: for saving, printing, opening, closing documents, and much more.

What You Will Find in This Part

HOW TO...
Learn the Basics

S ection 1 starts you off on the right foot. In this section, you'll learn the basics: how to start Word for Windows 95 and how to exit the program.

After you start Word, you'll explore using both the mouse and the keyboard, and how to change the size of the windows on your computer screen. You'll look into the basic components of Word: menus, dialog boxes, and Word's unique toolbars.

Finally, you'll learn how to move around the Word document window and how to look at the status of a document on-screen. You'll end this section with a tour of Word's full-featured help facility.

What You Will Find in This Section

Install Word for Windows 95

You can install Word for Windows 95 in several ways: from CD-ROM or disks, and as part of Microsoft Office or as a separate program. This task will demonstrate how to install Microsoft Word from disks and Microsoft Office, including Word, from CD-ROM.

> If your Word for Windows program is on disks, make copies of the disks before installation and store them in a safe place.

Before installing Word, you should have installed Windows on your computer system and followed the Windows guidelines for hardware and software requirements. Here are some recommendations:

- Your computer system should be an IBM-compatible computer based on an 80386DX processor or greater.

- You should have installed Windows 95 or above.

- You should have at least 8 megabytes of RAM on your computer. The more RAM you have, the better Windows 95 and Word for Windows 95 run.

  Random-access memory (RAM) is your computer's main memory; your computer uses RAM to run Windows and applications software, and to temporarily store information. When you turn off your computer, the contents of RAM are deleted.

- Additional memory, in any combination of extended and expanded memory, also helps Windows run better.

There are three types of RAM: conventional, extended, and expanded. *Conventional memory* (you can have as much as one megabyte) is the regular RAM that your computer uses. *Extended memory* is an extension to conventional memory. *Expanded memory* requires special software and often requires a special board; it is separate from conventional and extended memory.

- Your color monitor and video card should support VGA, SVGA 256-color, or greater.

  VGA stands for Video Graphics Array, which produces high resolution and lets you have 16 colors at a time on your system. SVGA stands for super VGA.

- A Microsoft-compatible mouse.

- To get the most from Word for Windows, a printer (either laser or dot-matrix) should be part of your computer system.

The Setup installation program gives you many choices, which cannot be covered in this space. These tasks show you two common paths through installation. If you can't follow this installation path strictly, remember that the Setup program guides you carefully through every step of your installation.

> Before starting installation, start your computer. After you turn on your computer, Windows 95 automatically starts.

Begin Guided Tour   Install Word for Windows 95 from Disks

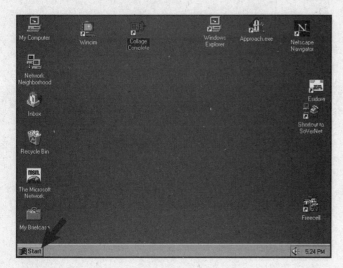

1 Click on the **Start** button.

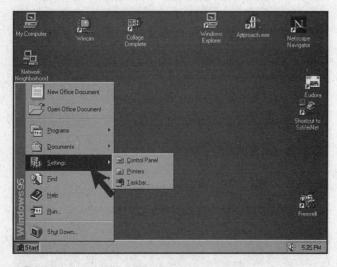

2 Select the **Settings** command.

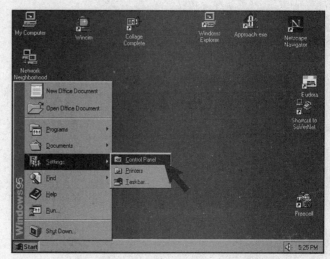

3 Select the **Control Panel** command. The Control Panel window appears.

4 Double-click the **Add/Remove Programs** icon. The Add/Remove Programs Properties dialog box appears.

(continues)

Guided Tour   Install Word for Windows 95 from Disks   *(continued)*

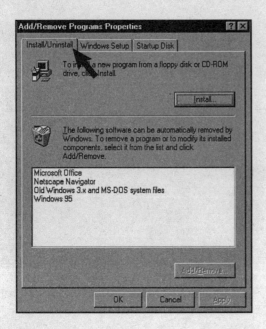

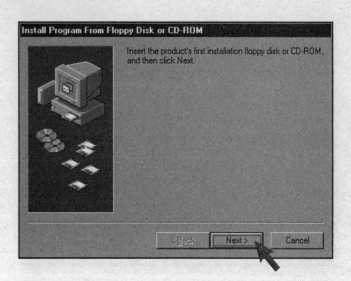

7 Insert Disk 1 - Setup in your floppy disk drive and click **Next**. Windows 95 looks for the installation program on the disk and searches for old copies of Microsoft Word on your computer.

5 Select the **Install/Uninstall** tab if the Install/Uninstall section of the Add/Remove Programs Properties dialog box is not displayed on your computer screen.

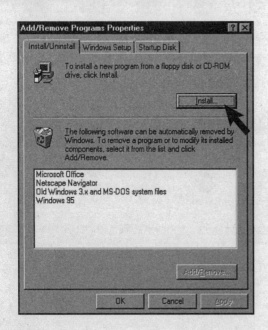

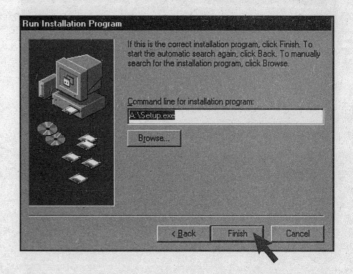

8 Click the **Finish** button. Word starts the Setup installation program. A Welcome dialog box appears.

6 Click the **Install** button. The Install Program From Floppy disk or CD-ROM dialog box appears.

Guided Tour   Install Word for Windows 95 from Disks

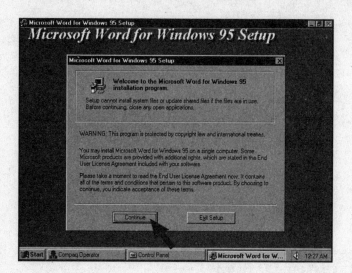

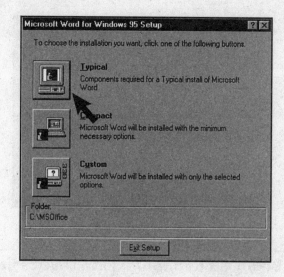

9 Click the **Continue** button. The Name and Organization Information dialog box appears.

11 Click the **Typical** button to install Microsoft Office with the components that most users require. Respond to prompts by clicking **Yes** or **No**. The Setup installation program copies files into the selected folder.

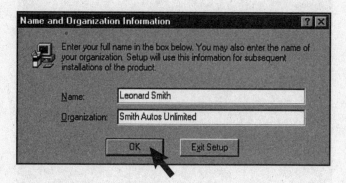

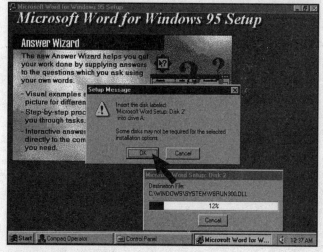

10 Type your name and organization name in the text boxes and click **OK**. Click **OK** again to confirm that the information you typed is correct. The Setup installation program displays the Product ID. Select **OK**. The Setup installation program searches for installed components.

12 When prompted, insert the next disk. Then click **OK**. Continue inserting program disks and following instructions.

(continues)

Guided Tour   Install Word for Windows 95 from Disks   *(continued)*

13 At the end of installation, to register online, click the **Online Registration** button. Otherwise, click on **OK**.

Begin Guided Tour   Install Microsoft Office from CD-ROM

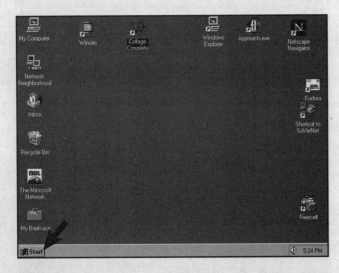

1 Click on the **Start** button.

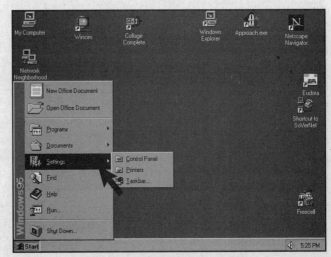

2 Select the **Settings** command.

Guided Tour Install Microsoft Office from CD-ROM

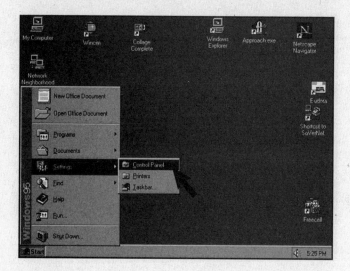

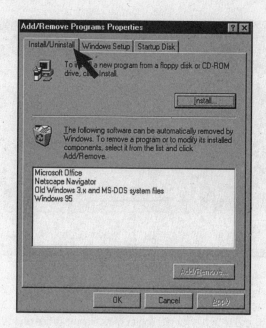

(3) Select the **Control Panel** command. The Control Panel window appears.

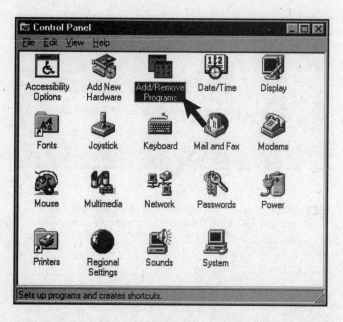

(5) Select the **Install/Uninstall** tab if the Install/Uninstall section of the Add/Remove Programs Properties dialog box is not displayed on your computer screen.

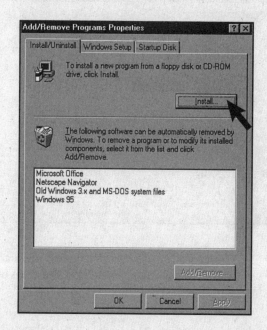

(4) Double-click the **Add/Remove Programs** icon. The Add/Remove Programs Properties dialog box appears.

If someone previously installed a copy of Word or Microsoft Office, you'll see it in the box in the middle of the dialog box. You don't have to remove it before installing a new version.

(6) Click the **Install** button. The Install Program From Floppy disk or CD-ROM dialog box appears.

(continues)

Guided Tour   Install Microsoft Office from CD-ROM   *(continued)*

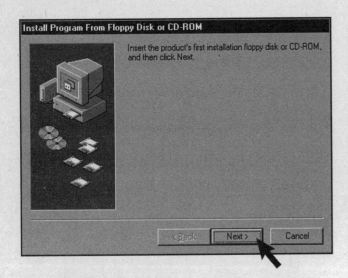

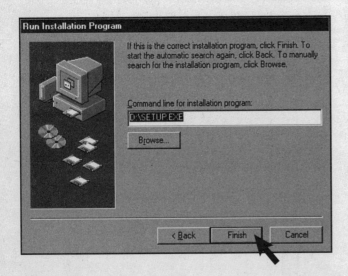

7 Insert the CD-ROM disk in your CD-ROM drive and click **Next**. Windows 95 looks for the installation program on the disk and searches for old copies of Microsoft Office on your computer.

8 Click the **Finish** button. The Setup installation program searches your hard drive for previously installed copies of Microsoft Office.

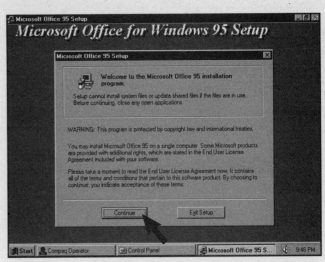

9 Select the **Continue** button. The Name and Organization Information dialog box appears.

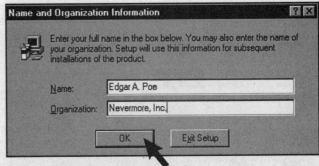

10 Type your name and organization name in the text boxes and click **OK**. Click **OK** again to confirm that the information you typed is correct.

Guided Tour   Install Microsoft Office from CD-ROM

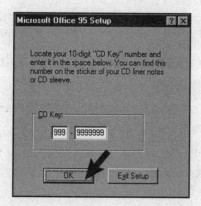

11 Type your CD Key number in the text box and select **OK**. (You'll find your CD Key number on the back of the CD case or on the sticker of your CD liner notes.) Click **OK** again to close the Microsoft Office 95 Setup dialog box after noting your Product ID. The Setup installation program searches for previous copies of Microsoft Office products.

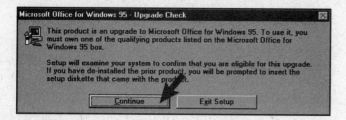

12 Select the **Continue** button. Another Microsoft Office 95 Setup dialog box appears.

13 Click **OK** to accept the Setup intallation program's suggestion of the folder in which the program files will be located. Setup searches for installed Microsoft Office programs and files previously installed on your computer.

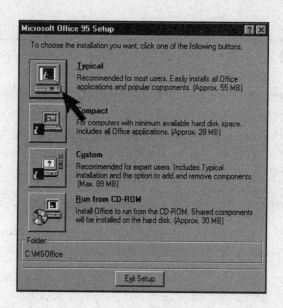

14 Click the **Typical** button to install Microsoft Office with the components that most users require. Respond to prompts by clicking **Yes** or **No**. The Setup installation program copies files into the selected folder.

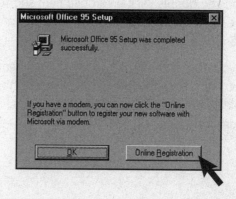

15 At the end of installation, to register online, click the **Online Registration** button. Otherwise, click **OK**.

Start and Exit Word for Windows 95

Before you start Word for Windows 95, start your computer, making sure that your surge protector and your peripherals, such as your printer, are also switched on. Windows 95 automatically starts when you turn on your computer. (If you are new to using the mouse, you may want to look over the "Work with a Mouse" task on page 17 before attempting the steps in this section.)

There are four ways to start Word for Windows.

- You can start the program from within Windows using the **Start** button.

- If you plan on using Word often, you can create a shortcut on your desktop from within the Windows 95 Find utility, the Windows Explorer or My Computer. (A following Guided Tour shows you how to use the Find utility to create a shortcut.)

- You can double-click on a document shortcut on the desktop or in the Windows Explorer or My Computer windows.

- If you have recently worked on a document that you want to reopen, select the **Start** button, select **Documents**, and then choose the file from the menu.

There are several ways to quit Word. You can...

- Open the **File** menu and select the **Exit** command.

- Click on the **Close** button (the **X** button at the top right part of the screen).

- Double-click either the **Application** or **Document Control** menu (the two buttons at the top left part of the screen).

- Press **Alt+F4**.

If a document is open when you try to quit Word, Word displays a dialog box that prompts you to save the document; you can click **Cancel** or press the **Esc** key to return to Word without quitting. To save the document, either press **Y**, click the **Yes** button, or press **Enter**. For detailed information on saving a file, see "Save a Document" on page 73. To quit Word without saving the file, click the **No** button.

If there is no open document, Word ends without prompting you.

Begin Guided Tour   Start Word for Windows 95

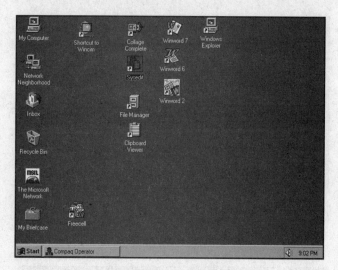

1 Click the **Start** button.

2 Select the **Programs** command.

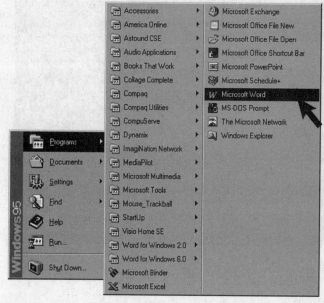

3 Select the **Microsoft Word** command.

Begin Guided Tour Create a Shortcut and Start Word for Windows 95

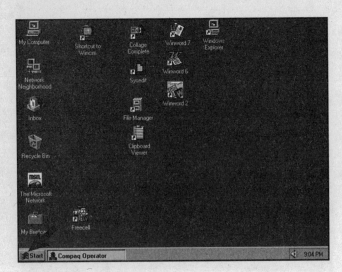

(1) Click the **Start** button.

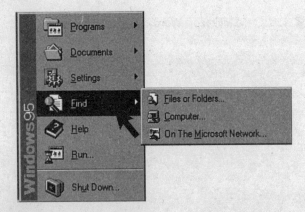

(2) Select the **Find** command.

(3) Select **Files or Folders**. The Find dialog box appears.

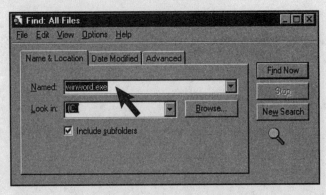

(4) In the **Named** text box, type **winword.exe**.

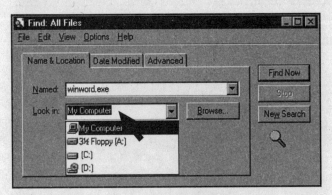

(5) If you are not sure of the hard drive or location in which Word is installed, select **My Computer** from the **Look in** drop-down list.

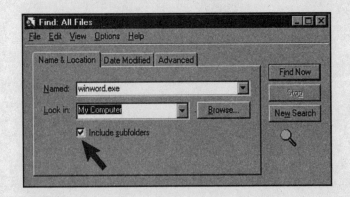

(6) Make sure to check the **Include Subfolders** check box.

Guided Tour Create a Shortcut and Start Word for Windows 95

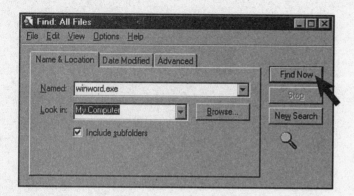

9 If you want to edit the shortcut name, click it twice (don't double-click), and edit as you would any text by using the **Backspace** and arrow keys.

7 Click the **Find Now** button, and wait for Windows to find the file.

Clicking twice on the shortcut name does not mean that you should double-click, which is rapid clicking and which will open the application. Make sure that you click, pause, and then click again. Then start editing the shortcut name.

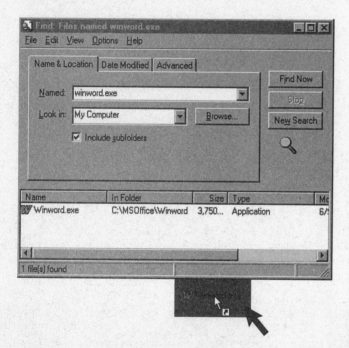

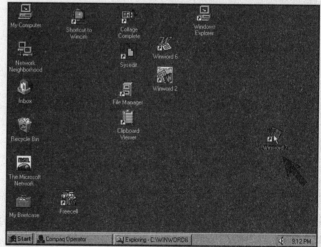

8 Click the **Winword.exe** file from the bottom of the Find window and drag it onto the desktop.

10 To start Word, double-click the shortcut icon on the desktop.

If you find a file using either the Windows Explorer or My Computer, you can create a shortcut by dragging the file onto the desktop.

Begin Guided Tour   Exit Word for Windows 95

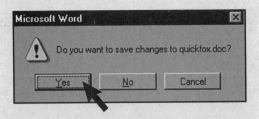

2 If you made any changes to a document, Word displays a dialog box. If you want to continue using Word, click **Cancel** or press **Esc**. To save the changes, either press **Y**, click the **Yes** button, or press **Enter**. To close Word without saving changes, click the **No** button.

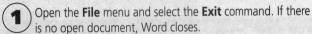

1 Open the **File** menu and select the **Exit** command. If there is no open document, Word closes.

Work with a Mouse

A mouse is an input device that you slide around on a desk, table, or other flat surface. As you move the mouse, a mouse pointer moves around on the computer screen in the same direction. So if you move the mouse in a circle, the mouse pointer copies your movement and moves in a circle on-screen.

When you move the mouse pointer, notice that it changes shape, depending on its location on the Word screen. Some of the most common mouse pointer shapes follow:

When you place the pointer in the text area, it looks like an I-beam, similar to a large I. Do not confuse the I-beam pointer with the flashing *insertion point*, which shows you the location of the next character that you type.

On a window border, the pointer is a two-headed arrow. You can use this type of pointer to change the size of the window: horizontally, vertically, or both (when you move the pointer to a corner of the window). For more information about changing window size, see "Change a Window's Size" on page 21.

Outside the *text area* (the area in which you create documents), and in a few other areas in which you enter text, the pointer is an arrow that points diagonally to the left. Use this arrow to point to parts of the window (for example, at the top of the screen), and click or double-click the mouse button to cause an action. You can point to *toolbar buttons*, which are small boxes usually containing small graphics that remind you of the action you can take or the format you can change. You can also point to menus from which you can choose commands.

When the pointer (pointing diagonally to the right) is in the *selection bar* (a vertical area from the top to the bottom in the left margin of the text area), you can highlight an entire line of text at once. You'll learn about selecting text in "Select Text" on page 92.

When Word is executing a command, the mouse pointer looks like an hourglass. This tells you that Word is busy and you must wait to take your next action.

You cannot only move the mouse pointer around the screen, you can also select with the mouse. The following table describes mouse actions.

Mouse Actions

Action	Description
Point	Move the mouse so the mouse pointer is located at a particular place on the screen.
Click	Quickly press and release the mouse button (usually the left button) once. Clicking usually selects an item on the screen.
Right-click	Quickly press and release the right mouse button once. Right-clicking usually opens a shortcut menu, which contains commonly used commands.
Double-click	Quickly press and release the mouse button twice. Many times, double-clicking is a shortcut for an action.
Drag	Press and hold the mouse button down while moving the mouse. For example, you can drag selected text and drop it elsewhere in a document. This is known as *drag-and-drop*.

Begin Guided Tour   Practice Using the Mouse

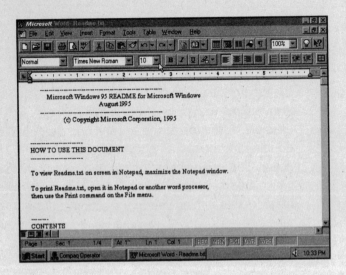

1 Move the mouse to the downward-pointing arrow to the right of the number 10 or 12 in the top center of the screen. Notice the mouse pointer becomes an arrow that points up and to the left.

2 Click the downward-pointing arrow. When Word opens a list, select an option. Word closes the list.

3 Move the mouse pointer to the left side of the screen. When the mouse pointer changes to a right-pointing arrow, you are in the selection area.

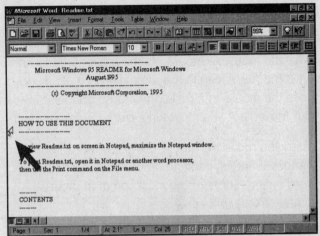

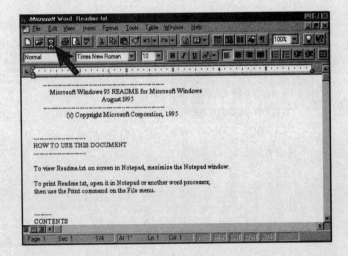

4 Point to the **Save** button, and click the left mouse button. Notice that the mouse pointer briefly changes to an hourglass.

Work with the Keyboard

or every Word command that you can act on using the mouse, there is a keyboard counterpart. So, if you don't have a mouse or don't like using it, you can still work in Word. However, if you have a mouse and you get more comfortable with Word, you'll probably find that you use a combination of the mouse and the keyboard.

Word has many commands; activate them by pressing single keys, *key combinations* (pressing two or three keys simultaneously), and *key successions* (pressing two or three keys one after another). In this book, key combinations are shown as two or three keys, each separated by a plus sign (+); and key successions are shown as two or three keys, each separated by a comma (,). For example, the key combination (or *shortcut keys*) for saving a file is **Shift+F12**, and the key succession used to open the File menu is **Alt, F**.

If you plan to use the keyboard to access menus, look at the *menu bar*, the area that displays the menu names. Notice that each menu has an underlined letter. Typically, the first letter in the menu is underlined. However, because some menus and commands start with the same letter (for example, **File** and **Format**), a letter within the word is underlined instead. You'll learn more about using menus in "Use Word Menus" on page 23.

To select a menu command using the keyboard, press and release the **Alt** key (because this is a key succession, you don't have to hold down the Alt key). Then press the underlined letter for the menu that you want. For example, to select the menu **File**, press **F**.

Word opens the menu and displays more choices, each with an underlined letter. Notice the text to the right of the Open, Save, Save As, Print, and Exit commands on the File menu. These are key combinations that you can press instead of opening the File menu. So rather than saving a document by pressing Alt, F (for File), and S (for Save), you simply press **Ctrl+S**.

You can also move along the menu bar, open menus, and select commands by pressing combinations of the left, right, up, and down arrow keys. Press the left or right arrow keys until the desired menu appears highlighted. Then open the menu by pressing the down arrow key. Select a command by pressing up or down arrow keys until the desired command appears highlighted. You can close a menu that you don't want to use by pressing the **Alt** key or **Esc** key and then leave the menu bar by pressing **Alt** or **Esc** again.

Begin Guided Tour   Select a Command with the Keyboard

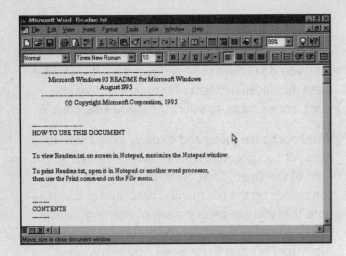

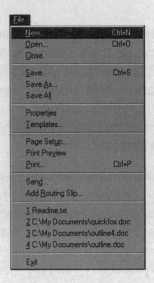

(1) To activate the menu bar, press and release the **Alt** key. If the mouse pointer is in the text area, notice that it changes to an upward-pointing arrow.

Many commands have key combinations you can use instead of pressing Alt and the menu and command selection letters. Look for these combinations on the menus next to the commands (for example, Ctrl+S saves a file). Look for others in "Word's Default Shortcut Keys and Key Combinations" on page 560. You also can save by holding down the **Shift** key while pressing **F12**.

(2) Press the underlined letter for the menu you want to open. To open the **File** menu, for example, press **F**. The menu lists commands with more underlined letters. Press the underlined letter for the command you want to select. For example, press **S** to select the **Save** command. Word closes the menu and executes the command you selected.

Change a Window's Size

When you first start Word for Windows, its *application window* (the area in which Word is running) covers the entire computer screen. This large window is a *full screen* or a *maximized* window. You can control the size of application windows and *document windows* (the areas in which documents appear) by using the buttons on the *title bar* (extending across the very top of the computer screen). The title bar displays the program name (Microsoft Word) followed by the name, if any has been specified, of the current document. If the document is unnamed, Word names it **DOCUMENT***n*, where *n* indicates a number that increases by 1 with each new unnamed document.

> With the exception of the first time, every time you start Word, the application window is either maximized (taking the entire width and height of the screen) or restored to the window's size in your most recent Word session.

The title bar includes these components:

 Application Control menu   Opens a menu with commands that manipulate the current program and its application window.

 Minimize button   Reduces the program to an icon in the taskbar, perhaps to run another program while Word still runs but without taking up screen space.

 Restore button   Only appears when the application window is maximized, to switch to a restored window, which is smaller than a maximized window.

 Maximize button   Only appears when the application window is restored, to maximize the restored window.

 Close button   Closes Word. This is equivalent to opening the **File** menu and selecting **Exit** (or pressing **Alt+F4**).

> Notice that, if the document window has been maximized, the menu bar also contains a Minimize, Restore or Maximize, and Close button, which closes the current document, as well as a Document Control menu, which you can use to manipulate the active document window. For more information about changing the size of application windows and document windows, see "Maximize, Minimize, and Restore the Application Window" on the next page.

Begin Guided Tour   Maximize, Minimize, and Restore the Application Window

1 Click the **Minimize** button on the top right corner of the application window. The window is minimized and moves to the taskbar (the bar at the bottom of your screen).

2 Click the **Word** icon in the taskbar. Word returns the application window to its previous state: restored or maximized.

3 Click the **Application Control** menu, and select **Restore** or **Maximize**, whichever is not dimmed. Word changes the size of the application window and changes either the Restore or Maximize button.

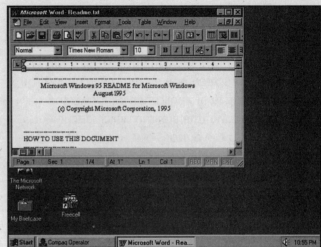

4 Click the **Restore** or **Maximize** button, whichever is available. Word changes the size of the application window and changes either the Restore or Maximize button.

Use Word Menus

The Word menu bar consists of nine menus, each of which contains related commands and submenus. Word's menus are known as *pull-down menus*, which means that after you click on a menu name, a menu opens or "pulls down" from the menu bar. *Menu commands* either perform Word functions immediately or open dialog boxes from which you can select options before the command is acted upon. Once a menu appears, you can select a command by clicking on it, or you can close the menu by clicking anywhere outside the menu. To open a menu using the keyboard, press the **Alt** key and the letter that is underlined in the menu name. Then press the underlined letter in the command's name or use the arrow keys to highlight a command and press **Enter**. To close a pull-down menu using the keyboard, press the **Esc** key.

The menus are:

File   These commands manage documents. Use this menu to save, create, retrieve, print documents, and to define page layout.

Edit   These commands manipulate text. You can copy, cut, and paste text; you can search for and replace text, characters, and symbols; you can use the **Undo** command to erase the most recent action; or use **Go To** to move to a specific place in the document.

View   These commands control how your document appears on-screen. You can show your document in Normal, Outline, or Page Layout mode and in various sizes. You also can display or hide Word toolbars; display or hide the Ruler on-screen; and work on a document on a screen without anything but the text area. You also can use this menu to add *footnotes* (additional information that enhances, but is not part of, your document) and/or *annotations* (reviewers' comments).

Insert   These commands allow you to insert other documents, files, special symbols, graphics, and more into your document. Use this menu to create a table of contents, figures, and authorities or an index.

Format   These commands control the appearance of characters and paragraphs in your document. Use this menu to specify tabs, apply styles, and change the number of columns.

Tools   These commands provide miscellaneous features. You can check spelling and grammar, find synonyms, hyphenate words in your document, work with *macros* (means by which you can save yourself repetitive steps), create envelopes and labels, and so on.

Table   These commands control tables and their rows and columns in your document; you can also sort selected elements in a document.

Window   These commands let you view a particular document from the list of open documents. In addition, you can use this menu to open and arrange multiple windows, so you can work on two or more documents at a time.

Help   These commands offer you immediate help with the program and with Windows 95.

Menus contain symbols and lines, each of which have specific meanings:

- Related commands on a menu are grouped together and separated from other groups of commands with a horizontal line.

- If a command looks dimmed or grayed, you cannot use it at this time. You may have to use another command first before you can use this command. For example, to use the Copy command in the Edit menu, you need to select text first.

- If a check mark precedes a command, the command can be turned on or off. For example, in the View menu, the Ruler command is turned on (will display on-screen) when a check mark is next to it and turned off (will not display on-screen) when there is no check mark next to it.

- If a command is preceded by a dot, the command function is the current selection; you can only select one command from that group of commands. For example, in the View menu, only Normal, Outline, Page Layout, or Master Document can be the current setting.

- If an *ellipsis* (three consecutive periods) follows a command, a dialog box will appear once you

select the command. For information about dialog boxes, see "Use Word Dialog Boxes" on page 26.

When a menu is open, you can see a brief description of the highlighted command in the *status bar* at the bottom of the document window. To move the highlight to a command without performing the command, repeatedly press the down or up arrow key. To select the highlighted command, press **Enter**. To use the mouse to move the highlight, just drag the mouse down the list of commands.

Begin Guided Tour   Practice Using a Word Menu

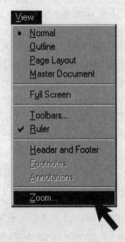

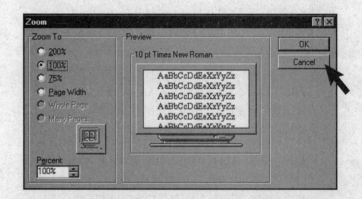

2 Click **Cancel** or press **Esc** to close the dialog box.

1 On the menu bar, open the **View** menu and then select **Zoom**. The Zoom dialog box appears.

Guided Tour   Practice Using a Word Menu

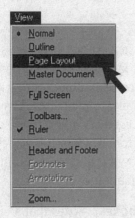

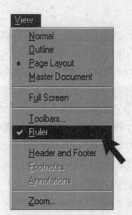

3 Open the **View** menu again, and click **Page Layout**.

5 Open the **View** menu and select **Ruler**. If the Ruler was on-screen, it disappears. If the Ruler was hidden, it appears.

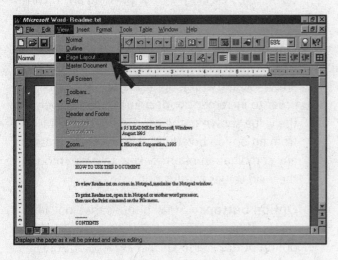

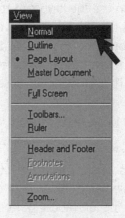

4 Word changes the look of the document and places a dot in front of the command.

6 Open the **View** menu and select **Normal** to change the look of the document once again.

Use Word Dialog Boxes

Many times, when you select a command, Word will display a *dialog box*. Dialog boxes usually appear when you must choose options such as how many copies to print, a particular look of selected text, or how you want your application window to look. The dialog box can contain other types of boxes, or it can contain buttons that might even open another dialog box. Some dialog boxes contain several sections. To reveal a particular section, click on the tab at the top of the dialog box or repeatedly press an arrow key until the section appears.

Using the mouse is the easiest way to navigate in a dialog box and its associated boxes and buttons. However, you can use the keyboard to move around a dialog box. Press the **Tab** key (to move from left to right and from top to bottom) or the **Shift+Tab** key combination (to move from right to left and from bottom to top). The following list describes the various components of a dialog box and explains how to use the mouse and keyboard with each component:

Text boxes   Boxes in which you enter text, such as a file name. To move to the text box, either click the left mouse button in the text box or press the **Tab** (or **Shift+Tab** to move backward) key until the cursor is in the text box. Type and edit your text just as you would in a document window.

Drop-down list boxes   Boxes from which you select an item. To use a drop-down list box, either click the list arrow (the underlined down arrow) at the right side of the list box or press any combination of arrow keys to reveal a list from which you can choose by clicking or pressing arrow keys. To close a drop-down list box without selecting it, click the list arrow again or press **Esc**.

List boxes   Boxes from which you select an item. To use a list box, which has a vertical scroll bar on its right side, click the desired item or press any combination of arrow keys. If the item that you want to select is not visible, scroll up or down the list by pointing to the arrows at the top or bottom of the scroll bar, and pressing and holding down the left mouse button, or pressing any combination of arrow keys.

Text/list boxes   Boxes that are combinations of text boxes and list boxes. You can either type a value in the text box or select a value from the open list by clicking on it or pressing any combination of arrow keys.

Option boxes   Boxes into which you can either type a value or click either the up or down arrow located at the right side of the box in order to increment or decrement, respectively, the value shown in the box. To select a value from an option box using the keyboard, press any combination of arrow keys to cycle through the valid values for this option.

Option buttons   Small buttons that look like circles. When a group of options is preceded by option buttons (also known as radio buttons), you can select only one button, or option, from the group. Option or radio buttons work similarly to buttons in a car radio: you can push only one button at a time, and you can select only one station at a time. To select a radio button, move the mouse pointer to the radio button and click with the left mouse button, or press any combination of arrow keys. A large black dot will appear in the button, indicating that you have selected the option.

Check boxes   Small square boxes that display an **X** when you turn a feature on; they are blank when you turn a feature off. When check boxes precede a group of options, you can select several options from this group. For each option that you want to select, move the mouse pointer to the check box and click with the left mouse button, or press the underlined letter.

Command buttons   Rectangular-shaped buttons that you can select only separately. There are five command buttons that you will see most often: OK, Cancel, Close, Apply, and Help. Some dialog boxes contain other command buttons, which will be described as they occur. To select a command button with the mouse, move the mouse pointer to the command button and click with the left mouse

button. To select a command button with the keyboard, you can type the underlined letter on the button (if there is one). Otherwise, press **Tab** or **Shift+Tab** until the button is selected; then press **Enter**. The following table describes commonly used command buttons.

When a command button, such as OK, is surrounded by a heavier border than other command buttons, it is the default, or the active button. Pressing **Enter** "clicks" the default button.

Do not press Enter when entering text in a dialog box. When typing text in a large text box with room for multiple lines, press the down arrow key to move to the next line.

Word's Command Buttons

Button	Description
OK	Closes a dialog box after completing the command.
Cancel	Closes a dialog box before completing the command. All settings return to their prior state.
Close	Closes a dialog box before completing the command. All settings that you have changed remain changed.
Apply	Completes the command but keeps the dialog box open for further action.
Help	Finds help about the functions or actions related to this dialog box.

Begin Guided Tour   Use Dialog Boxes

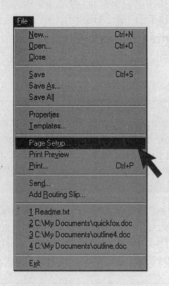

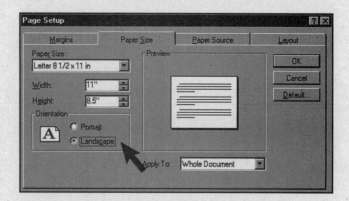

3 Select options to see the changes. For example, in the **Paper Size** section of the Page Setup dialog box, click the **Landscape** option button. Notice the change in the Preview box.

1 Display a dialog box by opening a menu and selecting a command with an ellipsis after it. For example, open the **File** menu and select **Page Setup**. Word opens the Page Setup dialog box.

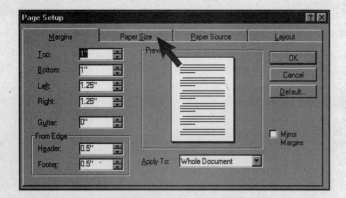

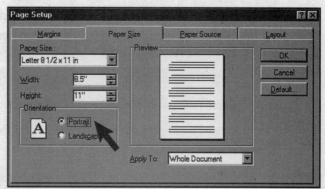

4 If you selected **Landscape**, click the **Portrait** option button. The Preview box changes again.

2 If you need to reveal a different section of the dialog box, click on a tab at the top of the dialog box. For example, click the **Paper Size** tab.

Guided Tour   Use Dialog Boxes

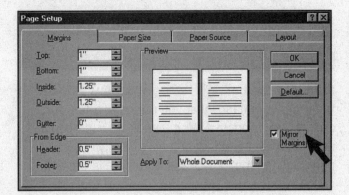

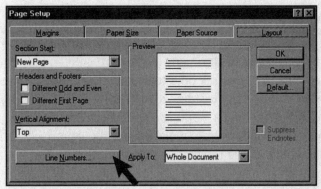

5 If the dialog box has multiple sections, click a tab at the top of the dialog box, and then select other options. For example, in the Page Setup dialog box, click the **Margins** tab, and click **Mirror Margins**. The Preview box changes again and the **Left** and **Right** options change to **Inside** and **Outside**, respectively. Click **Mirror Margins** again.

7 Click the **Line Numbers** button. Word opens the Line Numbers dialog box in front of the Page Setup dialog box.

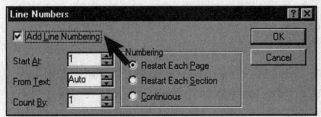

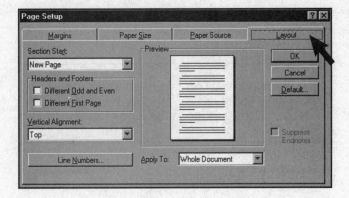

8 Click the **Add Line Numbering** check box. Parts of the dialog box become available. Then click **Cancel** to close the dialog box without making any changes; click **Cancel** again.

6 Move to another section of a multiple-section dialog box. For example, in the Page Setup dialog box, click the **Layout** tab.

Use Word Toolbars

Word's toolbars (horizontal bars containing buttons and sometimes drop-down list boxes) provide shortcuts for many of the most common commands. Just click on a toolbar button or select from a drop-down list box to perform a command without opening a menu and selecting a command or choosing options from a dialog box. You'll probably find most of the toolbars useful, so make sure that you know how to display or hide them. You also can drag any toolbars, including those that appear to be fixed in place, around the screen and reshape them by moving their borders. Toolbars that you have dragged away from the top or bottom of the screen (or that appear in that condition when revealed) are known as *floating toolbars*; they have title bars and Close buttons.

To display or hide toolbars, open the **View** menu and select the **Toolbars** command. When Word displays the Toolbars dialog box, click to place check marks in the check boxes for the toolbars you want to display, and remove the check marks from the check boxes for the toolbars that you want to hide.

A quick way to select toolbars is to use the shortcut menu for toolbars. Just right-click on a toolbar to open a menu with the names of all the toolbars and two commands: **Toolbars** (the same as the command on the **View** menu) and **Customize**.

Toolbars can take up a great deal of space on your screen, thereby leaving fewer lines of your document on-screen. If you use a toolbar quite often, keep it on your screen. However, if you don't use a toolbar constantly, it's a good idea to hide it and reveal it only when necessary.

The toolbars that you will use most often are:

Standard toolbar This series of buttons provides the Word commands that you use most often. Just click the appropriate button, and Word can open a new document window or a new file, save, edit, print, change the look of the document in the application window, and so on. For Standard toolbar details, see "Standard Toolbar" on page 536.

Formatting toolbar Click a button or select from a drop-down list box from the Formatting toolbar to control the appearance and size of text, as well as character and paragraph formatting. For Formatting toolbar details, see "Formatting Toolbar" on page 538.

The Standard and Formatting toolbars are those that you'll use most often. For that reason, they are shown by default.

Borders toolbar Contains buttons that allow you to turn on or off borders and lines, line styles, and shadings for parts of a document. You can turn on and off the Borders toolbar using a button at the end of the Formatting toolbar.

Drawing toolbar Enables you to add your own drawings to a document. You can turn on and off the Drawing toolbar by clicking on a button on the Standard toolbar. For Drawing toolbar details, see "Drawing Toolbar" on page 539.

Microsoft toolbar Provides buttons with which you can access eight other Microsoft applications—only those installed on your computer.

Tip Wizard toolbar Provides helpful hints with which you can create and edit each document. For Tip Wizard toolbar details, see "TipWizard Toolbar" on page 540.

Header and Footer Comprised of buttons with which you can create and customize headers and

footers. You will learn about headers and footers and the Header and Footer toolbar in "Add a Header and a Footer" on page 368 and in "Header and Footer Toolbar" on page 541. Note that you cannot display or hide the Header and Footer toolbar from the Toolbars dialog box; open the **View** menu and select the **Header and Footer** command.

> When you move your mouse pointer over a button or drop-down box on any toolbar, Word displays ToolTips, a small yellow box displaying the name of the button or box.

Begin Guided Tour Turn On and Off Toolbars

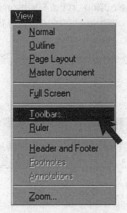

1 Open the **View** menu and select the **Toolbars** command. Word opens the Toolbars dialog box.

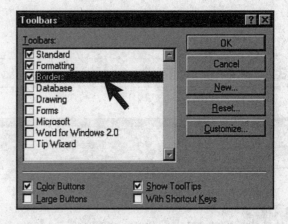

2 Click the boxes next to the names of the toolbars you want to display to select them; a check mark appears.

(continues)

Guided Tour Turn On and Off Toolbars   *(continued)*

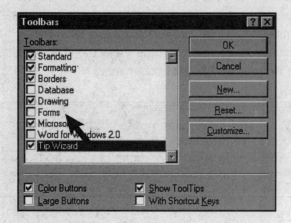

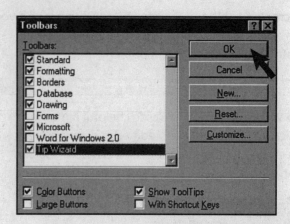

3 If a toolbar you don't want to display is selected, click its box to remove the check mark.

4 Click **OK** to close the dialog box.

5 Click the **Close** button on the Microsoft toolbar. You can close this and other floating toolbars in this way.

Begin Guided Tour Practice Using Toolbars

1 To use a list button on a toolbar, move the mouse pointer to the button and click it. For example, click the **Zoom Control** button. A drop-down list appears.

3 Click on another toolbar button. For example, click the **Drawing** button. Word adds the Drawing toolbar to the bottom of the screen and the Drawing button looks pressed down.

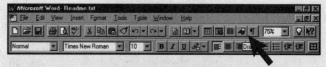

2 If you select the **Zoom Control** button, select a percentage from the drop-down list. For example, select **75%** from the list. Word closes the list, and the look of the document on the screen changes.

Guided Tour   Practice Using Toolbars

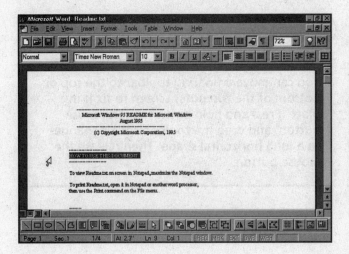

4 Move the mouse pointer to the left margin next to any line and click. Word highlights the entire line.

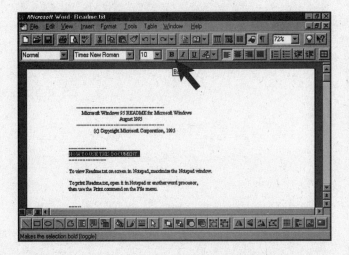

5 If you want to change the look of the selected line, move the mouse pointer to an enhancement button. For example, point to the **Bold** button and click. This turns on boldface for the selected text.

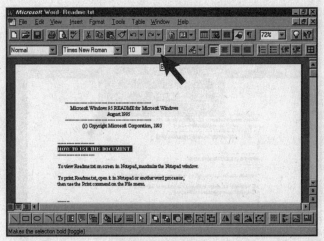

6 If you want to turn off the enhancement, click the button again. For example, point to the **Bold** button and click again. This turns off boldface for the selection.

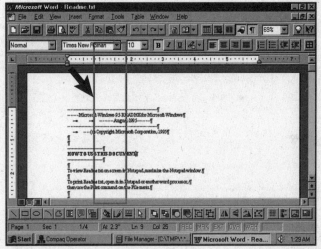

7 Drag a toolbar to the middle of the screen. For example, drag the Drawing toolbar.

(continues)

Guided Tour   Practice Using Toolbars

(continued)

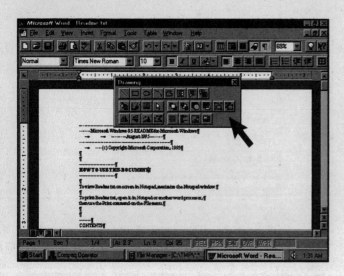

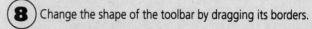 **8** Change the shape of the toolbar by dragging its borders.

You can move a floating toolbar to the top or bottom of the computer screen to fix it in place. Press and hold down the left mouse button, and drag the toolbar until it changes to a long horizontal shape. Then release the mouse button.

Use the Scroll Bars and the Status Bar

*S*croll bars allow you to use the mouse to move through a document from side to side and from top to bottom. There are two types of scroll bars: the vertical bar at the far right of the text area and the horizontal bar at the bottom of the text area. The arrows at the ends of the scroll bars and the *scroll box* (the box within the scroll bars) allow you to move around the document in the text area. The *scroll box* shows your current location in a document; the size of the scroll box indicates the size of the document. A large scroll box tells you that you can see a great deal of the document on the screen; a small scroll box denotes a long (or wide, if you are looking at the horizontal scroll bar) document.

There are three ways to move through a document by using a scroll bar: the scroll bar arrows, the scroll box, and the area within the scroll bar.

Scroll bar arrows   Point to a scroll bar arrow, click, and hold down the left mouse button. As the document scrolls up or down the screen (or side to side), the scroll box moves to show the part of the docu-

ment currently displayed. Clicking once on a scroll bar arrow scrolls the document up or down one line.

Within the scroll bar   Click the part of the scroll bar above or below the scroll box to move a screen minus two lines up or down.

> When you use the scroll bar to move up and down the pages of a document, you won't see a change in the page number displayed in the status bar at the bottom of the screen until you click in the document.

Scroll box   Point to the scroll box, click, and drag it to a new position on the scroll bar. As you drag, Word displays the page number. When you release the left mouse button, the document scrolls to a location in the document relative to the position of the scroll box. For example, if the scroll box is in the middle of the scroll bar, Word displays the middle of the document.

Begin Guided Tour   Use the Scroll Bars

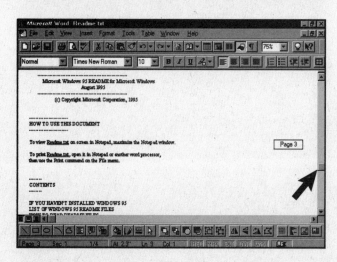

1 Point to the scroll box in the vertical scroll bar, and drag until the scroll box is about three-quarters down the scroll bar.

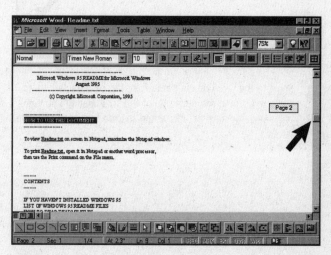

2 Point immediately below the top scroll arrow on the vertical scroll bar; press and hold down the left mouse button until the scroll box reaches Page 2.

(continues)

Guided Tour Use the Scroll Bars *(continued)*

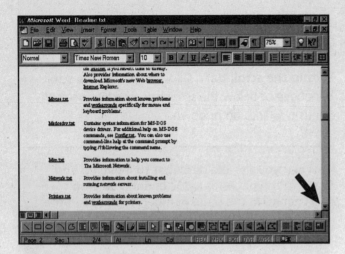

3 Point to the bottom scroll arrow on the vertical scroll bar, and click the left mouse button.

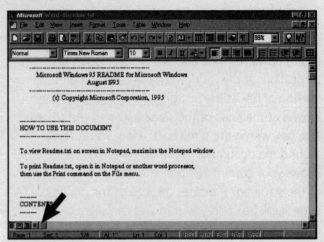

5 Point to the left scroll arrow in the horizontal scroll bar, press and hold down the left mouse button until the scroll box reaches the left side of the scroll bar.

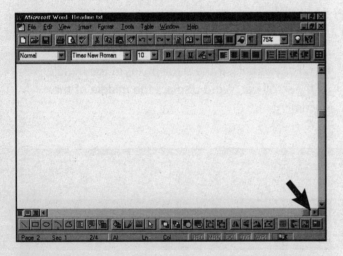

4 Point to the scroll box in the horizontal scroll bar, and drag the scroll box to the right side of the scroll bar. (If you were looking at a wide document, you would see the text near or at the right margin.)

Begin Guided Tour   Display and Hide the Scroll Bars

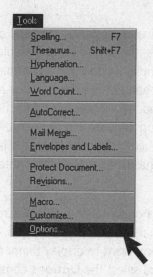

1 Open the **Tools** menu and select the **Options** command. Word displays an Options dialog box.

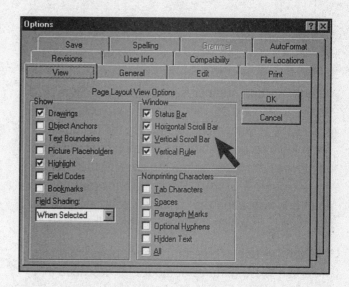

3 In the Window group, click to place check marks on both the **Vertical Scroll Bar** and the **Horizontal Scroll Bar** check boxes.

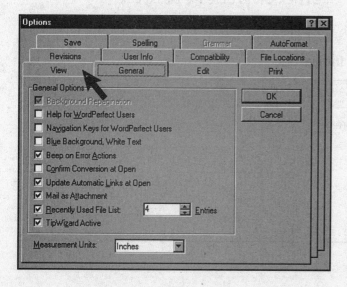

2 Click the **View** tab in the Options dialog box, unless the Options dialog box for the View category is on display.

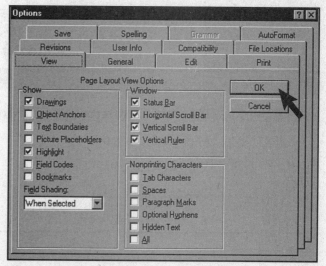

4 Select **OK** or press **Enter** to close the dialog box.

Understand the Status Bar

The *status bar*, at the bottom of the computer screen, contains three types of information. The left section shows the page location: current page number, section number (see "Start a New Page or Section" on page 56), and current page number, as well as the total number of pages in the document. The middle section shows the location of the insertion point: the distance from the top edge of the page, the line number of the line on which the insertion point is located, and the characters counted from the left margin, in which the insertion point is located.

The right section of the status bar displays indicators of certain Word features or modes, as described in the following table. If the indicators look dim, they are not available; if they look black, the features or modes are in use. For example, if you press the **Ins** or **Insert** key, the word **OVR** (which indicates that every character that you type replaces the character at the

insertion point) appears darker than the other indicators. Sometimes, the status bar also displays messages. For example, if you open a command menu, the status bar changes in order to show a description of the command. When you print a document, a small printer icon appears and the number of the page currently being printed. When the last page of the document has been sent to the printer, the icon disappears.

By default, the horizontal and vertical scroll bars and status bar should appear on your screen. If they are hidden and if you want to display them, open the **Tools** menu and select the **Options** command. In the Options dialog box, click the **View** tab. Make sure there are check marks in the **Status Bar**, **Horizontal Scroll Bar**, and **Vertical Scroll Bar** check boxes. Then click **OK** to close the dialog box.

Status Bar Indicators

Indicator	Description
REC	The Word macro recorder is turned on.
MRK	Mark Revisions is on.
EXT	The Extend Selection key (F8) is on.
OVR	Overtype mode is on.
WPH	WordPerfect help is on.

Get Help in Word

Word has a comprehensive online Help system, which you can access in the following ways:

- Press **F1** from any screen to display the Help Topics window for Microsoft Word. Then either click a tab or select a topic by double-clicking on it, or selecting it and clicking on the **Display** button. The sections of the Help Topics window are:

  Contents   Contains lists of how-to topics and subtopics. You can reveal, hide, or print topics and subtopics.

  Index   Displays an alphabetically arranged index of help information, including how-to's and definitions. You can quickly move to the desired index entry by typing one or more characters of the first word in the entry.

  Find   Use to create a list of all the words in the Word help facility. Once you create the list, you don't have to do it again. Then you can search the list for a key word in a help topic.

  Answer Wizard   Click this tab to ask the help facility a question and get an answer.

- When you are viewing help information, you can use the mouse or the keyboard to select a *jump term*: green, underlined text that reveals specific information about a term or "jumps" to another topic. To select a jump term using the mouse, point to the term and either click it or press and hold down the left mouse button (depending on the way in which the jump term was programmed). To select a jump term using the keyboard, press the **Tab** or **Shift+Tab** key to highlight the term; then press **Enter**.

- On any screen and in most dialog boxes, either press **Shift+F1** or click the question mark toolbar button to display a large question mark next to the mouse pointer. Move the mouse pointer to the command, button, or particular area of the screen; then click. Word displays information related to your selection. Press **Esc** to remove the question mark from the screen.

> In many dialog boxes, you can move the mouse pointer to an option and click with the right mouse button to display a short description of the option.

- Open the **Help** menu and select **Microsoft Word Help Topics**, **Answer Wizard**, **WordPerfect Help**, or **About Microsoft Word**, with the following results:

  Microsoft Word Help Topics   Reveals the last Help Topics window you accessed.

  Answer Wizard   Asks the Help facility a question and gets an answer.

  WordPerfect Help   For an experienced WordPerfect user who is a Word for Windows 95 beginner.

  About Microsoft Word   Displays version and copyright information about Word and information about the current status of your computer system.

To leave the help system, click the **Close** button or press **Esc**.

Begin Guided Tour　Use Help's Contents Section

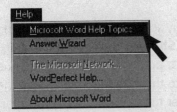

1 Open the **Help** menu and select **Microsoft Word Help Topics**, or press **F1**. Word opens the Help Topics Window.

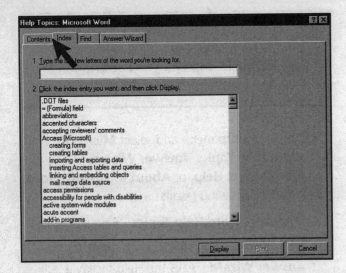

2 Click the **Contents** tab, if the Contents window is not on display.

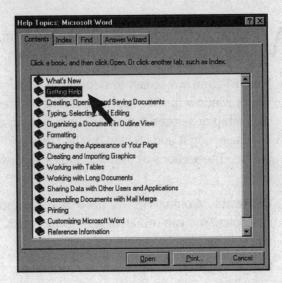

3 Double-click on a book icon (for example, **Getting Help**). Notice the book opens and a series of subtopics appear.

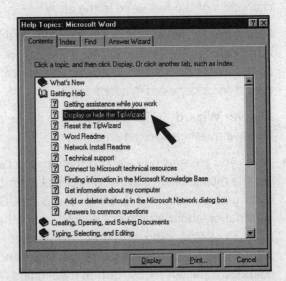

4 Select a Help subtopic. For example, select **Display or Hide the TipWizard**.

Guided Tour   Use Help's Contents Section

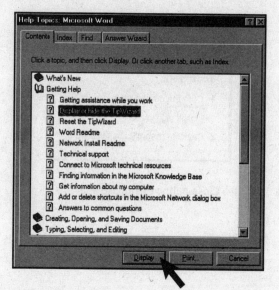

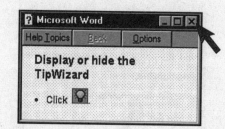

6 To close the topic, click the **Close** button.

5 To display the contents of the subtopic, click the **Display** button.

Begin Guided Tour   Use Help's Index Section

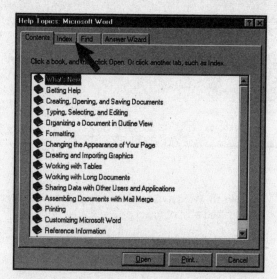

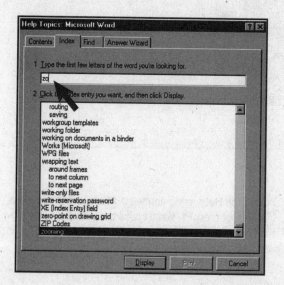

1 Open the **Help** menu and select **Microsoft Word Help Topics**, or press **F1**. Word opens the Help Topics Window. Click the **Index** tab.

2 Start typing the topic you are looking for, such as **Zooming**. As you type, Word starts the search. For example, after you type **zo**, Word highlights **zooming**. Then click the **Display** button.

(continues)

Guided Tour   Use Help's Index Section

(continued)

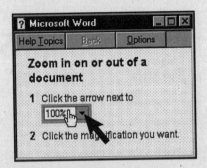

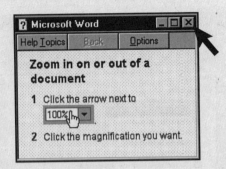

3 Move the mouse pointer around the Help topic window. If the pointer becomes a hand, click to get additional information about the topic.

4 Click the **Close** button to exit help.

Begin Guided Tour   Use Help's Find Section

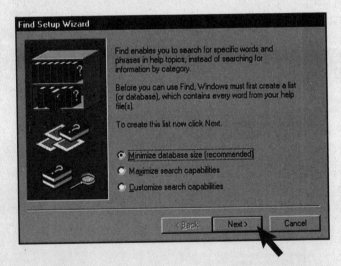

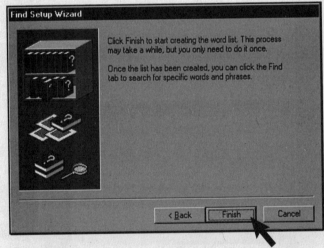

1 Open the **Help** menu and select **Microsoft Word Help Topics**, or press **F1**. Word opens the Help Topics Window. Click the **Find** tab. Word displays the first dialog box for the Find Setup Wizard. Click **Next**.

2 Click **Finish**. Word runs for several seconds and displays a word list and a list of topics.

Guided Tour Use Help's Find Section

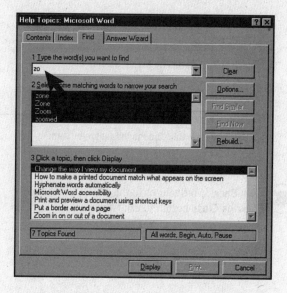

3 Start typing the name of the topic you are looking for, such as **Zooming**. As you type, Word starts the search. For example, after you type **zo**, Word moves to the bottom of the list. You can narrow the search even more by continuing to type additional letters or words.

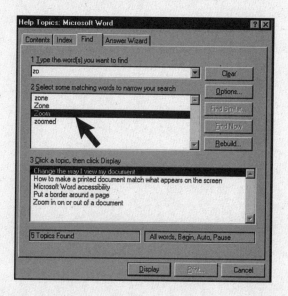

4 Select a word to refine the search. Word changes the list of topics.

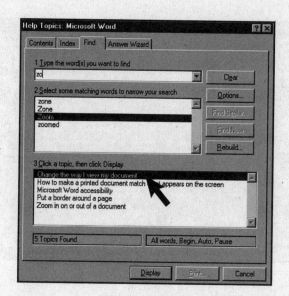

5 Select a topic. Then click the **Display** button.

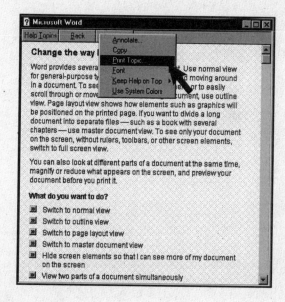

6 To print out the help on the top, click the **Options** button and select **Print Topic**. Word opens the Print dialog box.

(continues)

Guided Tour Use Help's Find Section *(continued)*

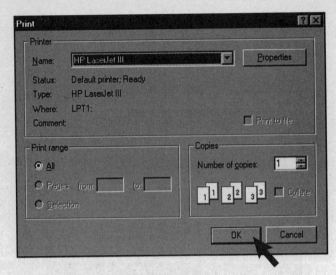

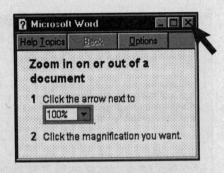

8 Click **Back**. Word returns to the previous help topic. Click the **Close** button to exit help.

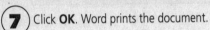

7 Click **OK**. Word prints the document.

HOW TO...

Enter Text and Manage a Document

Section 2 helps you to start using word processing in Word for Windows 95; and you learn how to view your document in several ways. In this section, you will learn how to create a new document using wizards, templates, and an empty document window. Then, you'll enter text and view it as text or in its current page layout.

You'll find out how to add pages and sections and how to move around a document from top to bottom. You'll learn how to magnify and reduce a document so that you can look at the text details or work with layouts of entire pages.

You'll explore printing your documents and adjusting print options. Finally, the section ends with information about saving documents, specifying save options, and closing documents with or without saving.

What You Will Find in This Section

Create a New Document

ord provides three ways to create a new document: with a wizard, a template, or from scratch.

- *Wizards* are the easiest way to create a new document. Using a series of wizard dialog boxes, you select a format that you like, answer questions, and fill in text boxes. Then Word assembles the document and presents it to you.

- *Templates* are formatted documents that contain some text. All you need to do is fill in the parts

that make the document your own. For example, if you use a fax template, type your name and your recipient's name, company name, address, and telephone numbers. Then you fill in the message, save the fax, and print it.

- Although creating a document from scratch may be more work and may sometimes be frustrating (especially when you're a beginner), the end result is your own design. If you have some extra time and a sense of design, creating your own document might be the way to go.

Begin Guided Tour   Create a Document with a Wizard

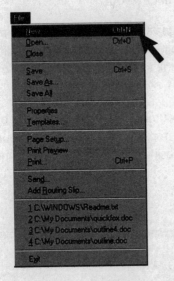

1 Open the **File** menu and select **New**. Word opens the New dialog box.

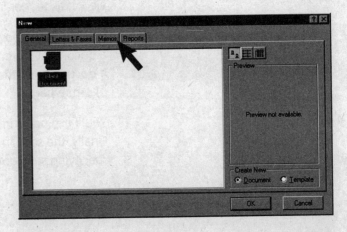

2 Click the tab that corresponds to the category of document you want to create. For example, click the **Memos** tab.

Guided Tour Create a Document with a Wizard

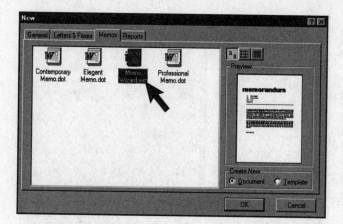

3 Double-click the icon with the WIZ extension. Word sets up the wizard for a few seconds and then displays the first dialog box.

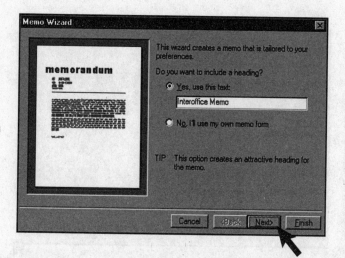

4 Answer the question in the dialog box by selecting the appropriate option button. In the example shown here, you can select **Yes** and edit the text in the text box to insert your own heading, or you can use your own memo stationery. When you finish, click **Next**. A different dialog box appears.

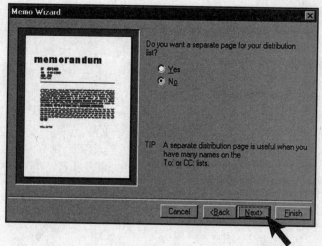

5 Answer the question in the dialog box by selecting the appropriate option button. Then click **Next** again. (If you change your mind about a previous dialog box, except for the first, you can click the **Back** button.) The next dialog box appears.

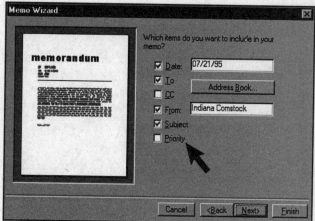

6 Check or clear the check boxes for items that you want to include or exclude, respectively. If you want, edit the date and/or your name. Then click **Next**.

(continues)

Guided Tour   Create a Document with a Wizard   *(continued)*

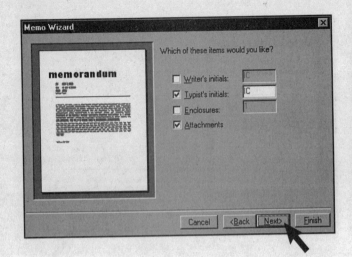

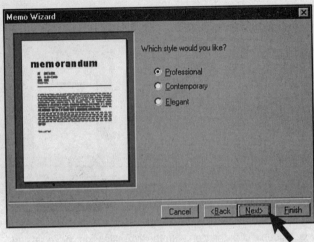

7 Check or clear the check boxes for items that you want to include or exclude respectively. For example, if you have attachments or enclosures that you want to send with the document, check the check boxes. Then click **Next**.

9 Click the option button that corresponds to the style you want to use or view before selecting. Then click **Next**.

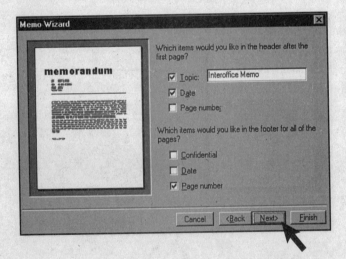

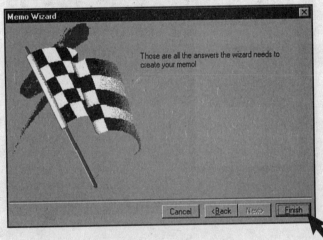

8 Check or clear the check boxes for items that you want to include or exclude respectively. For example, you can retype the **Topic** or have Word include **Confidential** at the bottom of each page. Then click **Next**.

10 Click the **Finish** button. Word processes your answers and creates the type of document you chose—a memo in this case.

Guided Tour   Create a Document with a Wizard

11 Click and then type text wherever you see **Click here** followed by instructions. To learn more about entering text, see "Enter Text" on page 53. When you finish entering text, you'll probably want to save your document. To learn about saving documents, see "Save a Document" on page 73.

Begin Guided Tour   Create a Document with a Template

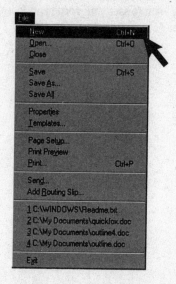

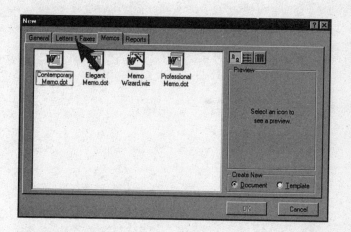

2 Click the tab that corresponds to the category of document you want to create. For example, click the **Letters & Faxes** tab.

1 Open the **File** menu and select **New**. Word opens the New dialog box.

(continues)

Guided Tour Create a Document with a Template *(continued)*

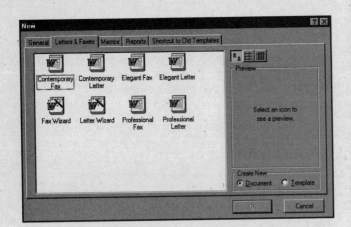

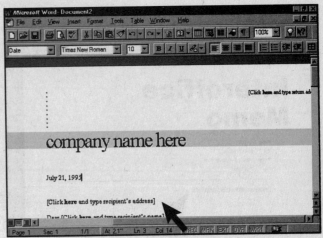

3 Select an icon with the DOT extension and view its format in the Preview box. Continue this until you find a format you prefer. Then double-click that icon. For example, double-click the **Contemporary Fax** icon.

4 Type text in place of **Click here and type return address** or wherever you see **Click here** followed by instructions. If you don't know how to enter text, wait until the next Guided Tour, "Enter Text," on page 53. When you finish entering text, you'll probably want to save your document. To learn about saving documents, see "Save a Document" on page 73.

Begin Guided Tour   Create a Document from Scratch

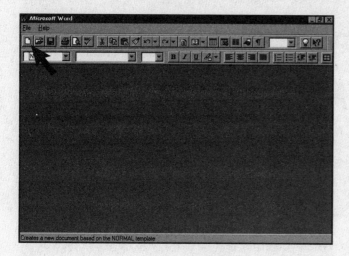

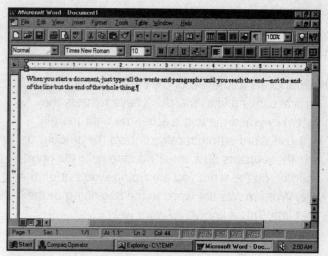

1 Click the **New** button or press **Ctrl+N** if the text area is dark. (If the text area has a white background or shows an empty page, there is no need to start a new document; you already have one.)

You can start a new document by opening the **File** menu and selecting **New**. When the New dialog box appears, click the **General** tab, if needed, and then double-click the **Blank Document** icon. When you open a blank document, you are still using a template although you don't see any formats. Word's default template, Normal, is in effect unless you specifically choose a different template.

2 Begin entering text. If you don't know how to enter text, wait until the next Guided Tour, "Enter Text," on page 53. When you finish entering text, you'll probably want to save your document. To learn about saving documents, see "Save a Document" on page 73.

Start Typing Your Document

Once you finish the steps to a wizard and have a template on the screen, the document window appears and you can start entering text. As you type, text appears to the left of the *insertion point*, the vertical blinking line. You don't have to press the Enter key when the text reaches the right margin because Word automatically controls the amount of text that appears on a line. If you are near the right margin and the word you are typing won't fit on the line, Word moves the word to the beginning of the next line. This is known as *word wrap*.

By default, Word aligns text with the left margin of the page and keeps the text at the right side of the page *ragged* (not aligned with the right margin). This is *left alignment*. (You can change the alignment if you want. Refer to "Format Pages and Paragraphs" on page 141.)

Whenever you want to start a new paragraph, press the **Enter** key. Word places a paragraph mark (¶), a special nonprinting symbol, at the end of the first paragraph.

Some documents require that you override the word-wrap feature and define your own lines. For example, if you are writing a poem, you might want to specify the number of lines in each paragraph. To create new lines within a paragraph, press **Shift+Enter**. Word places a new line mark (↵) at the end of the line.

To display the paragraph and new line marks as well as other nonprinting symbols, click the **Show/Hide** button, the paragraph symbol toward the end of the Standard toolbar. You can also control the display of nonprinting symbols from the Options dialog box for the View category. You'll learn more about View options in "Change View Options" on page 65.

When you enter text in Word, you have a choice of two typing modes: Insert or Overtype. In *Insert* mode, everything to the right of the insertion point is pushed ahead as you type; no text is deleted as you type. Insert mode is the default typing mode. In *Overtype* mode, Word erases characters and spaces to the right of the insertion point as you type. To get to Overtype mode from Insert mode, press the **Ins** key or double-click on the **OVR** indicator in the status bar. To switch back to Insert mode, press **Ins** or double-click on **OVR** again. The status bar indicates whether you are in Insert or Overtype mode. When the status bar displays a black **OVR**, you are in Overtype mode. If OVR looks dim, you are in Insert mode.

Begin Guided Tour   Enter Text

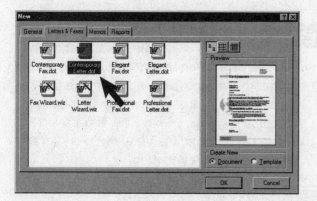

1 Create a document using one of the methods described in "Create a New Document" on page 46. For example, create a document with the Contemporary Letter template.

If you have a difficult time reading the tiny text used in some of the templates, zoom the document. Click the **Zoom Control** box near the end of the Standard toolbar and select a percentage such as **100%** from the drop-down list that appears. If you want to see more of the document at a later time, just select a smaller percentage or another option from the Zoom Control drop-down list.

2 Click where you want to enter text to move the insertion point. For example, click on **Click here and Type Return Address**. Then start typing.

You may see a jagged red line or the Tip Wizard appear as you type. The red line is triggered by the spell checker, which, by default, checks words automatically as you type. The Tip Wizard displays hints that might help you perform a task from beginning to end. To learn more about the Word spell checker and its options, see "Check Your Spelling" on page 118 and "Change Spelling and Grammar Options" on page 137. In the meantime, if you want to remove the red lines, press **F7** and repeatedly click **Ignore All** until Word prompts you to continue the spell check (click **Cancel**) or until the spell check is complete (click **OK**). To turn off the Tip Wizard, click on the **TipWizard** button (the light bulb) in the Standard toolbar.

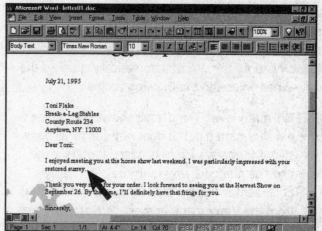

3 When you get to the end of a paragraph, press **Enter**. Continue typing and pressing **Enter** until you finish entering text. At this point, you may want to save your document. Refer to "Save a Document" on page 73 for instructions.

View Text in Different Modes

If you are writing a note to yourself, it doesn't matter whether you see the page layout (such as graphics, footnotes, and headers and footers—text that appears at the top and bottom of every page of a document) because there are probably none to see. However, if you are creating a letter for clients or a report using advanced desktop publishing tools, you'll want to view each page in WYSIWYG (what-you-see-is-what-you-get, pronounced "wizzy-wig") format, which shows exactly how the printed page will look.

You can use the View menu to display a document in one of three views: Normal, Page Layout, and Outline. You can also change views by clicking on one of three buttons to the left of the horizontal scroll bar at the bottom of the document window. You can tell which view you're in because its button will look pushed in.

Word performs some tasks only when you are in a particular view. For example, Word only allows you to draw in Page Layout view. However, you don't have to worry about this; Word automatically changes the view when you open the Drawing toolbar.

 Normal view The default shows text as you have formatted it, but does not display all page layout formats, such as headers, footers, page and line numbers, and footnotes. To display a document in Normal view, either select **Normal** from the **View** menu or click the **Normal View** button.

 Page Layout view Shows how the body text, headers, footers, and footnotes appear on the printed page. Page Layout view also shows the edges of the page, allowing you to see text relative to the edges of the paper. To display a document in Page Layout view, either select **Page Layout** from the **View** menu or click the **Page Layout View** button.

Outline view Shows the heading levels of your document, if you have applied heading styles using Word templates. To display a document in Outline view, either select **Outline** from the **View** menu or click the **Outline View** button. Word adds a toolbar and symbols to documents displayed in Outline view. Master Document view, which is related to Outline view and does not have a button on the status bar, allows you to display a long document as a whole or with only certain levels of headings.

You can also view a document as it will print. This is called *Print Preview*. For more information about Print Preview and its features, see "View Text as It Will Print" on page 67.

Begin Guided Tour Take a Look at the Different Modes

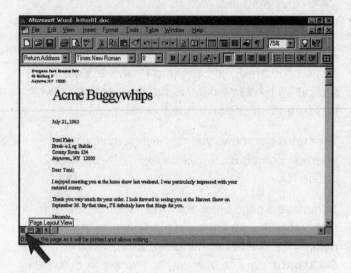

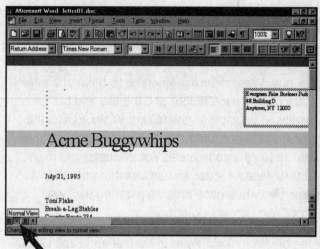

1 With an open document in the document window, open the **View** menu and choose **Page Layout**, or click the **Page Layout View** button. Word displays the document in Page Layout view.

2 To return to Normal View, open the **View** menu and choose **Normal**, or click the **Normal View** button. Word displays the document in Normal view.

Start a New Page or Section

When you fill up a page in a document, Word automatically inserts a *page break*, which marks the end of one page and the beginning of a new one. Word determines where to break the page by calculating page height and the top and bottom margins. If you add or delete text, Word adjusts the page breaks accordingly. From time to time, you may want to force a page break. For example, you may want to create a letter and an attachment—all in a single file with a page break separating the two. Forced page breaks do not adjust.

Page breaks look different in Normal and Page Layout views. In Normal view, page breaks inserted by Word are indicated with a dotted line. If you insert a page break, Word adds the text **Page Break** in the middle of the dotted line. In Page Layout view, page breaks look like the gap between two pieces of paper.

To embed a page break, open the **Insert** menu and choose the **Break** command. In the Break dialog box, Page Break is already selected by default; just click **OK**, and Word inserts the page break. To insert a page break without opening the Break dialog box, point to the place in which you want to insert a page break and press **Ctrl+Enter**.

You can also insert section breaks or column breaks (see "Add Multiple Columns to a Document" on page 165) using the Break dialog box. Use section formatting when there is a major change in your document: starting a two-column layout; changing page orientation (see "Use Portrait and Landscape Orientation" on page 148); placing a headline; or inserting new or reformatted page numbers, headers, or footers. Although the default is for Word to start a new page at a section break, you can start (and even end) a new section on the same page as the previous (or following) section, as shown in the following table.

The status bar shows you the section in which the insertion point is located (for example, Sec 1, Sec 2, or Sec 100).

To remove a page break that you have inserted or a section break, move the insertion point to the beginning of the line below the break, and press the **Backspace** key. The only way to remove an automatic page break that Word has inserted is to move the insertion point to a line that is above the page break and then to insert a page break. You may want to insert a page break rather than accepting the default. For example, you can insert a page break between the end of one chapter and the beginning of another. Or you might want to make sure that related text remains on the same page by inserting a page break above the text.

Paragraph and section marks both contain formats for their paragraphs or sections, respectively. If you delete a paragraph or section mark, the text preceding the deleted mark assumes the format of the following paragraph or section.

Section Break Types

Option	Starts the Next Section
Next Page	At the top of the next page.
Continuous	On the next line of the same page as the previous section.
Even Page	At the top of the next even-numbered page.
Odd Page	At the top of the next odd-numbered page.

Begin Guided Tour   Insert a Page Break

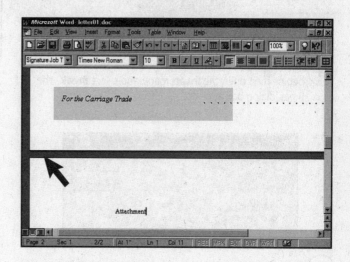

1 With the current document in Normal view, move the insertion point at the end of the line after which you want to start the new page. Open the **Insert** menu and select the **Break** command.

3 Click the **Page Layout View** button. Word shows the break between pages.

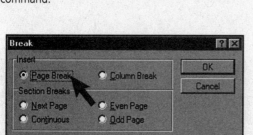

2 Select the **Page Break** option button and click **OK**. Word closes the Break dialog box, inserts the page break, and changes the page number in the status bar.

Begin Guided Tour Insert a Section Break

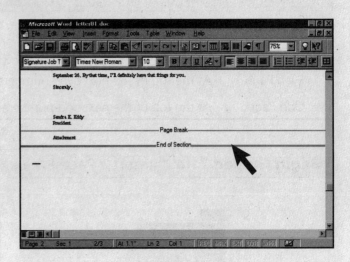

1 Place the insertion point where you want the section to begin. Then open the **Insert** menu and select **Break**. The Break dialog box appears.

3 Click the **Normal View** button. When you are in Normal view, section break marks are named **End of Section**.

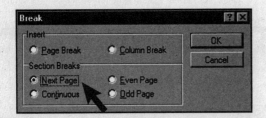

2 Select a section break option For example, select **Next Page**. Then click **OK**. Word closes the dialog box, places a section break mark at the insertion point, changes the section number and, optionally, the page number in the status bar.

Move Around a Document

ord offers three ways to move around a document: the mouse, the keyboard, and the Go To command. With the mouse or the keyboard, you can quickly scroll or jump around a document—from the top to the bottom or from the left margin to the right margin, or anywhere in between.

Using the mouse is an easy way to navigate in your document. You can either move the mouse pointer around the text area or you can use the mouse with parts of the scroll bar (see "Use the Scroll Bars and the Status Bar" on page 35). To use the mouse in the text area, click the left mouse button; hold and drag the mouse pointer in the direction you want to move. For example, to see the next page of a document, drag the mouse downward. As you drag the mouse, new parts of the document appear. The text that you drag over appears *highlighted* (that is, if text normally appears in black on a white background, it will now appear in reverse video, or white on a black background). If you release the left mouse button and then click the mouse outside the highlighted area, the highlight disappears.

Before making any changes to your document, make sure that you remove the highlight. If you don't and press the **Del** or **Backspace** key, you will delete the entire highlighted section. If that happens, quickly press **Ctrl+Z** before continuing. Ctrl+Z undoes the deletion. To learn more about undoing, see "Undo and Redo Actions" on page 105.

If you're typing or editing, sometimes it's faster to use keys to move around a document than to move your hand to the mouse. Also, if you have to move the mouse and then press and hold a mouse button (when pressing one key can accomplish the same purpose), it might be better to use the keyboard.

The following table lists the *navigation* or movement keys and describes the effect on the insertion point of pressing each key.

Word Navigation Keys

Press This Key	To Move the Insertion Point
Down arrow	One item down a list or down one line of text
Left arrow	One character to the left
Right arrow	One character to the right
Up arrow	One item up a list or up one line of text
Ctrl+down arrow	One paragraph down
Ctrl+left arrow	One word to the left
Ctrl+right arrow	One word to the right
Ctrl+up arrow	One paragraph up
Ctrl+End	To the end of the document
Ctrl+Home	To the beginning of the document

(continues)

Word Navigation Keys   Continued

Press This Key	To Move the Insertion Point
Ctrl+PgDn	To the bottom of a window
Ctrl+PgUp	To the top of a window
End	To the end of the current line
Home	To the beginning of the current line
PgDn	Down one screen
PgUp	Up one screen

Go to a Page, Line, or Section

When you know the number of the page, line, or section that you want to jump to in your document (especially if the document is very long), the **Go To** command on the **Edit** menu is a quick way of doing so. Go To is a very powerful command, which you can also use to jump to bookmarks, footnotes, fields, tables, graphics, equations, objects, and annotations, and so on. To choose what kind of item you want to go to, simply select the item from the **Go To What** list box in the Go To dialog box.

A quick way to open the Go To dialog box is to either press **F5** or **Ctrl+G**, or double-click the left side of the status bar.

Begin Guided Tour   Navigating a Document with the Mouse and Keyboard

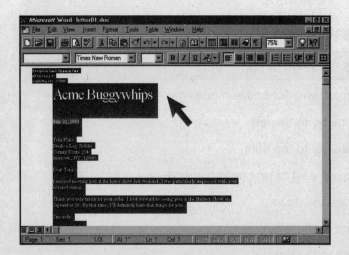

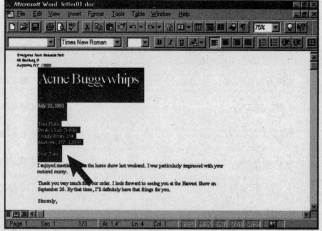

1 If you are at the top of the document, press **Ctrl+End** to move to the end. Then move the mouse pointer to the bottom of the text area, press and hold down the left mouse button, and drag toward the top of the screen. After releasing the left mouse button, click next to the text at the top of the document. You also can press **Ctrl+Home** to move to the top of the document.

2 With the insertion point at the top of the document, press and hold down the left mouse button, and drag down until the highlight is in the middle of the document. Press the **End** key to remove the highlight. You can also move down a document line by line by repeatedly pressing the down arrow key.

Guided Tour   Navigating a Document with the Mouse and Keyboard

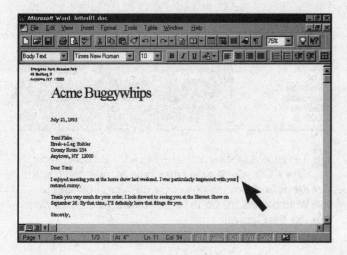

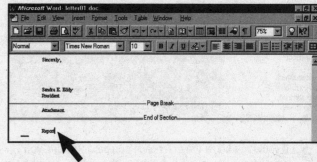

4 Press **PgDn** to move the insertion point down to another part of the document.

3 Move the insertion point to the beginning of a line by clicking in the space to the left of that line. Then press **End** to move the insertion point to the end of the line.

Begin Guided Tour   Moving to a Specific Page

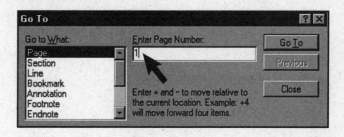

2 In the Go To dialog box, select **Page** in the **Go To What** list box. Then type a page number in the **Enter Page Number** text box. Then click the **Go To** button. Word displays the top of the page.

(continues)

1 With a document on-screen, open the **Edit** menu and select the **Go To** command. Or press **F5**, **Ctrl+G**, or double-click the left side of the status bar.

Guided Tour Moving to a Specific Page

(continued)

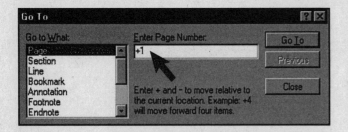

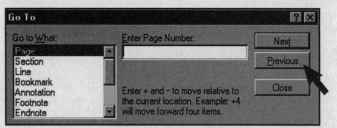

3 If you don't know the exact page number you want, you can enter a page number relative to the current insertion point. To go forward or back a specific number of pages, type **+n** or **-n**, where *n* represents the number of pages, in the **Enter Page Number** text box. For example, type **+1** to move one page ahead of where you are now. Then click the **Go To** button.

4 To return to the previous insertion point location, remove the characters from the **Enter Page Number** text box, and click **Previous**. When you remove the characters from the text box, Word changes the **Go To** button to **Next**. To close the dialog box, click the **Close** button.

Magnify or Reduce Your View of a Document

Word provides a feature that allows you to *zoom* a document: view it in different sizes from 200 percent of its size, which allows you to see the text but not the layout, to two facing pages, which enables you to view the layout but not necessarily the text—and many sizes in between. Page Layout view offers more zoom choices than Normal view.

To magnify or reduce the view, either open the **View** menu, select the **Zoom** command, and select choices in the Zoom dialog box; or click the **Zoom Control** button and choose from the drop-down list. The Zoom dialog box offers more viewing choices.

> **Begin Guided Tour**   Zoom a Document

1 Display a document in Normal view. Then open the **View** menu and select **Zoom**.

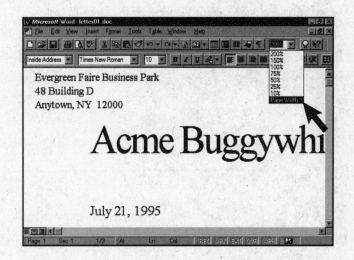

3 Click the **Zoom Control** drop-down list and select **Page Width**. This allows you to see all the text from the left margin to the right margin.

(continues)

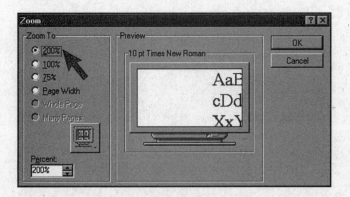

2 In the Zoom dialog box, click **200%**. Notice that the Preview box shows a sample document at the selected Zoom value. Then click **OK**. Word magnifies the document and changes the percentage in the Zoom Control drop-down list.

Guided Tour Zoom a Document *(continued)*

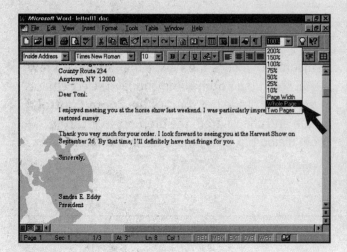

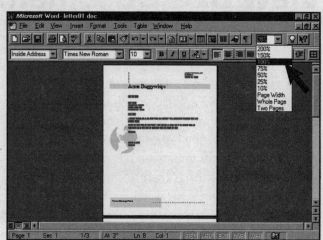

4 Click the **Page Layout View** button to change to Page Layout view. Click the **Zoom Control** drop-down list and select **Whole Page**, which along with **Two Pages** is available only in Page Layout view.

5 Notice that you can no longer read most of the text. Click the **Zoom Control** drop-down list and select **100%**. Then return to Normal view.

Change View Options

You can customize your copy of Word in many ways. With view options, you can change the look of documents and the document window. In addition, you can determine whether you can view certain types of nonprinting characters.

The quickest way to view or hide nonprinting characters is to click on the **Show/Hide** button (the paragraph symbol) on the Standard toolbar. It's useful to show all nonprinting characters. Then you'll be able to see whether you have two spaces between some words or are using a tab rather than spaces to indent a paragraph or line.

To change view options, open the **Tools** menu and select **Options**. Then click the **View** tab to display the Options dialog box for the View category. For a complete look at the options in this dialog box, see "Options Dialog Box—View Tab" on page 541.

The options in the Options dialog box for the View Category vary depending on the view; Page Layout offers a few more choices.

Begin Guided Tour Change View Options

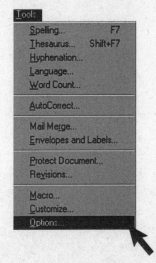

1 Display a document in Page Layout view. Then open the **Tools** menu and select **Options**.

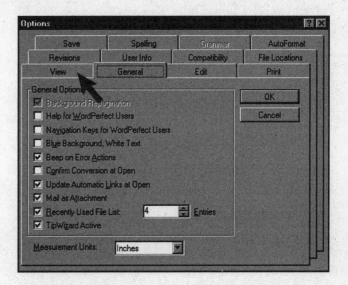

2 Click the **View** tab to display the Options dialog box for the View category if it is not already on display.

(continues)

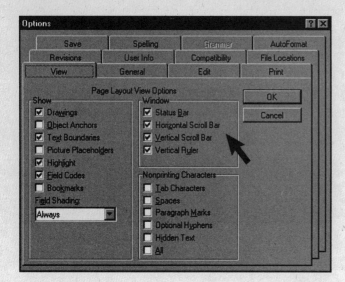

3 Select the items you want to show by clicking the appropriate check boxes. Word displays a check mark next to all the items that will appear. Then click **OK**.

View Text as It Will Print

Print Preview lets you look at and adjust the format, titles, headers and footers, margins, view text, and so on, of each page before you print, thereby saving on paper costs and printer toner.

In Print Preview, Word reduces the page so that it fits on your computer screen and allows you to review several pages simultaneously. You can access many commands while in Print Preview. For example, you can save the document, find text, and add text, pictures, and other objects.

At the top of the Print Preview window is a toolbar, which you can use to work on the document. Here is an overview of the buttons in the Print Preview toolbar:

 Print   Prints a document using the current printing defaults.

 Magnifier   Magnifies or reduces the displayed document and turns off editing mode. Clicking again turns off zooming and starts editing mode.

 One Page   Fits the page on the screen and shows the page as it is laid out.

 Multiple Pages   Displays from 1–18 pages. Click the button and then drag the resulting box to the number of pages you want displayed on the screen at one time. You can use this feature to show and edit *facing pages* (one even and one odd looking as they would appear if bound in an open book).

 Zoom Control   Clicking the arrow to the right of the text box reveals a list of percentages and values by which you can scale the pages. You also can type a percentage in the Zoom Control text box.

 View Ruler   Displays or hides horizontal and vertical rulers.

In Print Preview, you can use rulers to drag the margins to a new location. Either drag the left and/or right margins, or move the mouse pointer until a double-headed arrow replaces the standard upward-pointing arrow. Then press and hold down the left mouse button and drag the margin to a new position.

 Shrink to Fit   Word attempts to fit your document on just one page.

 Full Screen   Switches from the standard screen with a title bar, menu bar, toolbar, and status bar to a screen that shows only the toolbar. Click the button again to return the hidden elements to the screen.

 Close   Closes Print Preview and returns to your document.

 Help   Click this button and then click a section of the screen to display information about the clicked-on item. Press **Esc** to close the Help box.

To move through the document pages, use the vertical scroll bar or press **PgUp** (to move up one page) and **PgDn** (to move down one page).

Begin Guided Tour   Preview Text

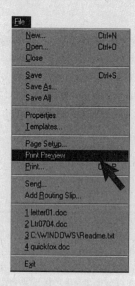

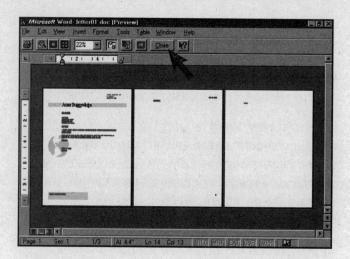

1 Open the **File** menu and select **Print Preview**, or click the **Print Preview** button.

3 If everything looks okay, click the **Print** icon to print the document using the defaults. If you need to make some changes, click the **Close** button to return to the document window.

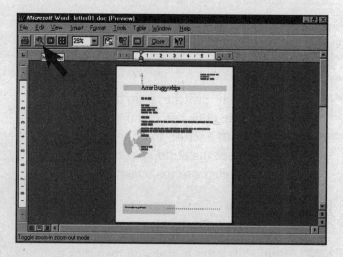

2 Look for any problems you need to correct before printing the document. Use the toolbar buttons to adjust the view of the document, as necessary.

Print a Document

Word for Windows has many printing options, but most times you print, you'll accept the default settings. The easiest way to print a document using the defaults is to click the **Print** button. This is the only way to print without opening the Print dialog box.

If you want to use some of Word for Windows 95's many printing options, you need to open the **File** menu and select the **Print** command; or press **Ctrl+Shift+F12** or **Ctrl+P**. Word opens a dialog box that offers a variety of options from which you can choose. You can print ranges of pages, all odd or even pages, an entire document, related material, or even to a file for later printing.

Both Word's **Print** button and **Print** command use Windows' printing facility. This means that to change certain options, you must use the Windows Control Panel and Windows commands. For example, many computers, through a network or additional cables, have access to two or more printers. To change the default printer (the printer to which Word and other Windows programs always print unless overridden temporarily), select the **Start** button, select **Settings**, and choose **Printers**; or double-click on the **Printers** icon in the Control Panel. Point to an icon representing a printer, open the **File** menu, and click on **Set As Default**. A check mark preceding **Set As Default** indicates the selected printer is the default printer.

With another Windows feature, you can check your print jobs. After you click **OK** in the Print dialog box, Windows sends your print job to the printer and adds a small printer icon to the right side of the task bar. To check printing, double-click on the icon. Windows opens the dialog box for the default printer and shows you the job in its position in the *print queue*, the list of jobs waiting to be printed or already printing. You can see the name of the document, its status, progress, and so on. In this dialog box, you also can temporarily or permanently stop printing, change printer properties, or specify the default printer.

For a complete description of the Print dialog box, see "Print Dialog Box" on page 554.

> You can also print from the Print Preview window. Just click the **Print** button in the Print Preview toolbar. Or open the **File** menu and select the **Print** command; or press **Ctrl+Shift+F12**.

Change Print Options

You can customize printing in many ways: you can process a print job while doing other work in Word or devote all your resources to print processing. When you print a document, you can include summary information, hidden text, and drawing objects. And you can specify the tray that feeds the paper on which documents will print.

To specify print options, open the **Tools** menu and select **Options**. Then click the **Print** tab to display the Options dialog box for the Print category. For descriptions of all the options in this dialog box, see "Options Dialog Box—Print Category" on page 545.

Begin Guided Tour Print a Document Using the Default Settings

1 With the document you want to print open on-screen, click the **Print** button.

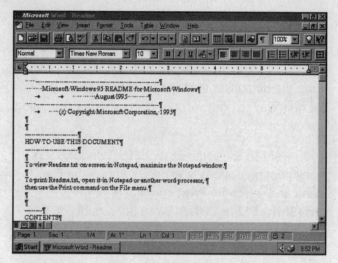

2 Word shows the print status and inserts an animated printer icon in the status bar. Windows adds a printer icon to the left of the time, and after a short time, Word starts printing.

Begin Guided Tour Print Select Parts of a Document

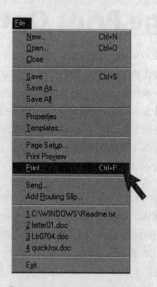

1 Open the document you want to print. Then open the **File** menu and select the **Print** command. You can also press **Ctrl+P** or **Ctrl+Shift+F12**. Word opens the Print dialog box.

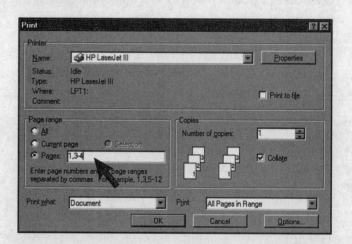

2 Select a Page range option. If you select the **Pages** option, enter the pages in the text box you want printed. Either type a single page number, specific page numbers separated by commas (for example, 1,3,6), ranges of pages (for example, 1–6), or a combination of particular page numbers and ranges (for example, 1, 3, 6–9).

Guided Tour   Print Select Parts of a Document

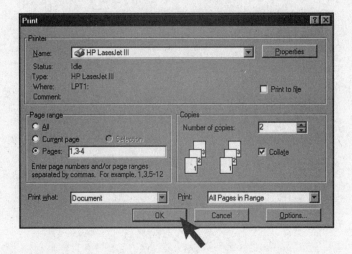

3 Type or select the number of copies that you want to print in the **Number of copies** text/option box. Print all the pages in the range, only odd pages, or only even pages by opening the **Print** drop-down list and making a selection. From the **Print what** drop-down list, select the part of the document that you want printed: the document, summary information (creation date, author, title, and so on), annotations, styles, autotext entries, or key assignments. When you finish selecting options, click **OK**.

Begin Guided Tour   Change Print Options

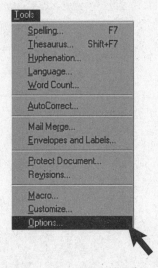

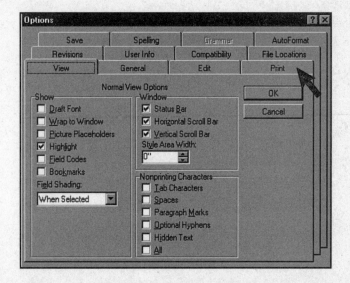

1 Open the **Tools** menu and select **Options**. (If there is no open document and the menu bar contains only the File and Help menus, click the **New** button.)

2 Click the **Print** tab to display the Options dialog box for the Print category if it is not already on-screen.

(continues)

Guided Tour   Change Print Options   *(continued)*

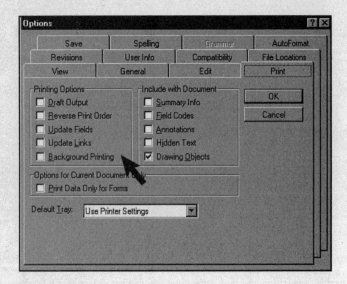

3 Select the options you want by clicking the appropriate check boxes. Then click **OK** to apply the changes and close the dialog box.

Save a Document

Whether you have created a new document or changed an existing document, the only way to store a permanent copy on your hard drive is to use one of the save commands. Without saving, when you exit Word or Windows, the document will be lost forever.

Save a document in the following ways:

- Open the **File** menu and select the **Save** command; press **Ctrl+S**. Or click the **Save** button whenever you want to save a complete copy of a document. The first time you save a document, Word opens the Save As dialog box, enabling you to name the document and place it in a particular drive and/or folder.

- Open the **File** menu; choose the **Save As** command to open the Save As dialog box to create a copy of a document under a new name and/or in a new location.

> You can use the **Save As** command to create a backup document on a floppy disk that you can store away from your computer or office.

- Using the Options dialog box for the Save category, you can automatically save a document every few minutes as you are working on it or create a backup file every time you save. For more information about Save options, see "Change Save Options" on page 76.

The fields in the Save As dialog box are:

- **Save In**   Open this drop-down list, and select the hard drive or floppy drive in which you want to save the file.

 Up One Level   Moves up to the drive or folder that is the parent of the current drive or folder. For example, when you are in My Documents, Word's default storage folder, clicking **Up One Level** will move you to the root folder, **C:**.

 Look in Favorites   Looks in the Favorites folder for a document previously stored there. The Favorites folder contains the documents that you want to store there. It's an excellent repository for documents that you will edit or use again and again.

 Create New Folder   Creates a new folder in which to save the file.

> If you want to store the same type of file or a group of chapters for a large document, it's a good idea to create a new folder.

 List   Displays up to four columns of folders and file names.

 Details   Displays file names and details: size, type, and the date it was last modified.

 Properties   Displays file names and file properties, including the title; author; revision number; number of pages, words, and characters; and its size.

 Commands and Settings   Press this button and select from the menu to perform miscellaneous actions, such as opening a file, printing one or more files, viewing properties, sorting, searching, and so on.

- **File name**   In this text box, type the name of the file that you want to save. Word suggests a name, either the first few words in the document or **Doc*n*.doc**, where n represents a unique number, but you will probably want a more descriptive file name.

• **Save as type**   If you don't want to save the file using the Word for Windows 95 format, select its file type from this drop-down list.

When you save a document for the first time, Word asks you to provide a file name. When naming a document, you can give it a long or short name. If you ever plan on transferring the file to a computer running Windows 3.1 or an earlier version, it's best to use a short file name of one to eight characters

(either letters, numbers, or the symbols ! @ # $ % & - ( ) _ { } ~ ^). Name files so that you can easily identify them a few days or a few months from now.

If you will be using Windows 95 exclusively, a file name can be up to 255 characters. When naming a file, do not use the symbols | ? : * " < > |. Windows reserves them for its own use. Using a long file name allows you to describe a file and display that description in the Windows Explorer.

Begin Guided Tour   Save a Document for the First Time

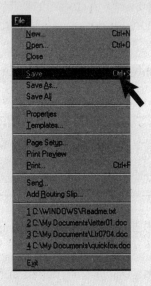

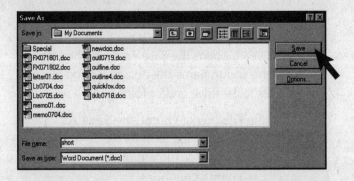

3 Click **Save**. Word saves the document, closes the dialog box, and displays the file name in the title bar.

From now on, when you save this document (or any other saved document), selecting the **Save** command, clicking on the **Save** button, or pressing **Ctrl+S** or **Shift+F12** will save the file without opening the Save As dialog box. To give a file a new name or place it in a new location, open the **File** menu and choose **Save As**.

1 Create a new document. (If you need help, review "Create a New Document" on page 46.) Then open the **File** menu and select the **Save** command. You can also click the **Save** button, press **Ctrl+S**, or **Shift+F12**. Word displays the Save As dialog box.

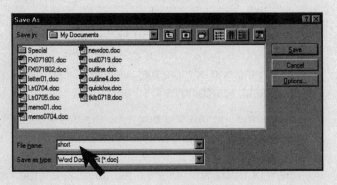

2 Type a file name in the **File name** text box.

Begin Guided Tour Save a File Under a New Name and in a New Location

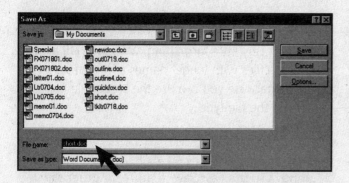

1 With a document on-screen, open the **File** menu and select the **Save As** command. Word opens the Save As dialog box with the contents of the File name text box highlighted.

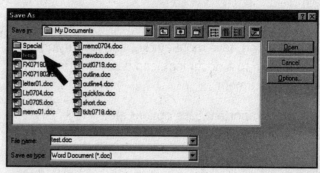

4 In the Save As dialog box, double-click the folder you just created. That folder's name now appears in the Save in text box.

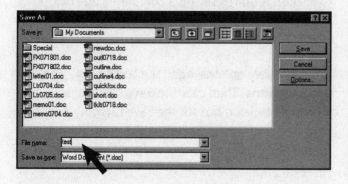

2 Type in the new name for your document. It will overwrite the highlighted name in the File name text box.

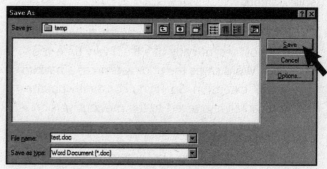

5 Click **Save**. Word saves the new document in its new folder. The original document remains in its original location.

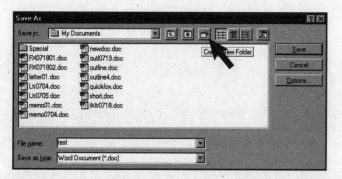

3 Click the **Create New Folder** button. Type a name for the new folder in the New Folder dialog box, and click **OK**. This creates a subfolder under the current folder.

Change Save Options

Word's save options enable you to automate saving, save more quickly, add identifying information to a document, and password-protect the current document.

The most important Save options are:

Automatic Save   Automatically saves the new changes document every few minutes as you are working on it. Simply tell Word that you want this feature turned on and then indicate the number of minutes between each save. This important feature allows you to recover a document if you lose power while editing.

Always Create Backup Copy   Instructs Word to save the most recent copy of a file. Every time you save a file, Word saves the prior version as a backup with a WBK extension. So, if you constantly update files, you can always revert to the previous version—for whatever reason.

Extensions are one-, two-, or three-character that identify the file type (such as DOC for document, EXE

for a file that runs a program, or TXT for text documents with very little formatting). Windows 95 allows you to save files with longer names and with no extension because you can use the longer file name to indicate the file type.

> If you have elected to save a backup copy, you cannot use the Fast Save feature, another save option, which saves only the part of the file that has changed. This saves time but since multiple copies of a file are saved with Fast Save, it does not save disk space. Creating a backup requires saving a complete copy of the file.

To specify save options, open the **Tools** menu and select **Options**. Then click the **Save** tab to display the Options dialog box for the Save category. For descriptions of all the options in this dialog box, see "Options Dialog Box—Save Category" on page 550.

Begin Guided Tour Automatically Save Documents

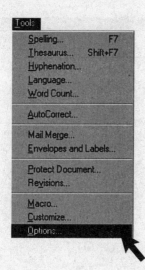

1 Open the **Tools** menu and select the **Options** command.

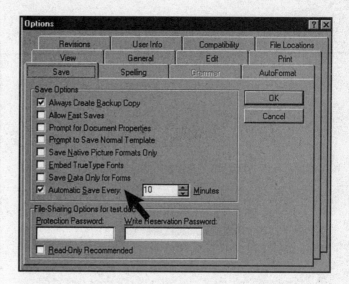

3 Click the **Automatic Save Every** check box, if it is not already checked.

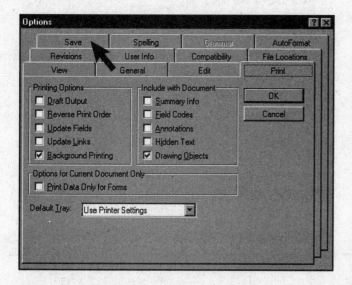

2 Click the **Save** tab to display the Options dialog box for the Save category if it is not already on-screen.

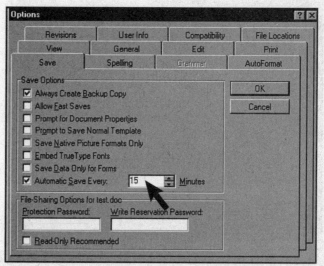

4 Choose the frequency with which you want Word to save (from 1 to 120 minutes). The default, and a good frequency, is 10 minutes. Click **OK** to close the dialog box.

Begin Guided Tour   Create Backup Copies

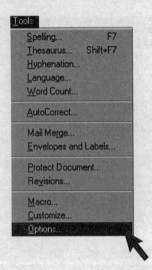

1 Open the **Tools** menu and select the **Options** command.

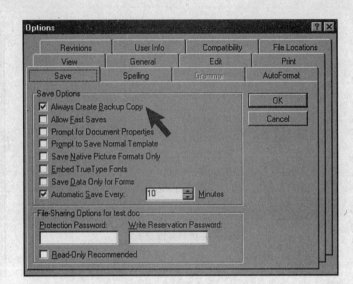

3 Check the **Always Create Backup Copy** check box. Click **OK** to close the dialog box.

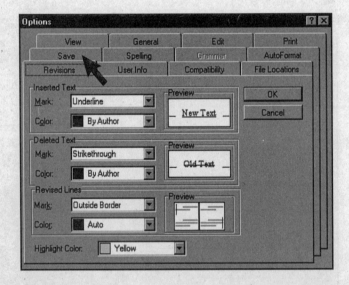

2 Click the **Save** tab to display the Options dialog box for the Save category if it is not already on-screen.

Open a Document

After you create and save a document, you'll probably want to retrieve it at some point in order to continue working on it. You can even save a great deal of time by opening an existing document and using its formats and page layouts as the basis for a new document.

To open a document, click the **Open** button (the open yellow folder at the top left of the screen) on the Standard toolbar. Open the **File** menu and select the **Open** command; or press **Ctrl+O** to display the Open dialog box from which you can retrieve an existing document.

The fields in the Open dialog box are:

- **Look in** Open this drop-down list and select the hard drive or floppy drive in which the file that you want to open is stored.

  Up One Level Moves up to the drive or folder that is the parent of the current drive or folder if the desired file is not in the current folder. When you are in **My Documents**, Word's default folder, clicking on **Up One Level** will move you to the root folder, **C:**.

  Look in Favorites Looks in the Favorites folder for a document that you stored there.

  Add to Favorites Adds the selected file to the \favorites folder.

  List Displays up to four columns of folders and file names.

  Details Displays file names and details: size, type, and the date it was last modified.

  Properties Displays file names and file properties, including the title; author; revision number; number of pages, words, and characters; and its size.

 Preview Press to view some of the contents of the selected file before you open it.

 Commands and Settings Press this button and select from the menu to perform miscellaneous actions, such as opening a file, printing one or more files, viewing properties, sorting, searching, and so on.

- **File name** In this text box, type the name of the file that you want to open.

- **Files of type** If the file is not formatted as a Word for Windows 95 file, you may need to select its file type from this drop-down list.

Look for a File to Open

If you don't know the name of the file that you want to retrieve, its file type, or its location, Word provides several ways to retrieve a document from the Open dialog box:

- To open a file whose name and file type you don't know, in the **Files of type** drop-down list, select the arrow button (the underlined down arrow). When the list of types opens, select the type that you think is the most likely to be correct or select **All files (*.*)**. Word displays all documents of that type in the box in the middle of the dialog box. If the desired file is displayed, double-click on it to open it.

> An asterisk (*) entered in place of a file name and/or file type is a *wild card*, which can represent any group of characters.

- To open a file whose name you don't know but with a file type that you do know, move the mouse pointer to the **Files of type** drop-down list, select the arrow button, and then select the file type. Word displays all documents of that type in the box in the middle of the dialog box. If the desired file appears, double-click on it to open it.

- To open a file whose name you know or whose name you know in part, but with a file type that

you do not know, type all or part of the file name in the File name text box. Then press Enter. Word displays a list of all files that match the letters that you typed.

- To display a complete list of files in the current folder, type ***.*** in the File name box or just look in the box in the middle of the dialog box.

Begin Guided Tour   Open a Document

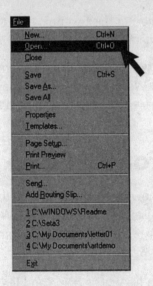

1 Open the **File** menu and select the **Open** command. Alternatively, you can click the **Open** button, or press **Ctrl+O**. Word displays the Open dialog box. The File name box lists the DOC files in the current folder.

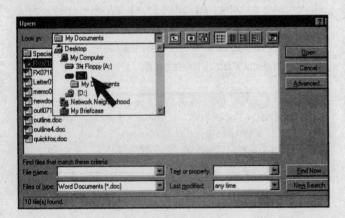

2 Click the **Look in** drop-down list and select the drive in which the file is located.

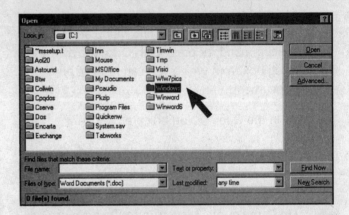

3 Double-click on the folder in which the file is located.

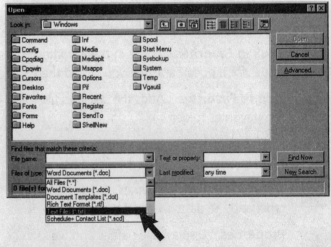

4 If necessary, select a file type from the **Files of type** drop-down list.

Guided Tour Open a Document

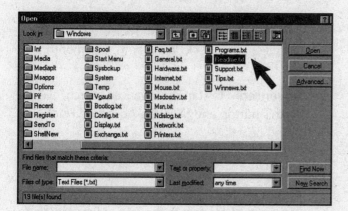

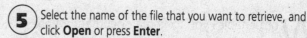

5 Select the name of the file that you want to retrieve, and click **Open** or press **Enter**.

A quick way to open a file is to double-click it. This selects and clicks **OK** in one step.

Find a Document

Word enables you to find a document whose complete name or location you don't remember. If you know part of a file name, a range of dates during which it was created or modified, or even some text within the document, you have a pretty good chance of finding a lost document.

Word provides two searches: simple and advanced. If you know the drive and folder location of a file but may not remember the exact name, you can use the simple search. Otherwise, select the advanced search. To find a document using either type of search, open the **File** menu and select the **Open** command. The Open dialog box appears.

If you plan to run a simple search, select the folder in which the file is located. Then choose from these options at the bottom of the Open dialog box:

- **File name**   Type as much of the file name as you can remember in this text box, or open the drop-down list and choose from the list of files that you previously typed. For information about the Open dialog box, see "Open a Document" on page 79.

> If you are not sure of the spelling of a file name for which you are searching, let Word start the search. For example, if you know the first few characters of a file name, type it in the **File name** text box. So, if you type **memo**, Word looks for all files beginning with **memo** and ending with any number of characters.

- **Files of type**   Select the type of file from this drop-down list.

- **Text or property**   Type any distinctive text that you remember is in the document in the text box, or open the drop-down list and choose from text that you previously entered.

- **Last modified**   If you can identify a range of dates during which you modified the document,

open this drop-down list and select from today, last week, this week, last month, this month, or any time.

- **Advanced**   To start an advanced search, click on this button and fill in the Advanced Find dialog box.

The options in the Advanced Find dialog box are:

- **Match all word forms**   Word search for all variations of the text in the Text or Property text box. For example, if you are searching for the word **drive**, Word also searches for **drives**, **drove**, and **driven**.

- **Match case**   Word search for an exact match for the combination of uppercase and lowercase characters in the Text or Property box.

> You can only check one of the Match all word forms and Match case check boxes; the other must remain clear.

- **Delete**   Select a search specification in the Find files that match these criteria list box; click the **Delete** button to remove the specification from the search.

- **New Search**   Clears the search specifications and starts a new search.

- **Define more criteria**   Fill in this group to further narrow the search. For example, select **And** or **Or** to indicate you are adding more criteria. Then select a property (a name, date, format, file type, and so on, on which Word will conduct the search) from the **Property** drop-down list, a condition (the property contains, starts with, or ends with if it's a name, or is yesterday, today, this week, and so on, if it's a date) from the **Condition** drop-down list, and type a value (any combination of characters or spaces) in the **Value** text box. If you select **And**, all sets of criteria must be true. If you select **Or**, all sets of criteria are tested but only one must be true.

You can find a file name that begins with **abc**; search for a file that was created, modified, or printed last week or on a specific date; or find a file that is larger than 10,000 characters. For example, if you have forgotten a file name but know that it contains the phrase **transcribed record**, define this criteria: **Text or property includes transcribed record**. Or if you know that the document is over 10 pages long, click on the **And** option button and add this criteria: **Number of pages at least 10**.

- **Add to List**   Adds the condition in the Define more criteria group and to the criteria in the box at the top of the Advanced Find dialog box.

- **Look in**   In this text box, enter a drive and/or folder in which to search, or select from the displayed drives and folders. To search your entire computer, select **My Computer**.

- **Search subfolders**   Searches all the folders under the drive and/or folder in which the search is to take place.

- **Find Now**   Starts the search. When the search begins, the name of the button changes to **Stop**. Click **Stop** to end the search at any time.

- **Save Search**   Opens a dialog box in which you can save all the search criteria to perform a future search.

- **Open Search**   Opens a dialog box from which you can select a saved search.

Begin Guided Tour   Find a Document Using a Simple Search

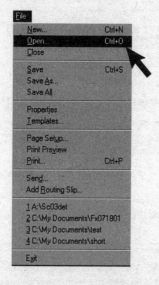

1 Open the **File** menu and choose the **Open** command, click on the **Open** button on the Standard toolbar, or press **Ctrl+O**.

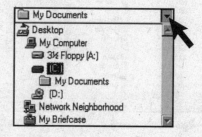

2 In the Open dialog box, click the down arrow to display the **Look in** drop-down list. Then double-click the drive in which the file is located.

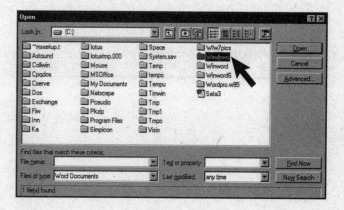

3 Double-click the folder in which the file is located.

(continues)

Guided Tour   Find a Document Using a Simple Search   *(continued)*

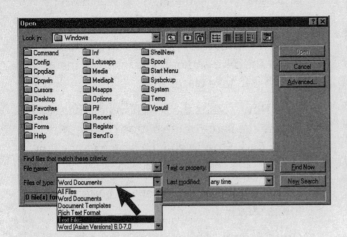

4 Select the type of file from the **Files of type** drop-down list. If you are not sure of the file type, select **All Files**.

5 Type as much of the file name as you can remember in the **File name** text box.

When you click anywhere in the dialog box, Word narrows your choice.

6 You can type text from within the document in the **Text or property** text box. If you have searched for this file before, open the drop-down list and select previously typed text.

7 Also, you can select a range of dates from the **Last modified** drop-down list.

Most times, you will either find the specific file or narrow your search so you can choose the desired file without clicking **Find Now**.

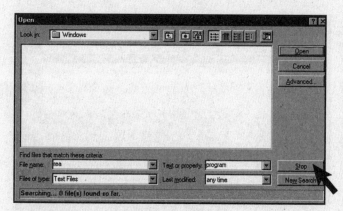

8 To start the search, if you have not already found the file, click the **Find Now** button. Word starts searching. Notice that the Find Now button is now called **Stop**.

9 After the search has been completed, you can double-click on a file to open it or change your choices and continue the search.

Begin Guided Tour   Find a Document Using an Advanced Search

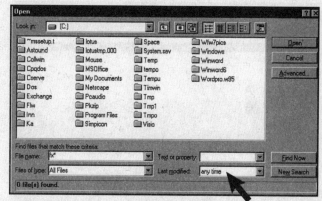

1 Open the **File** menu; choose the **Open** command. In the Open dialog box, select the type of file from the **Files of type** drop-down list; then type part of the file name followed by wild-card characters in the **File name** text box.

2 You can type text in the **Text or property** text box and/or select a range of dates from the **Last modified** drop-down list. Click the **Advanced** button.

(continues)

If you type an asterisk (*) after the characters in the **File name** text box, you're telling Word that the file name starts with those specific characters followed by any number of other characters.

Guided Tour Find a Document Using an Advanced Search *(continued)*

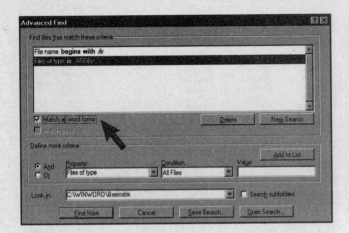

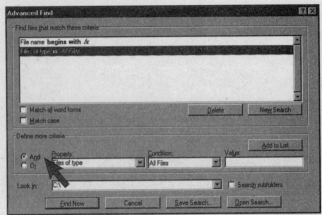

3 You can check the **Match all word forms** check box to have Word search for all variations of the text you entered in the Text or Property text box. Or you can check the **Match case** check box to match the exact combination of upper- and lowercase text.

5 To define another criterion, click the **And** or **Or** option button.

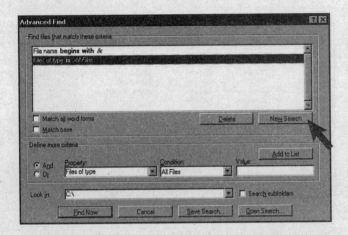

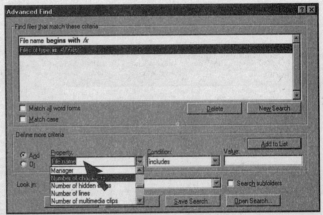

4 If you change your mind about a search criterion, select it and click the **Delete** button. (If you want to halt the search, click the **New Search** button.)

6 To continue to define the criterion, select an entry from the **Property** drop-down list.

Guided Tour   Find a Document Using an Advanced Search

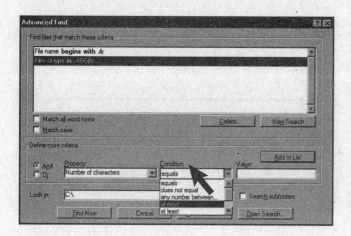

7 To continue to define the criterion, select an entry from the **Condition** drop-down list.

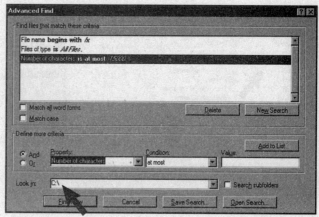

9 If the **Look in** text box/drop-down list is empty, type or select the drive and, optionally, the folder in which the file is located.

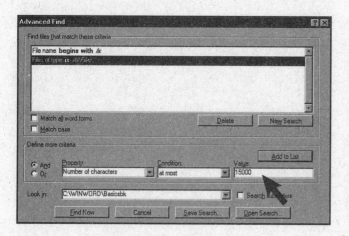

8 To continue, type text in the **Value** text box. Then click the **Add to List** button. Word adds the criteria to the **Find files that match these criteria** box and removes the value from the Value text box.

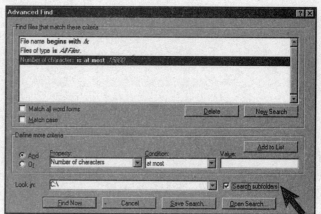

10 To search all subfolders under the drive and folder, check the **Search subfolders** check box.

(continues)

Guided Tour   Find a Document Using an Advanced Search   *(continued)*

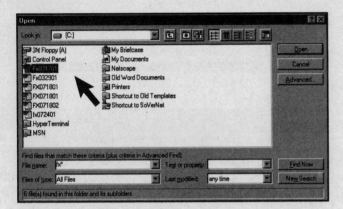

11 Click the **Find Now** button. Word closes the Advanced Find dialog box, performs the search, and shows the results. (To open a file, either double-click it or select it; then click the **Open** button.)

If you don't find any files, restart your search after either carefully correcting your spelling or using fewer search criteria (that is, don't search for text or use fewer characters in the file name).

Close a Document

If you have decided not to keep the current file, or you have just opened it to look at something, you don't have to save it.

To close a file, open the **File** command and select the **Close** command. If you have made any changes, Word prompts you to save the changes. Click **Yes** to save the changes, using the Save As dialog box; click **No** to close the document without saving it.

Whether you save a new file for the first time by opening the **File** menu and selecting the **Save** command or save an existing file after editing it by opening the **File** menu and selecting the **Save As** command, Word displays the Save As dialog box.

You also can close a document by closing the document window in which it is located or by exiting Word. In either case, Word prompts you to save the document if you have not done so.

Begin Guided Tour   Close a Document

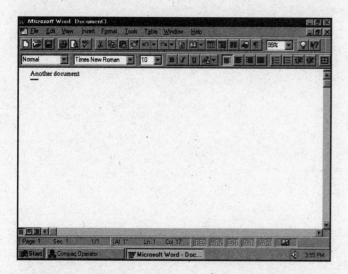

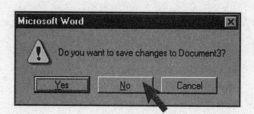

2 Click **No** to close the document without saving it. (To save changes, click **Yes**.)

1 Open or create a a document on-screen. (For help in creating a document, see "Create a New Document" on page 46.) Then open the **File** menu and select **Close**. Word prompts you to save your changes.

HOW TO...

Edit a Document

This section shows you how to edit a document. In this section, you will learn how to find a document; then you'll find out how to select text so that you can edit it. You'll discover how to manipulate text in many ways: delete it permanently; remove it and store it so you can paste it in another location; make a copy of it so the original remains in its current location and you can place a copy elsewhere.

You'll learn how to undo your actions. Then you will find and replace plain and formatted text, formats by themselves, and special symbols that you can't print. Then you'll learn how to check your document's spelling and grammar and replace words with synonyms. Finally, you'll discover how to change several of Word's options: General, Editing, Spelling, and Grammar.

What You Will Find in This Section

Select Text

Before you can copy, move, delete, or change formats for text, you must select it. As you work on a document, you can select blocks of text using the mouse, the keyboard, or both.

Regular text selection extends from the left margin to the right margin if you select one line or more of text. Word also enables you to select columns of characters and spaces. For example, if you have to edit a document with lines that have been indented by repeated pressing of the **Spacebar**, you'll start out with many spaces in front of the first character in every line. Rather than deleting the spaces line by line, you can delete a column of excess spaces.

To select a block of text using the mouse, move the mouse pointer to either the beginning or the end of the block of text to be selected. Then hold down the left mouse button and drag the mouse pointer toward the other end of the block of text. As you move the mouse, Word selects the block of text. When you reach the end of the selection, release the left mouse button. The highlight remains until you click the left mouse button or press a key.

> When you select text, pressing almost any key on your keyboard causes the highlighted text to disappear and be replaced by the character or symbol that you typed. If this happens inadvertently, immediately press **Ctrl+Z** to reverse your action and make the highlighted text reappear.

Word provides these mouse shortcuts for selecting specific blocks of text:

- Select a word by moving the mouse pointer to any character in the word and double-clicking the left mouse button. Word selects both the word and the space immediately to the right of the word.

- Select a line of text by moving the mouse pointer to the selection bar, the invisible column at the left edge of the text area. When the mouse pointer changes to an arrow pointing up and to the right, move the arrow to the left of the line to be selected and click the left mouse button. To select more than one line at a time, you can continue to hold the left mouse button down and drag the mouse up or down from the point at which you first clicked.

- Select a sentence by moving the mouse pointer anywhere within the sentence, holding down the **Ctrl** key, and clicking the left mouse button.

- Select a paragraph by moving the mouse pointer to the selection bar. Then move the mouse pointer in front of any line in the paragraph and double-click the left button.

- Select a paragraph by triple-clicking any word in the paragraph.

- Select multiple paragraphs by double-clicking in front of the first or last paragraph to be selected, continuing to hold down the left mouse button, and dragging the mouse pointer up or down within the selection bar.

- Select text without dragging by moving the mouse pointer to one end of the text to be selected and clicking the left mouse button. Then move the mouse pointer to the other end of the selection, hold down the **Shift** key, and click the left mouse button. Use this method when the text you want to select extends beyond the boundaries of the computer screen.

- Select the entire document by moving the mouse pointer into the selection bar, holding down the **Ctrl** key, and clicking the left mouse button.

- Select the entire document by moving the mouse pointer into the selection bar and triple-clicking.

- Select a column by moving the mouse pointer to the beginning of the column of text to be selected. Hold down the **Alt** key and drag the pointer diagonally down to the opposite corner of the column. If any character is at least half-way in the selection area, Word selects it. When you select all the text that you want, release the mouse button.

If you change your mind about the current selection, just move the mouse pointer off the selected text and click. Word turns off the selection. If you accidentally select too much text, you can "back up" by continuing to hold down the left mouse button and moving the mouse pointer to the end of the selection.

Almost every mouse action has a keyboard equivalent. For example, to start a selection using the keyboard, move the insertion point to a starting point and press **F8**. This action starts Extend Selection mode and turns on the **EXT** (that is, Extend Selection) indicator in the status bar. When Extend Selection mode is active, text selection is cumulative; each time you select text, Word adds the new selection to the text that you've already selected. Repeatedly press **F8** to add the next larger text block to the selection—from word, sentence, paragraph, section, to the entire document. No matter how large a block you selected, you can press a combination of arrow keys to adjust the characters selected. For example, pressing the left arrow causes the highlight to back up one character or space for every key pressed, and pressing the right arrow adds a character or space to the selection.

Text Selection Keys

To Select	Press
A document	Ctrl+5 (on the numeric keypad)
To the end of a paragraph	Ctrl+Shift+down arrow
To the beginning of a word	Ctrl+Shift+left arrow
To the end of a word	Ctrl+Shift+right arrow
To the beginning of a paragraph	Ctrl+Shift+up arrow
To the end of a document	Ctrl+Shift+End
To the beginning of a document	Ctrl+Shift+Home
One line down	Shift+down arrow
One character or graphic to the left	Shift+left arrow
One character or graphic to the right	Shift+right arrow
One line up	Shift+up arrow
To the end of a line	Shift+End
To the beginning of a line	Shift+Home
One screen down	Shift+PgDn
One screen up	Shift+PgUp

You can extend your selection to a specific character to the right of your current selection by pressing that character (letter, number, or symbol) on the keyboard. For example, in the text **The quick brown fox jumped over the lazy dog**, move the insertion point in front of quick and press **F8**. If you type **x**, the selection will be extended to the end of the word fox.

You can deselect text in reverse order of selection. Press **Shift+F8**, and the highlight will back up in the reverse order in which the text was selected. To turn off Extend Selection mode, either press the **Esc** key or perform an editing command. The following table summarizes Word's text selection keys.

A shortcut for selecting a large block of text is to move the insertion point to one end of the text you want to select, press **F8** (to start Extend Selection mode), press **F5** (the Go To command), type a page number in the dialog box, and press **Enter**. Then Word extends the selection to the top of the page to which you just jumped. If you change your mind about the selection, press **Shift+F5**; then Word places the insertion point back at the previous location. (For more information about using the Go To command, see "Move Around a Document" on page 59.)

Begin Guided Tour   Select Blocks of Text with the Mouse

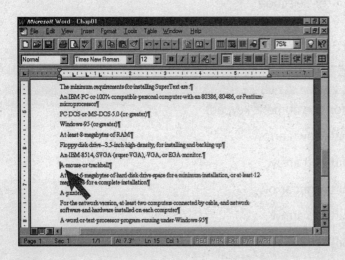

1 With an open document on-screen, move the mouse pointer to the first character to be selected. Then press and hold down the left mouse button. The insertion point remains at the first character you select.

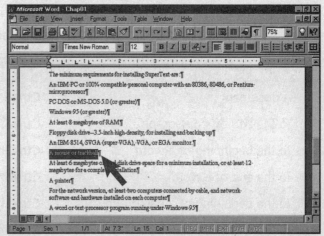

2 Drag the mouse to the other end of the selection and release the mouse button. Word highlights the selected text.

Guided Tour   Select Blocks of Text with the Mouse

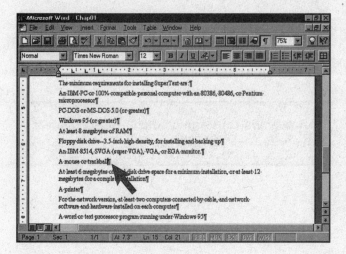

3 Click outside the highlighted area to "deselect" the selection.

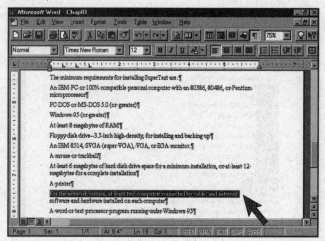

5 Move the mouse pointer into the selection area (in the left margin). When the mouse pointer points up and to the right, click to select a line.

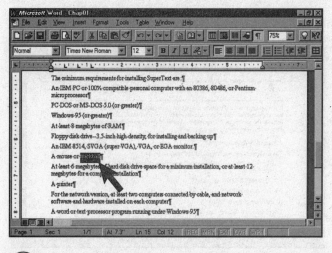

4 Double-click any word in the document to select it.

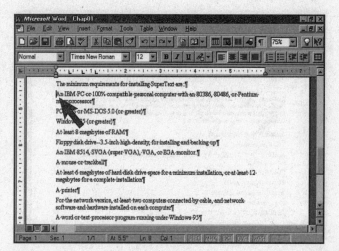

6 Move the mouse pointer to the beginning of a column of text you want to select.

(continues)

Guided Tour   Select Blocks of Text with the Mouse   *(continued)*

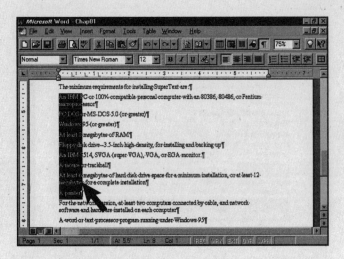

7 Press and hold down the **Alt** key to start Column Select mode. Then press and hold down the left mouse button and drag diagonally to the end of the column. Then click outside the selection to remove the highlight.

> Another way of starting Column Select mode is to press Ctrl+Shift+F8.

Begin Guided Tour   Select Blocks of Text with the Keyboard

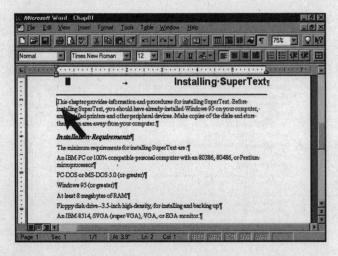

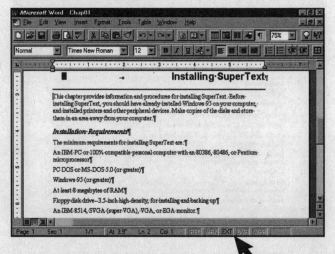

1 Use any combination of arrow, Home, and End keys to move the insertion point to either the beginning or the end of the area you want to select.

2 Press **F8** to turn on Extend Selection mode as indicated by the bold **EXT** in the status bar.

Guided Tour Select Blocks of Text with the Keyboard

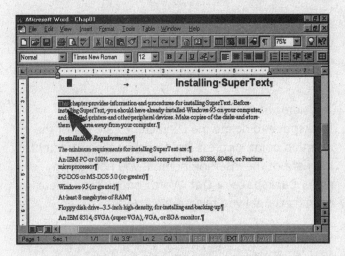

3 Press **F8** again to select a word. Press it again to extend the selection to the end of the sentence.

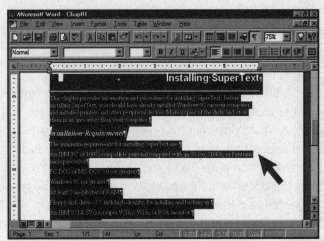

5 Press **Ctrl+5** (on the numeric keypad) to select the entire document. Then press the **Home** key to remove the highlight and go to the top of the document.

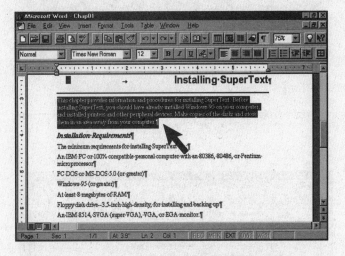

4 Press **F8** again to extend the selection to the end of the paragraph. To remove the selection, repeatedly press **Shift+F8** until the highlight is gone. Then press **Esc** to turn off Extend Selection mode.

Delete Text

Once you select text, you can do a great deal with it. You can change its appearance (for example, see "Add Emphasis to Selected Text" on page 170 and "Change Fonts and Font Sizes" on page 182). Or you can move it or place a copy of it in another location, either in the current document, in another Word document, or even in another Windows application. (See "Move Text" on page 99 and "Copy Text" on page 103.) You also can delete it from the document. For example, if your company no longer sells a particular product, you can erase all traces of it from your marketing literature or sales reports. Or if you have been editing a paragraph that can't be fixed, just delete it and start over.

To permanently delete selected text (see on "Select Text" page 92), either open the **Edit** menu and select the **Clear** command or press **Del**. This erases the selection without storing it in the **Clipboard**, an area in which Windows temporarily stores selections that are cut or copied using Word's (and other Windows applications) **Edit** menu's **Cut** or **Copy** commands, respectively. You'll learn more about the Clipboard in "Move Text" on page 99.

To delete characters from a document, press **Backspace** to delete the character to the left of the insertion point; or press **Del** to delete the character to the right of the insertion point. If you hold down either **Backspace** or **Del**, Word continues to delete characters until you release the key.

If you have inadvertently removed text, you can restore it to your document if you have not performed any action since the deletion. Either open the **Edit** menu and select the **Undo** command, or press **Ctrl+Z**. For more information about the Undo command, see "Undo and Redo Actions" on page 105.

Begin Guided Tour Delete Text

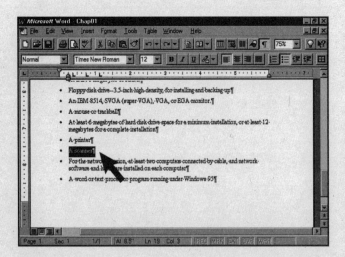

1 Select some text using the mouse or keyboard. For example, to select a line, move the mouse pointer to the selection bar and click the left mouse button.

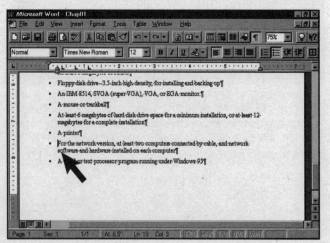

2 Open the **Edit** menu and select the **Clear** command, or press the **Del** key. The selected text disappears.

Move Text

After you select text, you can use the **Cut** and **Paste** commands on the **Edit** menu to move the selection to a new location. When you use the **Cut** command, Word stores the cut selection in the Clipboard.

> You also can copy a selection to place the copy elsewhere in a document while keeping the selection in its original location. A copied selection is also held in the Clipboard. For more information about copying text, see "Copy Text" on page 103.

The *Clipboard* is a Windows program, which is not only available for Word but also for other programs that run under Windows. When you cut a selection, Windows moves it to the Clipboard, and when you paste it, Windows inserts it from the Clipboard to the location of the insertion point in Word or another Windows application. The copy also remains in the Clipboard, so you can continue inserting it wherever you want in the document. The Clipboard stores only one selection at a time. Every time you cut (or copy) a selection to the Clipboard, the new selection replaces the prior contents. When you exit Word, but keep running Windows, the contents of the Clipboard remain. When you exit Windows, the Clipboard is emptied.

 To remove a selection from its original location, open the **Edit** menu and choose the **Cut** command, press a shortcut key combination, **Ctrl+X** or **Shift+Del**. Or click the **Cut** toolbar button, or right-click and select **Cut** from the shortcut menu. This places the selection in the Windows Clipboard in which it is stored until the next cut or copy. (See "Copy Text" on page 103.)

 To paste the selection into its new location, open the **Edit** menu and choose the **Paste** command, press a shortcut key combination, **Ctrl+V** or **Shift+Ins**. Or click the **Paste** toolbar

button, or right-click and select **Paste** from the shortcut menu. This places a copy of the contents of the Windows Clipboard at its new location.

You can paste the same selected text as many times as you like. For each copy to be pasted, choose the **Paste** command one time. Note that you can reposition the insertion point for each subsequent paste. Word remembers the pasted copy until you make another text selection and cut (or copy) it to the Clipboard.

> If you try to use the Cut command without selecting text first (or without having a selection in the Clipboard), Word displays the Edit menu or the shortcut menu with the Cut command dimmed. This is a reminder that you must select text before cutting it.

Word provides another shortcut method, *drag-and-drop*, for moving text. Make a selection, move the mouse pointer within the selection, press and hold down the left mouse button, and "drag" the selection to its new location. Then release the left mouse button, "dropping" the selection. During drag-and-drop, Word adds a dotted box to the tail of the mouse pointer and shows the current location of the insertion point using a vertical dotted line. As you drag, notice the position of the dotted insertion point. When it's where you want to drop the selection, release the left mouse button.

> To move selected text without changing the contents of the Clipboard, use drag-and-drop instead of selecting the Copy or Cut commands from the Edit menu, the shortcut menu, or clicking on the Copy or Cut toolbar buttons. Using either command or toolbar button replaces the contents of the Clipboard with new contents. Using drag-and-drop does not place anything in the Clipboard.

Begin Guided Tour   Cut and Paste Text

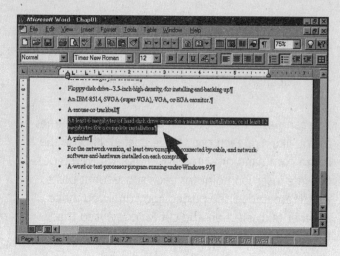

1 Select the text to be cut and pasted.

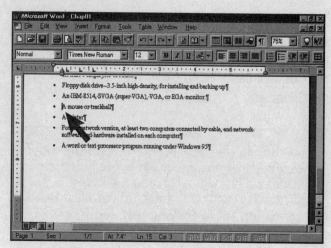

3 Click the location at which you want to paste the selection. This moves the insertion point.

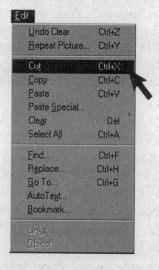

2 Open the **Edit** menu and select the **Cut** command. You also can click the **Cut** toolbar button, or press **Ctrl+X**, or press **Shift+Del** to cut a selection.

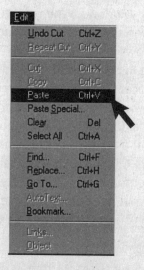

4 Open the **Edit** menu and select the **Paste** command. You also can click the **Paste** toolbar button, press **Ctrl+V**, or **Shift+Ins**.

Guided Tour Cut and Paste Text

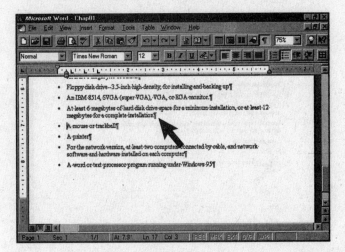

5 The text appears at the location of the insertion point. To paste the cut selection again, click the **Paste** toolbar button.

Begin Guided Tour Move Text with Drag-and-Drop

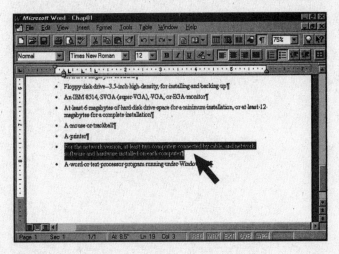

1 Select the text to be moved.

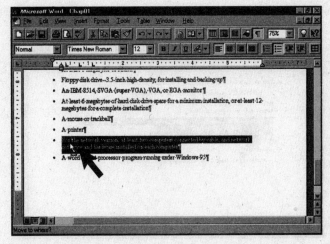

2 Move the mouse pointer anywhere within your selection. Notice that the mouse pointer becomes an arrow that points up and to the left, and a dotted vertical line marks the location of the insertion point and a box is added to the tail of the mouse pointer.

(continues)

Guided Tour   Move Text with Drag-and-Drop

(continued)

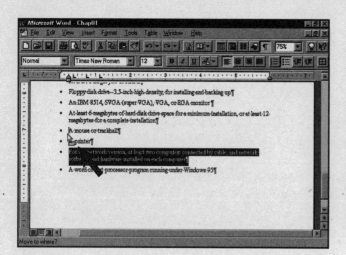

3 Press and hold down the left mouse button and drag the selected text toward its new location. The dotted vertical line indicates the current location of the insertion point.

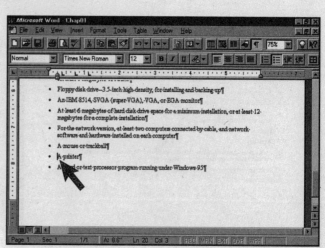

5 Click the left mouse button anywhere on the screen. Word turns off the highlight.

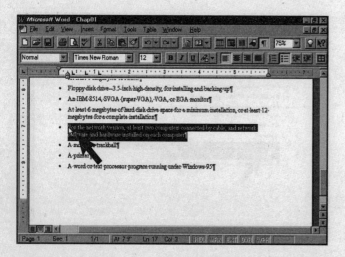

4 When you reach the new location, release the left mouse button. Word changes the mouse pointer back to its starting shape.

Copy Text

After you select text, you can use the **Copy** and **Paste** commands on the **Edit** menu to copy the selection to another location within your document while keeping the selection in its original location, too.

> If you try to use Copy without selecting text first or without a selection in the Clipboard, Word displays the Edit menu with these commands dimmed. This is a reminder that you must select text before using these commands.

 To copy a selection from its original location, open the **Edit** menu and choose the **Copy** command, press a shortcut key combination (**Ctrl+C** or **Ctrl+Ins**), or click the **Copy** toolbar button. This places the selection in the Windows Clipboard in which it is stored until the next copy or cut (see "Move Text" on page 99).

 To paste the selection into its new location, open the **Edit** menu and choose the **Paste** command, press a shortcut key combination (**Ctrl+V** or **Shift+Ins**), or click the **Paste** toolbar button. This places a copy of the contents of the Windows Clipboard at its new location.

You can paste the same selected text as many times as you like by repeatedly executing the **Paste** command. For each copy to be pasted, move the insertion point to the desired location and execute the **Paste** command one time.

> You can drag-and-drop to copy a selection, make a selection, move the mouse pointer within the selection, press and hold down the Ctrl key, press and hold down the left mouse button, and "drag" the copy of the selection to its new location. Then release the left mouse button, "dropping" the selection. During drag-and-drop, Word adds a dotted box and a box with a plus sign to the tail of the mouse pointer and shows the current location of the insertion point using a vertical dotted line. As you drag, notice the position of the dotted insertion point. When it's in the location at which you want to drop the selection, release the left mouse button.

Begin Guided Tour   Copy and Paste Text

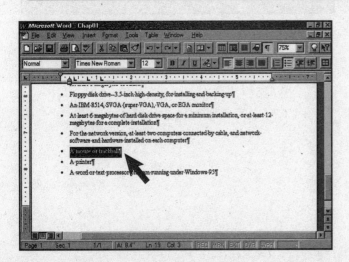

1 Select the text to be copied and pasted.

(continues)

Guided Tour Copy and Paste Text   *(continued)*

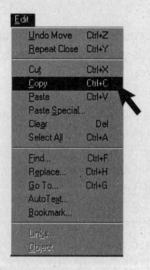

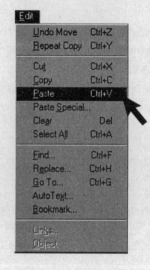

2 Open the **Edit** menu and select the **Copy** command. You also can click the **Copy** toolbar button, press **Ctrl+C**, or **Ctrl+Ins** to copy a selection.

4 Open the **Edit** menu and select the **Paste** command. You also can click the **Paste** toolbar button, press **Ctrl+V**, or **Shift+Ins**.

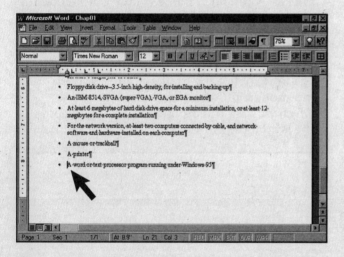

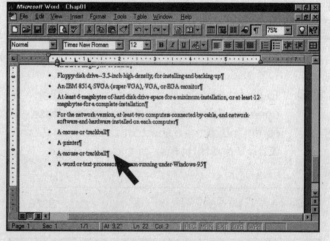

3 Click where you want to paste the selection. This moves the insertion point.

5 Word copies the text to the insertion point location. To paste the copied selection again, click the **Paste** toolbar button.

Undo and Redo Actions

As you go through all the steps in editing your document, you'll inevitably make some mistakes. To help you reverse mistakes, Word provides the very important Undo command on the Edit menu, the Ctrl+Z shortcut key combination, and the Undo toolbar button. Select the Undo command to cancel the last action, if Word allows.

 Word allows you to undo most editing and formatting changes. For example, you can undo copying or cutting a selection to a new location. However, saving, opening, or printing a document is impossible to undo.

 If you change your mind about an undo, you can reverse it, if Word allows. To redo an undo, open the **Edit** menu and select the **Redo** command, press **F4** or the **Ctrl+Y** key combination; or click the **Redo** button.

An advantage of using the Undo and Redo toolbar buttons is that you can select the action you want to undo or redo. Simply click the downward-pointing arrow next to the button to reveal a list of actions that you can undo or redo. Selecting an action from an Undo or Redo list also selects and acts on everything above that action.

Undo and Redo are context-sensitive commands, which means they adjust to your last action, and the type of action is displayed next to the command. For example, some typical Undo commands are Undo Typing, Undo Paste, and Undo Cut.

> **Begin Guided Tour** Undo and Redo Actions

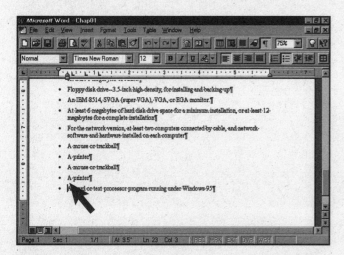

1 Open a document and then perform some action on the text. For example, copy and then paste a selection. (To learn how to open a document, see "Open a Document" on page 79. For information about copying and pasting, see "Copy Text" on page 103.)

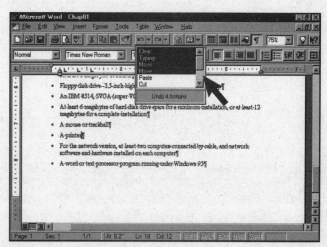

2 If you want to undo more than one of your changes, click on the **Undo** toolbar button, select an appropriate item on the list, and press **Enter**. Or you can undo one action by opening the **Edit** menu and choosing the **Undo** command. You also can click the **Undo** toolbar button without opening the list or press **Ctrl+Z**. Word reverses one or more actions.

(continues)

Guided Tour   Undo and Redo Actions

(continued)

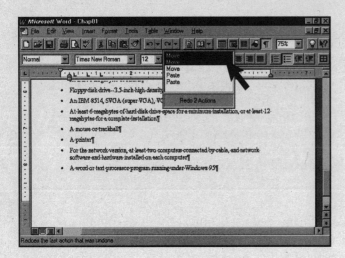

3 If you want to reverse more than one Undo, click on the **Redo** toolbar button, select an appropriate item on the list, and press **Enter**. Or you can redo one Undo by opening the **Edit** menu and choosing **Redo**. You also can click the **Redo** toolbar button without opening the list or press **Ctrl+Y**. Word repastes the pasted selection.

Find Text, Formats, and Symbols

Use the **Find** command on the **Edit** menu, or press **Ctrl+F**, to move to a place in a document in which a certain word, part of a word, phrase, set of characters, format, or symbol occurs. For example, you can look for the word **music**, or you can look for the sentence **I listen to classical music most of the time**. Or you can look for any italicized characters or even symbols such as a paragraph mark or tab mark. The characters, words, phrase, or symbol that you are looking for is the search string.

If you start a search from within a text selection, Word looks in the selection first and then asks if you'd like to continue the search in the rest of the document.

When you open the **Edit** menu and choose the **Find** command, Word opens the Find dialog box, which contains these options:

- **Find What**   Type the search string in this text box or open the drop-down list to select a previous search string.

- **Search**   Open this drop-down list and select **Up** to search from the insertion point toward the top, **Down** to search from the insertion point toward the bottom, or **All** to search throughout the entire document. Don't worry too much about choosing the direction, because once the search is at the beginning or end of the document, you are prompted to continue the search from the other end of the document.

- **Match Case**   Refines your search by specifying a matching combination of upper- or lowercase text. For example, to look for **White House** and avoid all occurrences of **white house**, check this box.

- **Find Whole Words Only**   Refines your search by telling Word to find complete words rather

than parts of words that match the search string. Suppose that you are looking for all the occurrences of the word **cap**. If you simply click **OK** or press **Enter**, Word will find cap and also caption, capitulate, cape, escape, and so on.

- **Use Pattern Matching**   Finds patterns of characters and *operators* (symbols that indicate actions, such as addition, multiplication, or comparisons, that take place on characters and/or numbers), part of Word's capability to perform advanced searches. If you select this option, you cannot use the Match Case or Find Whole Words Only options.

- **Sounds Like**   Finds words and phrases that sound like, but are not necessarily spelled like, the search string. If you select this option, you cannot use the Match Case or Find Whole Words Only options.

- **Find All Word Forms**   Word searches for all variations of the search string. For example, if you are searching for the word **drive**, Word also searches for drives, drove, and driven. If you select this option, you cannot use the Match Case or Find Whole Words Only options.

- **No Formatting**   Removes any formats that you have previously specified for searches.

- **Format**   Finds formats for paragraphs, frames, styles, tabs, fonts, and highlights.

- **Special**   Finds symbols that you won't find on your keyboard: for example, paragraph and tab marks; page, line, section, and column breaks; graphics, and so on.

Once you see (and learn) Word's codes for special characters, you can type them in the Find What text box. Commonly used codes to type are ^p (paragraph mark), ^t (tab mark), and ^l (new line mark).

- **Find Next**   Finds the next occurrence of the text in the Find What text box or the selected format or symbol.

- **Replace**   Opens the Replace dialog box. (For information about replacing text, formats, and symbols, see "Replace Text, Formats, and Symbols" on page 112.

You can continue to edit a document while searching. For example, as you are searching, you may see a spelling error. In that case, click outside the Find dialog box and make a correction. Then click inside the dialog box to activate it and continue your search.

Begin Guided Tour   Find Text

1 With a document on-screen, open the **Edit** menu, and select **Find**, or press **Ctrl+F**. Word displays the Find dialog box.

2 In the **Find What** text box, type the text you want to search for (otherwise known as the search string).

If you want to see text that is underneath the dialog box, simply move the mouse pointer to the dialog box title bar, press and hold down the left mouse button, and drag the dialog box to another part of the computer screen. You can even drag it partly off the screen. If you drag the dialog box so far off the screen that you can no longer see the title bar and cannot drag the dialog box to a better position, either click on the **Cancel** button or press the **Esc** key to close the dialog box; then open it again.

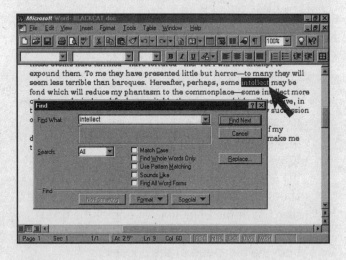

3 Select **Find Next**. If Word finds the search string, it selects it.

Guided Tour   Find Text

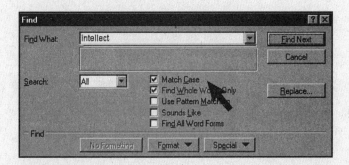

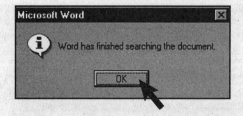

5 Click **Find Next** again. If Word does not find the search string before it reaches the end of the document, it displays a message. Click **OK** to return to the Find dialog box. Click **Cancel** or press **Esc** to close the dialog box.

4 If you want, check the **Find Whole Words Only** and **Match Case** check boxes to narrow your search. Select **Find Next** again. Word searches your document for the search string. If Word finds the search string, it selects it.

Begin Guided Tour   Find a Format

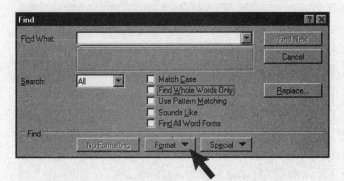

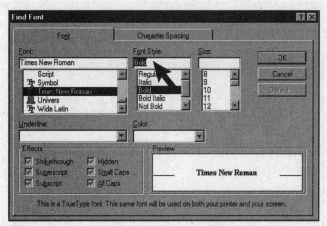

1 With a formatted document on-screen, open the **Edit** menu, and choose the **Find** command, or press **Ctrl+F**. When Word opens the Find dialog box, click the **Format** button.

3 From the dialog box, select one or more options; then click **OK**. Word adds the selected format(s) under the Find What text box.

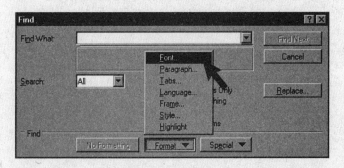

2 Select an option from the Format list, such as Font. Word opens a dialog box for the selected option.

You can combine a search for formats with or without a search for text. To search for text formatted in a particular way, simply fill in the Find What text box in the Find dialog box and then follow the steps under "Find a Format" on this page. To search for formats, leave the Find What text box empty and follow the steps under "Find a Format."

(continues)

Guided Tour   Find a Format   *(continued)*

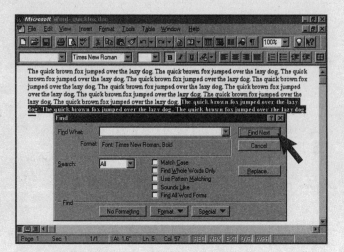

4 Click **Find Next**. If Word finds the search string, it selects it. If Word does not find the search string, it tells that it has finished the search and has not found the search item.

Before you start your next search if you have searched for formatting, click the **No Formatting** button to remove the formats from the Find dialog box. Otherwise, Word will include the formats in your next search, causing inaccurate results. For example, Word may tell you that it can't find a word that you are sure is in a document. The reason for this is that Word is searching for both the word and the formatting that was not removed from the Find dialog box.

Begin Guided Tour   Find a Symbol

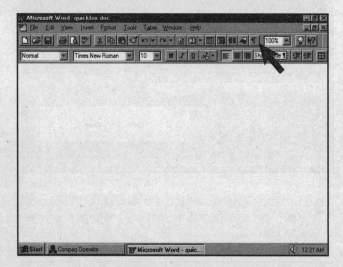

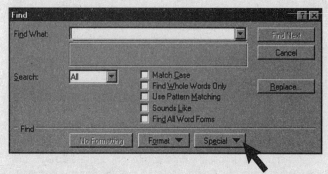

2 With a document on-screen, open the **Edit** menu, and choose the **Find** command, or press **Ctrl+F**. When Word opens the Find dialog box, click the **Special** button.

1 Click the **Show/Hide** toolbar button to reveal all the nonprinting symbols in the document on-screen. (Although Word finds nonprinting symbols whether or not they are displayed, it's a good idea to see them as Word finds and selects them.)

Guided Tour Find a Symbol

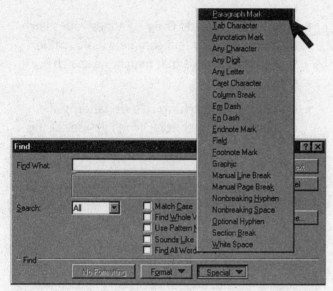

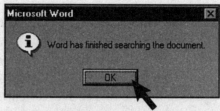

5 Repeatedly click **Find Next** to find new occurrences of the special character. If Word does not find the search string before it reaches the end of the document, it displays a message. Click **OK** to return to the Find dialog box. Click **Cancel** or press **Esc** to close the dialog box.

If you want, you can click on the **Show/Hide** toolbar button to hide nonprinting symbols.

3 Select a special character from the list, such as Paragraph Mark. Word adds the symbols representing the special character to the Find What text box.

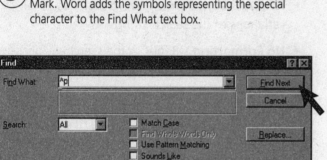

4 Click **Find Next**. If Word finds the special character, it selects it.

Replace Text, Formats, and Symbols

When you are editing, you sometimes have to make the same change throughout a document. For example, if you want to replace every instance of the word **pie** with the word **cake**, it could be a chore to look for and find each occurrence of pie, move out of the dialog box, delete the word **pie**, type **cake**, and then repeat the process several times until the end of the document. Word's Replace command searches for a string of characters and replaces that string of characters with a replace string. You can use the Find and Replace features to search for and optionally change groups of characters, words, phrases, punctuation, and formatting, saving a lot of time.

You can open the Replace dialog box by opening the **Edit** menu and selecting the **Replace** command, pressing the **Ctrl+H** keys, or by clicking the **Replace** button in the Find dialog box.

The options in the Replace dialog box are very similar to those in the Find dialog box (see "Find Text, Formats, and Symbols" on page 107):

- **Find What**   Type the search string in this text box or open the drop-down list to select a previous search string.

- **Replace With**   Type the replace string in this text box or open the drop-down list to select a previous replace string.

- **Search**   Select **Up** to search and optionally replace from the insertion point toward the top, **Down** to search and optionally replace from the insertion point toward the bottom, or **All** to search and optionally replace throughout the entire document.

- **Match Case**   Refines your search by specifying a matching combination of upper- or lowercase text.

- **Find Whole Words Only**   Refines your search by telling Word to find complete words rather than parts of words that match the search string.

- **Use Pattern Matching**   Finds patterns of characters and operators. When you select this option and click **Special**, Word reveals a list of symbols, such as Beginning of Word (<) or End of Word (>). For example, if you select Beginning of Word and type **a** next to the **<** symbol, Word searches for every word starting with the letter **a**.

- **Sounds Like**   Finds words and phrases that sound like, but are not necessarily spelled like, the search string.

- **Find All Word Forms**   Word searches for all variations of the search string.

- **No Formatting**   Replaces the searched-for formats with no formatting.

- **Format**   Replaces found formats with formats for paragraphs, frames, styles, tabs, fonts, and highlights.

- **Special**   Replaces found symbols with symbols that you won't find on your keyboard: for example, paragraph and tab marks; page, line, section, and column breaks; graphics, and so on.

You also can replace text and other keyboard characters with special symbols using the **Special** option. In the AutoCorrect dialog box, you will find several examples. For example, an e-mail emoticon, :-), is replaced with a happy face symbol, and user-created arrows are replaced by arrow symbols. For more information about the AutoCorrect feature, see "Automatically Correct Typos" on page 121.

- **Find Next**   Finds the next occurrence of the text in the Find What text box or the selected format or symbol.

- **Replace**   Replaces this occurrence of the search string with the replace string.

- **Replace All**   Replaces all occurrences of the search string with the replace string in one fell swoop.

Begin Guided Tour   Replace Text

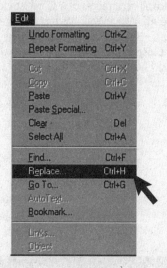

1 Open the **Edit** menu and select the **Replace** command, or press **Ctrl+H**. Word displays the Replace dialog box.

If you have used the Find command earlier in this Word session, your last search string will appear in the Find What box.

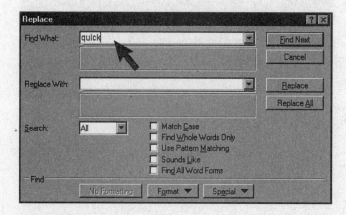

2 In the Find What text box, type the text that you would like to replace (the search string), such as **quick**. Word makes the Find Next and Replace All buttons available.

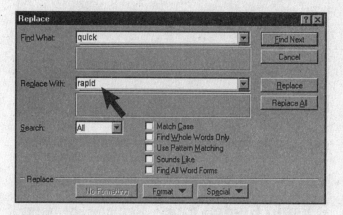

3 In the Replace With text box, type the replace string— **rapid**, for example.

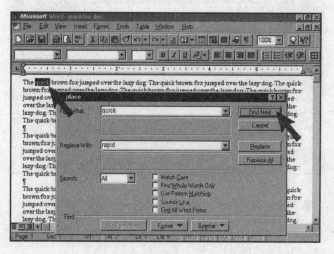

4 To find the first occurrence of the search string after the insertion point, click **Find Next**. Word selects the search string but does not replace it.

(continues)

Guided Tour   Replace Text *(continued)*

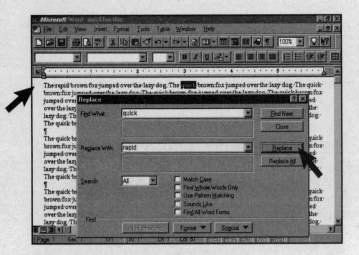

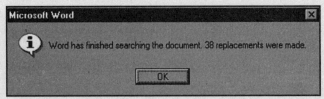

6 To replace all occurrences of a search string at once, select **Replace All**. When Word has replaced all occurrences, a message appears. Click **OK** to close the message box. At any time, you can select **Close** in the Replace box to stop the find-and-replace process.

5 Click **Replace**. Word replaces the highlighted search string and select the next occurrence of the search string.

Begin Guided Tour   Replace Formats

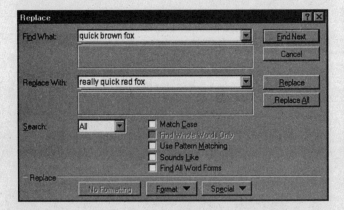

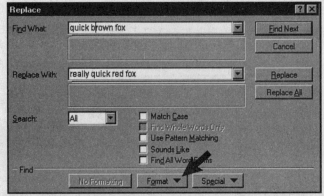

1 Open the Replace dialog box by choosing the **Edit** menu and the **Replace** command, or pressing **Ctrl+H**. Optionally, type the search string and replace string in the **Find What** text box and in the **Replace With** text box, respectively.

2 Click in the **Find What** text box, and click the **Format** button.

Guided Tour   Replace Formats

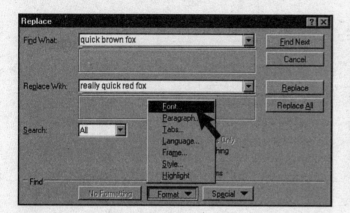

3 Select an option from the open list, such as **Font**. Word opens a dialog box.

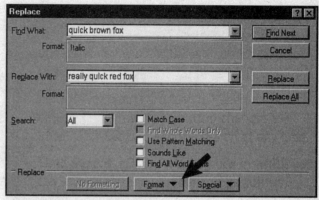

5 Click in the **Replace With** text box, and click the **Format** button.

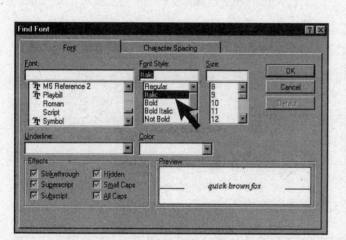

4 Select one or more options from the dialog box. Then click **OK**. Word closes the dialog box and displays the options under the Find What text box.

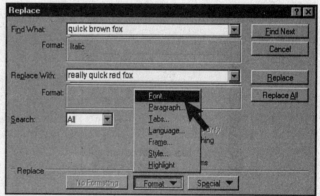

6 Select an option from the open list. Word opens a dialog box.

(continues)

Guided Tour Replace Formats *(continued)*

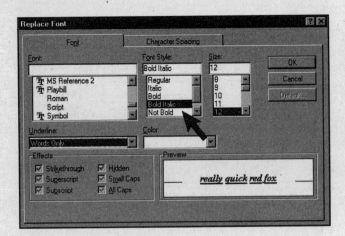

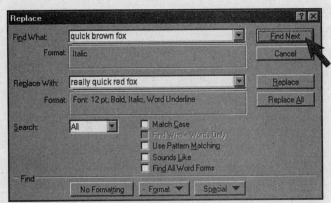

7 Select one or more options from the dialog box. Then click **OK**. Word closes the dialog box and displays the options under the **Replace With** text box.

8 To find the first occurrence of the search string after the insertion point, click **Find Next**. Word selects the search string but does not replace it.

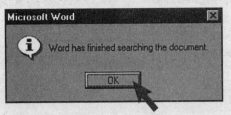

9 Click **Replace**. Word replaces the highlighted search string and select the next occurrence of the search string, if there is one. Otherwise, a message appears. Click the **OK** button to close the message box.

Begin Guided Tour Replace Symbols

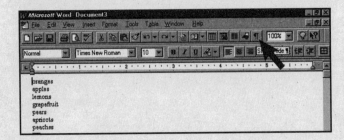

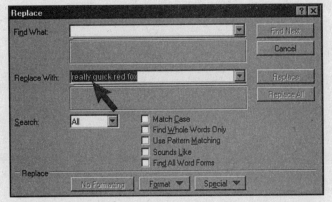

1 Open or create a document, and if the **Show/Hide** button is not active, click it. (Although Word finds nonprinting symbols whether or not they are displayed, it's a good idea to see them as Word finds and selects them.

2 Open the Replace dialog box by choosing the **Edit** menu and the **Replace** command, or pressing **Ctrl+H**.

Guided Tour Replace Symbols

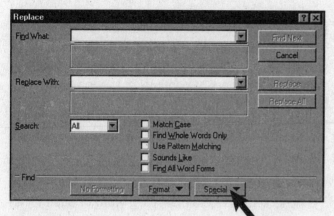

3 Click in the **Find What** text box, and click the **Special** button.

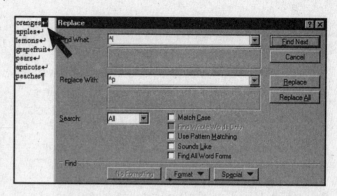

6 To find the first occurrence of the search string after the insertion point, click **Find Next**. Word selects the search string but does not replace it.

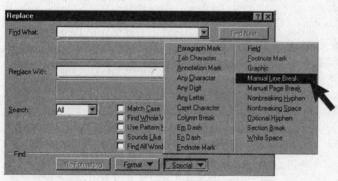

4 Select a special character from the list. You can repeat steps 3 and 4 to replace multiple special characters.

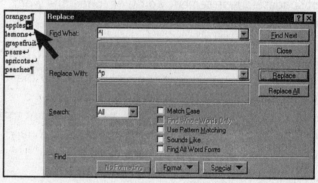

7 Click **Replace**. Word replaces the highlighted search string and select the next occurrence of the search string, if there is one. Otherwise, a message appears.

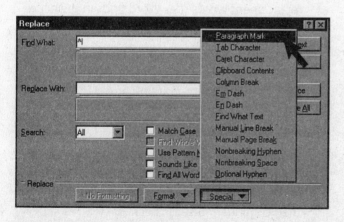

5 Click in the **Replace With** text box, and click the **Special** button, and select a special character from the list. You can repeat this for multiple special characters.

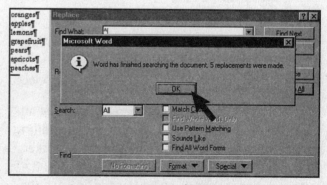

8 Click **Replace All**. Word replaces the remaining search strings and displays a message. Click **OK** to close the message box; click the **Close** button to close the Replace dialog box.

Check Your Spelling

After you have created a document, it's important to review it, not only for its look but also its content. After you have edited one or two drafts of a document, check your spelling with Word for Windows' spell checker and use the other proofing tools: the thesaurus (see "Use the Thesaurus" on page 127), and the grammar checker (see "Check Your Grammar" on page 129).

By default, Word checks a document as you are creating it and underlines misspelled words or those not in a dictionary with a jagged, red line. Point to the line and click with the right mouse button to see a list of suggested replacement words, or correct the word to remove the line. For more information on this and other Word spelling options, see "Change Spelling and Grammar Options" on page 137. Although Word is always checking your spelling (unless you clear the Automatic Spell Checking check box in the Spelling section of the Options dialog box), you might want to run the spell check after selecting a custom dictionary or adding words to a custom dictionary.

Word uses a large main dictionary, which cannot be modified or even viewed, as well as custom dictionaries into which you add words and terms that are unique to your occupation, business, or hobby. For more information about custom dictionaries, see "Use a Custom Dictionary" on page 123.

You can use Word's spell checker to review an entire document, part of a document, or a single word—depending on how much of the document you select.

To run the spell checker, either open the **Tools** menu and select **Spelling**, press **F7**, or click on the **Spelling** button on the Standard toolbar. As the spell checker runs, it looks through the main dictionary and all the custom dictionaries that you have made active. If the spell checker finds any errors, it displays the Spelling dialog box; otherwise, it displays a message telling you that the spell check is complete.

If you didn't start the spell check at the top of the document and Word doesn't find another word in your selection, it displays a dialog box asking if you want the spell check to continue at the top of the document. When the spell check is complete, Word displays an informational message.

The Spelling dialog box contains these options:

- **Not in Dictionary** In this box, the spell checker displays a misspelled word or one that is not in the main dictionary or any active custom dictionary.

- **Change To** This text box contains the first word in the Suggestions box, or, if there are no suggestions, the word in the Not in Dictionary box. You can either accept one of the suggested words or type a replacement word. You can also delete a word from your document by deleting the word in the Change To box. When you press **Delete** to delete the word in the Change To box, Word alters the Change and Change All buttons to read Delete and Delete All, respectively. Then click the **Delete** or **Delete All** button.

- **Suggestions** In this list box are potential replacement words that Word finds in the active dictionaries.

- **Add Words To** This box lists the name of the custom dictionary to which you can add a word. Click the downward-pointing arrow to reveal the names of all active custom dictionaries and to select one, if you want.

- **Ignore/Ignore All** Click either of these buttons to skip the selected word or all occurrences of the selected word, respectively, and then continue the spell check.

When the Spelling dialog box is open, you can work in your document. Just click in the document and start typing or editing. During this time, the **Ignore** button in the Spelling dialog box changes to **Resume**. When you're ready to continue the spell check, click the **Resume** button.

- **Change/Change All**   Change the selected word or all occurrences of the selected word, respectively, and then continue the spell check.

- **Delete/Delete All**   Delete the word or all occurrences of the selected word, respectively, from the active custom dictionary. These buttons are available only if you have deleted all the text from the Change To box. Once the word or words are deleted, the spell check continues.

- **Add**   Places the selected word in the custom dictionary named in the Add Words To box.

- **Suggest**   Type a word in the Change To box so that you can see suggestions based on that word.

If the Suggest button is dimmed (the default), the Always Suggest box in the Options dialog box for the Spelling category is checked and Word automatically suggests words. To clear the Always Suggest box and activate both the Suggest button and the Change To box, open the **Tools** menu, select **Options**, click the **Spelling** tab, click **Always Suggest**, and click **OK**.

- **AutoCorrect**   Adds the misspelled word and correction to the AutoCorrect dialog box. (To learn more about the AutoCorrect feature, see "Automatically Correct Typos" on page 121.)

- **Options**   Displays the Options dialog box for the Spelling category, which is explained in "Change Spelling and Grammar Options" on page 137 and in "Options Dialog Box—Spelling Category" on page 551.

- **Undo Last**   Changes the last word replaced back to the original word and moves back to the last word.

Begin Guided Tour   Check the Spelling in a Document

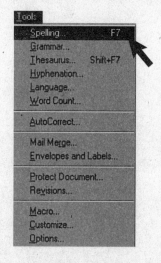

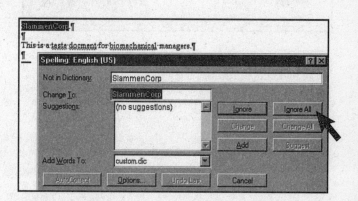

1 Select the part of the current document that you want Word to check. Then open the **Tools** menu and choose the **Spelling** command, press **F7**, or click on the **Spelling** button on the Standard toolbar. Word selects the first word not found in a dictionary, and opens the Spelling dialog box.

2 To ignore this occurrence or all occurrences of the word, click the **Ignore** or **Ignore All** button, respectively. The spell check continues. If the spell checker finds another word, it selects the word and names replacement words.

(continues)

Guided Tour Check the Spelling in a Document *(continued)*

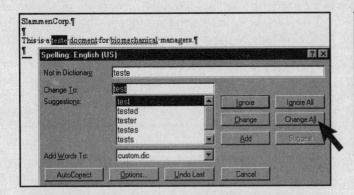

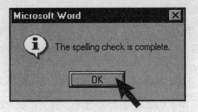

While running the spell check, you can edit your document. For example, as the spell checker selects words, you may see a problem with a word in the area. Click outside the Spelling dialog box and correct the word. To restart the spell check, click the **Resume** button.

3 To change this occurrence or all occurrences of a selected word using Word's suggestions, click a suggestion, and click the **Change** or **Change All** button, respectively. To manually correct the spelling of the selected word, edit it in the **Change To** box and click **Change**. The spell check continues. If it finds another word, it selects it and names replacement words.

5 Click **OK** to return to your document.

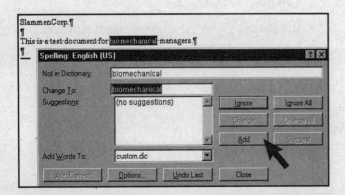

4 To add a word to the active custom dictionary, select the **Add** button. The spell check continues. If it finds another word, it selects it and names replacement words. If the spell check is complete, Word displays a message.

Automatically Correct Typos

To automatically correct words that you often type incorrectly (such as, **dialgo** instead of **dialog**, or **thier** rather than **their**), open the **Tools** menu and choose the **AutoCorrect** command. In the AutoCorrect dialog box, type both the incorrect version and the correct version of the word and click **OK** or press **Enter**. From this point on, in any new document, as you type, Word automatically corrects the misspellings. In fact, you can use AutoCorrect to save yourself keystrokes. Type a shortcut version of a word (for example, **org**) as the incorrect version, and then type the long version (for example, **organization**) as the correct version.

During a spell check, you also can use the AutoCorrect feature. When the spell checker finds a misspelling and you identify the correct spelling, just click the **AutoCorrect** button to have Word automatically correct this mistake in the future. See "Check Your Spelling" on page 118.

> In the AutoCorrect dialog box, you can indicate characters to be replaced by special symbols not found on your keyboard. For examples of characters replaced by symbols, see the first few entries in the dialog box.

The AutoCorrect dialog box includes these options:

- **Correct TWo INitial CApitals** (the default)   Changes the second uppercase letter to lowercase when you inadvertently type a pair of uppercase characters.

- **Capitalize First Letter of Sentences** (the default)   Changes the first letter following a period to uppercase.

- **Capitalize Names of Days** (the default) Capitalizes names of the days of the week.

- **Correct accidental usage of cAPS LOCK Key** (the default)   Detects and changes uppercase to lowercase and lowercase to uppercase when the Caps Lock key is active.

- **Replace Text as You Type** (the default) Corrects automatically as you type text in documents.

- **Replace**   Type an incorrectly spelled word to be replaced in this text box. To insert an incorrect word in this text box automatically, select the word in the document; then open the AutoCorrect dialog box.

- **With**   Type the correct text in the text box and click the **Plain Text** (the default) or **Formatted Text** option button to store the text without or with formatting that you have applied, respectively.

- **Exceptions**   Opens the Exceptions dialog box in which you can select exceptions for certain corrections: you can select abbreviations ending with periods that will not trigger the Capitalize First Letter of Sentences option, and you can add words that have two initial uppercase letters not to be corrected by the Correct TWo INitial CApitals option.

- **Add**   Adds the incorrect and corrected entries to the list box at the bottom of the dialog box.

- **Delete**   Click this button after selecting an incorrect and correct pair of words to delete them from the list box at the bottom of the dialog box.

> If you don't need all the pairs of words the Word developers placed in the AutoCorrect dialog box, remove selected words (just click a pair and then click the **Delete** button). You might do this because you never misspell, mistype, or never use certain words on the list; or even if you want to make sure that Word's speed is not slowed by unnecessary text.

Begin Guided Tour Add a Word to AutoCorrect

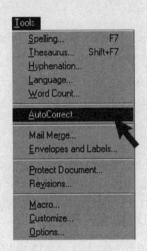

1 With or without a document on-screen, open the **Tools** menu and select the **AutoCorrect** command. (In order for the Tools menu to be available, you must have a document—even an empty one— open.

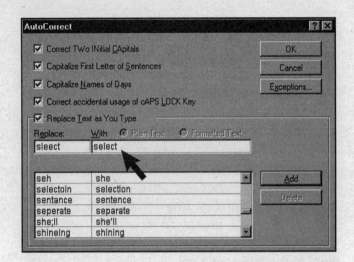

3 Type the correct version of the word in the **With** text box.

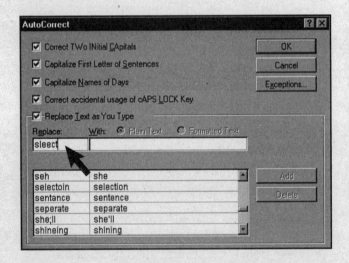

2 In the AutoCorrect dialog box, type a word that you often misspell in the **Replace** text box. As you type, Word shows the closest words already on the list.

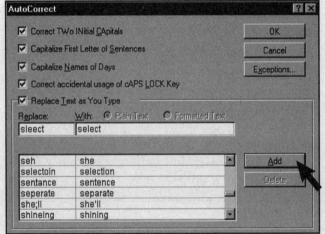

4 To save the pair of words but keep the dialog box open, click the **Add** button. To save the words and close the dialog box, click **OK**.

Use a Custom Dictionary

If you write or edit medical or legal papers, or write technical reports, you can use one or more custom dictionaries. Word starts out with a custom dictionary, CUSTOM.DIC, already installed. However, you can create as many different custom dictionaries as you want, but you can use only ten at a time.

To specify particular custom dictionaries, open the **Tools** menu and select the **Options** menu. Click on the **Spelling** tab to reveal the Spelling section of the Options dialog box. Then click on the **Custom Dictionaries** button. All the custom dictionaries are listed in the **Custom Dictionaries** group. Check the check boxes preceding the custom dictionaries that you want to use (or clear the check boxes for the dictionaries that you don't need for this spell check. Then click on **OK** two times.

Custom dictionaries can not only contain terms specific to an occupation or hobby but also can include proper names of companies and individuals. So when you're writing a letter, the spell checker will not find names and terms not found in the main dictionary. This avoids irritating and unnecessary interruptions.

> You can also create a custom dictionary while checking spelling in your document. In the Spelling dialog box, click the **Options** button, and Word opens the Options dialog box for the Spelling category.

The simplest way to add words to a custom dictionary is during a spell checker session. Make sure that you have chosen the custom dictionary to which you want to add words. Then check one or more documents and add words where needed.

If you want to add several words to the custom dictionary at one time, you can create a special document containing the words, each separated by a space. Then run the spell checker against this document. When Word finds a word that is not in either the standard or the custom dictionary, you can add it.

From the Spelling section of the Options dialog box, you can open the custom dictionary and add a series of words, pressing **Enter** after each word so that each word appears on its own line. You also can modify and delete words in the custom dictionary. To add, modify, or delete words in a custom dictionary, open the **Tools** menu and select the **Options** command. Click the **Spelling** tab (if the Spelling section of the Options dialog box is not on-screen), and then click on the **Custom Dictionaries** button. Select the dictionary in which you want to work and click the **Edit** button. (Clicking the **New** button creates a new dictionary, clicking **Add** adds a custom dictionary to the list of dictionaries that the spell checker uses, and clicking **Remove** removes the selected custom dictionary.)

Begin Guided Tour   Create a Custom Dictionary

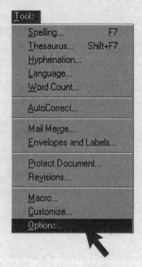

1 Open the **Tools** menu and select **Options**. Word opens the Options dialog box.

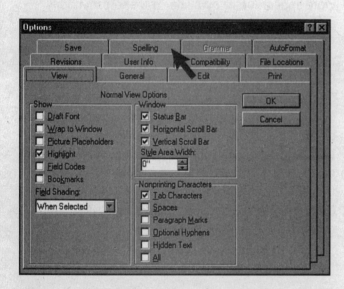

2 Click the **Spelling** tab. Word opens the Options dialog box for the Spelling category.

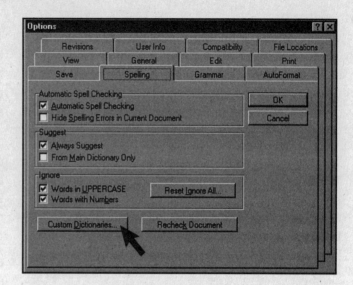

3 Click the **Custom Dictionaries** button. Word opens the Custom Dictionaries dialog box.

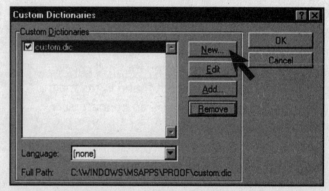

4 Click the **New** button. Word opens the Create Custom Dictionary dialog box.

Guided Tour   Create a Custom Dictionary

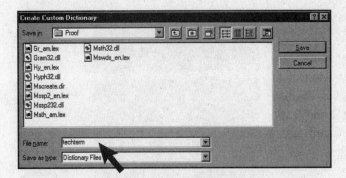

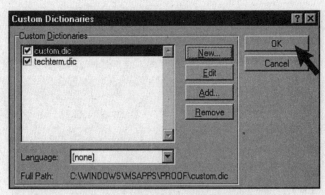

5 Type the name you would like to give the dictionary in the **File name** text box. Then click the **Save** button. Word saves the dictionary, closes the dialog box, and makes the new dictionary active.

6 Click **OK**. Word returns to the Options dialog box for the Spelling category. Click **OK** again to close the Options dialog box.

Begin Guided Tour   Modify a Custom Dictionary

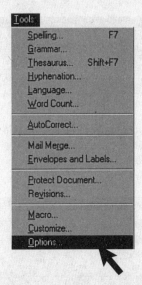

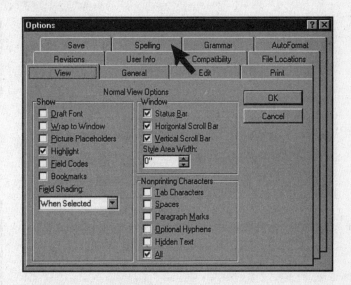

1 Open the **Tools** menu and select **Options**. Word opens the Options dialog box.

2 Click the **Spelling** tab. Word opens the Options dialog box for the Spelling category.

(continues)

Guided Tour Modify a Custom Dictionary

(continued)

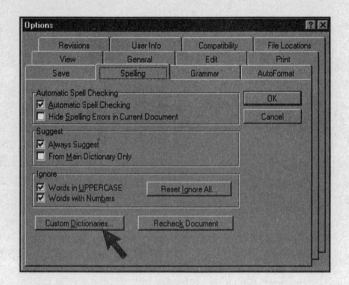

3 Click the **Custom Dictionaries** button. Word opens the Custom Dictionaries dialog box.

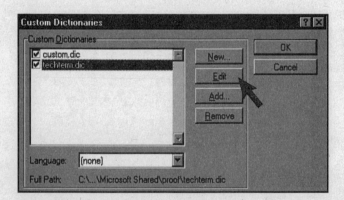

4 Click the **Edit** button. Then click the **OK** button to close the information box. Word opens a document with the name of the custom dictionary.

5 Start typing terms, pressing **Enter** after each.

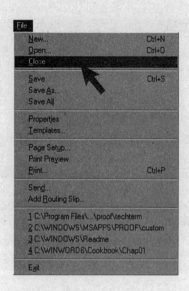

6 Open the **File** menu and select the **Close** command. Word asks if you want to save the document.

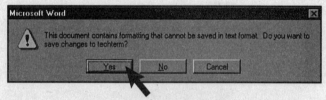

7 Click **Yes**. Word informs you that the dictionary is a Text Only document and asks you to save it as a Word document or as a Text Only document.

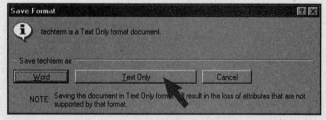

8 Click **Text Only**. Word saves and closes the dictionary.

Use the Thesaurus

The thesaurus adds variety to your documents by letting you choose words with similar meanings instead of using the same word repeatedly. You also can use the thesaurus to choose a word that is slightly closer to what you mean in a sentence. For example, does the word improve mean advance or repair? Does loud mean deafening or powerful? In both examples, the groups of words are synonyms but the meanings are not identical.

Word's **Thesaurus** command on the **Tools** menu allows you to replace a word with a synonym from a list. The Thesaurus dialog box includes these options:

- **Looked Up**   This drop-down list displays the word or phrase that you selected to be checked. If there is no synonym for a selected word, the box is labeled **Not Found** instead.

- **Meanings**   This list box displays definitions, Antonyms, or Related Words (other forms, such as adjectives, verbs, and nouns) of the selected word so you can make an informed decision. If there is no meaning, this box is labeled **Alpha-**

betical List and the thesaurus displays words or phrases that are in the same area alphabetically as the selected word but are not synonyms.

- **Replace with Synonym**   Displays the suggested replacement word or phrase. If you're starting a new document and select the thesaurus, this box is labeled **Insert**. If you select **Antonym** from the **Meanings** box, this text box is labeled **Replace with Antonym**.

- **Replace/Insert**   Replaces the selected word or phrase with the word or phrase in the **Replace with Synonym** box.

- **Look Up**   Displays synonyms for the replacement word that you select from the **Meanings** list box.

- **Previous**   Displays the word that was previously in the **Looked Up** text box. When you have reached the first word in the series of those that you looked up, Word dims the button, making it unavailable.

Begin Guided Tour   Use the Thesaurus

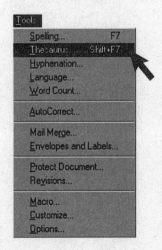

1 In a document, move the insertion point within a word or to its immediate right. Then open the **Tools** menu and choose the **Thesaurus** command, or press **Shift+F7**. Word displays the Thesaurus dialog box with the selected word in the **Looked Up** box.

(continues)

Guided Tour   Use the Thesaurus   *(continued)*

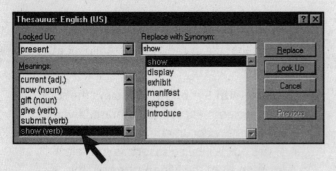

② Select the meaning you want (either a synonym or antonym) in the **Meanings** list box. For the selected word in the Meanings box, Word displays synonyms (or antonyms, depending what meaning you picked) in the **Replace with Synonym** (or sometimes **Replace with Antonym**) list box.

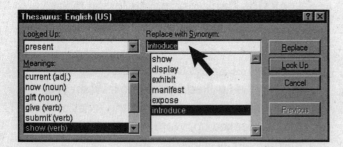

③ Select an appropriate word in the **Replace with Synonym** (or **Replace with Antonym**) list box. Word places the selected word in the Replace with Synonym (or Replace with Antonym) text box.

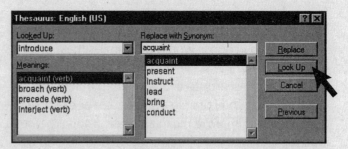

④ To further investigate the word in the Replace With Synonym (or Replace with Antonym) text box, click the **Look Up** button. Word displays meanings and synonyms from which you can select.

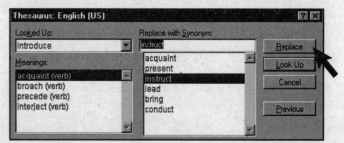

⑤ To replace the original word with the selected word, click the **Replace** button. (Or you can return to the original word by opening the **Looked Up** drop-down list and selecting it; then click **Cancel**.) Word closes the dialog box and returns to the current document.

Check Your Grammar

Another way to improve a document while editing it is to run Word's grammar checker. You can set the grammar checker to one of three levels and then customize the settings within the selected level. This means you can use the grammar checker to polish a document, or you can use it as a tool to improve your grammar and style. By using the readability statistics, you'll know whether the document is aimed at the appropriate audience.

> Before the grammar checker evaluates the grammar in a document, it runs the Word spell checker.

To run the grammar checker, open the **Tools** menu and choose the **Grammar** command. Word displays the Grammar dialog box, which contains these options:

- **Sentence**   The grammar checker displays a sentence that you should evaluate and perhaps correct.

- **Suggestions**   The grammar checker either describes the problem or offers one or more corrections.

- **Ignore**   Skips to the next error in a sentence or

to the next incorrect sentence without changing the current error or sentence.

- **Next Sentence**   Ignores the errors in a sentence and finds the next incorrect sentence.

- **Change**   The grammar checker corrects a sentence with its suggestion. If the button is not available, move the insertion point to the document and make the change or make the edit in the Sentence box.

- **Ignore Rule**   Ignore the errors in a sentence and similar errors in other sentences. The grammar checker then finds the next incorrect sentence.

- **Explain**   Displays a small window expanding the explanation in the Suggestions box.

- **Options**   Opens the Grammar/Options dialog box, which allows you to select specific grammar and style rules, show readability statistics, and customize settings. Refer to "Change Spelling and Grammar Options" for more information on this dialog box.

- **Undo Last**   Reverses the last change and returns to the sentence or phrase the grammar checker previously selected.

Begin Guided Tour   Check Your Grammar

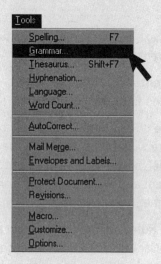

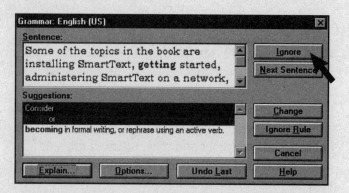

3 If the Grammar dialog box appears, correct your document or ignore the suggestions by clicking on the **Ignore** or **Change** button. The grammar checker continues.

1 Select the part of the document that you want Word to check. If you want Word to check the entire document, you don't have to select anything. Then, open the **Tools** menu and select the **Grammar** command. If the grammar checker finds a sentence that is grammatically incorrect or contains a misspelled word, Word opens the Grammar dialog box or Spelling dialog box.

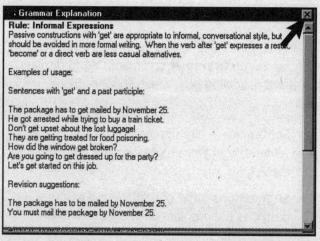

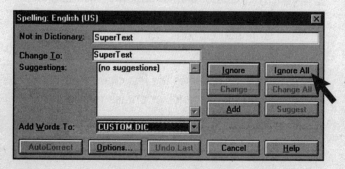

2 If the Spelling dialog box appears, correct your document or ignore the suggestions using the options described in "Check Your Spelling" on page 118. The grammar checker continues.

4 To see a description of any suggestion, click the **Explain** button. (You can drag the borders to increase the size of the Grammar Explanation window.) To close the window, click the **Close** button.

Guided Tour Check Your Grammar

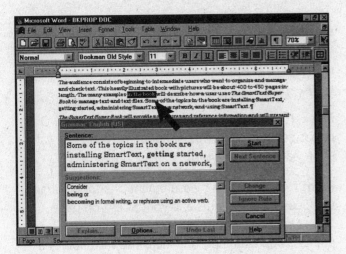

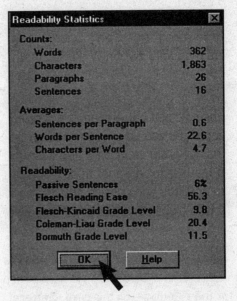

5 To switch from the Grammar dialog box to your document, move the insertion point outside the dialog box and click. Word dims the dialog box. (You can change the selected parts of your document inside the Sentence box.)

7 Continue correcting your document or ignoring the suggestions. When the grammar checker has completed its evaluation of selected text, Word displays readability statistics. Click **OK** to return to the document.

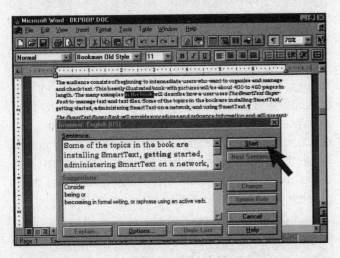

6 To switch back to the dialog box and start the grammar checker, select **Start** in the dialog box.

Change General Options

Word provides miscellaneous options in the Options dialog box for the General category. Included are two options for WordPerfect users, the list of recently used documents on the File menu, and the unit of measure. For descriptions of each option in this dialog box, see the "Options Dialog Box— General Category" on page 543.

> For most Word users, it's best to keep the default options set as they are.

To open the Options dialog box, open the **Tools** menu and choose the **Options** command. Then click the tab for the category—in this case, **General**.

One of the more important options in this dialog box is the unit of measure. Most people in the United States measure small objects in inches; throughout the rest of the world, the comparable unit of measure is the centimeter. Printing and typography experts are more likely to measure in picas or points. Word allows you to choose the unit of measure with which you are most comfortable for all your documents or for a particular one. From time to time, especially if you use Word for desktop publishing, you may want to select a unit of measure that allows you to move graphics and set specific dimensions on a fine scale. If so, you may want to switch, at least temporarily, to centimeters or points.

Inch   The standard unit of measure for those not using the metric system; the default unit of measure for Word. One inch is equivalent to 2.54 centimeters. Valid abbreviations for inch are **in** and **"**.

Centimeter   The standard small unit of measure in the metric system. One centimeter is equivalent to .4040 inch. The valid abbreviation for centimeter is **cm**.

Pica   The standard unit of measure for printers. One pica is equal to 12 points or about 1/6 inch. The valid abbreviation for pica is **pi**.

Point   The standard measurement of a font character. (See "Change Fonts and Font Sizes" on page 182.) One point is roughly 1/72 of an inch, so 72 points is approximately one inch. The valid abbreviation for point is **pt**.

> You also can select **Lines** as the unit of measure for paragraph spacing. (See "Control Spacing of Paragraphs and Lines" on page 159.) Word automatically changes a Lines value to points. The valid abbreviation for lines is **li**.

To temporarily specify a different unit of measure in a Format menu dialog box, type a value followed by the abbreviation for the unit. (If you type a value and don't add an abbreviation, Word assumes that you mean the default unit.) When you click **OK**, Word closes the dialog box and automatically translates the entered value to the default unit of measure.

> You must use decimal equivalents for fractions (for example, .75 instead of 3/4 or .5 rather than 1/2) because you cannot enter fractions.

Begin Guided Tour Change General Options

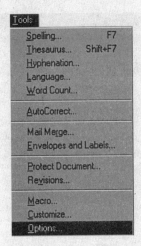

1 Open the **Tools** menu and select the **Options** command. Word displays the previous Options dialog box used during this Word session.

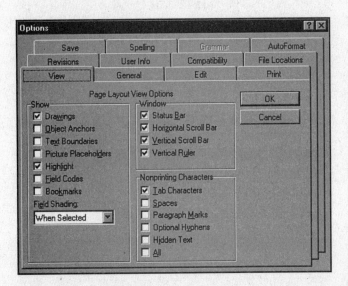

2 Click the **General** tab to change to the Options dialog box for General options.

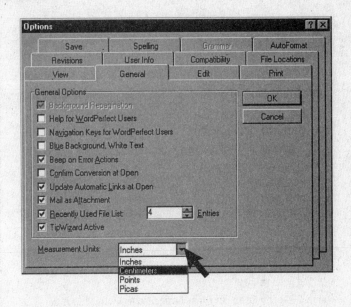

3 Click the underlined arrow in the **Measurement Units** drop-down list to open the list. Then choose a unit of measure.

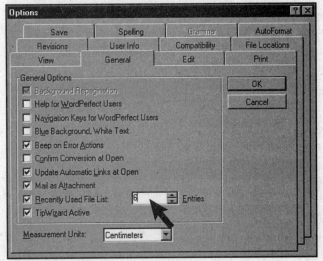

4 In the **Entries** text box/list box, type the number of recent documents to appear at the bottom of the File menu. You may want to increase this number if you work on many documents over a short period of time. However, if you increase the number, the File menu may be forced to appear next to File rather than under it.

(continues)

Guided Tour   Change General Options

(continued)

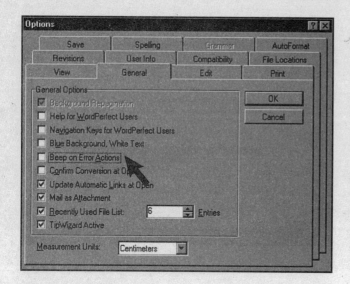

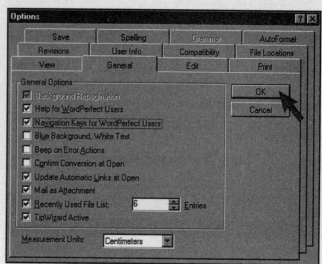

5 Clear the **Beep on Error Actions** check box. You may want to turn off the beep if you work in a quiet office environment or if you don't feel that you need an audible reminder.

7 Click **OK** to save your changes and close the dialog box.

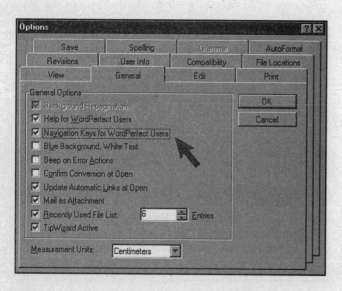

6 If you are a WordPerfect user, check the **Help for WordPerfect Users** and **Navigation Keys for WordPerfect Users** check boxes.

Customize Editing Options

You can customize the way in which you edit your documents. For example, if you don't want to take the chance of having Word delete a selection when you press a key, or want to automate left indents, clear check boxes in the Options dialog box for the Edit category.

Among the important options in this dialog box are Drag-and-Drop Text Editing, Automatic Word Selection, and Use Smart Cut and Paste. Drag-and-drop (see "Copy Text" on page 103 and "Move Text" on page 99 is an excellent way to move or copy text. Just select some text and drag it to a new location on-screen. Automatic Word Selection allows you to select entire words at a time. Simply, start dragging over a word, and Word expands the selection to the entire word and the space immediately after. Smart Cut and Paste removes or adds extra spaces between words when you cut text to the Clipboard or insert text from the Clipboard. In standard word processors, for example, when you insert blocks of text from the Clipboard, the result may be two spaces before the

new text, and no spaces after. Smart Cut and Paste evaluates a selection and corrects excess or missing spaces automatically.

> If you are a beginner to Word, a checked Typing Replaces Selection option can be dangerous. For example, if you select several paragraphs for formatting and accidentally press any key on the keyboard, Word deletes the selection. (Remember that you can open the **Edit** menu and select **Undo**, press **Ctrl+Z**, or click on the **Undo** button to reverse this.) Consider clearing this check box until you become more experienced.

To display this dialog box, open the **Tools** menu and select **Options**; then click the **Edit** tab. For a description of each option in the Options dialog box for the Edit category, see "Options Dialog Box—Edit Category" on page 544.

Begin Guided Tour   Customize Editing Options

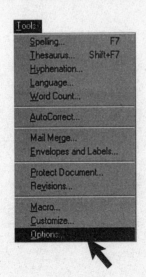

1 Open the **Tools** menu and select the **Options** command. Word displays the previous Options dialog box used during this Word session.

(continues)

Guided Tour Customize Editing Options *(continued)*

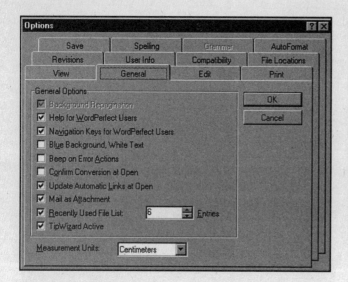

2 Click the **Edit** tab to change to the Options dialog box for Edit category.

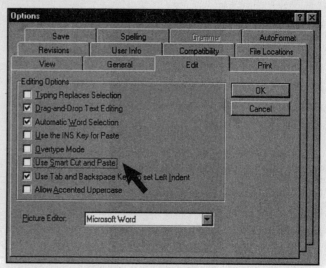

4 If you want to control cut and paste operations manually, clear the **Use Smart Cut and Paste** check box. Then click **OK**.

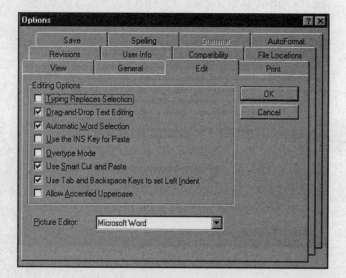

3 If you want to manually delete selected text rather than have Word delete it when you start typing, clear the **Typing Replaces Selection** check box.

Change Spelling and Grammar Options

The Options dialog box for the Spelling category allows you to customize a spell check. You can have Word run the spell checker as you work in a document and to suggest a list of correctly spelled words when it encounters a misspelling. From the Spelling Options dialog box, you also can create new custom dictionaries and activate them.

The Options dialog box for the Grammar category enables you to customize the grammar and style rules that the grammar checker uses. You can choose from and customize Strictly (all rules), For Business Writing, For Casual Writing, and up to three Custom rules that you specify. You also can indicate whether you want to show readability statistics or check spelling before proofing.

To open the Options dialog box, select the **Tools** menu and then choose **Options**. In the Options dialog box, click either the **Spelling** or **Grammar** tab. For descriptions of all the options in both categories, see "Options Dialog Box—Spelling Category" on page 551 and "Options Dialog Box—Grammar Category" on page 552.

To set your own grammar and style rules, click the **Customize Settings** button. In the Customize Grammar Settings dialog box, select a set of rules:

- **Strictly (all rules)**   Enforces most grammar and style rules in the grammar checker.

- **For Business Writing**   Enforces most grammar rules and some style rules.

- **For Casual Writing**   Enforces most grammar rules and eight style rules.

- **Custom 1**, **Custom 2**, or **Custom 3**   Allow you to set your own rules.

The three preset levels of grammar and style rules allow you to change grammar rules to fit your environment. For example, if you are writing a business plan that will cause your business to succeed or fail, consider applying the strictest grammar rules. On the other hand, if you're writing an informal note to your best friend, you can loosen the rules somewhat.

> For most users, it's best to keep the default settings in this dialog box. Eventually, you can fine-tune options, depending on your spelling and grammar strengths and weaknesses.

Begin Guided Tour   Change Spelling Options

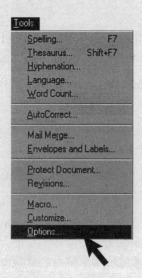

1 Open the **Tools** menu and select the **Options** command. Word displays the previous Options dialog box used during this Word session.

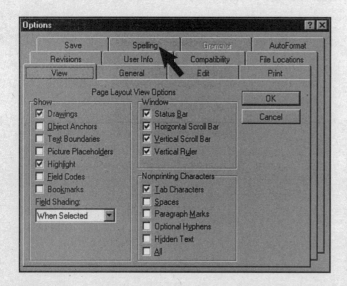

2 Click the **Spelling** tab to change to the Options dialog box for Spelling category.

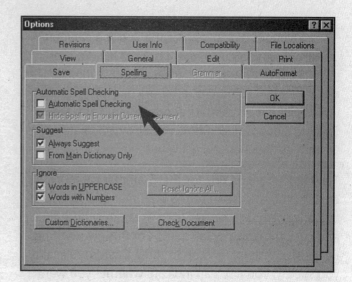

3 To run the spell checker when you want to rather than having Word run it all the time, clear the **Automatic Spell Checking** check box.

To learn more about the results of clicking on the Custom Dictionaries button, see "Use a Custom Dictionary" on page 123.

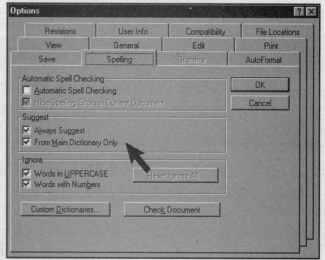

4 To run the spell check against the main dictionary only, check the **From Main Dictionary Only** check box. Then click **OK**.

Begin Guided Tour   Select and Customize Grammar Rules

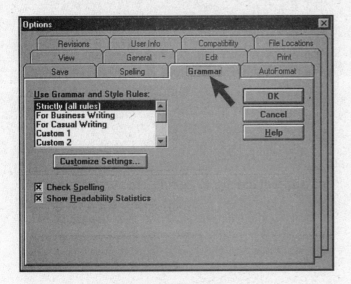

1 Open the **Tools** menu and select the **Options** command. Then click the **Grammar** tab to change to the Options dialog box for Grammar category.

3 Select settings in the **Grammar** and/or **Style** boxes to ease or tighten the rules. In the Catch group, you can adjust the settings. Just click on the downward pointing arrow on the right side of the drop-down list. Then select from the list.

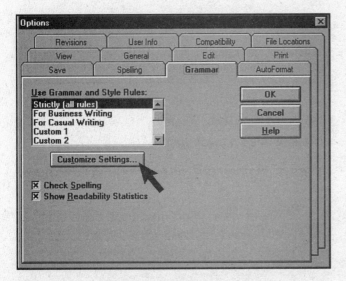

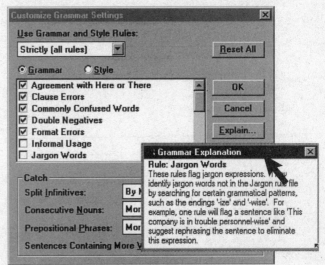

2 Choose a level of grammar and style rules, or click the **Customize Settings** button to display the Customize Grammar Settings dialog box.

4 If you don't understand a Grammar or Style entry, select it, and click the **Explain** button. Click the **Close** (**X**) button to close the Grammar Explanation box (which you can size); click **OK** to close the dialog box. Click **OK** again to close the Options dialog box.

HOW TO...
Format Pages and Paragraphs

This section informs you about formats: document-wide and paragraph-based. In this section, you will learn how to change margins, paper size, and page orientation. You'll find out how to create headers and footers and how to specify the pages on which they appear. You'll not only see how to insert page numbers in headers and footers, but you'll also find out how to change page number formats and the numbers themselves.

You'll explore how to control the location of a paragraph on a page: at the bottom of one page or the top of the next; on a single page or divided between two pages; or with the previous paragraph on the same page.

You will find out almost everything there is to know about paragraph formatting: indenting, inserting spaces before and after, and aligning with the left margin, the right margin, both, or centered on the page. You'll also learn about setting line spacing. You'll learn how to set tabs, how to choose a tab type, and how to clear tabs. Finally, the section ends with information about defining and formatting multiple columns within a document.

What You Will Find in This Section

Change Margins

Margin settings control the amount of space between the edge of the paper and the text on the page. Most letters, reports, and memos look great with Word's default top, bottom, left, and right margins. However, if you are preparing a one-page flyer or an advertisement with plenty of white space and graphics, consider increasing some or all of the margins. Or, if you need to control the number of pages in a document, consider decreasing margins.

You can set margins using either a dialog box or the Rulers:

- You can set all margins with the Margins category in the Page Setup dialog box. If you format a single page at a time (the default), you can set the Top, Bottom, Left, and Right margins. If you want to balance the text and graphics by looking at two facing pages at once, click the **Mirror Margins** check box. Then you can set the Top, Bottom, Inside, and Outside margins.

- You can set the left and right margins using the horizontal Ruler. (If the Ruler is not displayed, open the **View** menu and choose the **Ruler** command.)

- Or you can set the top and bottom margins with the vertical Ruler (available only in Page Layout mode). For information on viewing modes, see "View Text in Different Modes" on page 54.

To open the Margins category of the Page Setup dialog box, open the **File** menu, choose the **Page Setup** command, and click the **Margins** tab, if necessary. The Page Setup dialog box for Margins provides these options:

Top   Type or select the measurement from the top edge of the paper to the top of the first line of text in this text box. The default measurement is 1 inch.

Bottom   Type or select the measurement from the bottom edge of the paper to the bottom of the last line of text in this text box. The default measurement is 1 inch.

Left   Type or select the measurement from the left edge of the paper to the left edge of text in this text box. The default measurement is 1.25 inches.

Right   Type or select the measurement from the right edge of the paper to the right edge of text in this text box. The default measurement is 1.25 inches.

Gutter   In this text box, type or select the *gutter* margin measurement, which allows for binding or hole-punching on the left side of a page printed on a single side of the paper, leaving the other side blank. Word adds the gutter margin measurement to the left margin, resulting in a larger left margin.

Header   In this text box, type or select the measurement from the top edge of the paper to the top of the first line of the header, which is within the top margin. The default measurement is 0.5 inch.

Footer   In this text box, type or select the measurement from the bottom edge of the paper to the bottom of the last line of the footer, which is within the bottom margin. The default measurement is 0.5 inch.

Preview   In this box, look at the sample page to see how your margin settings affect the document.

Apply To   Open this drop-down list to change the margins for the entire document or from the location of the insertion point forward, or, if you have selected text, change margins for the entire document or for the selection. If you are working with sections, you can apply margins to selected sections.

Mirror Margins Check this check box to turn on *mirror margins*, which allow for binding or hole-punching of a page printed on both sides; the inside margins "mirror" each other.

Default Click this button to make these new margins the default for every document in the future.

Using the horizontal or vertical Ruler to set margins is completely visual. If you have a document on-screen, you can see immediately how new margins will look

when you use the Ruler. This is a quicker way to change margins, although it's a little more difficult to select exact numeric measurements.

On the horizontal Ruler, a single pointer represents the right margin. All text ends at or before the right margin, depending on paragraph alignment. Two pointers indicate the left margin. The top pointer controls the location of the first character in the paragraph's first line; the bottom pointer controls the left margin of the remaining lines in the paragraph.

Begin Guided Tour   **Change Margins with a Menu Command**

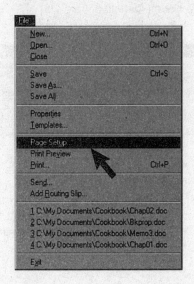

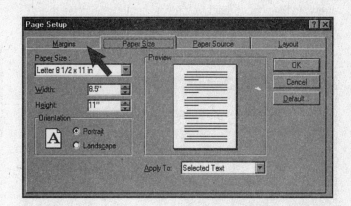

1 To change the margins of selected text, first select the appropriate text. (You don't need to select text if you want to change margins for the entire document or from the insertion point forward.) Then open the **File** menu and select the **Page Setup** command or double-click on the gray area of the Ruler.

2 In the Page Setup dialog box, click the **Margins** tab, if needed.

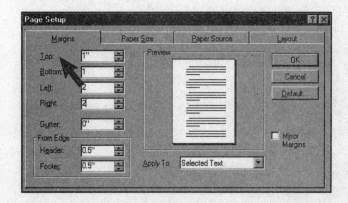

3 Set any combination of **Top**, **Bottom**, **Left**, or **Right** margins, either typing a number in the text box or moving the mouse pointer to one of the arrows to the right of that box, pressing and holding down the left mouse button, and releasing it when the desired number appears.

(continues)

Guided Tour Change Margins with a Menu Command *(continued)*

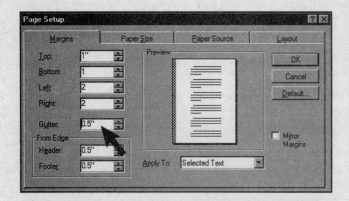

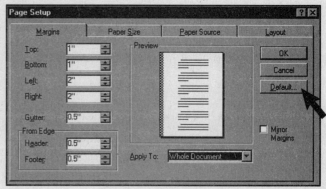

4 Change the gutter margin, either typing a number in the **Gutter** text box or moving the mouse pointer to one of the arrows to the right of that box, pressing and holding down the left mouse button, and releasing it when the desired number appears.

6 If you want to use the new margin settings as the default measurements for every Word document you create from now on, click the **Default** button.

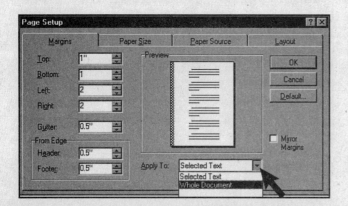

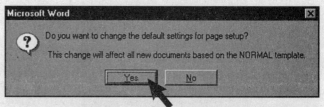

7 Word asks you if you want to use the new settings as the default. Select **Yes** to change all new documents or **No** to change just this document. (The Normal template contains a set of predefined styles and formats that you can apply to Word documents.) Then select **OK** to close the Page Setup dialog box.

5 Click the drop-down list arrow next to **Apply To** and select **Whole Document**, **Selected Text** (if you have selected text), or **This Point Forward** (if you have not selected text).

Begin Guided Tour   Change Margins with the Ruler

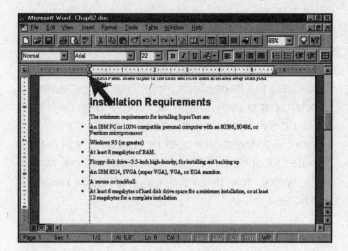

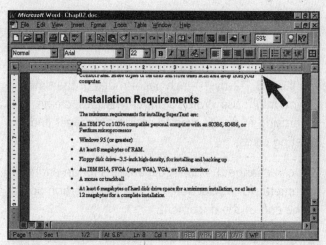

1 To change the left margin for selected text only or for the current paragraph, move the mouse pointer to the small rectangle below the left margin and first-line pointers on the ruler. Hold the mouse button down and drag the left margin to its new location. The dotted line indicates the current left margin location.

3 To change the right margin for the current paragraph or selected text, move the mouse pointer to the pointer on the right side of the Ruler. Then hold the mouse button down and drag the margin to its new location. The dotted line indicates the current right margin location.

If you can't find the right margin marker on the Ruler, drag the horizontal scroll bar box to the right until you see the right margin of the document and the right margin marker.

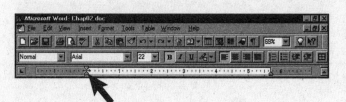

2 If you are in Page Layout view, another way to change the left margin is to move the mouse pointer to the place at which the left margin pointers meet and the Ruler changes from gray to white. When the mouse pointer changes to a double-headed arrow, hold the mouse button down and drag the left margin to its new location. This changes the left margin for the entire document, whether or not you have selected text or paragraphs.

4 To display measurements as you set margins by dragging within either Ruler, press and hold down the **Alt** key. For example, if you are working in the horizontal Ruler and use this technique, Word displays the width of the margins and the text between the margins.

Change Paper Size

You won't always use 8 1/2-by-11-inch paper printed along the 8 1/2-inch dimension (or narrow edge of the page). If you work in a law office, you'll use 8 1/2-by-14-inch paper much of the time. Or you might use Word to print envelopes, create advertising flyers, or even to design notepaper and greeting cards.

You can change the paper dimensions for an entire document, for a selection, or from the insertion point to the end of the document.

> If you change dimensions for a section (that is, less than the entire document), Word automatically inserts a section break before and after the area in which paper dimensions are different from the rest of the document. To learn how to insert a section break, refer to "Start a New Page or Section" on page 56.

To change paper dimensions, open the **File** menu, choose the **Page Setup** command, and click the **Paper Size** tab. In the Page Setup dialog box for Paper Size, the **Paper Size** drop-down list provides standard paper sizes, which vary, depending on the active printer. For example, the Hewlett-Packard LaserJet III provides nine options, and an Epson FX86E provides six options. To specify unique paper dimensions, type or select values in the **Width** and **Height** text boxes.

Begin Guided Tour   Select Paper Size

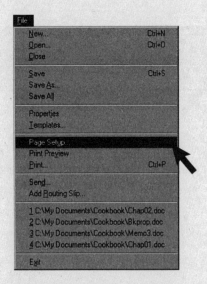

1 Open the **File** menu and select the **Page Setup** command. The Page Setup dialog box opens, and the section of the dialog box in which you last worked is on display.

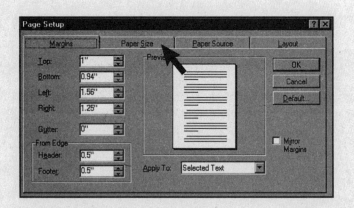

2 Click the **Paper Size** tab, if needed. Word changes the Page Setup dialog box to display page size and orientation options.

Guided Tour   Select Paper Size

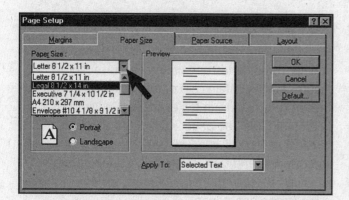

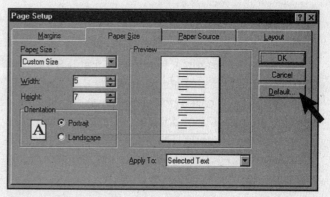

3 To choose a standard paper size, open the **Paper Size** drop-down list and select an item on the list. The sample in the Preview box changes.

5 If you want to make the dimensions you've established the default for this and future Word documents, click the **Default** button. Word asks you if you want to use the new settings as the default.

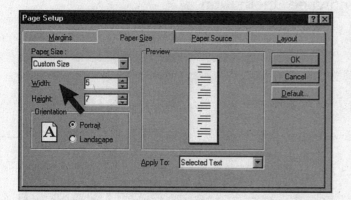

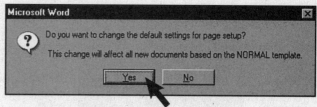

6 Click **Yes** (change all new documents based on the Normal template, the default styles and formats for Word documents) or **No** (just this document), to return to the Page Setup dialog box without making these dimensions the default. Then click **OK** to close the Page Setup dialog box.

4 To choose a custom size, type dimensions in the **Width** box, the **Height** box, or both. Or move the mouse pointer to one of the arrows to the right of either box; then press and hold the mouse button until the desired value appears. Notice that the **Paper Size** box displays **Custom Size**.

Use Portrait and Landscape Orientation

A typical document, such as this book, is printed with the text oriented to the smaller dimension of the page. For example, with paper that is 8 1/2-by-11-inches, the text is printed across the 8 1/2-inch dimension. This is called *portrait* orientation, which is used for the majority of documents, such as most letters and memoranda. The main reason that portrait orientation is so popular is that the eye can easily scan across the text that can fit on a line.

To present a great deal of information, which does not have to be read line by line, on a page, use

landscape orientation, in which the text is printed across the long dimension of a page. Today, the most popular use of landscape orientation is for spreadsheets, which contain cells of information rather than lines of text, or certain tables created in Word (see "Create a Table" on page 202). You don't read a spreadsheet line by line; you jump up and down rows and columns and from cell to cell. Certain tables, especially those with many columns, look much better in landscape orientation.

Begin Guided Tour Use Portrait and Landscape Orientation

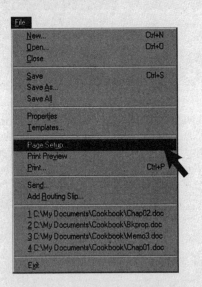

(1) Open the **File** menu and choose the **Page Setup** command. The Page Setup dialog box opens, and the section in which you last worked is on display.

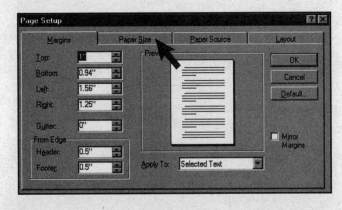

(2) Click the **Paper Size** tab, if needed. Word changes the Page Setup dialog box to display page size and orientation options.

Guided Tour Use Portrait and Landscape Orientation

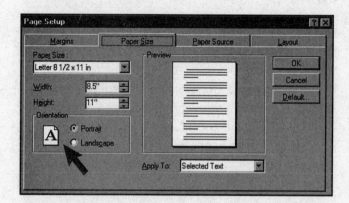

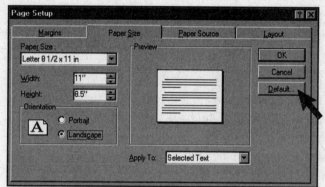

3 In the Orientation group, select either the **Portrait** or the **Landscape** option button. Word changes the illustration in the Preview box.

4 To make the selected orientation the default, click the **Default** button and select **Yes** when prompted. Then click **OK** to close the Page Setup dialog box and return to your document.

Insert Page Numbers

When creating multiple-page documents, such as reports and proposals, showing the number of each page makes the document look much more professional. Sometimes, you create a document that is made up of several files. With Word's customized page numbering, you have the ability to define the starting page number for each new file (see "Insert Page Numbers" below).

Word always adds page numbers to *headers*, text and graphics that appear on the top of the page, or *footers*, text and graphics that appear at the bottom of the page. When you add a page number to a header or footer (see "Add a Header and Footer" on page 368), Word starts counting page numbers. You can control where Word starts counting page num-

bers or page number formats by opening the **Insert** menu and choosing the **Page Numbers** command. When Word displays the Page Numbers dialog box, click the **Format** button. In the Page Number Format dialog box, select a number format and determine whether your pages continue from the last page number or start at a specific number that you designate.

> If you are working in Normal view, you won't see page numbers (or the headers or footers, for that matter). However, if you go to **Page Layout** view, you'll be able to see the page numbers as they will print.

Begin Guided Tour   Insert Page Numbers

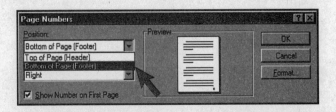

1 Open the **Insert** menu and select the **Page Numbers** command. Word displays the Page Numbers dialog box.

2 Click the **Format** button. Word displays the Page Number Format dialog box. The default starting page number appears in the text box next to the **Start At** radio button. Open the **Position** drop-down list and choose to put the page number in the header (at the top of the page) or in the footer (at the bottom of the page). By default, Word places the page number in the footer.

Guided Tour Insert Page Numbers

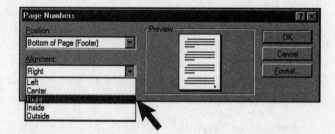

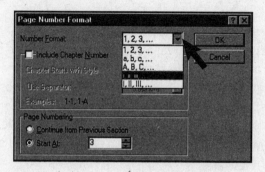

3 Open the **Alignment** drop-down list and select the location of the page number in the header or footer. If you choose **Left**, **Center**, or **Right**, the page number is always in the same location on the page. If you choose **Inside** or **Outside**, the location of the page number varies (either always inside or always outside) depending on whether the page is even-numbered or odd-numbered. Type the starting page number in the box, or move to one of the arrows to the right of the box; press and hold the mouse button down until the value that you want appears. For example, to start the numbering on page three, type a **3** in the box.

4 Click the **Format** button to display the Page Number Format dialog box. Open the **Number Format** drop-down list by clicking the down arrow next to it. Click the format you want. Click **OK** to close the Page Number Format dialog box. Click **OK** again to close the Page Numbers dialog box.

Many professionally prepared documents do not show the page number on the first page. To start page numbers on the second page, clear the check mark from the **Show Number on First Page** check box.

Control When a New Page Starts

An automatic page break sometimes splits a paragraph between two pages. A single line of a paragraph ending a page is called an *orphan* line; a single line starting a page is a *widow* line. In most cases, you don't want a single line at the beginning or end of a page. The Word default ensures that at least two lines of a paragraph remain at the beginning or end of a page.

To check the status of widow and orphan lines, open the **Format** menu and choose the **Paragraph** command, or right-click within the paragraph and select Paragraph from the shortcut menu. Then click the **Text Flow** tab. When Word displays the Paragraph dialog box for **Text Flow**, see whether the **Widow/ Orphan Control** check box in the Pagination group is checked (widow and orphan control is turned on) or clear.

With Widow/Orphan Control turned on, a paragraph can still print with two or three lines on one page and

two or three lines on the next. The other options in the Pagination group are:

Keep Lines Together   Check this box if you want to force a paragraph to print on one page.

Keep with Next   Check this box to force two paragraphs to remain on the same page.

Page Break Before   Check this box to insert a page break before a selected paragraph.

Be careful when selecting multiple paragraphs and activating the Page Break Before option. The result will be page breaks before every paragraph—potentially pages and pages of white space and very little text.

Begin Guided Tour   Control Page Breaks for Selected Paragraphs

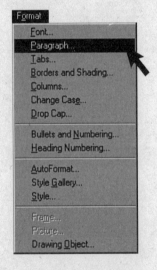

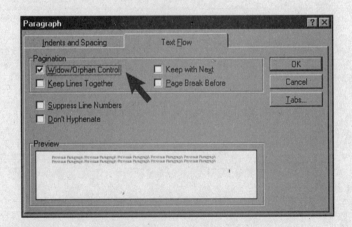

1 Select one or more paragraphs. (If you want to format a single paragraph, just click within it.) Open the **Format** menu and select the **Paragraph** command. Word displays the Paragraph dialog box. If needed, click the **Text Flow** tab to open the Text Flow section of the Paragraph dialog box.

2 In the Pagination group, you can check or clear any combination of **Keep Lines Together**, **Keep with Next**, and **Page Break Before**. Then click **OK** to close the dialog box.

Indent Paragraphs

Indentation moves either an entire paragraph or the first line away from the left and/or right margin of the document. There are three main types of indents:

First-line indent Start the first line of a selected paragraph further away from the left margin than succeeding lines, which are all aligned.

Hanging indent Start the first line in a selected paragraph closer to the left margin than succeeding lines, which are all aligned.

Left or right indent Indent all the lines of a paragraph from either or both margins. This is also known as a *block indent*.

When you use the **Format** menu and the **Paragraph** command, you can set indentation in the Indentation group of the Paragraph dialog box. For a description of Paragraph dialog box options, see "Paragraph Dialog Box" on page 557.

Use the Ruler's left margin markers and right margin marker to set indentation. The left margin markers are two pointers: the top pointer is the first-line indent marker, and the bottom pointer is the left margin marker. To indent paragraphs from the left, move the bottom pointer. To create first-line or hanging indents, move the top pointer. The right margin marker on the Ruler is a single pointer. To indent paragraphs from the right, move the right margin marker.

Word also provides these key combinations for paragraph indentation, as shown in the following table.

 Unindent button Click this toolbar button to decrease the amount of indentation.

 Indent button Click this toolbar button to increase the amount of indentation.

Indenting Paragraphs with the Keyboard

Key	Type of Indent	Description
Ctrl+T	Hanging Indent	Indents all but the first line of selected paragraphs. Press again to increase the indent to the next tab stop.
Ctrl+M	Indent	Indents all the selected paragraphs from the left margin, one tab stop at a time.
Ctrl+Q	Remove all indents	Removes all indents from the selected paragraphs.

Begin Guided Tour   Indent Paragraphs with a Menu Command

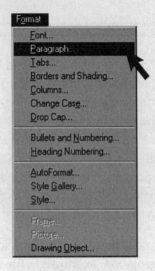

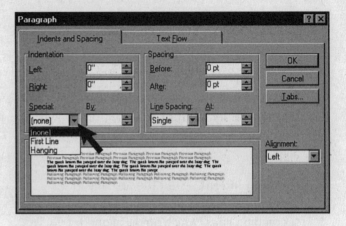

3 From the **Special** drop-down list, select **First Line** or **Hanging**. Word changes the illustration in the Preview box.

1 Select one or more paragraphs. (If you want to select a single paragraph, simply click anywhere within it.) Open the **Format** menu and select the **Paragraph** command. Word displays the Paragraph dialog box.

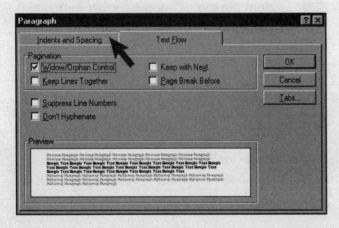

2 If needed, click the **Indents and Spacing** tab.

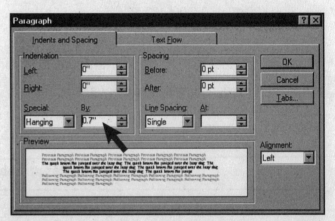

4 In the **By** box, type any positive number from 0 to 22 (if the unit of measure is inches), including decimal fractions, if you want (for example, .25, .6, or .2). You don't have to type the unit of measure mark (for example, ") after typing the value; Word automatically assumes that you are using the default unit of measure. Word indents the first line in the paragraph by the value in the **By** box.

Without changing the unit of measure, you can specify a particular measurement in the Format dialog box. For example, you can make the left margin 5 cm (centimeters), 32 pt (points), 2 pi (picas), or if you have changed the unit of measure from inches, to 0.5 in or 1". After you click **OK**, Word converts the value that you entered into the standard unit of measure.

Guided Tour   Indent Paragraphs with a Menu Command

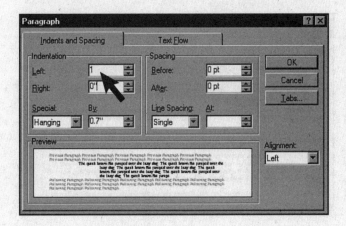

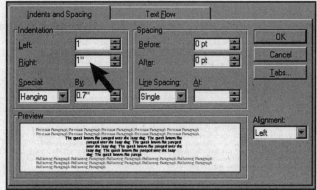

5 If you want, in the **Left** box, type a value that represents the left margin. When you click outside the **Left** box, Word changes the illustration in the Preview box.

6 If you want, in the **Right** box, type a value that represents the right margin. When you click outside the **Right** box, Word changes the illustration in the Preview box. Then click **OK** to close the Paragraph dialog box.

Begin Guided Tour   Indent Paragraphs with the Horizontal Ruler

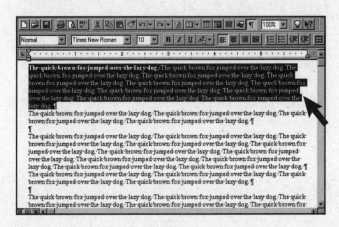

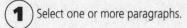

1 Select one or more paragraphs.

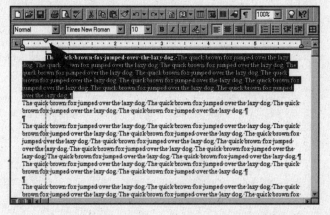

2 To adjust the first line, move the mouse pointer to the first-line indent marker, hold down the mouse button, and drag the marker to where you want it. The vertical line represents the present location of the first line of the selected paragraph.

(continues)

Guided Tour Indent Paragraphs with the Horizontal Ruler

(continued)

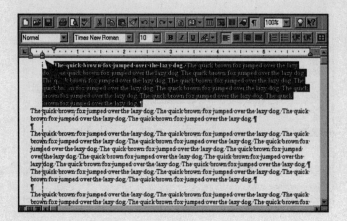
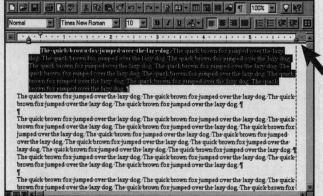

3 To adjust the left margin, move the mouse pointer to the left margin marker, hold down the mouse button, and drag the marker to where you want it. The vertical line represents the present location of the left margin of the selected paragraph.

4 To adjust the right margin, move the mouse pointer to the right margin marker, hold down the mouse button, and drag the marker to where you want it. The vertical line represents the present location of the right margin of the selected paragraph.

Align Paragraphs

You can align paragraph text so that it is flush with either the left or the right margin, centered between the margins, or flush with both the left and the right margins (*justified*). To change paragraph alignment to left, right, centered, or justified, you can use the **Format Paragraph** command, Formatting toolbar buttons, or key combinations, as shown in the following table. (For descriptions of all the Formatting toolbar buttons, see "Formatting Toolbar" on page 538.)

 Align Left button   The default, aligns the selected paragraph to the left margin.

 Center button   Centers the selected paragraph between the left and right margins.

 Align Right button   Aligns the selected paragraph to the right margin.

 Justify button   Aligns the selected paragraph with both the left indent and the right margin.

Types of Paragraph Alignment

Alignment Options	Keys	Description
Left	Ctrl+L	Text aligns with the left margin. The right margin is ragged.
Right	Ctrl+R	Text aligns with the right margin. The left margin is ragged.
Center	Ctrl+E	Text is centered between the margins.
Justified	Ctrl+J	Text aligns with both the left and right margins by adding extra spaces between words.

Begin Guided Tour   Align Paragraphs

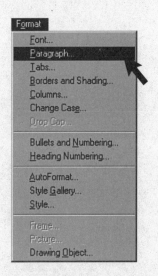

1 Select one or more paragraphs to align. Open the **Format** menu and select the **Paragraph** command. Word opens the Paragraph dialog box.

(continues)

Guided Tour Align Paragraphs *(continued)*

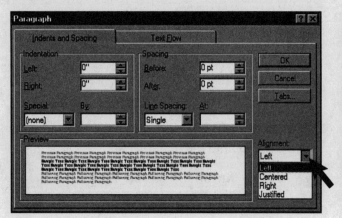

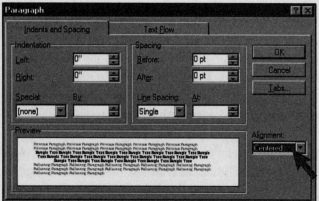

2 Click the **Indents and Spacing** tab, if necessary. Open the **Alignment** drop-down list by clicking on the text in the box or the downward-pointing arrow to the right of the box. Word displays your choices: **Left**, **Centered**, **Right**, and **Justified**.

3 Select one of the alignments. Word changes the alignment in the highlighted paragraph in the Preview box. Click **OK** to close the dialog box.

Control Spacing of Paragraphs and Lines

Paragraph spacing adjusts spacing above and below a paragraph. Word's default paragraph spacing is no space between paragraphs. You can select **Format Paragraph** and use the **Before** and **After** text boxes or press key combinations to adjust spacing between paragraphs. To add or remove an extra space before one or more selected paragraphs, press the **Ctrl+0** key combination. There is no keyboard shortcut for adding spacing after a paragraph.

Line spacing adjusts the space between the lines of text within a paragraph. As the size of the type in a document increases, Word increases the white-space measurement as well. Use **Format Paragraph** to

choose line spacing. Then select an option from the **Line Spacing** drop-down list. For a description of each option in the Paragraph dialog box, see "Paragraph Dialog Box" on page 557. The following table shows the line spacing keyboard combinations.

Line Spacing Keyboard Combinations

Keys	Description
Ctrl+1	Sets single spacing
Ctrl+5	Sets one-and-one-half spacing
Ctrl+2	Sets double spacing

Begin Guided Tour   Adjust Space between Paragraphs

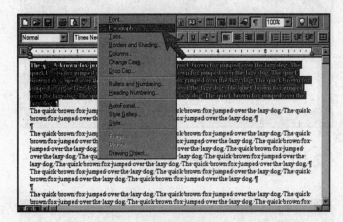

1 Select one or more paragraphs. Then open the **Format** menu and choose the **Paragraph** command. Word displays the Paragraph dialog box.

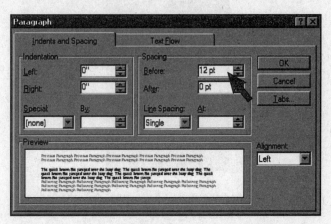

2 Select the **Indents and Spacing** tab, if necessary. Type a value in the **Before** box. Alternatively, press and hold down the left mouse button on either the up or the down arrow (located to the right of the box) until the desired value appears.

(continues)

Guided Tour   Adjust Space between Paragraphs

(continued)

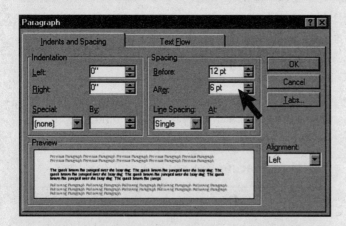

3 Type a value in the **After** box. Alternatively, press and hold down the left mouse button on either the up or the down arrow until the desired value appears. As you change the settings, Word changes the Preview document in the dialog box. Then click **OK** to close the Paragraph dialog box.

Begin Guided Tour   Adjust Space Between Lines

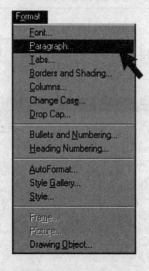

1 After selecting one or more paragraphs, open the **Format** menu and select the **Paragraph** command. Word opens the Paragraph dialog box.

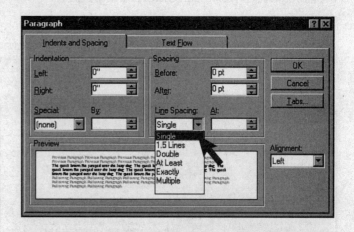

2 Select the **Indents and Spacing** tab, if necessary. Open the **Line Spacing** drop-down list and select an option.

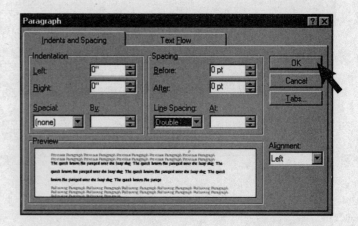

3 Click **OK**. Word closes the dialog box and adjusts the line spacing of the selected paragraphs as you just saw in the Preview box.

Set and Clear Tabs

Use tabs to indent text within a line or paragraph. For example, to format multiple columns of data or text that you don't want to make into a table (a company's telephone list or a college's room assignments), you may need to place parts of each line at specific *tab stops*, locations of tabs between the left and right margins, or indent some lines using the same tab positions. Either accept Word's default tab stops (every 1/2-inch) on the Ruler or change the tab settings in the Tabs dialog box. Then, in your document, press the **Tab** key to start text at the next tab position. On the Ruler, the default tab positions appear as small vertical lines on the bar just below the Ruler scale line.

Use the Ruler to set, change (by dragging), and clear tab stops and to change tab alignment: Left, Center, Right, and Decimal. Use the **Format Tabs** command, double-click on the gray border at the bottom of the Ruler, or click on the **Tabs** button in the Paragraph dialog box to open the Tabs dialog box. This will set and clear tab stops; clear some or all tab positions; determine the type of *leader* (the dotted lines between a title and a page number in some tables of contents) to use; and set or change five types of tab alignments: Left, Center, Right, Decimal, and Bar.

> To find out the relative location of a tab stop along the width of a document, move the mouse pointer to the tab stop you want to check, press the **Alt** key and click the mouse button. Word displays the measurements of the tab stop to the left margin and to the right margin. As you drag a tab stop along the Ruler to change its position, press the **Alt** key to see its current position.

The following table lists each tab alignment setting and provides a description for each.

Tab Alignment Types

Tab Alignment Button	Setting	Description
L	Left	The leftmost character aligns with the tab position. The rest of the text flows to the right.
⊥	Center	The text is centered on the tab position.
⌐	Right	The rightmost character aligns with the tab position. The rest of the text flows to the left.
⊥.	Decimal	Any decimal point aligns with the tab position. The remaining digits flow left and right from the decimal point. If there is no decimal point, this setting behaves like a right tab.
N/A	Bar	Word draws a vertical line through the selected text at a specific position. The bar is not really a tab because you can't tab to it. However, when you set a bar, Word places a symbol on the Ruler. Bars can only be set using the Tabs dialog box.

Use the **Format Tabs** command, click on the **Tab** button in the Paragraph dialog box, or double-click on the bottom gray border of the Ruler to open the Tabs dialog box in order to set tabs at regular or varying intervals.

- To set tabs at regular intervals (for example, every .75-inch), type a value in or select a value from the **Default Tab Stops** text box in the Tabs dialog box.

- To set tabs at varying intervals (for example, .5", 1.5", 3.3") for tabs, type measurements between –22" and 22", one at a time, in the **Tab Stop Position** text box. (You can use a negative number for tabs within hanging indents.)

A feature that is not available when you use the Ruler is defining a *leader*, typically a dotted line that extends from the last character or space in the text (which usually starts close to or at the left margin) and the tab (which is usually close to the right margin). The most common use of leaders is in tables of contents to guide the reader's eye from a heading to its page number.

To quickly display the Tabs dialog box, double-click any tab mark on the Ruler. Another way to open the Tabs dialog box is to open the **Format** menu, select the **Paragraph** command, and click the **Tabs** button.

You can clear one specific tab stop or all tab stops.

- To clear a tab stop from the Ruler, select a tab position and drag it down off the Ruler toward the bottom of the computer screen.

- To clear a tab stop from within the Tabs dialog box, open the **Format** menu and select the **Tabs** command. Select the tab stop from the list in the **Tab Stop Position** box, click the **Clear** button, and click **OK**.

- To clear all tab stops from within the Tabs dialog box, open the **Format** menu and select the **Tabs** command. Click the **Clear All** button and click **OK**.

Begin Guided Tour   Set Tab Stops Using the Ruler

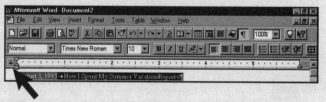

1 Select the text or click in the line for which you want to define tab stops. (If you want to set tabs for a single line without affecting other lines in the document, press **Enter** to add a new line, which will keep the default tab stops. Then select only the line in which you want to define tab stops.)

2 Repeatedly click on the **Tab Alignment** button until the one that you want is on the Ruler.

Guided Tour   Set Tab Stops Using the Ruler

3 On the Ruler, click at the position at which you want a tab stop. When you insert a tab stop, it causes all of the default tab stops to the left of the one you just inserted to disappear, and Word changes the format.

4 Continue selecting tab alignment buttons and placing tab stops.

Begin Guided Tour   Set Tab Stops Using the Tabs Dialog Box

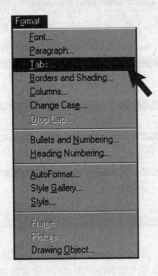

1 Select one or more paragraphs. Open the **Format** menu and select the **Tabs** command. Word displays the Tabs dialog box.

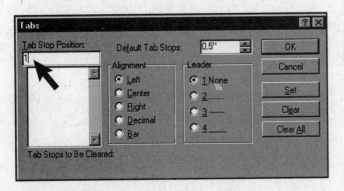

2 In the **Tab Stop Position** text box, type a number representing the tab stop.

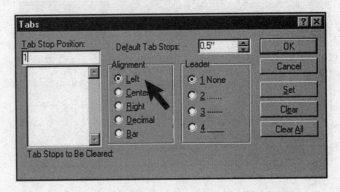

3 Click the type of alignment (**Left**, **Center**, **Right**, **Decimal**, or **Bar**) for the tab position.

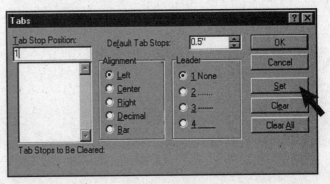

4 Click the **Set** button to save the new tab stop but keep the dialog box open.

(continues)

Guided Tour Set Tab Stops Using the Tabs Dialog Box *(continued)*

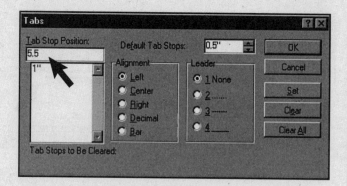

5 To set another tab stop, type a number representing the tab stop in the **Tab Stop Position** text box.

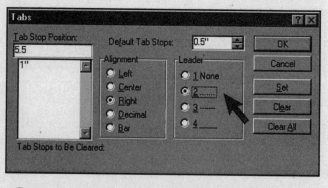

7 To select a leader, choose one of the four leader types.

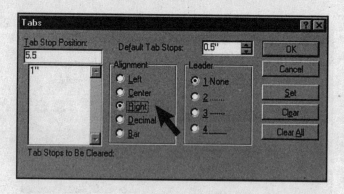

6 Click the type of alignment: **Left**, **Center**, **Right**, **Decimal**, or **Bar**.

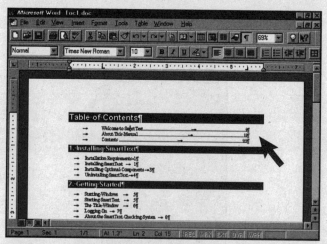

8 When you finish setting tab stops, click **OK** to close the dialog box. (If you want to continue setting tab stops, click the **Set** button.) Word returns to your document, places the new tab setting on the Ruler, and formats the selected text. Click to remove the highlight.

Add Multiple Columns to a Document

To create a newsletter or any document with multiple columns of equal width, you'll use *snaking columns*, which simply means the text continues from the bottom of one column up to the top of the next.

When you add columns to a document, Word automatically places section breaks before and after the columns. (If you are in Page Layout view, you can see the columns as they will print.) Word also attempts to balance the columns so they are approximately the same length. If you are combining *single-column* format (which is one line of text stretching from left to right margin) and multiple columns, insert a section break between the two types of columns.

 You can define columns of exactly the same width and spacing between them or vary both the width and spacing. The **Columns** toolbar button allows you to define the number of columns (depending on page size, layout, and orientation) but you cannot adjust width or spacing. Using the Columns dialog box, you cannot only define a number of columns, but you also can adjust width and spacing. In the Columns dialog box, you can choose from five preset column layouts.

It is much easier to work with columns in Page Layout view, which allows you to see the columns as they will print and to be able to format them and adjust their length. Normal view shows multiple columns as a single column.

The options in the Columns dialog box are:

Presets   Click a button in this group to select from five predefined column layouts.

Number of Columns   In this text box, either type or select the number of columns, by default, from 1 to 10. You can specify more columns by decreasing the left and right margins or by going to landscape mode.

Line Between   Check this check box to place a vertical line between columns.

Width and Spacing   Use this group to specify the **Width** of a column and the **Spacing** between columns. Check or clear the **Equal Column Width** check box to keep identical columns or to define widths of individual, unequal columns.

Apply To   Open this drop-down list to change the columns for this section or from the location of the insertion point forward.

Preview   View the results of the chosen options.

Start New Column   Check this box to insert a column break, after selecting **This Point Forward** from the **Apply To** drop-down list.

Begin Guided Tour   Add Columns Using a Toolbar Button

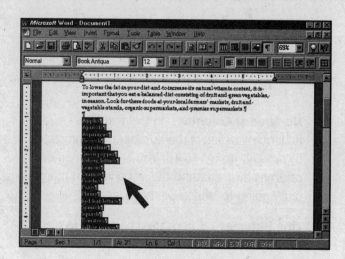

1 To see the results of these steps, look at your document in Page Layout view. Select a section of text to become columns or move the insertion point to the section in which you want to create columns. Then click the **Columns** toolbar button.

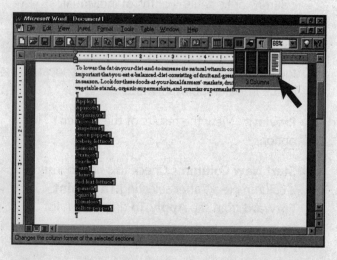

2 While pressing and holding down the left mouse button, drag across the number of columns to be selected.

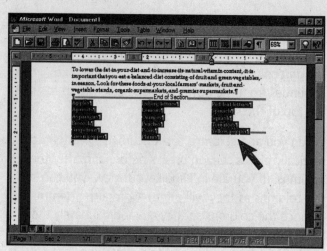

3 Release the mouse button. Word changes the format of the selected section and places section breaks before and after the selected text.

Begin Guided Tour Add Columns Using a Menu Command

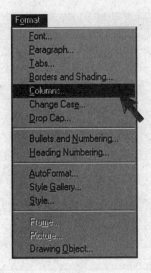

1 Either select or click in a section of text to become columns, or move the insertion point to the section in which you want to create columns. Then open the **Format** menu and choose the **Columns** command. Word displays the Columns dialog box.

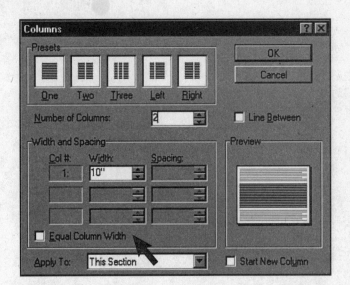

3 If you intend to use uneven columns, clear the Equal Column Width dialog box if it is checked.

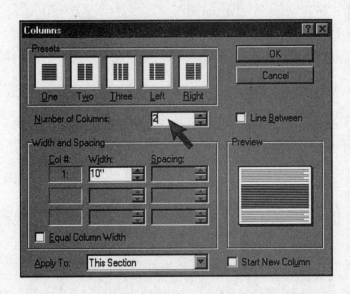

2 Either select a **Presets** format or type a value in or select a value from the **Number of Columns** text box. Word changes the document in the **Preview** box and calculates the width of the columns and the space between the columns.

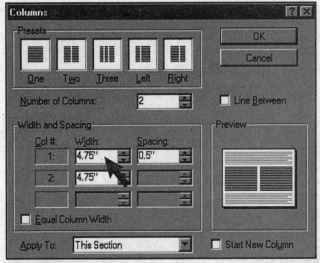

4 Click in the **Width** list box. Word activates the options in the **Width and Spacing** group.

(continues)

Guided Tour Add Columns Using a Menu Command *(continued)*

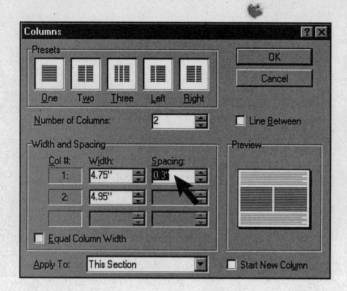

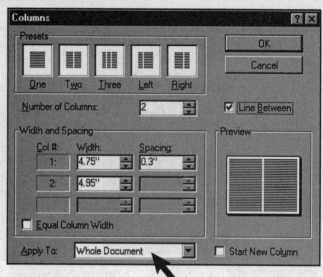

(5) Type or select a value for the space between columns in the **Spacing** list box for Col #1. Word calculates a new width for Col #2.

(7) Select the part of the document to apply formatting in the **Apply To** box. Then click **OK** to close the Columns dialog box.

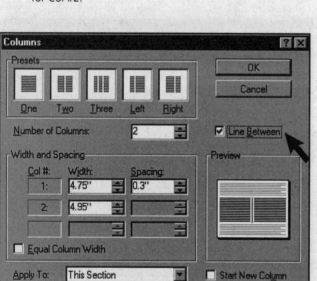

(6) To insert a vertical line between the columns, check the **Line Between** box. Word shows the results in the **Preview** box.

HOW TO...
Enhance a Document

Section 5 covers character formatting; you'll find out how to add emphasis such as boldface, italics, and underlines to your documents. You'll learn how to hide text, reveal it, and print it. You'll learn about *kerning* (adjusting spacing between characters), how to change the look of a document by selecting a different *font* (typeface design), and *point size* (the size of the type).

You'll find out how easy it is to format a drop cap (a larger and usually decorative letter at the beginning of a paragraph, especially the first paragraph in a document) and how to insert special symbols in your documents.

Bulleted and numbered lists allow you to simplify your text. In this section, you'll find out how to use and customize bulleted and numbered lists.

Finally, you will learn about Word's automatic formatting features: AutoFormat and the Style Gallery.

What You Will Find in This Section

Add Emphasis to Selected Text

Character formatting, or emphasis, changes the appearance of an individual character. Keeping the same type design and size, you can change the appearance of a character to give it greater emphasis. You can underline it in several ways, slant it, make its lines thicker, move it above or below other characters (*superscript* and *subscript*), or even change its color.

You can apply character enhancements from within the Font dialog box, by clicking on Formatting toolbar buttons, or by pressing key combinations.

> To use the Formatting toolbar, it must appear on-screen. If the Formatting toolbar does not appear on-screen, open the **View** menu and choose the **Toolbars** command. Place a check mark in the Formatting check box, and click on **OK**. You also can move the mouse pointer to any toolbar on-screen, right-click, and select **Formatting** from the shortcut menu. (If no toolbar is on-screen, you must use the View Toolbars command; the shortcut menu will not appear.)

To display the Font dialog box, open the **Format** menu and select the **Font** command. The following table describes each of the formatting options in the Font dialog box with the shortcut keys for these formats. For a complete description of all the options in the Font dialog box, see "Font Dialog Box" on page 556.

The easiest way to format characters is to use the Formatting toolbar (and, in one case, the Standard toolbar). The Formatting toolbar not only enables you to manipulate characters but also shows you how the characters are formatted.

Font drop-down list   Shows you the current *font* (the typeface design) and enables you to choose a new font from the fonts installed on your computer. For more information about fonts, see "Change Fonts and Font Sizes" on page 182.

Font Size drop-down list   Shows you the current point size of the current text and enables you to choose a new point size. For more information about point size, see "Change Fonts and Font Sizes" on page 182.

Bold   Applies boldface to or removes boldface from the selected text.

Italic   Applies italics to or removes italics from the selected text.

Underline   Applies a single underline to or removes the underline from the selected text.

Highlight   Applies a highlight to or removes a highlight from the selected text.

Format Painter   On the Standard toolbar, copies the format of the selected text to other text.

> To change the case of selected text, open the **Format** menu and choose the **Change Case** command. In the Change Case dialog box, click one of the option buttons, and select **OK** or press **Enter**. You can also cycle through a list of cases from which to choose. Just press **Shift+F3** until the selected text appears the way you want.

Font Dialog Box Formats

Option	Key Combination	Description
Bold	Ctrl+B, Ctrl+Shift+B	Applies boldface to selected text.
Italic	Ctrl+I, Ctrl+Shift+I	Applies italics to selected text.
Strikethrough	None	Strikes through selected text.
Hidden	Ctrl+Shift+H	Hides selected text.
Small Caps	Ctrl+Shift+K	Changes selected text to small capitals.
All Caps	Ctrl+Shift+A	Changes selected text to full-size capitals.
Underline		
None	N/A	
Single	Ctrl+U, Ctrl+Shift+U	Underlines all selected text, including spaces between words.
Words Only	Ctrl+Shift+W	Underlines all selected text, excluding spaces between words.
Double	Ctrl+Shift+D	Applies double underline.
Superscript	Ctrl+=	Moves selected text higher relative to other text on the line.
Subscript	Ctrl+Shift+=	Moves selected text lower relative to other text on the line.
Regular	Ctrl+Spacebar	Removes character formatting from the selected text.
	Ctrl+Shift+Z	

Begin Guided Tour   Emphasize Text Using a Menu Command

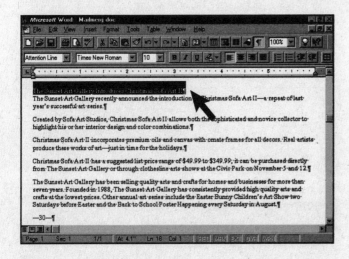

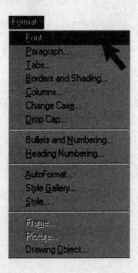

 Select existing text that you want to format or move the insertion point to the location at which you want to type formatted text.

2 Open the **Format** menu, and select the **Font** command; or right-click on the selected text and select **Font**. Word displays the Font dialog box.

(continues)

Guided Tour Emphasize Text Using a Menu Command *(continued)*

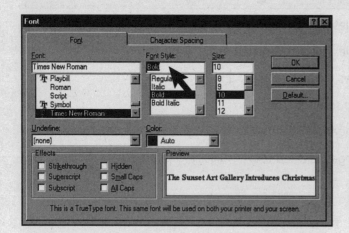

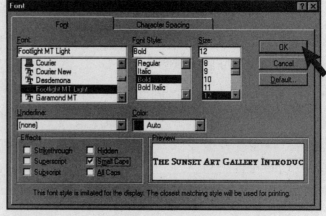

3 Choose from the **Font Style** text/list box. In the **Preview** box, Word displays the format that you selected.

5 To change additional character formats, select other options from the dialog box (and see the results in the **Preview** box). When you complete your selections, click **OK**.

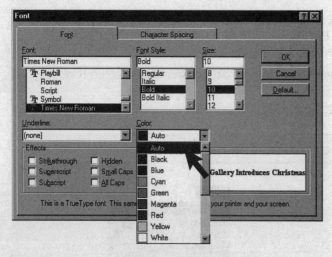

4 If you have a color monitor, printer, or plotter, open the **Color** drop-down list and select from the list of colors.

Begin Guided Tour   Use the Formatting Toolbar

1 To enhance selected text, click one or more buttons on the Formatting toolbar. When you select a button, it appears to be pressed.

3 To turn off or undo a character enhancement, select the enhanced text and click the button that controls that enhancement. The buttons that you click no longer appear to be pressed.

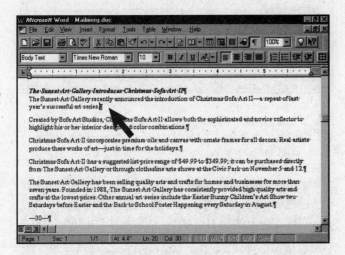

2 To enhance text that you have not yet typed, move the insertion point to the place at which you want to start typing. Then click one or more buttons on the Formatting toolbar.

Begin Guided Tour Use the Format Painter

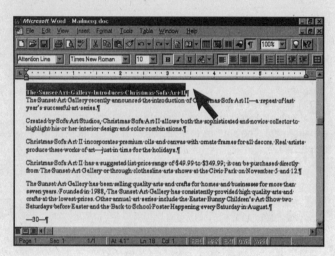

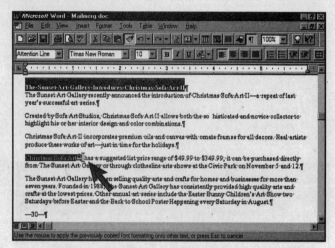

1 Select text with a format that you want to copy.

2 Click the **Format Painter** button. The mouse pointer looks like a paintbrush.

3 Click the left mouse button and drag over text that you want to change. After applying the format, Word deactivates the Format Painter.

You can keep the Format Painter turned on until you choose to turn it off. Just double-click the **Format Painter** toolbar button and Word keeps the button activated. To turn off the Format Painter, click on the **Format Painter** toolbar button.

Begin Guided Tour   Use Superscript and Subscript

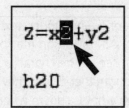

1 Select the text to be formatted with superscript.

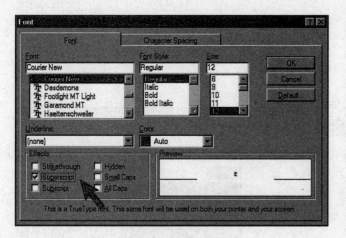

2 Open the **Format** menu and select the **Font** command. Word displays the Font dialog box. Check the **Superscript** check box. Click **OK**.

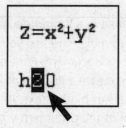

3 Select the text that you want to format with subscript.

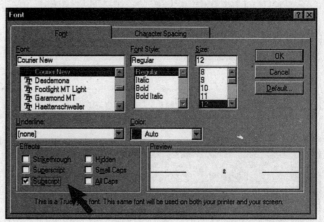

4 Open the **Format** menu and select the **Font** command. Word displays the Font dialog box. Check the **Subscript** check box. Click **OK**.

Hide Text and Reveal Hidden Text

Y ou can hide text in a Word document. Use hidden text to make notes to yourself or to others throughout a document. For example, if you're a teacher, you can create a document for a test and include the answers as hidden text. After the test is over, you can reprint the document with the answers and give it to your students.

Before hiding text or typing hidden text, be sure to turn on the **Show All** button on the Formatting toolbar so you can see all the characters and symbols in your document, whether or not they are hidden. You can determine what is shown when you click the **Show/Hide** button by following the steps in the "Display or Conceal Hidden Text" Guided Tour on the next page.

A shortcut for hiding selected text is to press **Ctrl+Shift+H**. Press **Ctrl+Shift+H** again to reveal selected hidden text.

Begin Guided Tour   Hide and Reveal Text

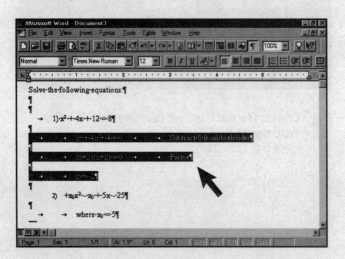

1 Select existing text, or move the insertion point to where you want to type hidden text.

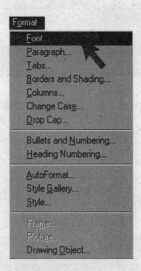

2 Open the **Format** menu and choose the **Font** command. Word displays the Font dialog box. If needed, click the **Font** tab to display the Font section of the dialog box.

Guided Tour   Hide and Reveal Text

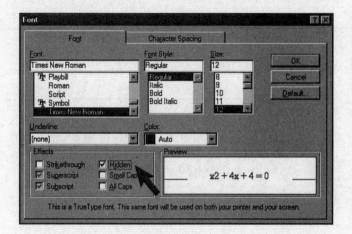

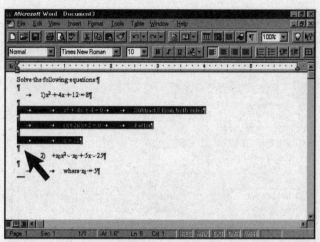

3 In the Style box, place a check mark in the **Hidden** check box. Then click **OK**. Word indicates that the text is hidden with a dotted underline.

4 To switch back to normal text, repeat steps 1 and 2, clear the Hidden check box, and then click **OK**.

Begin Guided Tour   Display or Conceal Hidden Text

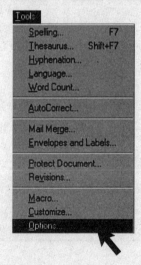

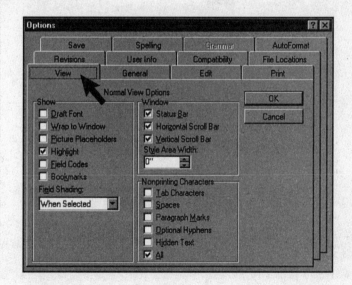

1 Open the **Tools** menu and choose the **Options** command. Word displays the Options dialog box.

2 Click the **View** tab. Word displays the Options dialog box for the View category.

(continues)

Guided Tour Display or Conceal Hidden Text

(continued)

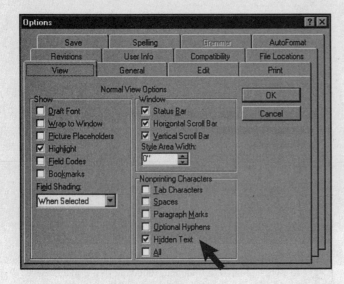

3 To display hidden text, under **Nonprinting Characters**, place a check in the **Hidden Text** check box. To conceal hidden text, remove the check from the Hidden Text check box. Then click **OK**.

If you check the **All** check box, all nonprinting characters are affected by your clicking on the **Show/Hide** toolbar button. Then, there is no need to check the **Hidden Text** check box.

Begin Guided Tour Print a Document With or Without Hidden Text

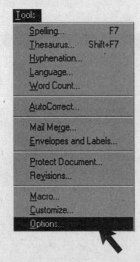

1 Open the **Tools** menu and select the **Options** command.

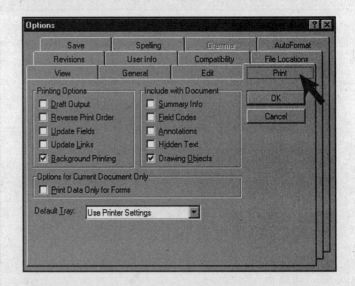

2 Click the **Print** tab. Word displays the Options dialog box for the Print category.

Guided Tour Print a Document With or Without Hidden Text

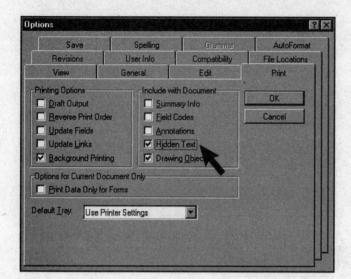

3 To print hidden text, place a check in the **Hidden Text** check box. To exclude hidden text from being printed, remove the check from the Hidden Text check box. Then click **OK**. Word returns to the current document from which you can print.

Adjust Spacing Between Characters

Reducing or tightening the space between characters is known as *kerning*. Kerning is particularly important for large text, such as headlines. An unkerned headline just looks like a series of letters; when you tighten the space between letters, they look like words.

If you select more than two characters at a time for kerning, it's difficult to fine-tune the separation between letters. However, if all the letters need to be moved, kerning is a good way to start; then you can adjust pairs of letters. Many times, you'll find that some letters don't need to be moved at all.

Use kerning to reformat a paragraph when the last line of the paragraph consists of only one word. Kern the letters and words in the preceding line of the paragraph so that Word moves the single word up from the last line.

Begin Guided Tour   Adjust Spacing Between Characters

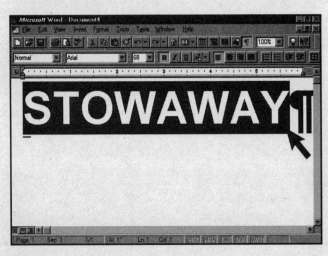

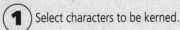

1 Select characters to be kerned.

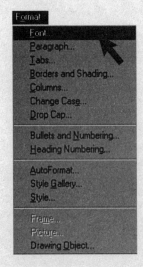

2 Open the **Format** menu and select the **Font** command.

Guided Tour   Adjust Spacing Between Characters

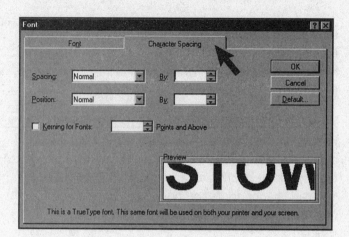

3 In the Font dialog box, click the **Character Spacing** tab, if needed. Word displays the Font dialog box for Character Spacing.

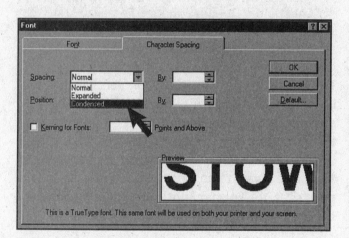

4 Select **Condensed** from the **Spacing** drop-down list. Click **OK**.

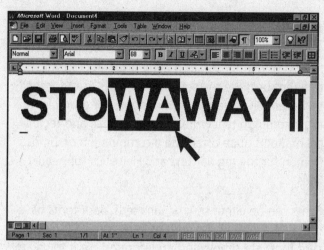

5 After viewing the condensed text, select a pair of characters that need further kerning.

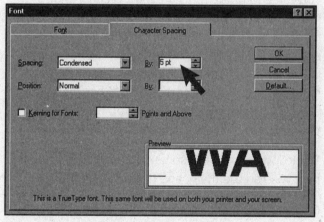

6 Open the **Format** menu and select the **Font** command to display the **Character Spacing** tab of the Font dialog box. Increase the number in the **By** text/option box. Then click **OK**. Repeat this with other pairs of characters until the selected text appears the way you want.

> To decide whether the number in the **By** text/option box is sufficient, click in another text box. Word then changes the display in the Preview box. Continue to change the number and click outside the **By** text/option box until you are satisfied. Then click **OK**.

Change Fonts and Font Sizes

Fonts are families of typeface designs. For example, two pages of text from different documents (a typewritten letter versus a page from a book) will look different because the sets of characters used for the text probably have different designs. For example, the most common typewriter font is Courier, and technical manuals quite often use a combination of Times Roman for the regular text and Helvetica for headlines.

Fonts can be either serif or sans serif. *Serif* fonts have decorative lines at the ends of letter strokes, and *sans serif* fonts are simple and undecorated. Serif fonts are generally considered to be easier to read, so most body text falls into the serif category.

You can also divide fonts into proportional and monospace (or nonproportional) fonts. *Proportional* fonts use different widths for each character. For example, the space for the letter *I* is much narrower than the space used for *W*. Every character in a *monospace* (or nonproportional) font has the same width, which is very useful when you have to align text vertically or at specific column locations.

The following table lists some common Windows fonts, how you can use them, and their characteristics.

Characters also can differ in size. The size of a character in a font is measured in *points*, hence point size or font size. The higher the point number is, the larger the character. A point is 1/72 of an inch, so a 72-point character measures approximately one inch from top to bottom, depending on the design.

When you start Word, a default font (Times New Roman) and point size (10) is assigned to the new document. For a particular document, you may decide that the default font isn't appropriate for your needs. You can change fonts and point sizes by using either the **Format Font** command or the Formatting toolbar.

> If you prefer to use a font other than 10 point Times Roman for most of your documents, read "Change the Default Font and Font Size" on page 336.

The **Format Font** command is more versatile than the Formatting toolbar. Both allow you to change the font and point size, but the **Format Font** command opens the Font dialog box, which provides other formatting options not available with the Formatting toolbar. Thus, if you want to do more than define fonts and point sizes, the **Format Font** command is probably the better choice.

Commonly Used Fonts

Font	Usage	Description
Times New Roman	Standard body text	Serif/Proportional
Courier New	Letters	Serif/Monospace
Line Printer	Tables	Serif/Monospace
Century Schoolbook	Textbooks	Serif/Proportional
Book Antigua	Textbooks	Serif/Proportional
Helvetica	Headlines	Sans serif/Proportional
Arial	Headlines	Sans serif/Proportional

Whether you use the **Format Font** command or the Formatting toolbar, the way in which you select a font or point size is very similar; you'll select from a list. In the **Font** drop-down list on the Formatting toolbar or the Font text/list box in the Font dialog box, either type the name of a font installed on your computer system or printer, or open the list of fonts and click your choice. To select a point size, use the same procedures: either select from the **Font Size** drop-down list on the Formatting toolbar or the **Size** text/list box in the Font dialog box.

> To increase the size of selected text by one point, press **Ctrl+]**. Press **Ctrl+[** to decrease the size of selected text by one point.

When selecting fonts, keep these notes in mind:

- Don't use more than two fonts per page, especially if you are working with a document that must look good (for example, an advertising flyer or brochure). With more than two fonts, your document will start to look like a ransom note.

- If you are working with technical documents, make sure that your font clearly shows the difference between the zero (*0*) and the letter *O*; the uppercase letter *Z* and the number *2*; and the lowercase letter *l*, the uppercase letter *I*, and the number *1*.

- If you use a copier to duplicate your documents, see how the font that you have chosen copies. Since copied text may appear lighter than the original, is the text still easy to read? If not, select a font with heavier lines.

- If your readers are older people, think about increasing the point size and selecting an easy-to-read font.

Begin Guided Tour Select a Font and Font Size Using a Menu Command

1 Select your entire document by pressing **Ctrl+5** (on the numeric keypad), or select a smaller portion of the document.

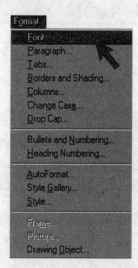

2 Open the **Format** menu and select the **Font** command, or right-click and select **Font** from the shortcut menu. Word displays the Font dialog box.

(continues)

Guided Tour   Select a Font and Font Size Using a Menu Command   *(continued)*

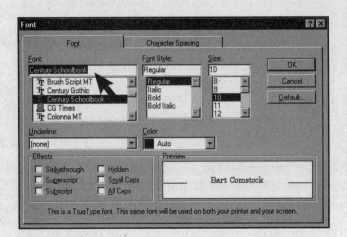

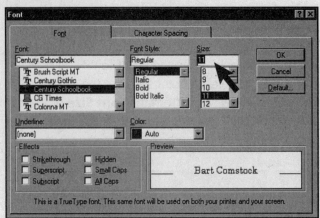

3 If the Font section of the Font dialog box is not displayed, click on the **Font** tab. Select a font from the **Font** text/list box. View the sample in the **Preview** box.

4 Select a point size from the **Size** text/list box. View the sample in the **Preview** box. Then click **OK**.

Begin Guided Tour   Select a Font and Font Size Using the Formatting Toolbar

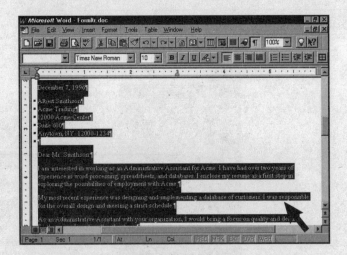

2 Open the **Font** drop-down list and select a font. For your convenience, Word displays the names of the most recently used fonts at the top of the list, separated from the rest by a double line.

1 Select your entire document by pressing **Ctrl+5** (on the numeric keypad), or select a smaller portion of the document.

3 Open the **Font Size** drop-down list and select a point size.

Insert a Drop Cap

Initial drop caps add elegance to a document, and they're easy to create. Word does all the work for you and places the selected character in a *frame*, a box that encloses an object and that allows for manipulation of both the object and the text that surrounds it.

To add a drop cap, simply click anywhere in the paragraph in which you want the drop cap to appear; open the **Format** menu and select the **Drop Cap** command. In the Drop Cap dialog box, select the position of the drop cap:

- **None**   The default, which indicates that the selected character is not a drop cap. To remove a drop cap, select **Drop Cap** from the **Format** menu, and click **None**.

- **Dropped**   A drop cap in a frame surrounded by text.

- **In Margin**   A drop cap in a frame in the left margin.

If you select **Dropped** or **In Margin**, you can change the font, specify the number of lines that the character drops below the other characters on its text line, and set the distance that the drop cap is separated from the surrounding text. If you select **None**, you cannot manipulate the selected character at all.

> If you are working in Normal view, after you close the Drop Cap dialog box, Word asks you if you want to be in Page Layout view to see the drop cap and the formats that you apply. Click the **Yes** button to switch to Page Layout view; click the **No** button to remain in Normal view and format the drop cap. Or click the **Cancel** button to stop formatting the drop cap.

After you close the dialog box, you can adjust the size of the frame or move the frame by dragging its borders or the entire frame.

Begin Guided Tour   Insert a Drop Cap

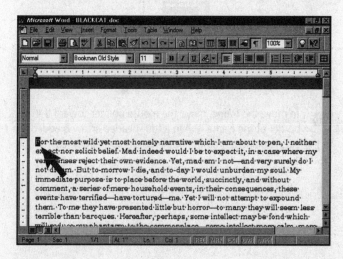

1 Click anywhere in the paragraph in which you want the drop cap.

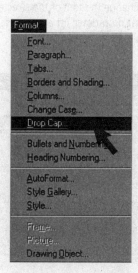

2 Open the **Format** menu and choose the **Drop Cap** command.

(continues)

Guided Tour   Insert a Drop Cap   *(continued)*

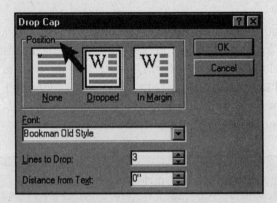

3 In the Drop Cap dialog box, select a position: **None**, **Dropped**, or **In Margin**.

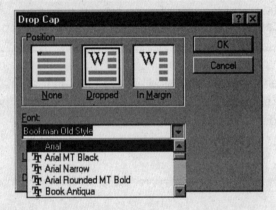

4 If you want, change the font of the selected character. Open the **Font** drop-down list and choose one from the list of fonts installed on your computer.

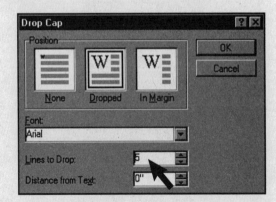

5 In the **Lines to Drop** text/option box, type or select the number of lines that you want the selected character to drop (that is, the height of the character).

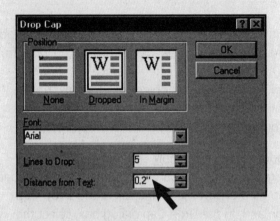

6 In the **Distance from Text** text/option box, type or select the distance between the frame and the text that will surround it. Then click **OK**.

7 To adjust the size of the frame surrounding the drop cap, move the mouse pointer to a handle (it looks like a little black square). When the pointer changes to a double-headed arrow, drag the frame border to the desired location.

8 To move the frame, move the mouse pointer toward the border of the frame. When a four-headed arrow is added to the mouse pointer, drag the frame border to the desired location.

Guided Tour   Insert a Drop Cap

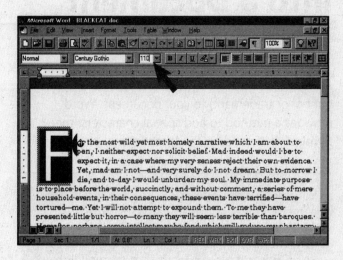

(9) To change the font of the character in the frame, select the character, open the **Font** drop-down list, and select a font from the list.

If the Show/Hide button is active, showing nonprinting characters such as the anchor (which shows the paragraph to which the drop cap is "anchored"), click it to view the document without those characters. Inactivating the Show/Hide button does not hide the frame, but when you print your document, the frame will not print.

(10) To change the font size of the character in the frame, select the character, open the **Font Size** drop-down list, and either type a value or select a value from the list.

Insert Special Characters into a Document

At times, you'll need to add a special character not found on your keyboard (such as a copyright symbol or trademark) to your document. Word provides a method to add special characters: the **Symbol** command on the **Insert** menu.

You can use the numeric keypad to insert ANSI (American National Standards Institute) or ASCII (American Standard Code for Information Interchange) symbols. First, press the **Num Lock** key if it is not already activated (a small light on most computers shows that NumLock is turned on); then press and hold down the **Alt** key. Then press keys on the numeric keypad to enter a three- or four-digit code in an ANSI or ASCII chart.

When you use the **Insert Symbol** command to display the Symbol dialog box, notice that one symbol appears highlighted. If you click **Insert**, Word inserts the highlighted symbol into your document. If you press and hold down the left mouse button or press an arrow key, Word "magnifies" that symbol so you can see it in detail.

Most standard text fonts have their own unique set of ANSI symbols. When you find a font that has the symbol you need, just embed the symbol. A few fonts, which may include some text characters, don't use the ANSI character set. Examples of this type of font are Symbol and Wingdings, often used to insert special symbols to emphasize parts of documents. Unfortunately, not all of Word's character formatting capabilities are available for enhancing these non-ANSI symbols. However, you can apply some formats, such as bold and italics.

You can insert some commonly used special characters by pressing shortcut keys. Press **Alt+Ctrl+C** to insert a copyright symbol, press **Alt+Ctrl+T** to insert a trademark symbol, and press **Alt+Ctrl+R** to insert a registered trademark symbol. By default, Word's AutoCorrect feature allows you to type **(c)**, **(tm)**, and **(r)**, respectively, to automatically insert the copyright symbol, trademark symbol, and the registered trademark symbol.

Begin Guided Tour   Insert Special Characters

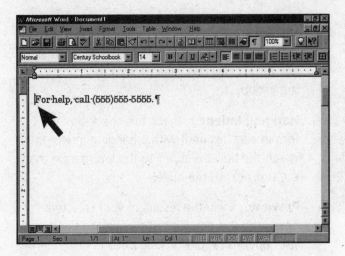

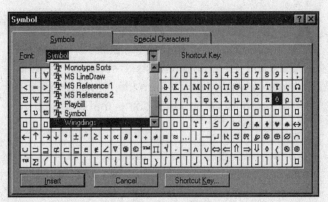

1 Move the insertion point to the place at which you want to embed the symbol.

3 In the **Font** drop-down list, type or select the name of the font that contains the symbol you want.

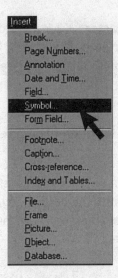

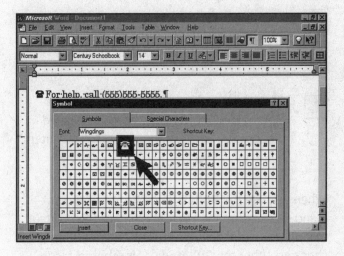

2 Open the **Insert** menu and select the **Symbol** command. Word displays the Symbol dialog box.

4 Select the desired character. As you choose, Word displays your choice in a magnified view. Double-click the character. Then click **Close**.

Create Bulleted and Numbered Lists

An effective way to emphasize text in a list is to precede each list item with a bullet or a number. Typically, you use numbered lists to show the steps in the order in which you perform them to accomplish a task; bulleted lists emphasize points that are in no particular order.

Word provides three ways to create bulleted and numbered lists: using the **Numbering** and **Bullets** buttons on the Formatting toolbar; using the **Format** menu and the **Bullets and Numbering** command; and using the shortcut menu's **Bullets and Numbering** command.

 Click the **Bulleted List** button to create a bulleted list from one or more selected paragraphs. Each paragraph becomes an item in the list.

 Click the **Numbered List** button to create a numbered list from one or more selected paragraphs. Each paragraph becomes an item in the list.

When you use the **Bullets and Numbering** command (from either the **Format** menu or the shortcut menu), you can modify the bullets and/or numbers by choosing either the **Bulleted** or **Numbered** tab in the Bullets and Numbering dialog box and then clicking the **Modify** button to display another dialog box.

Both the Modify Bulleted List dialog box and the Modify Numbered List dialog box provide these options:

Alignment of List Text   To align the bullet between the left margin and the bullet text, select **Left**, **Centered**, or **Right** from this drop-down list.

Distance from Indent to Text   To adjust the amount of indentation of the text, select a value from 0 to 22 inches in this list box.

Distance from Bullet/Number to Text   To adjust the distance from the bullet to the first line of text, select a value from 0 to 22 inches in this list box.

Hanging Indent   Check this check box to format each list item with a hanging indent in which the bullet is closer to the left margin than the text next to the bullet.

Preview   View the results of your selected options in this box. This allows you to fine-tune your options before clicking **OK**.

The Modify Bulleted List dialog box provides these options:

Bullet Character   Click a button to choose a bullet character to be replaced. Then click the **Bullet** button to select a replacement bullet character.

Point Size   Type or select the size of the bullet character in this text/option box. Valid values are 1 to 1638.

Color   From this drop-down list, select one of 17 colors. Auto, the default, represents black or the color that you have set in the Windows Control Panel.

The Modify Numbered List dialog box provides these options:

Text Before   In this text box, type characters that will precede the number.

Number   From this drop-down list, select the number format: none, uppercase Roman and Arabic numerals, alphabetic characters, textual numbers, and so on.

Text After   In this text box, type a character (for example, a period) that follows the number.

Font   Click this button to open the Font dialog box from which you can select a font, font style, size, and other character enhancements for the numbers.

Start At   Type or select a starting number for the list in this text/option box.

To create a multilevel list, which can include a combination of bulleted and numbered items, select **Format Bullets and Numbering**, click the **Multilevel** tab, and select the desired list.

Begin Guided Tour   Create a Bulleted List Using a Menu Command

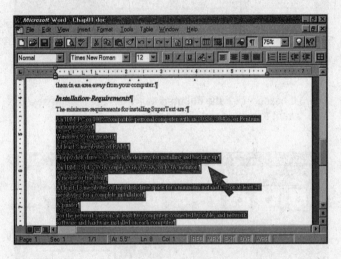

1 Select the part of the document to which you want to add bullets.

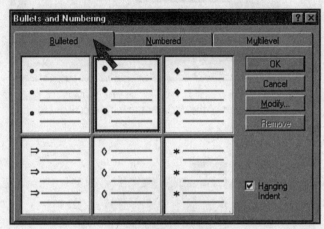

3 If needed, click the **Bulleted** tab. Click one of the six bullet examples. Then click **OK**.

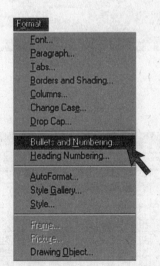

2 Open the **Format** menu and select the **Bullets and Numbering** command. Or you can click the **Bullets** button on the Formatting toolbar.

Begin Guided Tour Select a New Bullet Symbol

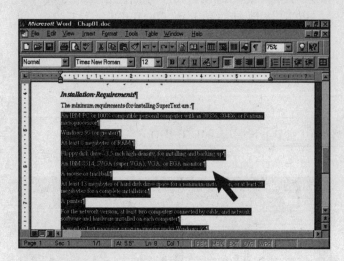

1 Select the part of the document to which you want to add bullets.

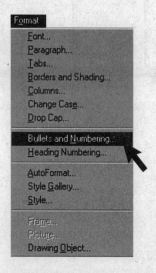

2 Open the **Format** menu and select the **Bullets and Numbering** command, or right-click and choose **Bullets and Numbering**.

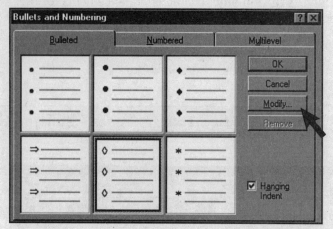

3 If needed, click the **Bulleted** tab. Select the bullet that you want to replace and click **Modify**.

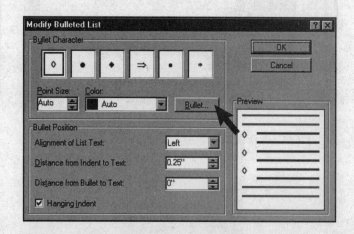

4 In the Modify Bulleted List dialog box, click the **Bullet** button.

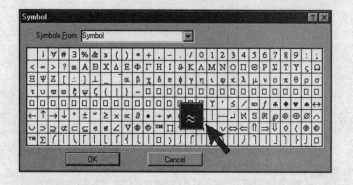

5 Click a symbol and click **OK**. Word returns to the Modify Bulleted List and replaces the selected bullet with your new choice. Click **OK** to close the dialog box and return to your document.

Begin Guided Tour Create a Numbered List

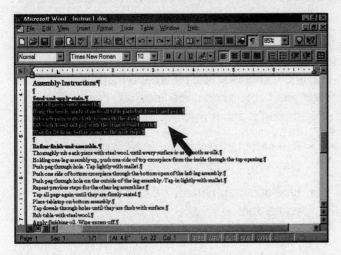

1 Select the part of the document that you want numbered.

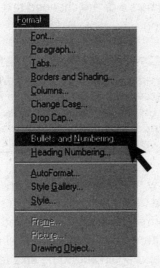

2 Open the **Format** menu and select the **Bullets and Numbering** command, or right-click and choose **Bullets and Numbering**.

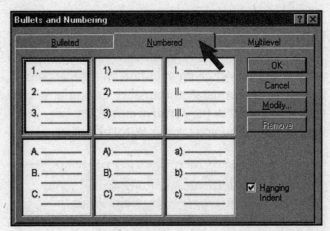

3 If needed, click the **Numbered** tab. To select a standard numbering system, choose one of the six samples. Then click **OK** to close the dialog box. To modify the numbering system or format, click **Modify**.

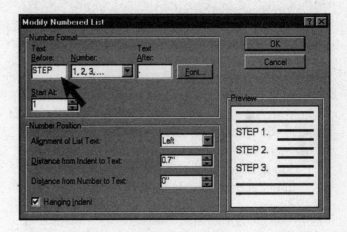

4 In the Modify Numbered List dialog box, set the options you want, as described in the text accompanying this Guided Tour. When you have completed your selections and when you approve of the sample in the Preview box, click **OK**.

Use Automatic Styles (AutoFormat)

Word enables you to style a document automatically, using the AutoFormat feature in two ways: using the AutoFormat button on the Standard toolbar or the Format AutoFormat command. Just type your text, click the **AutoFormat** button, or open the **Format** menu and choose **AutoFormat**.

By default, Word automatically applies some formats as you type. For example, Word replaces straight quotes with Smart Quotes, which are typographically correct. Word also replaces the **st** in **1st** with a superscript st and fractions, such as **1/2**, with ½. To see the formats that are automatically applied (and to select automatic formatting options), open the **Tools** menu, select the **Options** command, and click on the **AutoFormat** tab in the Options dialog box. For more information about the options in the AutoFormat section of the Options dialog box, see "Options Dialog Box—AutoFormat Category" on page 553.

 If you want to automatically format a document without reviewing, accepting, or rejecting changes, click the **AutoFormat** button on the Standard toolbar.

If you want to have more control over the changes, choose the **Format AutoFormat** command. After reformatting the current document, Word allows you to review the results, reject all the changes, accept the changes, or select a style from the Style Gallery. (For more information about using the Style Gallery, see "Use the Style Gallery" on page 199.)

You can use the Review AutoFormat Changes dialog box to review your document paragraph by paragraph before you accept the changes. You can accept the changes to a particular paragraph by clicking on one of the **Find** buttons, or you can reject the changes by selecting the **Reject** button. If you change your mind about rejecting a change, you can select

the **Undo Last** button. When you display the Review AutoFormat Changes dialog box, the look of your document changes. The paragraph marks appear in different colors and underlines; you can add strikethroughs and revision bars.

- Red paragraph marks indicate that AutoFormat removed or added a paragraph mark.

- Blue paragraph marks indicate unchanged paragraphs.

- An underline indicates added characters.

- A strikethrough indicates that AutoFormat deleted text and spaces.

- Revision bars indicate changed text or formatting.

If you change your mind about a format that you have accepted, either open the **Edit** menu and select the **Undo** command; press **Ctrl+Z**; or click the **Undo** button on the Standard toolbar.

You can display the newly formatted document with or without the formatting marks. If you select **Hide Marks**, no formatting marks appear and all the formatting buttons are "dimmed." To show the formatting marks again and to be able to change formats, select **Show Marks**. At any time, you can return to the AutoFormat dialog box by selecting **Close** (if you made changes) or **Cancel** (if you didn't make changes).

You can move between the Review AutoFormat Changes dialog box and your document. When you need to return to the document to correct text or change a style, click in the document. To return to the dialog box, click in it.

Begin Guided Tour   Format a Document Using AutoFormat

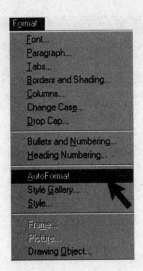

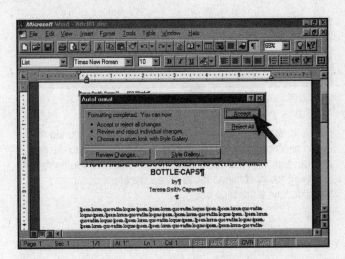

1 Create or open a document. Open the **Format** menu and select the **AutoFormat** command. (To have Word automatically format the document without your being able to reject or accept changes, click the **AutoFormat** button.)

3 To return to your document without making changes, click **Reject All**. To review other available styles, click **Style Gallery**. To accept all the changes, click **Accept**. To review changes, continue to step 4.

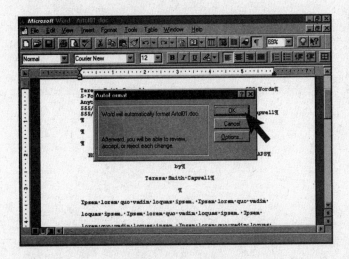

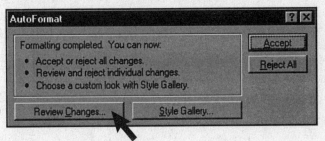

4 To review the changes before accepting or rejecting them, select **Review Changes**. Word displays the Review AutoFormat Changes dialog box, in which you can review each paragraph and either reject or accept the changes.

2 Click **OK**. Word formats the document and displays a changed AutoFormat dialog box.

5 Click a **Find** button or select parts of the document to read the description of a specific change.

(continues)

Guided Tour Format a Document Using AutoFormat

(continued)

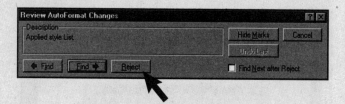

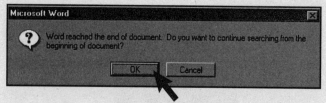

6 To reject the change, click the **Reject** button. To undo the rejection, click the **Undo Last** button. To move to the next change, click the **Find** button. Repeat this step until you finish reviewing the document. (If you review the entire document, Word displays a message box.)

7 At the end of the review (and at the bottom of the document), click **OK** to continue the search at the top of the document, or click **Cancel** to close the information box. Click the **Close** button to close the Review AutoFormat Changes dialog box.

Change Automatic Format Options

In the Options dialog box for the AutoFormat category, Word provides two types of options: for AutoFormat and for AutoFormat As You Type. Before you run AutoFormat, you can determine the types of formats that are applied: for headings, borders, bulleted and numbered lists, other lists, and para-graphs that are not headings. In addition, you can have Word replace certain characters, such as frac-tions and straight quotes, with related symbols. For descriptions of each option in this dialog box, see the "Options Dialog Box—AutoFormat Category" on page 553.

Begin Guided Tour   Change Automatic Format Options

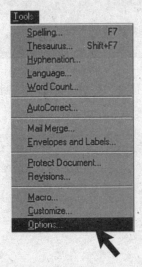

1 With a document on-screen, open the **Tools** menu and select the **Options** command. Word displays the most recently used category of the Options dialog box.

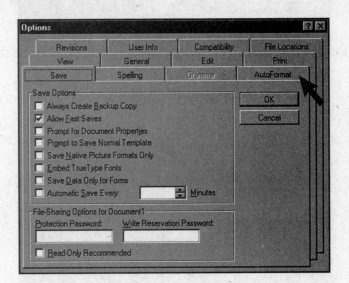

2 Click the **AutoFormat** tab.

(continues)

Guided Tour   Change Automatic Format Options   *(continued)*

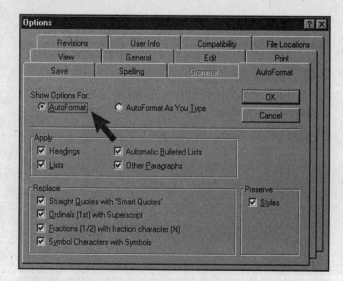

3 Click the **AutoFormat** option button.

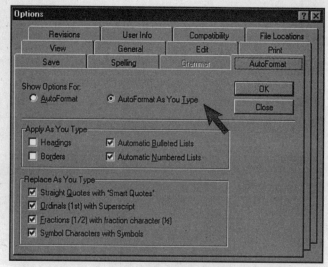

5 Click the **AutoFormat As You Type** option button.

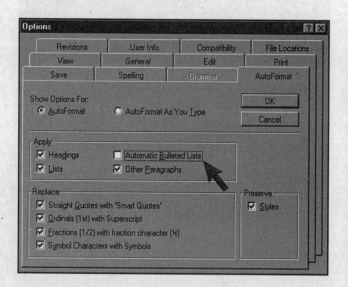

4 Check the options you want in the **Apply** and **Replace** areas, and clear the options you don't want. For example, if you do not want Word to automatically format bulleted lists, clear the Automatic Bulleted Lists check box.

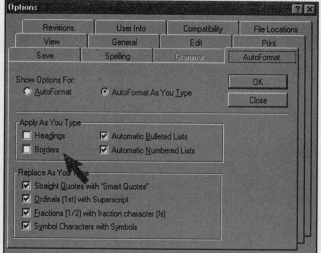

6 Check the options you want in the **Apply as You Type** and **Replace As You Type** areas, and clear the options you don't want. For example, if you do not want Word to automatically format borders, clear the Borders check box. Then click **OK**.

Use the Style Gallery

Word's Style Gallery offers you a long list of *templates* (collections of related styles) from which you can choose. These templates use different paragraph formats to change the look of all elements of a document. For example, you can select from contemporary, elegant, and professional templates for business and personal letters, and you can choose from three press release formats.

To start the Style Gallery, open the **Format** menu and select the **Style Gallery** command. To view a template before accepting it, select from the **Template**

scroll list or type its name in the text box. You can view your document, a sample document, or style samples in the **Preview of** box by clicking on the **Document**, **Example**, or **Style Samples** option button, respectively.

> When you start a new document by choosing the **File New** command, in the New dialog box, you can select from the same templates that appear in the Style Gallery.

Begin Guided Tour Use the Style Gallery

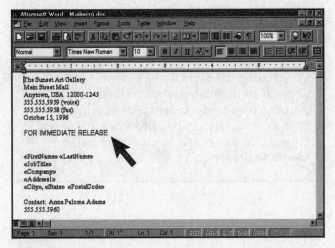

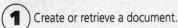

1 Create or retrieve a document.

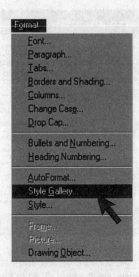

2 Open the **Format** menu and choose the **Style Gallery** command. Word displays the Style Gallery dialog box with your document in the **Preview of** box as it is currently formatted.

(continues)

Guided Tour   Use the Style Gallery   *(continued)*

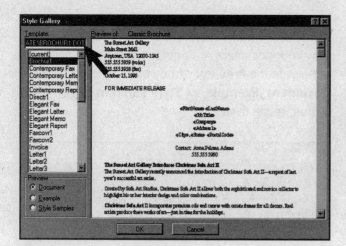

3 To view your document using another style, click an item in the **Template** list box.

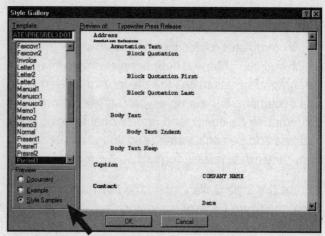

5 To view styles for elements of a sample document (for example, headings and other paragraphs), click an item in the **Template** list box; then click the **Style Samples** option button. When you find the template you want to use, select it from the list box and click **OK**. Word automatically reformats the document.

> When using the Style Gallery, don't restrict yourself to templates whose names fit the purpose of your document. For example, to style a memorandum, try **Brochure**, **Present1**, **Presrel2**, and **Report2**, in addition to all the **Memo** templates.

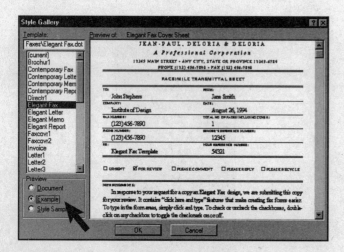

4 To view a sample document using another style, click an item in the **Template** list box; click the **Example** option button.

HOW TO...
Work with Tables

In this section, you will learn how to create, format, and edit another multiple-column format: *tables*. Word's table columns can be of unequal widths and can extend up to the full width of a page. You can select, edit, manipulate, and format tables and their contents in the same way in which you work with other text in your documents.

Word tables consist of *cells*: the intersections of rows and columns, which are actually small documents in which you can control contents, formats, and enhancements. In contrast, a multiple-column section of a document snakes from the beginning of the section to the end. Although you can change the look of multiple columns by specifying the number of columns, determining the place at which a column breaks, and formatting selected text, a table allows much more regulation. Use a table when you want to create a chart or diagram. You can even use a Word table to create a spreadsheet with its own formulas.

Here, you find out how to create and navigate a table; how to edit and format a table; and how to change text into a table and a table into text. You'll learn how to sort text in a document, and, finally, you'll find out how to calculate numbers entered in a table.

What You Will Find in This Section

Create a Table

Word lets you create a table as if it were a spreadsheet. When you create a table, Word divides the space between the left and right margins into equal *columns*, information aligned vertically. In addition to columns, a table also consists of *rows*, information aligned horizontally. The height of a *cell* (the intersection of a row and a column) expands to hold all the text you enter into that cell. The height of a row is the height of the largest cell in the row.

There are two ways of creating a table: using a menu command or the Insert Table button on the Standard toolbar. To create a table using a menu command, open the **Table** menu and choose the **Insert Table** command. When Word displays the Insert Table dialog box, define the size of the table. In the **Number of Columns** text/option box, type a value or cycle through the range of values (from 1 to 31). In the **Number of Rows** text/option box, type a value or cycle through the range of values (from 1 to 32767). To define the width of a column, type a value or cycle through the range of values (from 0 to 22 inches) in the **Column Width** box. You can also accept Word's column width, Auto, which is based on the width between the margins and the number of columns. The ranges of values for the Insert Table dialog box are also affected by computer memory, paper width and height, and other factors. Therefore, you may not be able to use the full range of values that Word provides.

 Click the **Insert Table** button to insert a table into the document at the insertion point. When Word displays the table template, drag the mouse to define the number of rows and columns in the table. Drag to the left or right to determine the number of columns; drag up or down to set the number of rows; or drag diagonally to change both rows and columns.

Your screen resolution determines the maximum number of rows and columns in a table you can create by clicking on the **Insert Table** button. The finer the resolution, the more rows and columns you can insert.

Whether you use the **Insert Table** command or the **Insert Table** button to create a table, you can always insert more rows and/or columns. The easiest way is to select a row (if you want to add another row), column (to add another column), or even multiple rows or columns (to insert multiple rows or columns), respectively. Then click the **Insert Table** button.

When you insert a table in a document, notice that dots surround each cell. The dots show the boundaries of the cell and do not print. To turn off the dots, known as *gridlines*, open the **Table** menu and click the **Gridlines** command to remove the check mark that indicates the command is active. Another way to turn off gridlines is to select the **Tools Options** command, and select the **View** tab. Then clear the **Table Gridlines** check box, and click **OK**.

You can create a table using the *Table Wizard*, which is available when you open the **File** menu and select the **New** command or when you choose the **Table Insert Table** command. When you use a wizard to design a document, Word leads you through the creative process, making suggestions along the way.

Begin Guided Tour   Create a Table Using a Menu Command

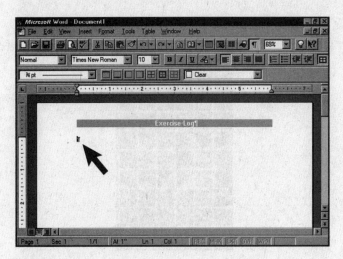

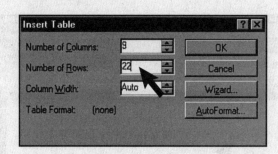

(3) Type or select the number of columns in the **Number of Columns** text/option box. Type or select the number of rows in the **Number of Rows** text/option box. Then click **OK**. (If the table were a maximum of 14 rows by 10 columns, you could have clicked on the **Insert Table** button instead.)

(1) Move the insertion point to the place in your document at which you want to insert the table.

(2) Open the **Table** menu and select the **Insert Table** command. Word displays the Insert Table dialog box.

Begin Guided Tour   Create a Table Using a Toolbar Button

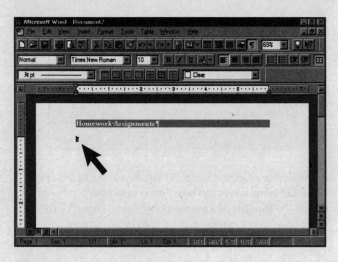

1 Move the insertion point to the place in your document at which you want to insert the table.

3 Drag down and to the right until you have selected the desired number of rows and columns. Then release the mouse button.

2 While pointing to the **Insert Table** button, press and hold down the mouse button.

Move Around in a Table

You can use the keyboard or the mouse to move around a table. To move around a table using the mouse pointer, move the mouse pointer to the cell in which you want to add text, and click the left mouse button to place the insertion point.

To navigate a table using the keyboard, use the keys and keyboard combinations in the following table.

You cannot move down to the next cell in a table by pressing Enter; when you press Enter, a new paragraph is added to the cell. If you move the mouse pointer to the right of the bottom right cell in a table, outside the grid lines, pressing **Enter** adds a new row to the bottom of the table.

Word's Table-Navigation Keys

Key	Description
Down arrow	Moves the insertion point down one line within the table or out of the table. Within a cell, press the down arrow to move down lines of text.
Up arrow	Moves the insertion point up one line within the table or out of the table. Within a cell, press the up arrow to move up lines of text.
Right arrow	Moves the insertion point to the next cell. Within a cell, press the right arrow to move to the right, one character or space at a time.
Left arrow	Moves the insertion point to the previous cell. Within a cell, press the left arrow to move to the left, one character or space at a time.
Tab	Moves the insertion point to the next cell. (Use **Ctrl+Tab** to insert a tab within a cell.) If you press **Tab** in the last cell of a table, you create a new row.
Shift+Tab	Moves the insertion point to the previous cell.
Alt+Home	Moves the insertion point to the first cell in the current row.
Alt+End	Moves the insertion point to the last cell in the current row.
Alt+PgUp	Moves the insertion point to the top cell in the column.
Alt+PgDn	Moves the insertion point to the bottom cell in the column.

Begin Guided Tour Move Around in a Table

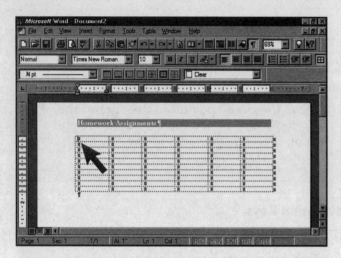

1 Click the top left row in a table to move the insertion point.

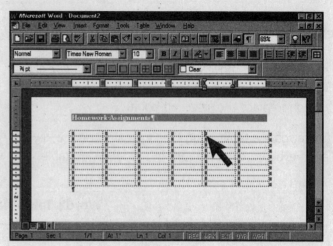

3 Press the left arrow key to move the insertion point to the previous cell in the row.

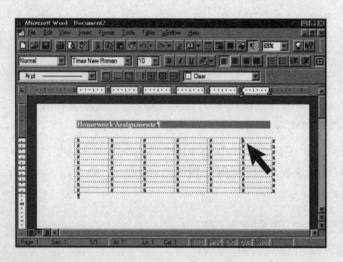

2 Press **Alt+End** to move the insertion point to the last cell in the row.

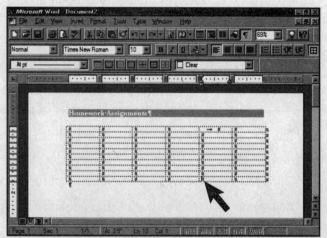

4 Press **Alt+PgDn** to move to the bottom row of the current column.

Select Information in a Table

When you select text in one or more cells using any of the keys in the table in the "Select Text" task on page 92, the selection starts at the location of the insertion point and extends from there. You also press **F8** to turn on and press **Esc** or **Tab** to turn off **Extend Selection** mode when selecting text in a table. The following table provides a list of table selection keys and a description of each.

Word's Table Selection Keys

Key	Description
Without Extended Selection Mode	
Alt+5 (on the numeric keypad, with NumLock inactive)	Selects the entire table.
Shift+up arrow	Selects the current cell and the cell above. (Deselect" by pressing **Shift+down arrow**.)
Shift+down arrow	Selects the current cell and the cell below. (Deselect by pressing **Shift+up arrow**.)
Shift+left arrow	Selects the current cell and then the prior cell one character at a time. (Deselect by pressing **Shift+right arrow**.)
Shift+right arrow	Selects the current cell and then the next cell one character at a time. (Deselect by pressing **Shift+left arrow**.)
Shift+Alt+Home	Selects all the cells from the insertion point to the first cell in a row.
Shift+Alt+End	Selects all the cells from the insertion point to the last cell in a row.
Shift+Alt+PgDn	Selects all the cells from the insertion point to the last cell in a column.
Shift+Alt+PgUp	Selects all the cells from the insertion point to the first cell in a column.
Tab	Moves to a cell and selects all its text.
In Extended Selection Mode	
Up arrow	Selects the current cell and the cell above.
Down arrow	Selects the current cell and the cell below.
Left arrow	Selects the current cell one character at a time and then, with every press, each adjacent cell to the left.
Right arrow	Selects the current cell one character at a time and then, with every press, each adjacent cell to the right.
Home	Selects the contents of the prior cell.
End	Selects the contents of the next cell.

To use the mouse to select cell information, use the following techniques:

- To select text with the mouse, click the left mouse button on specific cells, or click the left mouse button and drag the pointer across several cells of a table.

- To select a row of cells with the mouse, move the mouse pointer to the selection bar in the left

margin. When the mouse pointer changes to an arrow pointing up and to the right, click the left mouse button. Word highlights the entire row.

- To select a column of cells with the mouse, move the mouse pointer to the top border of the top cell. When the mouse pointer changes to a down arrow, click the left mouse button.

Begin Guided Tour   Select Table Information

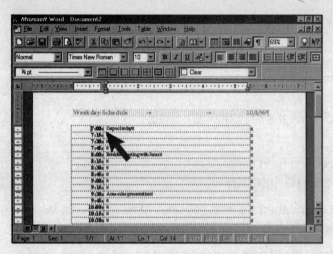

1 Click the top left row in a table to move the insertion point.

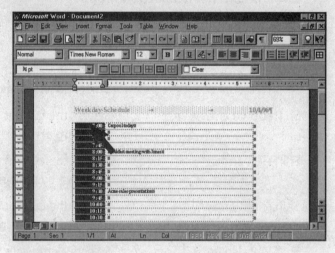

2 Press **Shift+Alt+PgDn** to select all the cells in the column.

Guided Tour   Select Table Information

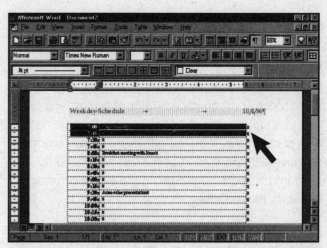

3 Move the mouse pointer to the left of the text in the top cell in the column. When the mouse pointer changes to point up and to the right, click the left mouse button to select the entire cell.

5 Press **End** to highlight the first cell and its contents. Press **End** to extend the selection to the second cell and its contents. Press the down arrow to extend the selection to the second row.

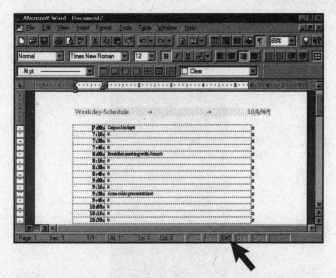

4 Press **F8** to turn on Extended Selection mode. Notice that the **Ext** indicator in the status bar is bold.

> A quick way to *deselect* all the selections in a table is to press keys that are the opposite of those you have just pressed (for example, press **Home** instead of End, and press the up arrow rather than the down arrow).

Copy and Move Information in a Table

You can move and copy cells using the Cut, Copy, and Paste commands from the Edit menu or the shortcut menu. (For more details on how these commands work, refer to "Copy Text" on page 103 and "Move Text" on page 99.) To copy, cut, and paste text in a table, select all the text in a cell including the end-of-cell mark. Then use either the **Copy** command to move cell information or the **Cut** command to copy information. At this point, the **Paste** command becomes **Paste Cells**.

When you paste, the cell that you are pasting over-writes the cell to which you are pasting. When you copy or cut multiple cells, the area into which you paste must have the same row-by-column dimensions

as the cut or copied cells. However, there is a way around this: rather than selecting all the cells into which you want to paste, click at the upper left corner of the area into which the cut or copied cells will be pasted. Then when you issue the **Paste Cells** command, Word will paste the cut or copied cells into the table starting with the cell in which you clicked.

> To see the end-of-cell marks in a table, click the **Show/Hide** button on the Standard toolbar. This displays all nonprinting symbols including the end-of-cell mark.

Begin Guided Tour   Copy Information in a Table

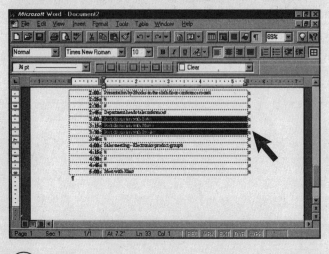

1 Drag the mouse to select some cells in a table.

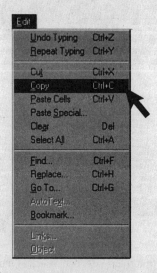

2 Open the **Edit** menu and select the **Copy** command. Or you can click the **Copy** toolbar button, press **Ctrl+C**, or right-click and select the **Copy** command.

Guided Tour Copy Information in a Table

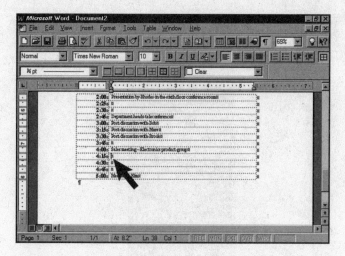

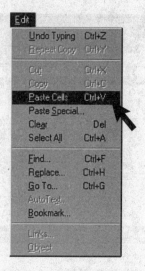

3 Move the insertion point to the location at which you want to insert the selected cells.

4 Open the **Edit** menu and select the **Paste Cells** command. Or you can click the **Paste** toolbar button, press **Ctrl+V**, or right-click and select the **Paste Cells** command.

Begin Guided Tour Move Information in a Table

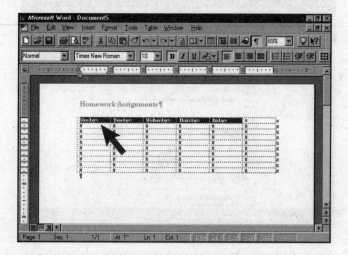

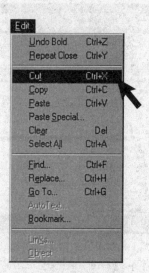

1 Click-and-drag the mouse to select the cells you want to move.

2 Open the **Edit** menu and select the **Cut** command. Or you can click the **Cut** toolbar button or press **Ctrl+X**.

(continues)

Guided Tour **Move Information in a Table** *(continued)*

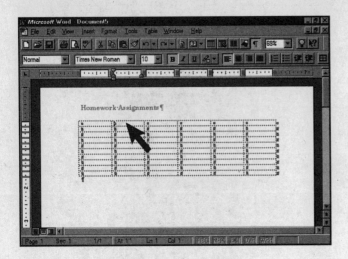

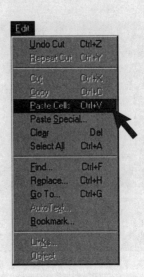

3 Move the insertion point to the location at which you want to insert the selected cells.

4 Open the **Edit** menu and select the **Paste Cells** command. Or you can click the **Paste** toolbar button or press **Ctrl+V**.

Begin Guided Tour **Drag and Drop in a Table**

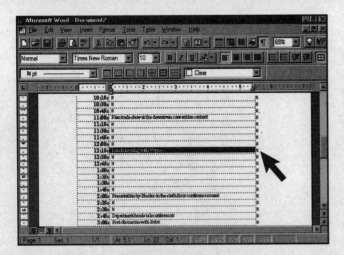

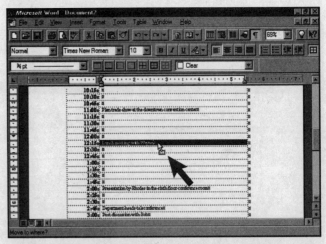

1 Select the text you want to move.

2 Move the mouse pointer anywhere within your selection. The mouse pointer becomes an arrow that points up and to the left, and a dotted vertical line marks the location of the insertion point; Word adds a box to the tail of the mouse pointer.

Guided Tour   Drag and Drop in a Table

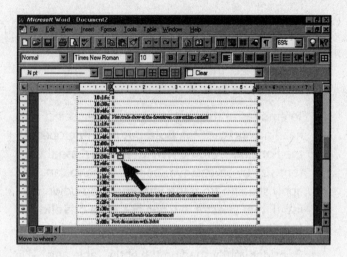

3 Press and hold down the left mouse button and drag the selected text toward its new location. The dotted vertical line indicates the current location of the insertion point.

4 When you reach the new location, release the left mouse button. Word changes the mouse pointer back to its starting shape.

Format a Table

Each cell in a table is like a miniature document; each has its own margins and format. Text within cells follows the cell format, not the document format. Just as you would format the text in a document, you can format cells or the contents of cells in a table. Select the entire cell (by making sure that you have selected the end-of-cell mark) or the text within a cell to be formatted. Then use the formatting commands you learned in the "Enhance a Document" section starting on page 169.

When working with tables, consider these formatting notes:

- You can emphasize the cells in a table by clicking the **Borders** button and then clicking both the **Outside Border** and **Inside Border** buttons.

- You can bring attention to a table with horizontal lines only. Select the entire table, open the **Format** menu and choose **Borders and Shading**. Click the **Box** button, click the top, middle, and bottom lines in the **Border** box, making sure not to click near the borders or center of the lines (you don't want to add vertical lines). Then click **OK**.

- Put special emphasis on the lines above and below the headings and at the bottom of the table. Select either the **1 1/2 pt** or **2 1/4 pt lines** from the **Line Style** drop-down list.

Then select the heading row and click both the **Top Border** and **Bottom Border** buttons. Finally, select the last row in the table and click the **Bottom Border** button.

- To emphasize the heading row further, select the heading and click the **Bold** button. Then open the **Font Size** drop-down list and increase the font size by at least two points. You also can apply shading from the **Shading** drop-down list. (Either select a low percent value or **Solid (100%)**).

- Consider lightly shading the entire table and applying a darker level of shading to the heading row. Select the entire table and select **5%** or **10%** from the **Shading** drop-down list . Then select the heading row and select **12.5%**, **20%**, or **Solid (100%)**.

You can also format tables using ready-made templates. Simply click in a table, open the **Table** menu, and select the **Table AutoFormat** command. When the Table AutoFormat dialog box appears, select a format from the list in the **Formats** list box, and apply other formats to the entire selection or parts of the table. You can try varying combinations of borders, shading, text enhancement, color, and the way the table fits on the page. The best way to learn about the **Table AutoFormat** command is to experiment with it.

Guided Tour Change Cell Formatting

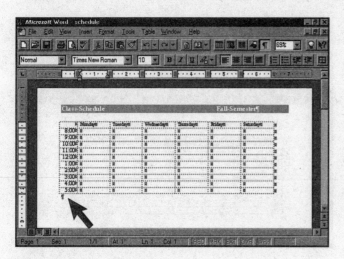

1 Open or create a table.

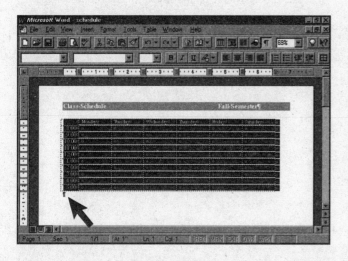

2 Press **Alt+5** (on the numeric keypad, with NumLock turned off) to select the entire table.

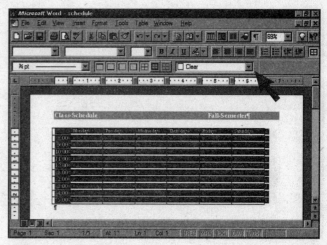

3 Click the **Borders** button. Click the **Inside Borders** button. Click the **Outside Borders** button.

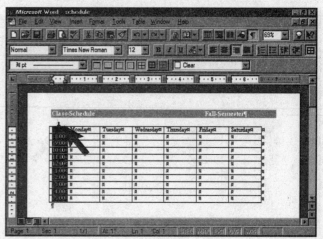

4 Select the leftmost column by moving the mouse pointer above the column until it changes to a downward-pointing arrow and clicking the left mouse button.

(continues)

Guided Tour Change Cell Formatting *(continued)*

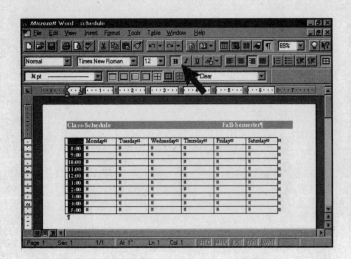

5 Click the **Bold** button. Open the **Font Size** drop-down list and select **12**.

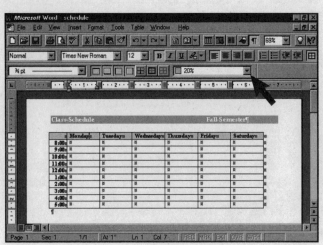

7 Open the **Font Size** drop-down list and select **12**. Click the **Bold** button. Select **20%** from the **Shading** drop-down list. Click anywhere on the screen to deselect the selection.

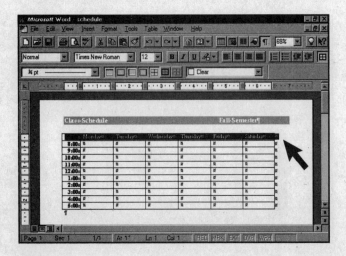

6 Select the top row by moving the mouse pointer to the selection bar and clicking the left mouse button.

Begin Guided Tour   Use AutoFormat

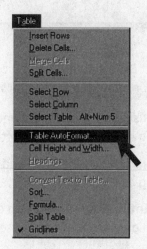

1 Select or click in the table you want to format. Then open the **Table** menu and select the **Table AutoFormat** command.

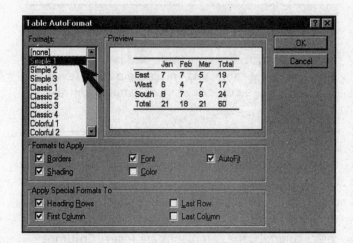

2 In the Table AutoFormat dialog box, select a format from the **Formats** list box. The Preview box shows what the format looks like. In the **Formats to Apply** and **Apply Special Formats To** groups, check boxes for default formats are checked or cleared.

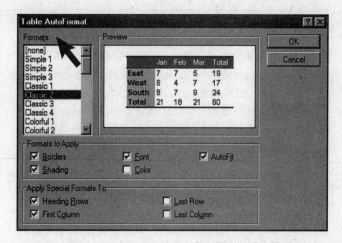

3 Select formats from the **Formats** list box, until the sample in the **Preview** box shows a format that you like. Then click **OK**.

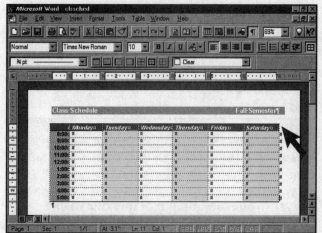

4 Further enhance the table formats by selecting all or part of the table and clicking on buttons or selecting options from the Formatting toolbar. Or you can open the **Format** menu, select the **Fonts** command, select options from the Fonts dialog box, and click **OK**.

Insert and Delete Rows, Columns, and Cells

When you insert cells, you can shift current cells at the same time or insert entire rows and columns. Select the location of the cells to be inserted, open the **Table** menu, and select **Insert Cells**. Choose one of the following options from the Insert Cells dialog box:

- **Shift Cells Right**   Inserts cells and shifts the selected cells one cell to the right, whether or not the new cells go beyond the right margin

- **Shift Cells Down**   Inserts cells and shifts the selected cells one row down, whether or not the new cells go beyond the bottom margin of the page.

- **Insert Entire Row**   Inserts an entire row at the insertion point or above the selected row.

- **Insert Entire Column**   Inserts an entire column at the insertion point or to the left of the selected column.

There are two shortcut methods for adding new rows, columns, or cells to a table. You can move the mouse pointer to the table, select the number of columns, rows, or cells that you want to add, and then click the **Insert Table** toolbar button. Or you can right-click and select the **Insert Columns, Insert Rows**, or **Insert Cells** commands (depending on whether you selected columns, rows, or cells). To add a row to the end of a table, move the mouse pointer to the last cell on the right side and press **Tab**.

To delete cells and shift the remaining cells at the same time, select the cells or click in the cell that you want to delete. Either open the **Table** menu or right-click and select **Delete Cells**. Choose one of the following options from the Delete Cells dialog box:

- **Shift Cells Left**   Deletes cells and shifts the remaining cells one cell to the left.

- **Shift Cells Up**   Deletes cells and shifts the remaining cells one row up.

- **Delete Entire Row**   Deletes an entire row at the insertion point or the entire selected row.

- **Delete Entire Column**   Deletes an entire column at the insertion point or the entire selected column.

To delete the contents of a table but not the table itself, select the table and press **Del**. One simple way to delete a table and its contents is to select the table and one piece of text (even a single character or paragraph mark) and then press **Del**.

Depending on the type of selection you make (rows, columns, or cells), the command on the **Table** menu changes. For example, if you select rows, you'll see the **Insert Rows** or **Delete Rows** command. If you select columns, the commands are **Insert Columns** or **Delete Columns**. If you select one or more cells, you'll see **Insert Cells**.

If you change your mind about an insertion or deletion, immediately select the **Edit Undo** command or press **Ctrl+Z** to put the table back the way it was. Or you can undo the insertion or deletion as well as all actions taken after the insertion or deletion by clicking the **Undo** button on the Standard toolbar and selecting the **Insert** or **Delete** command on the drop-down list.

Begin Guided Tour Insert Rows, Columns, and Cells Using a Toolbar Button

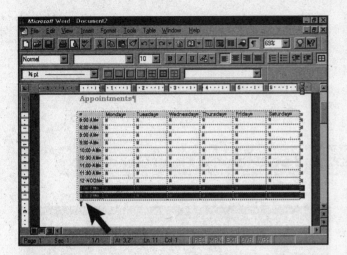

1 Create or go to a table, and select one or more rows by moving the mouse pointer to the left margin and clicking, or by clicking and dragging up or down.

2 Click the **Insert Rows** button, as the Insert Table button is known when rows are selected. Word adds a number of rows equal to the rows that you have highlighted.

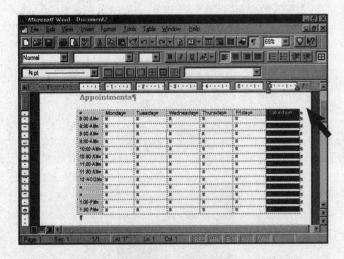

3 Select one or more columns by moving the mouse pointer to the top of the column(s). When the pointer changes to a downward-pointing arrow, click.

4 Click the **Insert Columns** button, the name of the Insert Table button when columns are selected. Word inserts a number of columns equal to the columns that you have highlighted.

If needed, edit the column and row labels that may have been moved or add labels to empty cells.

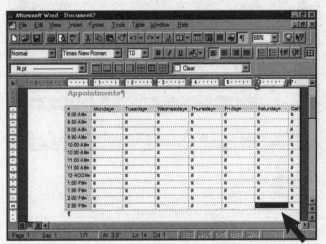

5 Move the mouse pointer to a cell. When it changes to an arrow that points up and to the right, click to select the entire cell.

6 Click the **Insert Cells** button, the name of the Insert Table button when cells are selected. Word opens the Insert Cells dialog box.

(continues)

Guided Tour Insert Rows, Columns, and Cells Using a Toolbar Button

(continued)

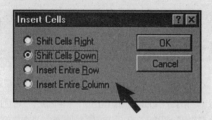

7 Click an option button. Then click **OK**.

Begin Guided Tour Insert Rows, Columns, and Cells Using a Menu Command

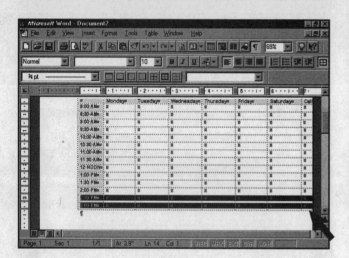

1 Create or go to a table, and select one or more rows by moving the mouse pointer to the left margin and clicking, or by clicking and dragging up or down.

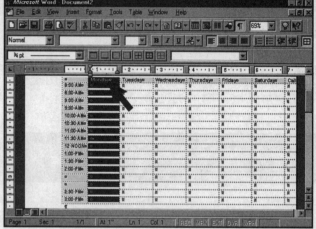

3 Select one or more columns by moving the mouse pointer to the top of the column(s). When the pointer changes to a downward-pointing arrow, click.

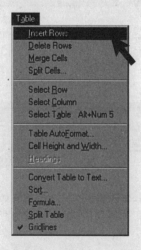

2 Open the **Table** menu, or right-click and choose the **Insert Rows** command. Word inserts the number of rows you selected.

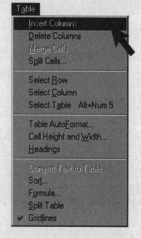

4 Open the **Table** menu, or right-click and select the **Insert Columns** command. Word inserts the number of columns you selected.

Guided Tour   Insert Rows, Columns, and Cells Using a Menu Command

When you add many columns to a table, consider shifting to Landscape orientation. Open the **File** menu and select **Page Setup**. Click the **Paper Size** tab, and click the **Landscape** option button. Make sure that you choose **Whole Document** in the **Apply To** drop-down list, and click **OK**.

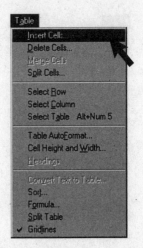

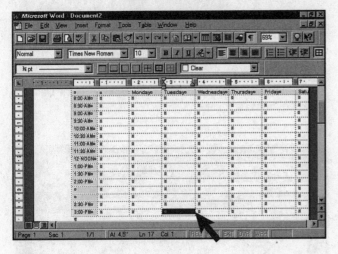

(6) Open the **Table** menu, or right-click and select the **Insert Cells** command. Word opens the Insert Cells dialog box.

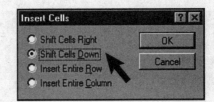

(5) Select a cell.

(7) Click an option button and click **OK**.

Begin Guided Tour   Delete Cells, Columns, and Rows

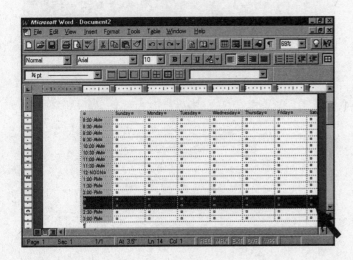

(1) Create or go to a table; select one or more rows you want to delete by moving the mouse pointer to the left margin and clicking, or by clicking and dragging up or down.

(continues)

Guided Tour Delete Cells, Columns, and Rows *(continued)*

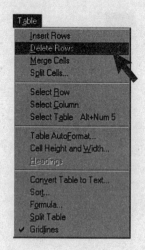

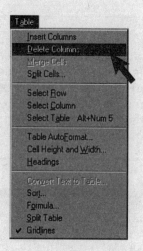

2 Open the **Table** menu, or right-click and choose the **Delete Rows** command.

4 Open the **Table** menu, or right-click and select the **Delete Columns** command.

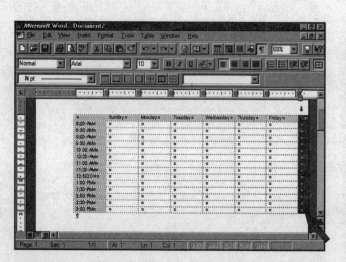

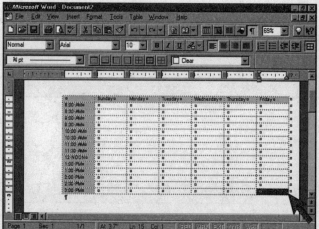

3 Select one or more columns that you want to delete by moving the mouse pointer to the top of the column(s). When the pointer changes to a downward-pointing arrow, click.

5 Select a cell you want to delete.

Guided Tour   Delete Cells, Columns, and Rows

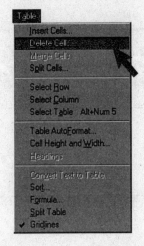

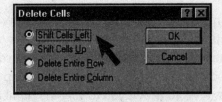

7 Word opens the Delete Cells dialog box. Click an option button and click **OK**.

6 Open the **Table** menu, or right-click and select the **Delete Cells** command.

Merge or Split Cells

At times, you'll need to have a table with rows or columns that contain different numbers of cells. For example, you may want to keep track of specific times or dates in one row or column and keep notes in the next. Word allows you to vary the number of cells in a selected row by opening the **Table** menu and selecting the **Merge Cells** or **Split Cells** command.

Whether or not you select rows or columns to be split or merged, Word always splits or merges the cells horizontally.

Begin Guided Tour   Merge Cells

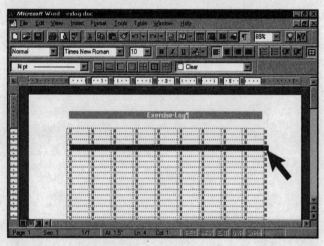

1 Select cells to be merged.

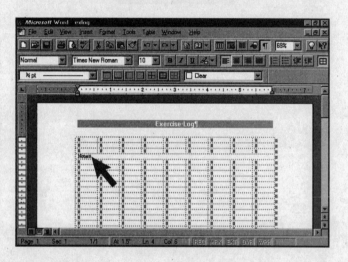

3 Click the left mouse button, and type some text in the merged cells.

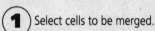
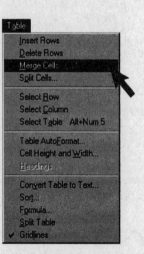

2 Open the **Table** menu and select the **Merge Cells** command.
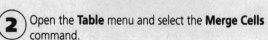

Begin Guided Tour   Split Cells

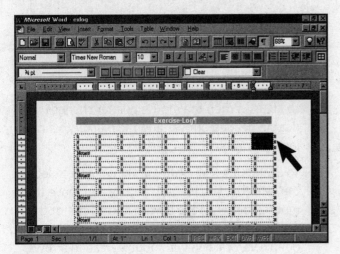

1 Select cells to be split.

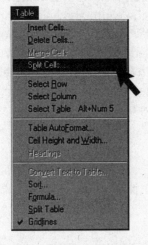

2 Open the **Table** menu and select the **Split Cells** command.

3 In the **Number of Columns** text/option box, type or select a number. Then click **OK**.

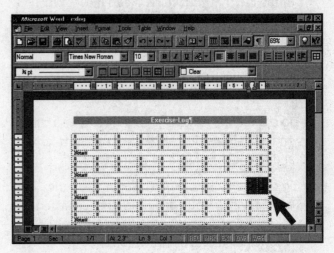

4 Continue selecting and splitting cells until you finish.

Change Column Width and Row Height

If you need to change the width of a column, you can use the mouse, the mouse with the Ruler, and a menu command. When you change the size of a column, you can also decide whether to let that change affect the overall width of the table.

- To change the width of a column using the mouse, move the mouse pointer to the border of the cell that you would like to move. When the mouse pointer changes to two parallel lines with double-headed arrows, click the left mouse button and drag the border to its new location. This technique works only on vertical (width) lines and not on horizontal ones.

- To change the width of a column and keep the original table width, hold down the **Shift** key and follow the preceding instructions.

- To change the width of a column, keep the original table width, and resize the remaining columns equally, hold down the **Ctrl** key and follow the preceding instructions.

- To change the width of a column using the mouse and the Ruler, either place the insertion point anywhere within a table or select cells.

Then, on the Ruler, move the mouse pointer to the Column Width marker (the gray bar overlaying the Ruler) that is directly above the vertical column line marking the border that you want to adjust. When the mouse pointer changes to a double-headed arrow, drag the marker to a new location on the Ruler.

- To change the cell widths within a table, select the cells that you want to widen, and move the mouse pointer to the border to the right of the cell(s). When the mouse pointer changes to a double vertical line with double-headed arrows, drag the border to a new location.

- You can open the **Table** menu, or right-click and select the **Cell Height and Width** command to change the width and height of rows and columns in a table. With this method, the changes made to a column (or row) affect the entire width (or height) of the table. You can also change the width of certain cells in a table by selecting only the cells that you want to change.

Begin Guided Tour Adjust Column Width

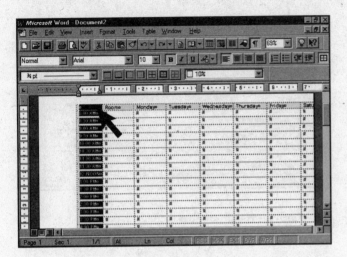

1 Create or go to a table, and select the column or cell whose width you want to change.

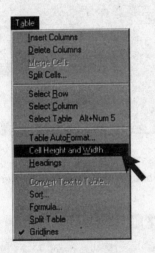

2 Open the **Table** menu, or right-click and choose the **Cell Height and Width** command. Word displays the Cell Height and Width dialog box.

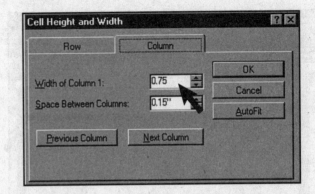

3 If needed, click the **Column** tab at the top of the dialog box. In the **Width of Column** text/option box, type or select a new width for the selected column.

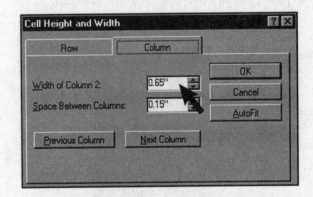

4 To change the width of any other columns, select the **Previous Column** or **Next Column** button, and fill in the **Width of Column** text/option box. When you finish specifying column widths, click **OK**.

Begin Guided Tour Adjust Row Height

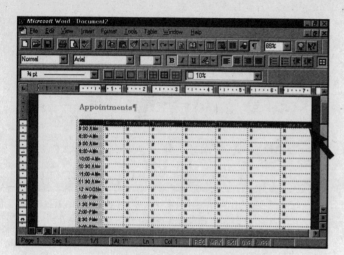

1 Select the row whose height you want to change.

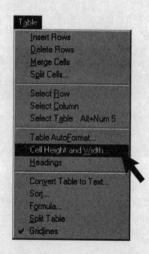

2 Open the **Table** menu and choose the **Cell Height and Width** command. Word displays the Cell Height and Width dialog box.

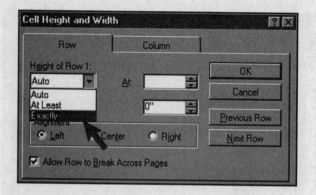

3 Open the **Height of Row** drop-down list and select **Exactly**.

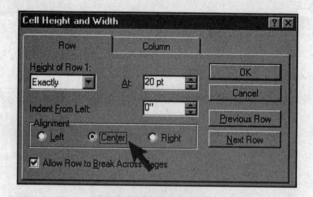

4 To change the alignment of the text in the row, click an **Alignment** option button: **Left**, **Center**, or **Right**.

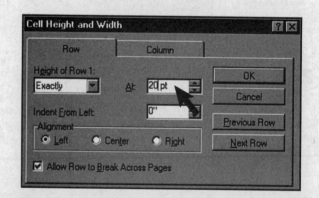

5 Type or select a new height for the selected row. To change the height of any other rows, select the **Previous Row** or **Next Row** button and repeat steps 3 and 4. When you have adjusted all the rows that you want to change, click **OK**.

Change Text into a Table

If a document contains text that would look better as a table, there is an easy way to convert that text into table format. When you select text to convert it to a table, make sure that the segments of text that will make up table cells are separated by paragraph marks, tabs, or commas. If you have combined paragraph marks with either tabs or commas, Word treats each paragraph mark as the end of a row. If you use all three marks to divide the text, Word asks you to choose the mark that represents the division between cells.

To convert text to a table, select the text that you want to convert, open the **Table** menu, and choose the **Convert Text to Table** command. If Word detects a combination of characters used to separate the text, it displays the Convert Text to Table dialog box; otherwise, it returns to your document and converts the text to a table.

 You can convert text to a table using a toolbar button. Simply select text and click the **Insert Table** button on the Standard toolbar.

Begin Guided Tour   Change Text into a Table

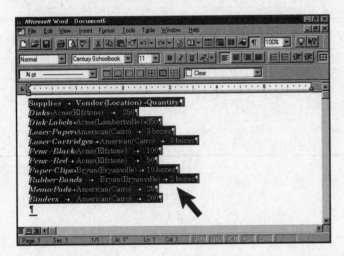

1 Select text to be converted to a table.

2 Open the **Table** menu and select the **Convert Text to Table** command. If you have more than one type of separator between units of text, Word displays the Convert Text to Table dialog box.

(continues)

Guided Tour   Change Text into a Table

(continued)

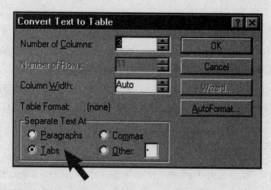

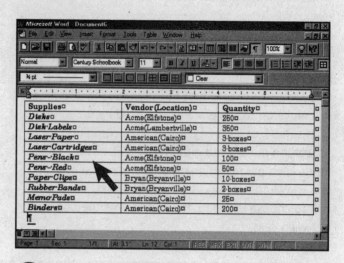

3 If the Convert Text to Table dialog box appears, select the mark that represents the division between cells. (If you want to format the table, click the **AutoFormat** button.) Then click **OK**. Word returns to the current document and makes a table.

4 Edit the table using the information in the preceding tasks.

Change a Table into Text

Word also allows you to convert a table to text. For example, if you are writing a manual and originally planned to include a table of terms, you may decide that the table would look better as a glossary. To convert the table back to text, first select it. Then open the **Table** menu and choose the **Convert Table to Text** command.

When you select all or part of a table, the **Table** menu contains the **Convert Table to Text** command. If you select nontable text, the command becomes **Convert Text to Table**. If no text or table is selected, the command is dimmed.

Begin Guided Tour Change a Table into Text

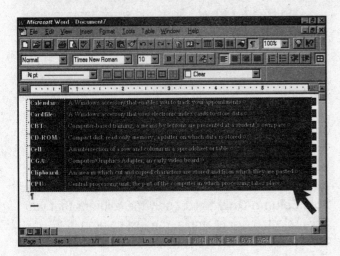

1 Select the table that you want to convert.

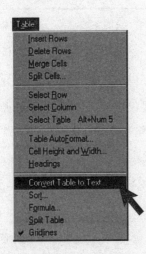

2 Open the **Table** menu and choose the **Convert Table to Text** command. Word opens the Convert Table to Text dialog box.

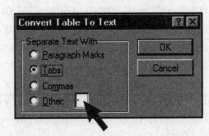

3 Select a character (in this case, press the **Spacebar** to insert a space) with which the table elements will be separated when Word converts the table to text. Then click **OK**. Word converts the table to text.

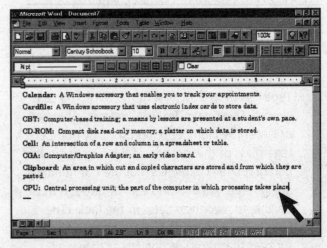

4 Format the text as needed. (In this case, the **Format Paragraph** command was used to add 6 pt spacing after each paragraph.)

Sort Text

When creating documents, you might like to order the information within or outside a table—alphabetically, numerically, or by date. To sort selected information, open the **Table** menu and choose the **Sort** command. Word ignores blank spaces, tabs, and indents; it sorts by the first alphanumeric character that it finds.

When you select the **Table Sort** command, Word displays the Sort dialog box, which enables you to specify three levels of sort: **Sort By**, **Then By**, and **Then By**. For example, if you maintain a list of employees, their departments, building, room, and telephone extension, you can sort that list by one, two, or three of these categories. You can produce a telephone list arranged alphabetically by last name (a single level of sort), or list employees by department and within department alphabetically by last name (two levels).

Word sorts text in and outside tables differently. To sort nontable text, you must select it all, but you only need to have the insertion point inside a table for all its contents to be sorted. However, whether or not you are sorting nontable text or a table, the contents of a line of text or table row remain together.

Options in the Sort dialog box are:

Type A drop-down list from which you can choose a sort type: Text (the default), Number, or Date. The Number option sorts by number, regardless of the location of the number in the paragraph; all characters that are not numbers are ignored. For Word to sort by dates, it must be able to recognize dates in the table. The date formats in the following table are the only formats that Word recognizes as dates; it ignores all other text.

Ascending Sorts from the lowest to the highest alphanumeric character.

Descending Sorts from the highest to the lowest alphanumeric character.

Header Row Indicates that you are sorting the contents of a table with a header row (that is, the first row does not contain detailed information; it consists of field names or labels). Word sorts everything but the top row. When the table contains a header row, Word uses the words in the header row as labels; otherwise, Word counts the words in a row and names them Word 1, Word 2, (or, in a table, Field 1, Field 2) and so on.

No Header Row Sorts the entire table, even the top row.

Normally, Word treats upper- and lowercase letters the same. However, you can specify that Word be sensitive to case. Just click the **Options** button in the Sort dialog box to open the Sort Options dialog box in which you can check the **Case Sensitive** check box; Word puts uppercase letters before lowercase (for example, *S* before *s*, but not before *B* or *b*). Select **Sort Column Only** to sort only the columns that you have selected (for example, the first column in a table). Click **OK** to return to the Sort dialog box.

Word's Date Formats

Format	Example
MM/DD/YY	04/17/67
MM-DD-YY	04-17-67
Month Day, Year	April 17, 1967
	Apr 17, 1967
DD-Mon-YY	17 April 67
	17 Apr 67
Month-YY	April-67
	Apr-67
MM-DD-YY hh:mm PMIAM	04-17-67 08:55 PM

Begin Guided Tour   Sort Text

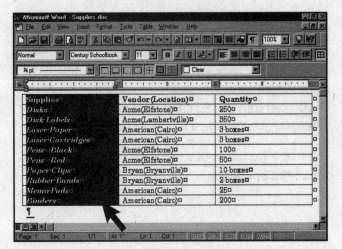

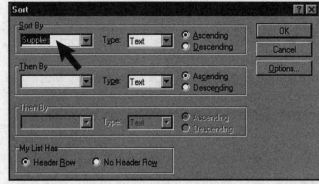

③ Select options in the Sort dialog box. Then click **OK**.

① Select part of a document to be sorted.

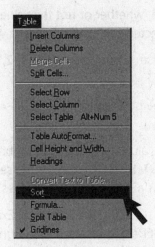

② Open the **Table** menu and select the **Sort** command.

Calculate Numbers in a Table

Word enables you to calculate numbers in a table using a combination of *functions* (pre-defined mathematical formulas) and *operators* (mathematical symbols or logical statements with which you act on the functions). In essence, Word enables you to create a small spreadsheet within a document.

You can use Word formulas for many purposes. For example, you can count the number of employees

listed on a distribution list or telephone list. You can average the number of hours you work per day over a month, or you can even calculate your vacation days as you keep track of your accumulated pay for a year. Or you can total a column of numbers and recalculate whenever you change a number in the column.

The following tables describe each function and the supported operators.

Word's Calculation Functions

Function	Description
ABS(x)	Returns the positive value of x, a number or formula, whether or not the value is positive or negative. (Examples: =ABS(-11) inserts 11 in the selected cell; =ABS(4) inserts 4.)
AND(x,y)	Returns 1 if x **and** y are true; returns 0 if x **or** y is false. (Examples: =AND(3>2,1+3=4) inserts 1 in the selected cell; =AND(3=2,1+3=4) inserts 0.)
AVERAGE()	Computes the average of the list of values within the parentheses. (Example: =AVER-AGE(1,3,5,7) inserts 4 in the selected cell.)
COUNT()	Counts the number of elements (either numbers or values representing numbers) in the list of values within the parentheses. (Examples: =COUNT(1,2,3) inserts 3 in the selected cell; =COUNT(1,A,2,3,8) inserts 4, if A does not represent a number, or 5, if it does.)
DEFINED(x)	Evaluates the expression x and returns 1 if x is valid; returns 0 if x is invalid. (Examples: =DEFINED(2+3) inserts 1 in the selected cell; =DEFINED(2>3) inserts 1 although the expression is false; =DEFINED(A=5) inserts 0 because A is not a number, making the expression invalid.)
FALSE	Returns 0 in the selected cell. (Example: =FALSE inserts 0 in the selected cell.)
IF(x,y,z)	Evaluates the expression x; inserts y (Yes, True, or 1) if x is true, and inserts z (No, False, or 0) if x is false. (Examples: =IF(2>3,7,2 inserts 2 because the expression is false; =IF(7+7=14,1,0) inserts 1 because the expression is true.)
INT(x)	From the formula or value x, returns the numbers to the left of the decimal point. (Example: =INT(2.1413) inserts 2 in the selected cell.)
MAX()	Finds the largest value in the list of values within the parentheses. (Example: =MAX(2.5,3,4.2,9.1) inserts 9.1 in the selected cell.)
MIN()	Finds the smallest value in the list of values within the parentheses. (Example: =MIN(2.5,3,4.2,9.1) inserts 2.5 in the selected cell.)

Function	Description
MOD(x,y)	Returns the remainder of dividing x by y. (Examples: =MOD(15,9) inserts 6 in the selected cell; =MOD(18,9) inserts 0.0.)
NOT(x)	Returns 0 (false) if the expression x is true; returns 1 (true) if x is false. (Examples: =NOT(5+3=8) inserts 0 in the selected cell; =NOT(2>4) returns 1.)
OR(x,y)	Returns 1 if either the expressions x **or** y are true; returns 0 if both x **and** y are false. (Examples: =OR(2<3,2=3) inserts 1 in the selected cell; =OR(8*9=54,2+3=7) inserts 0.)
PRODUCT()	Returns the product of multiplying a list of the values within the parentheses. (Example: =PRODUCT(3,3,3,5) inserts 135 in the selected cell.)
ROUND(x,y)	Rounds the number of formula x to the decimal places y. (Example: =ROUND(2.333*3.25,3) inserts 7.582 in the selected cell.)
SIGN(x)	Returns 1 if x is positive; returns -1 if x is negative. (Examples: =SIGN(593) inserts 1 in the selected cell; =SIGN(-593) inserts -1.)
SUM()	Sums the list of the values within the parentheses. (Examples: If the cells above the formula =SUM(ABOVE) contain 1, 4, and 7, the result 12 is inserted in the selected cell; if the cells to the left of the formula =SUM(LEFT) contain 1, 5, 9, 4, and 5, the result 24 is inserted; =SUM(1,5,9,4,5) inserts 24.)
TRUE	Returns 1. (Example: =TRUE inserts 1 in the selected cell.)

Word's Calculation and Logical Operators

Operator	Purpose	Use
+	Addition	2+3
–	Subtraction	98–34
*	Multiplication	9*3
/	Division	15/3
%	Percentage	
^	Powers/Roots	
=	Equal to	8=8
<>	Not equal to	8<>4
<	Less than	8<9
<=	Less than or equal to	5<=5
>	Greater than	8>4
>=	Greater than or equal to	8>=4

When you open the **Table** menu and select the **Formula** command, Word opens the Formula dialog box and suggests a particular SUM formula in the **Formula** text box. If the insertion point is at the bottom of a column of values or formulas, Word displays **SUM(ABOVE)**; if the insertion point is at the end of a row of values, Word displays **SUM(LEFT)**.

In the dialog box, you can select a number format for the calculated value, and you can paste a function at the end of the formula in the **Formula** text box. To select a number format, open the **Number Format** drop-down list.

- Pound signs (#) represent optional locations of numbers. If the result of a formula is large enough, the numbers replace the pound signs. If the result of the formula is small, the pound signs are ignored.

- Zeroes (0) represent required locations of numbers, whether or not the results of a formula are large enough.

- $ and % are the required dollar sign and percent sign.

For example, if you select the format **#,##0**, valid results might include **9** or **9,999** or **650**. Or if you select **$#,##0.00($#,##0.00)** valid results might include **$9.99** or **$0.05**.

Word lists names of all valid functions in the Paste Function drop-down list box/text box. You can either select a function, which includes parentheses if the syntax allows, and type the expressions or values within the parentheses; or you can type a complete formula in the text box. If you're a beginner, it's best to choose from the **Paste Function** drop-down list so that you use the correct format. Then click **OK**, and Word closes the dialog box and inserts the value in the cell in which the insertion point is located.

Begin Guided Tour   Add Numbers in a Table

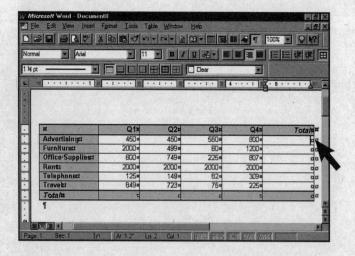

1 In a table, click in a cell that you want to contain the result of the calculation, the sum in this case. Word will put the formula in this cell.

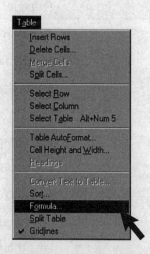

2 Open the **Table** menu and select the **Formula** command. Word opens the Formula dialog box with a SUM formula in the **Formula** text box.

Guided Tour Add Numbers in a Table

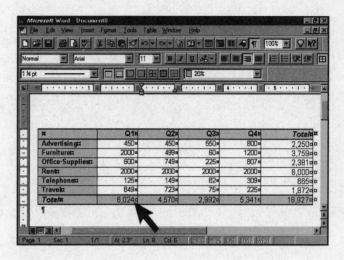

3 Select a number format, and then click **OK** to add the numbers. (If you want to do something besides add the numbers, edit the contents of the Formula box and then click **OK**.)

4 Word displays the sum in the cell you selected. Repeat steps 1, 2, and 3 until you have completed adding formulas.

Whenever you change numbers in a table, even if you add cells to the row or column in which you are calculating, you can have Word recalculate a formula. Select the cell containing the result and press **F9**.

HOW TO...

Add Graphics to a Document

This section gives you an overview of how to enhance your documents using the Microsoft WordArt text formatting *applet* (a small program that you can use inside Word and some other Windows-based programs), Microsoft Drawing, and clip art—from within Word and from other applications and folders on your computer. Both Microsoft WordArt and Microsoft Drawing create items that are called *objects*, individual components that make up a graphic (or a document). Examples of objects are rectangles, lines, and ellipses in Microsoft Drawing and text that is converted to a single graphic in Microsoft WordArt. Also in this section, you'll learn how to insert and edit frames and add captions.

What You Will Find in This Section

Convert Text to Graphics with WordArt

Microsoft's WordArt application, which runs under Word and some other Windows-based programs but cannot run independently, enables you to change a block of text to a graphic and then manipulate it as you would other graphics. You can use WordArt to enhance a heading, or to design a certificate, a handout, or even a simple logo.

To start WordArt, open the **Insert** menu and select the **Object** command. When the Object dialog box appears, select **Microsoft WordArt**; then click **OK**. The WordArt toolbar and menu bar replace the Word toolbars and menu bar. In addition, a small WordArt window appears. In the WordArt window, type the text that you want to convert. At this point, WordArt changes the text into a graphic; you can edit the whole but not the individual characters.

Select from the combination of formatting options:

Line and Shape From this drop-down list, select from the patterns in which your text will bend or to which it will conform.

Font From this drop-down list, select a font just as you do elsewhere in Word.

Font Size Select the size of the text or let WordArt decide by selecting **Best Fit**.

Bold Switches between normal and bold-face.

Italic Switches between normal and italics.

Even Height button Makes lowercase letters the same height as uppercase letters.

Flip button Turns the text from left to right to top to bottom.

Stretch button Stretches the text horizontally and vertically when you adjust the size of the frame with the graphic.

Alignment button Opens a drop-down menu from which you can choose alignment: Center, Left, Right, Stretch Justify, Letter Justify, or Word Justify.

Character Spacing button Opens the Spacing Between Characters dialog box in which you can specify spacing between characters.

Special Effects button Opens the Special Effects dialog box in which you can rotate and change the angle of the text.

Shading button Opens the Shading dialog box from which you can select patterns and colors for the graphic. Your selections do not have an effect on the background behind the graphic.

Shadow button Displays eight types of shadows. If you select **More**, WordArt opens the Shadow dialog box from which you can choose a shadow and/or select a shadow color for the text.

Border button Displays the Border dialog box from which you can select border styles and colors for the text.

Whenever you select an option, WordArt changes the look of the graphic in the document window. To exit from WordArt and return to your document, click anywhere on the document window.

To edit a WordArt graphic from within WordArt, simply double-click the graphic. When the WordArt window appears, the WordArt toolbar replaces the Word toolbars, and the WordArt menu bar replaces the Word menu bar; you can start editing. You can change the appearance of a WordArt graphic on-screen by sizing it. To size a graphic, click a *handle*, a small black box at the corners and in the middle of each border of a graphic.

- Move the mouse pointer to a corner handle. When the mouse pointer changes to a double-headed diagonal arrow, press and hold down the left mouse button, and drag to size two

sides of the border and change the look of the graphic.

- Point to a handle in the middle of a border. When the mouse pointer changes to a double-headed vertical or horizontal arrow, press and hold down the left mouse button, and drag to move the "clicked-on" side of the border and change the look of the graphic.

Begin Guided Tour   Create a WordArt Graphic

1 With an open document on-screen, open the **Insert** menu and select the **Object** command.

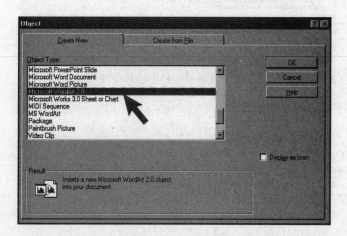

2 In the Object dialog box, double-click **Microsoft WordArt 2.0**. The WordArt toolbar and dialog box appear.

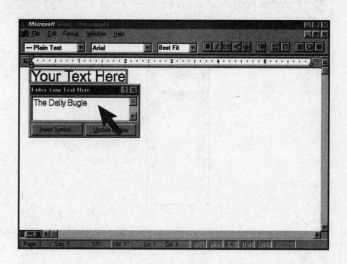

3 Type the text that you want to convert, and press **Enter** to end each line. Then click **Update Display**.

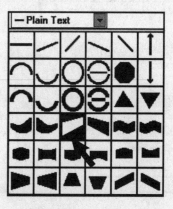

4 From the **Line and Shape** drop-down list, select a pattern to which the text will conform.

(continues)

Guided Tour   Create a WordArt Graphic   *(continued)*

(5) From the **Font** drop-down list, select a font.

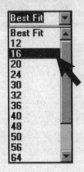

(6) From the **Font Size** drop-down list, select a point size.

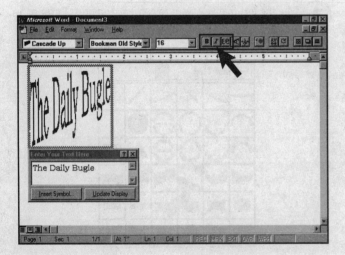

(7) To enhance the text, click the **Bold**, **Italic**, and/or **Even Height** buttons.

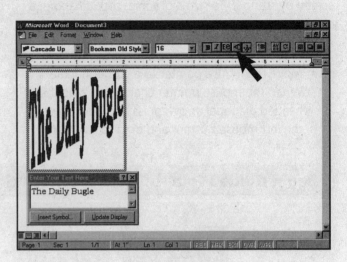

(8) Click the **Flip** button to flip the text from side to side to top to bottom. You can click the button again to turn off the Flip effect.

(9) Click the **Stretch** button to stretch the text when you change the size of the frame which holds the graphic.

Guided Tour   Create a WordArt Graphic

10 Click the **Alignment** button if you want to change the alignment of the graphic. You can choose from **Center**, **Left**, and **Right**, which correspond to Left, Centered, and Right alignment in Word, as well as **Stretch Justify**, **Letter Justify**, and **Word Justify** which align two or more lines of text with both the left and right margins. Stretch Justify justifies by changing the font size of individual lines, Letter Justify justifies by inserting spaces between the characters, and Word Justify justifies by inserting spaces between words.

12 In the **Tracking** group, in which you can specify the spacing between individual characters, either click an option button or select a custom percentage. Option buttons range from Very Tight (80%) to Normal (100%, the default) to Very Loose (150%). With Custom, you can specify a particular percentage from 0 to 500%). Check the **Automatically Kern Character Pairs** check box to adjust the spacing between characters automatically. Then click **OK**.

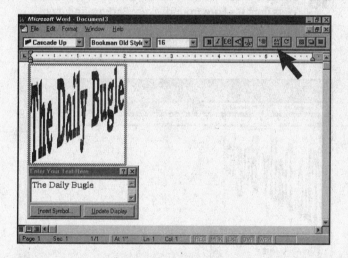

Because of their size and space between them, large "unkerned" characters look like separate characters, not words. Turning on kerning tightens the spaces between characters, resulting in words that look like words—not groups of letters that happen to be on the same line.

11 Click the **Character Spacing** button. WordArt opens the Spacing Between Characters dialog box.

13 Click the **Special Effects** button. WordArt opens the Special Effects dialog box.

(continues)

Guided Tour   Create a WordArt Graphic   *(continued)*

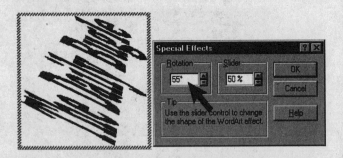

14 To rotate the graphic around the center of its frame, type or select a value from the **Rotation** text/list box. The default is **0**. To change the slant of the graphic, type or select a value from the **Slider** text/list box. The default is **50%**. Then click **OK**.

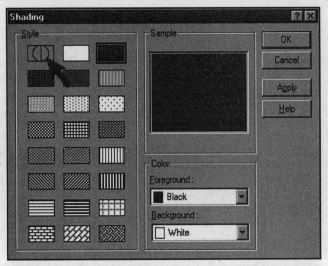

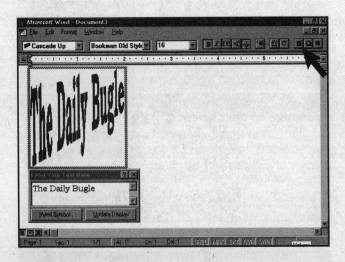

16 Click to choose a pattern from the **Style** group. Select colors from the **Foreground** and/or **Background** drop-down list. The Sample box shows the look of the graphic text as you make your selections. Then click **OK**.

15 Click the **Shading** button. WordArt opens the Shading dialog box.

17 Click the **Shadow** button. WordArt opens the Shadow dialog box.

Guided Tour Create a WordArt Graphic

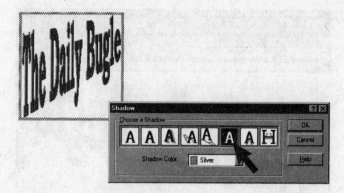

18 Select a shadow. To change the color of the shadow, open the **Shadow Color** drop-down list and select. Click **OK**.

20 To add a border to the text, select a border style from the **Thickness** group. To change the color of the border, choose from the **Color** drop-down list. Then click **OK**.

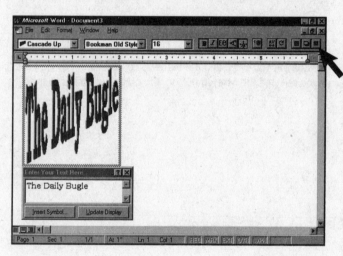

19 Click the **Border** button. WordArt opens the Border dialog box.

21 Close WordArt by clicking anywhere on the document window except on the WordArt text box.

(continues)

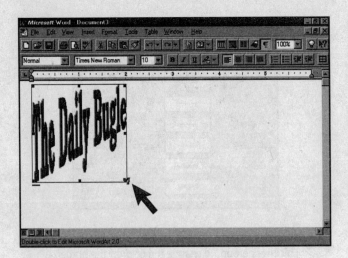

22 To size two sides of the graphic, move the mouse pointer to a handle at the corner of the border surrounding the graphic. When the mouse pointer changes to a double-headed arrow, drag the border. As you drag, the mouse pointer changes to crosshairs, and the border is composed of dashed lines. If you selected the **Stretch** button, the graphic stretches to the newly sized borders.

23 To size one side of the graphic, move the mouse pointer to a center handle. When the mouse pointer changes to a double-headed arrow, drag the border. The mouse changes to a crosshair as you drag, and the border is composed of dashed lines. If you selected the **Stretch** button, the graphic stretches to the newly sized borders.

Insert Pictures and Clip Art

Like any word processor, the main job of Word for Windows 95 is processing words. But often, adding an image spices up documents and makes them clearer and more complete. For example, if you are creating a family newsletter and are talking about a family picnic, why not add some clip art with a picnic theme? This not only illustrates your story but also makes the entire document more attractive.

Or perhaps you are creating an invitation to a party at your home. You can create a map to your home with another program, such as a drawing program and then import it into Word to illustrate your directions to the party.

In precomputer times, newspapers and advertisers had books of illustrations from which they would cut (clip) and paste pieces of art onto their pages, hence the name *clip art*.

You can obtain images from many places. Word comes with a clip art collection for illustrating your documents. You can find Word's clip art collection in the **\Clipart** subfolder in the **MSOffice** folder. Windows graphics, such as the bitmap files used for wallpaper, are in the **\Windows** folder. You can download images from most online services, such as America Online and CompuServe. You also can purchase collections of images or create them yourself. You even can have your own snapshots developed and stored on a CD-ROM disc rather than with traditional paper development in a format called Kodak Photo CD. You then can easily transfer your photos from the disc to your Word documents. Call your film processor to see if he can develop your film using this process.

You can illustrate a document by inserting symbols (see "Insert Special Characters into a Document" on page 188). When you add a symbol to a document, consider increasing its size by increasing its font size.

During Word's installation process, you must specify the graphics formats that Word can handle. There are dozens of graphics file formats, but the most common formats are Windows metafile, CompuServe GIF, Paintbrush (from Windows 3.1), and bitmaps. If you can't add an image, chances are you didn't specify that specific type of file format while installing Word. You can run the installation program again, however, and specify those formats. Similarly, you must install Word's collection of clip art in order to insert this art into a document.

To insert a picture into a document, open the **Insert** menu and select the **Picture** command. Word opens the Insert Picture dialog box, which has most of the options of the Open dialog box. (For information about the Open dialog box, see "Open a Document" on page 79.)

To preview a picture before inserting it in the document, click on the **Preview** button, the next-to-last button at the top of the dialog box. Word splits the dialog box into two panes, with files listed on the left and the picture of the currently selected file on the right. When you find a picture that you want to insert into the document, simply double-click on the file.

Options unique to the Insert Picture dialog box are Link To File and Save with Document. When you place a check mark in the **Link To File** check box, Word links the picture to the document. Linking a picture means that whenever you edit the picture using its original application, you can automatically update the picture in the document. Double-click the picture, return to the source application, and change the picture. When you return to your document, the picture in the document is automatically updated.

Checking the **Save with Document** check box makes the picture and all its possible link information part of the document, which can increase the size of the document a great deal. If you do not link the picture to the document, Word automatically saves the picture with the document.

Begin Guided Tour   Insert Clip Art

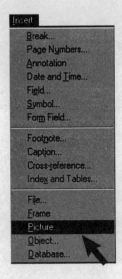

1 With a document on-screen, position the insertion point where you want the graphic to appear. Then open the **Insert** menu and choose the **Picture** command.

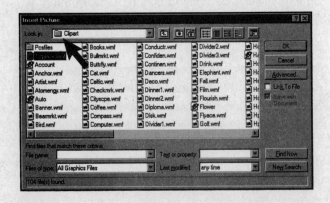

2 Open a folder or subfolder that holds the desired graphics file.

3 Click the **Preview** button. The dialog box now shows the selected picture.

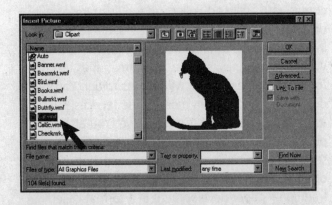

4 Double-click the graphics file. Word inserts it into your document.

Edit a Picture

Once you add a picture to a Word document, you can make more changes to it. You can change an object's size, crop (cut) pieces off, and add space between the object and text. You can use drag-and-drop to move a picture or you can place it in a frame and then drag the frame. For information about frames, see "Insert a Blank Frame" on page 263, "Move Framed Objects on a Page" on page 268, and "Edit an Object in a Frame" on page 271.

Before editing a picture, you must select it. There are two ways of selecting: either click the left mouse button anywhere within the object, or move the insertion point to the left of the object and then press **Shift+right arrow**. Word surrounds the object with a border containing eight handles, which enable you to change the dimensions of the border and, hence, the picture.

When you crop an object, you remove parts that you don't want to display. You can crop with the mouse or a menu command.

- To crop using the mouse, select the picture. Then move the mouse pointer to a handle in the middle of the border at which the cropping will occur. When the mouse pointer changes to a double-sided arrow, press and hold down the **Shift** key. When the mouse pointer changes to overlapping right angles, drag the handle toward the center of the object. Word removes the section between the original and new locations. To reverse the cropping, press and hold down **Shift**, and drag the handle toward its original position.

- To crop using a menu command, select the picture, open the **Format** menu, and select **Picture**. In the Picture dialog box, either type or select values in the **Left**, **Right**, **Top**, and/or **Bottom** box, making sure the specified value is a positive number. To reverse your action, click the **Reset** button.

Adding white space between the picture and the nearby text is another way to both enhance and emphasize a picture. You can add white space with the mouse or a menu command.

- To add white space using the mouse, select the picture. Then move the mouse pointer to a handle in the middle of the border. When the mouse pointer changes to a double-sided arrow, press and hold down the **Shift** key. When the mouse pointer changes to overlapping right angles, drag the handle away from the center of the picture. Word adds white space between the original and new locations of the handle. If you have previously cropped the object, Word returns the cropped portion before adding white space.

- To add white space using a menu command, select the picture, open the **Format** menu, and select **Picture**. In the Picture dialog box, either type or select a value in the **Left**, **Right**, **Top**, and/or **Bottom** boxes, making sure the specified value is a negative number. To reverse your action, click the **Reset** button.

You can *scale* (increase or decrease the size of pictures) with the mouse or a menu command.

- To scale using the mouse, select the picture, and then drag a handle. If you select a handle at the corner of the border, you'll scale two sides up or down and keep the original proportions of the picture. If you select a handle between the corners, you'll adjust that one edge of the object and lose the original proportions. When you scale an object, look in the status bar for the percentages that the height and width change from the original dimensions.

- To scale using a menu command, select the picture, open the **Format** menu, and select **Picture**. In the Picture dialog box, either type or select values representing the picture's original proportions in either set of **Width** and **Height** text/option boxes. In the **Scaling** group, these values represent percentages of the original dimensions. Or in the **Size** group, type or select a value representing the actual measurements in the **Width** and **Height** text/option boxes. To reverse your action, click the **Reset** button.

The **Original Size** group shows the original width and height of the picture.

At any time, you can return an object to its original size. Select the object and then select **Format Picture**. When Word displays the Picture dialog box, click the **Reset** button.

Begin Guided Tour Drag-and-Drop a Picture

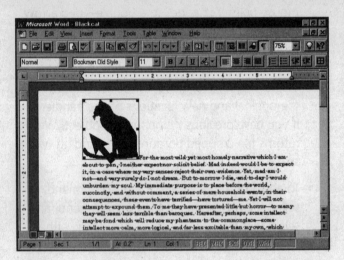

1 Select a picture. Word surrounds the picture with a border.

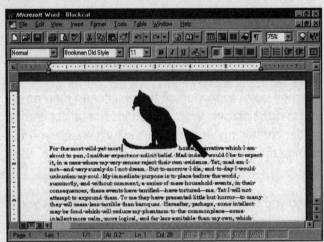

3 Drag the picture to its new location. Release the left mouse button.

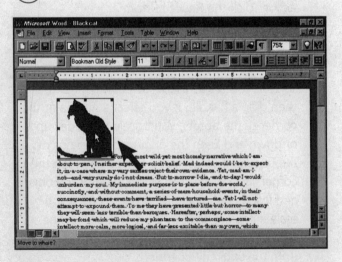

2 Move the mouse pointer within the picture. Press and hold down the left mouse button. Word adds a box to the tail of the mouse pointer. Either a dotted horizontal line under the picture when the mouse pointer is in the picture or a dashed vertical line when the mouse pointer is away from the picture shows the current location of the insertion point.

Begin Guided Tour Crop a Picture Using the Mouse

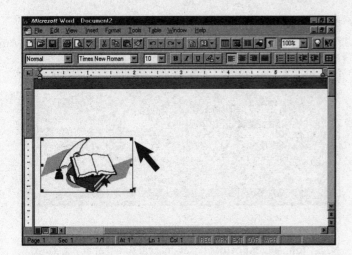

3 Press and hold down **Shift**. Then drag the handle toward the center of the picture. Word removes the section between the original and new location.

1 Select the picture. Word adds handles to the corners and sides of the border of the picture.

4 To reverse the cropping, press and hold down **Shift**, and drag the sizing handle toward its original position.

2 Move the mouse pointer to a handle in the middle of the border. The mouse pointer changes to a double-sided arrow.

Begin Guided Tour Crop a Picture Using a Menu Command

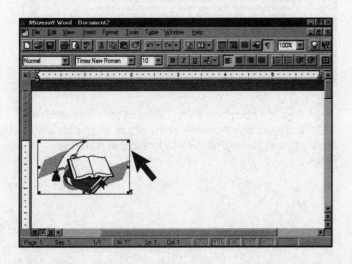

1 Select the picture. Word adds handles to the corners and sides of the border of the picture.

(continues)

Guided Tour Crop a Picture Using a Menu Command

(continued)

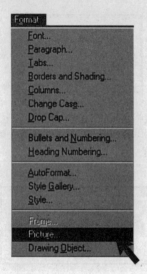

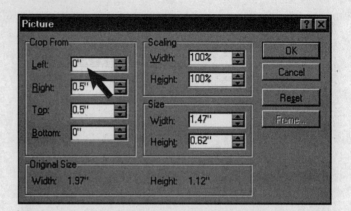

③ To crop the picture, type or select values in the **Left**, **Right**, **Top**, and/or **Bottom** boxes, making sure that any specified value is a positive number. (To reverse cropping, click the **Reset** button.) Click **OK**.

② Open the **Format** menu and select the **Picture** command. Word opens the Picture dialog box.

Begin Guided Tour Add White Space to a Picture Using the Mouse

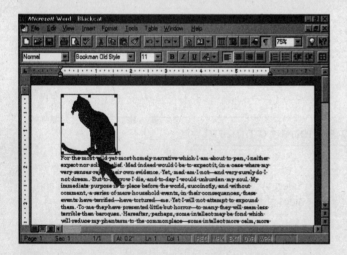

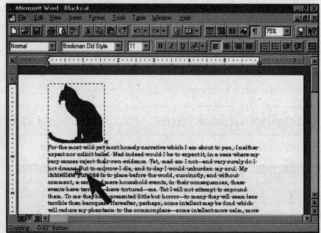

① Select the picture. Word adds handles to the corners and sides of the border of the picture. Move the mouse pointer to a handle in the middle of the bottom border. The mouse pointer changes to a double-sided arrow.

② Press and hold down **Shift**. Then drag the handle down and away from the center of the picture. Word adds white space between the original and new locations of the sizing handle.

Guided Tour Add White Space to a Picture Using the Mouse

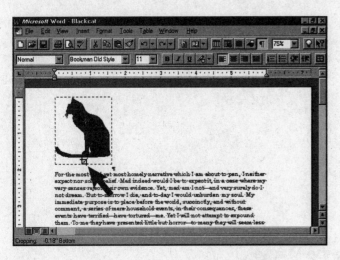

3 To reverse the changes, press and hold down **Shift**, and drag the sizing handle toward its original position.

Begin Guided Tour Add White Space to a Picture Using a Menu Command

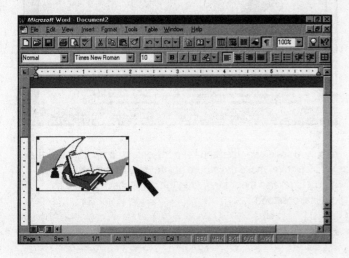

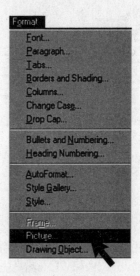

1 Select the picture. Word adds handles to the corners and sides of the border of the picture.

2 Open the **Format** menu and select the **Picture** command. Word opens the Picture dialog box.

(continues)

Guided Tour   Add White Space to a Picture Using a Menu Command (continued)

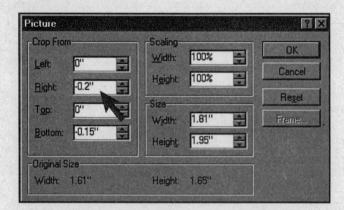

3 To add white space to the picture, type or select values in the **Left**, **Right**, **Top**, and/or **Bottom** box, making sure that the specified value is a negative number. (To reverse your action, click the **Reset** button.) Click **OK**.

Begin Guided Tour   Scale a Picture Using the Mouse

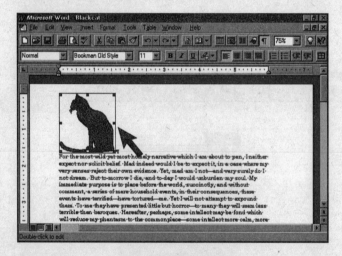

1 Select the picture. Word adds handles to the corners and sides of the border of the picture.

2 To scale two sides and keep the original proportions of the picture, move the mouse pointer to a corner handle and drag. (To reverse the scaling, drag the corner back toward its original position.)

Guided Tour Scale a Picture Using the Mouse

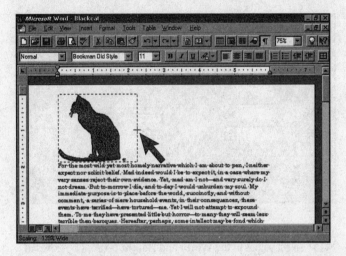

3 To scale one side of the picture and lose the original proportions, move the mouse pointer to a handle in the middle of a border and drag. (To reverse the scaling, drag the border back toward its original position.)

Begin Guided Tour Scale a Picture Using a Menu Command

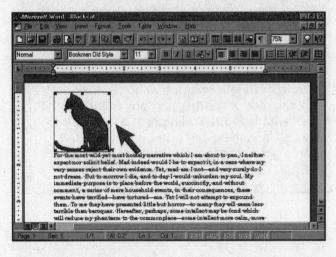

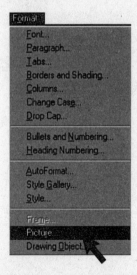

1 Select the picture. Word adds handles to the corners and sides of the border of the picture.

2 Open the **Format** menu and select the **Picture** command. Word opens the Picture dialog box.

(continues)

Guided Tour   Scale a Picture Using a Menu Command   *(continued)*

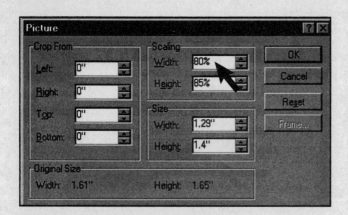

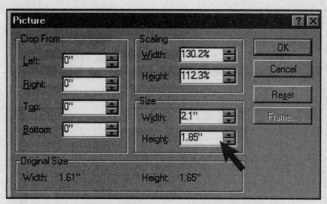

3 To scale the picture using original proportions, type or select percentage values in the **Width** and **Height** text/option boxes in the **Scaling** group. (To reverse your action, click the **Reset** button.) Then click **OK**.

4 To scale the picture using original measurements, type or select values in the **Width** and **Height** text/option boxes in the **Size** group. (To reverse your action, click the **Reset** button.) Then click **OK**.

Using the Size options may result in a picture that has lost its original proportions. If you want to keep a picture's proportions but must use one specific measurement (for example, a two-inch width), type that measurement in the **Width or Height** text/option box in the **Size** group, click in another text box to look at the percentage in the **Scaling** group (for example, 124%), and make the other dimension the same percentage in the **Width or Height** text/option box in the **Scaling** group.

Add Lines and Shading

If you want to emphasize one or more paragraphs in a document, or cells and borders in a table, consider adding borders, lines, and/or shading by opening the **Format** menu and selecting the **Borders and Shading** command or by selecting buttons on the **Borders** toolbar. If you select several paragraphs, Word places borders or lines around the entire selection.

When you choose the **Format Borders and Shading** command, Word displays the Paragraph Borders and Shading dialog box, which has two categories: Borders and Shading. The options in the Borders category of the dialog box are:

- **Presets**   Click one of three buttons, which allows you to select the border type: **None**, which represents no border; **Box**, which is a standard border; and **Shadow**, which is a drop-shadow border.

- **Border**   In this box, you can change the options and view an illustration of the current borders.

- **From Text**   Select or type a value in this text/option box in order to determine the amount of white space between the text and the border of a selection.

- **Line**   Click one of these illustrations of line styles to select it, or click **None**, which means no line and is the default.

- **Color**   From this drop-down list, choose one of 17 border colors.

The options in the Shading category are as follows:

- **None**   Click this option button to have no shading or coloring.

- **Custom**   Clicking on this button indicates that you will choose a pattern and/or colors for selection. Then, in the **Shading** list box, select from levels of gray or patterns. From the **Foreground** and **Background** drop-down lists, choose colors for the foreground and background of the selected pattern.

The Borders toolbar allows you to apply lines and shading, but not color or spacing from text, to a selection with these buttons:

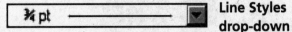

Line Styles drop-down list   Selects a border line.

Top Border button   Adds or removes a line at the top of the selection.

Bottom Border button   Adds or removes a line at the bottom of the selection.

Left Border button   Adds or removes a line at the left margin of the selection.

Right Border button   Adds or removes a line at the right margin of the selection.

Inside Border button   Adds or removes a horizontal and vertical line between each of the selections.

Outside Border button   Adds or removes a line at the top of the selection.

No Border button   Removes all lines from the selection.

Shading   Open this drop-down list box to apply shading within the borders of the selection.

Begin Guided Tour Apply Borders Using a Menu Command

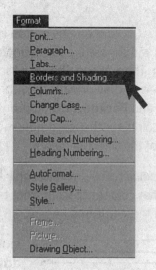

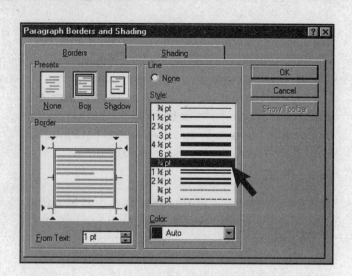

1 After selecting two or more paragraphs or table cells or clicking in one paragraph to select it, open the **Format** menu and select the **Borders and Shading** command. Word displays the Paragraph Borders and Shading dialog box.

3 From the **Style** box, select the appropriate border.

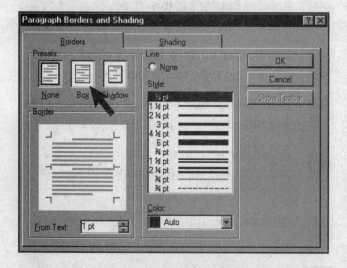

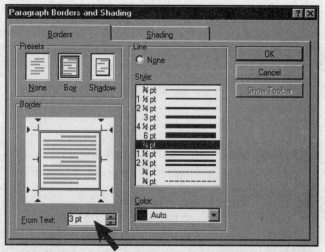

2 If needed, click the **Borders** tab. Then click **Box**, if you want to surround the selection, or **Shadow** to surround the selection with a shadowed border.

4 To adjust the distance of the border lines from the top and bottom of the selection, type or select a value in the **From Text** text/option box.

If you want to place lines above, below, to the left, and/or to the right, you can click between the corner markers in the Border box. For example, to add a line above the selection, click between the markers at the top of the Border box.

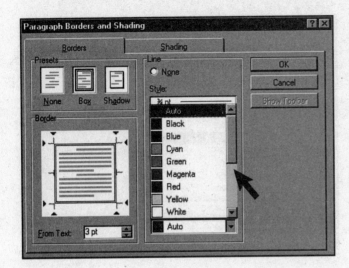

5 To display or print in color (if you have a color monitor, printer, or plotter), choose the **Color** drop-down list.

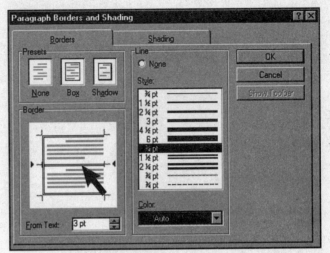

7 If you have selected two or more paragraphs (or cells) and want to place inside horizontal (or vertical) lines, click in the middle of the illustration in the **Border** box. Add or remove lines as desired.

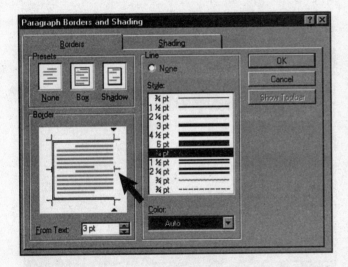

6 To add or remove a line from the border, click the line in the **Border** box. Repeat this as needed.

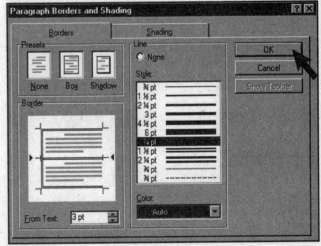

8 Click **OK** when you finish making your selections.

Begin Guided Tour   Apply Shading Using a Menu Command

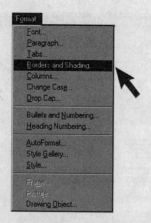

1 Select one or more paragraphs or table cells. Open the **Format** menu and choose **Borders and Shading**; the Borders and Shading dialog box appears.

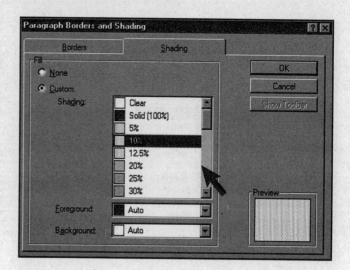

3 Click a pattern in the **Shading** list box. Word automatically selects the **Custom** option button and shows the pattern in the Preview box.

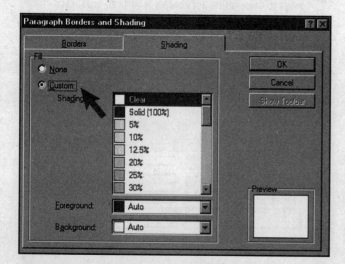

2 Click the **Shading** tab.

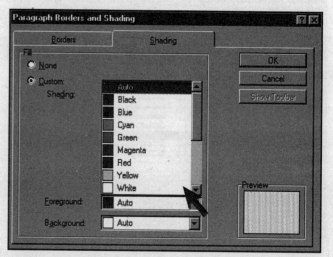

4 To add a foreground color to the selected pattern, select from the **Foreground** drop-down list.

Guided Tour   Apply Shading Using a Menu Command

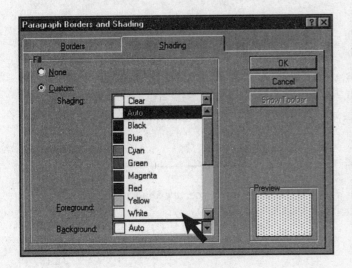 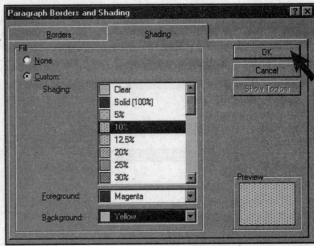

5 To add a background color to the selected pattern, select from the **Background** drop-down list.

6 Click **OK**.

Begin Guided Tour   Add Borders and Shading Using the Borders Toolbar

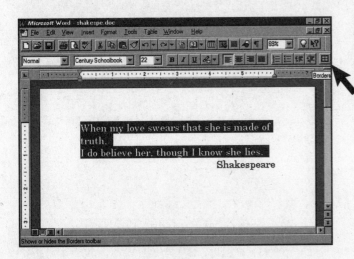

To open the Borders toolbar using a menu command, open the **View** menu and select the **Toolbars** command. In the Toolbars dialog box, click the **Borders** check box and click **OK**.

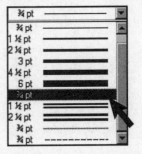

1 Select one or more paragraphs or table cells. To open the Borders toolbar, click the **Borders** button on the Formatting toolbar.

2 Open the **Line Style** drop-down list, and select a line size and style.

(continues)

Guided Tour   Add Borders and Shading Using the Borders Toolbar

(continued)

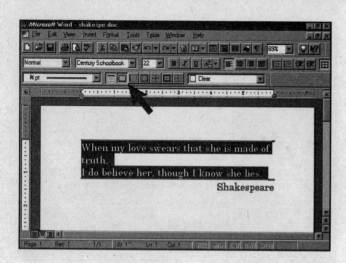

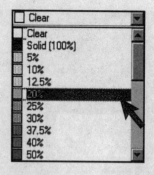

4 To choose a pattern, open the **Shading** drop-down list, and click your selection.

3 Click one or more of the line or border buttons. Word changes the selection.

Insert a Frame

rames are borders that allow text to flow around an object. You can insert a frame around an object already in your document or to make room for an object that you will place in the frame at a later time. Adding a frame allows for manipulation of both the object and the text that surrounds it.

To insert a frame around an object already in your document, select the object. Then open the **Insert** menu and select the **Frame** command. To insert a frame for an object to be added later, just select the **Insert Frame** command. When you click the new frame, notice that the Ruler shows the frame's left and right margins and that handles have been added on its corners and in the middle of its borders.

If you try to insert a frame and are not working in Page Layout view, Word prompts you to change to that view. After you answer **Yes**, Word inserts the frame.

To remove a frame, click to select it (so that handles appear on the border), open the **Format** menu, and select the **Frame** command. When Word opens the Frame dialog box, click the **Remove Frame** button. You also can delete a frame by selecting it and pressing the **Delete** key.

Begin Guided Tour   Insert a Blank Frame

1 With an open document on-screen, open the **Insert** menu and select the **Frame** command. Word changes the mouse pointer to a cross.

2 Move the mouse pointer to the first corner of the empty frame. Pressing and holding down the left mouse button, drag the mouse pointer diagonally. As you drag, a dotted rectangle shows you the size of the frame.

(continues)

Guided Tour   Insert a Blank Frame

(continued)

3 Release the left mouse button. Word places a frame surrounded by a border.

Begin Guided Tour   Frame an Object

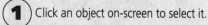

1 Click an object on-screen to select it.

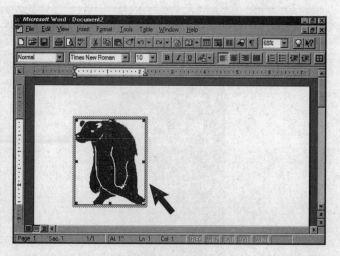

2 Open the **Insert** menu and choose the **Frame** command. Word surrounds the object with a frame.

Add a Caption

When a document contains many illustrations that may be misunderstood unless clearly identified, adding a caption helps the reader. To add a caption to the bottom of an object surrounded by a frame, follow the steps in the Guided Tour.

Word also enables you to add numbered captions to objects such as tables, figures, and equations (from Word's Equation Editor, which is not covered in this book). To insert a numbered caption, select the object, open the **Insert** menu, and select the **Caption** command. The options in the Caption dialog box are as follows:

>   **Caption**   After the figure number in this text box, insert a colon or a dash and then type a caption.

>   **Label**   If you are captioning an object other than a figure, open this drop-down list and select **Equation** or **Table**.

>   **New Label**   To "caption" another type of object, click on this button. In the **Label** text box in the New Label dialog box, type a label name.

>   **Delete Label**   To remove a new label, select it, and click this button. You cannot delete

Equation, Figure, or Table labels; when selecting any of these labels, the Delete Label button is dimmed.

>   **Position**   Open this drop-down list and select whether to place the caption above or below the selected object.

>   **Numbering**   Click this button to select a numbering format or include the chapter number in the label and select chapter options.

>   **AutoCaption**   Click this button to automatically add captions to specified objects from Word or from other Windows-based programs. You can format a caption as you would any other paragraph. For example, to align a caption under the object, select the caption, and then click the **Align Left**, **Center**, or **Align Right** button on the Formatting toolbar; or open the **Format** menu and select the **Paragraph** command. To learn how to format captions, see "Align Paragraphs" on page 157, "Add Emphasis to Selected Text" on page 170, and "Change Fonts and Font Sizes" on page 182.

Begin Guided Tour   Add a Caption

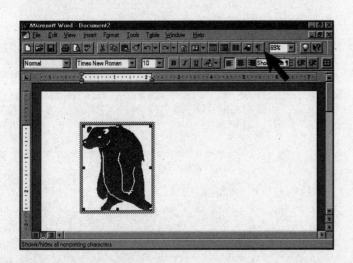

1. With a framed object on a page, click the **Show/Hide** button to show all nonprinting characters.

(continues)

Guided Tour Add a Caption *(continued)*

2 Move the insertion point to the lower right corner of the object and click.

Each anchor on the page indicates the location at which a frame is "anchored" to a paragraph. So, when you move the paragraph associated with the paragraph mark, the frame will move as well. If there is very little or no text on a page, the anchor will be very close to the frame. On pages with a great deal of text, the anchor may be further away. For information about moving frames, see "Move Framed Objects on a Page" on page 268.

3 Press **Enter**. Word adds room to the bottom of the frame and inserts a new paragraph mark at the bottom left margin of the frame.

4 With the insertion point to the left of the new paragraph mark, type the caption.

5 Select and format the caption.

Begin Guided Tour   Insert a Numbered Caption

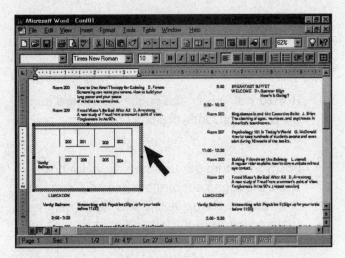

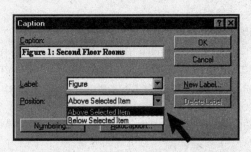

3 Open the **Label** drop-down list and select an object type. In the **Caption** text box, insert a colon or dash and type caption text. Open the **Position** drop-down list and select the position of the caption. Click **OK**. Word inserts the caption, automatically adding a caption number.

1 Select an object such as a figure, a table, or an equation. Word adds handles or a highlight to the selection.

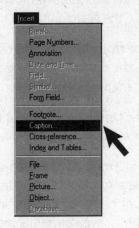

2 Open the **Insert** menu and select the **Caption** command. Word opens the Caption dialog box.

Move Framed Objects on a Page

You should place any object that you want to move in a document into a frame. You can move a frame and its contents anywhere on a page containing text by dragging it or by opening the **Format** menu or right-clicking and choosing the **Frame** command from the shortcut menu.

When you insert an object without a frame into a document, Word makes room for the object by clearing the area of the object, from the left margin to the right margin. If you insert a frame around an object, Word's default is to wrap text around the object.

To move a framed object using the mouse, move the mouse pointer to the border of the frame. When the mouse pointer adds a four-headed arrow tail, press and hold down the left mouse button, and drag the frame anywhere on the page. When you have moved the frame to the desired location, release the left mouse button.

To move an object using the **Format Frame** command, Word opens the Frame dialog box, which contains these options:

> **Text Wrapping**   In this group, click **None** to turn off *text wrapping*, running lines of text all around the frame, or click **Around** (the default) to turn on text wrapping.
>
> **Size**   In this group, change the width and height of the frame.
>
> **Width**   From this drop-down list, select **Auto** to allow Word to set the width of the frame, or select **Exact** and type or select a measurement in the **At** text/option box.
>
> **Height**   From this drop-down list, select **Auto** to allow Word to set the height of the frame; select **Exact** and type or select a measurement

in the **At** text/option box; or select **At Least** and type or select a minimum measurement in the **At** text/option box.

> **Horizontal**   Using the options in this group, select the horizontal position of the frame on the page.
>
> **Position**   From this text/drop-down list box, select the alignment of the frame: to the inside or outside of the page, left side, right side, centered between the left and right sides of the page, margin, or column; or type an actual measurement.
>
> **Relative To**   From this drop-down list, specify whether the horizontal position of the frame is relative to the Margin, Page, or Column.
>
> **Distance from Text**   In this text/list box, type or select the distance from the frame to the text near the frame.
>
> **Vertical**   Using the options in this group, select the vertical position of the frame on the page.
>
> **Position**   From this text/drop-down list box, select the alignment of the frame: to the top, bottom, or center of the Margin, Page, or Paragraph; or type an actual measurement.
>
> **Relative To**   From this drop-down list, specify whether the vertical position of the frame is relative to the Margin, Page, or Paragraph.
>
> **Distance from Text**   In this text/list box, type or select the distance from the frame to the text near the frame.
>
> **Move with Text**   If you check this check box, and if you move the text with which this frame is associated, the frame moves as well. If the Move with Text check box is clear, the frame remains in its present position.

Lock Anchor If you check this check box, the frame remains anchored to the margin, page, or paragraph to which it is currently anchored.

Remove Frame Click this button to delete the selected frame.

When an object is in a frame, you can move the object around the page to adjust the length of the lines of text and breaks from line to line.

Begin Guided Tour Move a Framed Object Using the Mouse

1 Select the frame. Move the mouse pointer within the frame until it adds a four-headed arrow as a tail.

2 Press and hold down the left mouse button, and drag the framed object. When it reaches its new location, release the mouse button.

Begin Guided Tour Move a Framed Object Using a Menu Command

1 Click the object to select it.

(continues)

Guided Tour　Move a Framed Object Using a Menu Command

(continued)

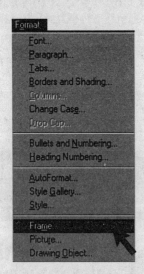

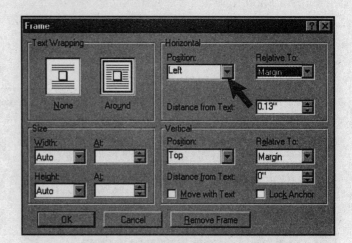

2 Open the **Format** menu and select the **Frame** command. Word opens the Frame dialog box, which shows the current location of the frame.

3 To change the frame's position, select a location or type a measurement in one or both of the **Position** text/drop-down list boxes. To change the frame's position relative to a page element, choose from the **Relative To** drop-down lists. Then click **OK**.

Edit a Frame

Using the Frame dialog box, you can change the size of the frame or indicate whether text should wrap around the frame. To display the Frame dialog box, open the **Format** menu and select the **Frame** command. (To learn about all the Frame dialog box options, see "Move Framed Objects on a Page" on page 268.)

With the mouse, you can size the frame using the techniques with which you edit pictures in Word documents.

Begin Guided Tour Edit an Object in a Frame

1 Click the object to select it.

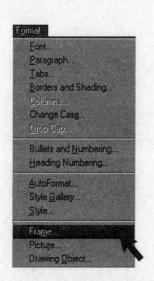

2 Open the **Format** menu and select the **Frame** command. Word opens the Frame dialog box.

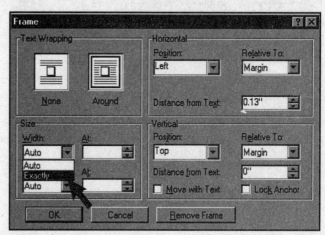

3 Open the **Width** drop-down list and select **Exactly**.

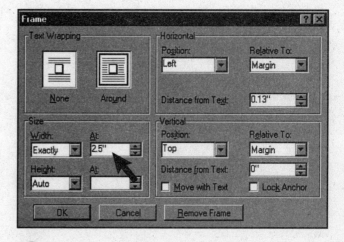

4 Type or select a value in the **At** text/option box.

(continues)

Guided Tour   Edit an Object in a Frame   *(continued)*

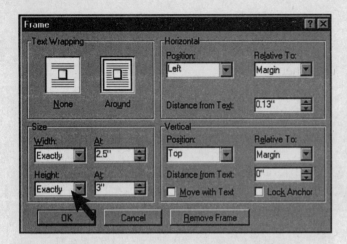

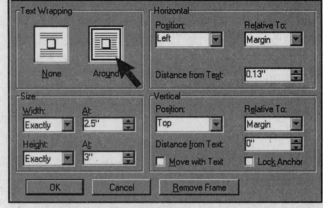

5 Repeat steps 3 and 4 for the **Height** drop-down list and its **At** text/option box.

6 To have text wrap around all margins of the frame, click the **Around** button. To have text not wrap (that is, it is before the top margin and after the bottom margin of the frame), click **None**. Then click **OK**.

Start and Exit Microsoft Drawing

The Microsoft Drawing application creates and edits pictures within Word documents. You can create flow charts, diagrams, organization charts, and illustrations for reports and proposals using Microsoft Drawing. Microsoft Drawing works from the Drawing toolbar, which you can open by clicking the **Drawing** button on the Standard toolbar. To close Microsoft Drawing, click the **Drawing** button again.

You also can open Microsoft Drawing from a menu. Open the **View** menu, select the **Toolbars** command, select the **Drawing** check box, and click **OK**. To close Microsoft Drawing from the menu bar, select **View Toolbars**, clear the Drawing check box, and click **OK**. For more information about Word toolbars, see "Use Word Toolbars" on page 30.

Begin Guided Tour   Start and Exit Microsoft Drawing

1 To start Microsoft Drawing, click the **Drawing** button to select it. The Drawing button looks pushed in and the Drawing toolbar appears at the bottom of the screen.

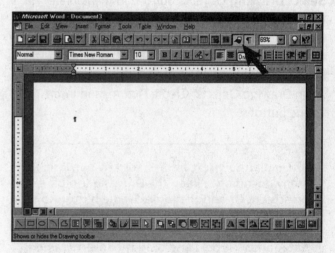

2 To close Microsoft Drawing, click the **Drawing** button to deselect it. The Drawing toolbar disappears from the screen.

Draw a Picture with Microsoft Drawing Tools

Once you start Microsoft Drawing (refer to the preceding Guided Tour), you can use the buttons on the Drawing toolbar to draw almost any type of picture, from a simple company logo to an illustration in a technical manual. Use the Line, Rectangle, Ellipse, Arc, Freeform, Text Box, and Callout buttons for creating a picture. Then enhance the picture using the Format Callout, Fill Color, Line Color, and Line Style buttons.

To select one or more objects in a drawing, use the **Select Drawing Objects** button. To manipulate objects, select Bring to Front, Send to Back, Bring in Front of Text, Send Behind Text, Group, Ungroup, Flip Horizontal, Flip Vertical, Rotate Right, and Reshape. Aids to working with pictures are the Snap to Grid, Align Drawing Objects, Create Picture, and Insert Frame buttons.

If you plan to insert frames, for any purpose, in many documents, keep the Drawing toolbar on-screen. Or add the Insert Frame button to the Standard or Formatting toolbar. Open the **Tools** menu, select **Customize**, click **Insert** in the **Categories** list box, and drag the **Insert Frame** button to a space on the desired toolbar. For more information about frames, see "Insert a Blank Frame" on page 263, "Move Framed Objects on a Page" on page 268, and "Edit an Object in a Frame" on page 271.

A small anchor on a page indicates the location at which a frame is "anchored" to a paragraph. So, when the paragraph associated with the paragraph mark moves, the frame will move as well.

For a description of each Drawing toolbar button, see "Drawing Toolbar" on page 539.

Normally, you click a Drawing toolbar button to use it, and Microsoft Drawing automatically "deselects" it after you have completed your work. (Pressing the **Esc** key also deselects a drawing button.) To keep a Drawing toolbar button selected until you decide to "deselect" it, double-click the button.

Begin Guided Tour Draw a Line

1 Click the **Line** button on the Drawing toolbar. (For a description of the Line button, see "Drawing Toolbar" on page 539.)

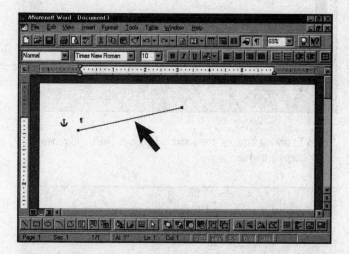

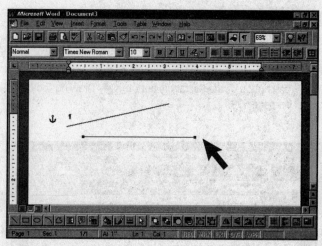

3 To draw a line at an angle at 0, 30, 45, 60, 90, and so on (where a complete revolution is 360 degrees), press and hold down **Shift**, click the left mouse button, and repeat steps 1 and 2.

2 Move the mouse pointer to the drawing area, and click to indicate one end of the line. Press and hold down the left mouse button, and drag to the other end of the line. Then release the mouse button.

Begin Guided Tour Draw a Rectangle or Square

1 Click the **Rectangle** button on the Drawing toolbar. (For a description of the Rectangle button, see "Drawing Toolbar" on page 539.)

2 To draw a rectangle, move the mouse pointer to a starting point in the drawing area. Press and hold down the left mouse button, and drag away from the starting point. When the rectangle is the desired size and shape, release the mouse button.

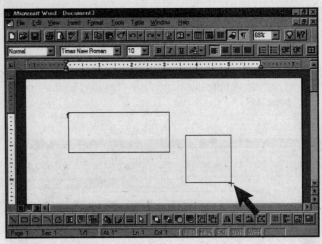

3 To draw a square, press and hold down **Shift** and repeat steps 1 and 2.

To draw a rounded rectangle, draw a rectangle. Then open the **Format** menu or right-click and select the **Drawing Object** command. In the Drawing Object dialog box, click the **Line** tab and check the **Round Corners** check box. Any changes that you make to the options in the Drawing Object dialog box will affect any objects drawn from that point on.

Begin Guided Tour Draw an Ellipse or Circle

1 Click the **Ellipse** button. (For a description of the Ellipse button, see "Drawing Toolbar" on page 539.)

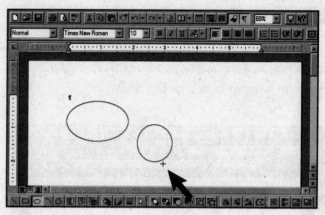

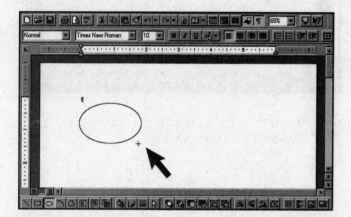

3 To draw a circle, press and hold down **Shift** and repeat steps 1 and 2.

2 To draw an ellipse, move the mouse pointer to a starting point in the drawing area. Press and hold down the left mouse button, and then drag away from the starting point. When the ellipse is the desired size and shape, release the mouse button.

Begin Guided Tour   Draw an Arc

1 Click the **Arc** button. (For a description of the Arc button, see "Drawing Toolbar" on page 539.)

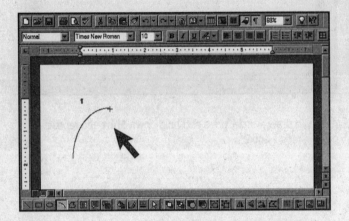

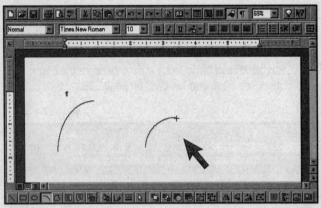

3 To draw an arc that is a segment of a circle, press and hold down **Shift** and repeat steps 1 and 2.

2 To draw an arc, move the mouse pointer to a starting point in the drawing area. Press and hold down the left mouse button, and drag away from the starting point. When the arc is the desired size and shape, release the mouse button.

Begin Guided Tour Draw a Freeform

1 Click the **Freeform** button. (For a description of the Freeform button, see "Drawing Toolbar" on page 539.)

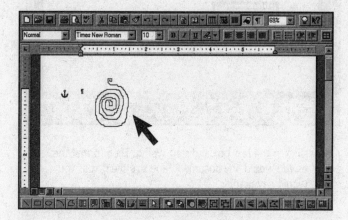

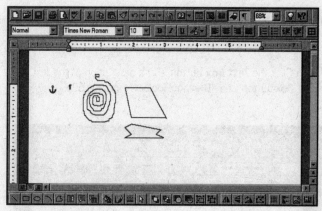

3 To draw a freeform made up of lines, move the mouse pointer to a starting point in the drawing area. Press and hold down the left mouse button and drag the lines, or click at the beginning and end of each line. When the last line touches or is near the starting point, Microsoft Drawing completes the object.

2 To draw a freeform, move the mouse pointer to a starting point in the drawing area. Press and hold down the left mouse button, and then drag in curves and lines. When the freeform object is complete, either double-click or press **Esc**.

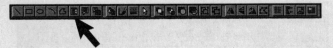

Begin Guided Tour Draw a Text Box

1 Click the **Text Box** button. (For a description of the Text Box button, see "Drawing Toolbar" on page 539.)

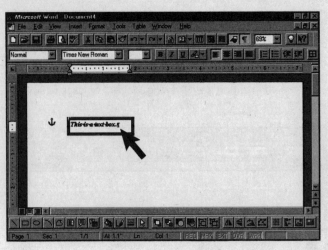

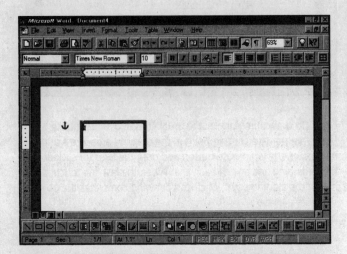

3 Click in the text box and start typing. Then format the text as you would any document, and size the box as you would any graphic.

2 To draw a text box, move the mouse pointer to a starting point in the drawing area. Press and hold down the left mouse button, and drag away from the starting point. When the text box is the desired size and shape, release the mouse button. (To draw a square text box, press and hold down **Shift** and repeat step 1 and this step).

Edit a Microsoft Drawing Picture

Once you have inserted objects in the drawing area, you may want to move them around or change their appearance. Before you manipulate a Microsoft Drawing picture, you must select it.

To select an object within a picture, move the mouse pointer to the object, and click the left mouse button. Microsoft Drawing places handles at either end of a line or around a two-dimensional object. To change the shape or size of a drawing object, move the mouse pointer to a handle, click the left mouse button, and drag in any direction. The border moves in the direction you drag the mouse pointer. To move the object, place the mouse pointer within the object and click the left mouse button. When a four-headed arrow is added to the mouse pointer, drag the object to its new location.

The Drawing toolbar also provides editing functions. For example, you can select the **Bring to Front** button to move the selected object to the front of all other objects in the picture. Or you can select the **Send to Back** button to move the selected object to the back of all other objects in the picture. You can flip an object horizontally or vertically using the **Flip Horizontal** and **Flip Vertical** buttons, respectively.

You also can specify options for future drawing objects using the Drawing Defaults dialog box. Just open the **Format** menu and select the **Drawing Object** command.

You can size a drawing object by selecting it, moving to a handle on the border surrounding the object, or clicking and holding down the left mouse button and dragging. Pressing and holding down the **Ctrl** key while dragging adjusts two sides (the top and bottom or the left and right) of the object at once.

Selecting the **Group** button allows you to make a selected group of objects into a single object. This command works well when you must move several objects to make room for new objects; just group them and move them as a whole. When you finish moving them, click the **Ungroup** button. There are two ways to select several objects to be grouped: click the **Select Drawing Objects** button and drag a border around all the objects, or press and hold down the **Shift** key and click on each object. In either case, you'll see handles around all the selected objects, so if you have selected two objects, you'll see 16 handles—8 for each object.

Begin Guided Tour   Edit a Microsoft Drawing Picture

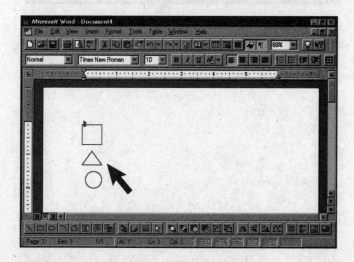

1 Create several objects using the buttons on the Drawing toolbar. (For help, refer to "Draw a Picture with Microsoft Drawing Tools" on page 274 and "Drawing Toolbar" on page 539.)

(continues)

Guided Tour   Edit a Microsoft Drawing Picture   *(continued)*

2 Select an object and change its fill color by clicking on the **Fill Color** button and selecting from the palette. Repeat for other objects. The example shows a red rectangle with a medium black border, a cyan triangle with a heavy blue border, and a green circle with no border.

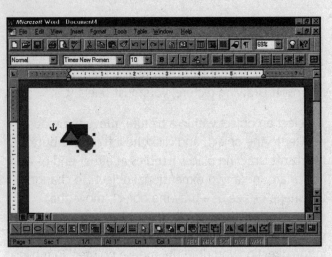

4 Select objects and drag them so they overlap. In the figure, the triangle is in front of the rectangle, and the circle, which is selected, is being dragged in front of the other objects.

3 Select objects and change them using other Drawing toolbar buttons. In the figure, the triangle is selected.

5 Select an object and click the **Send to Back** button.

Guided Tour Edit a Microsoft Drawing Picture

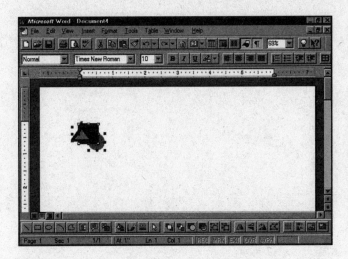

6 Either click the **Select Drawing Objects** button and drag a border around all the objects, or press and hold down **Shift** while clicking on objects to select all of them. Notice that each object has its own handles.

7 Click the **Group** button. The handles change. You can now move or format the objects as a group. To ungroup them, click the **Ungroup** button.

HOW TO...
Use Mail Merge

Through its mail merge feature, Word enables you to produce letters, envelopes, and mailing labels that are custom-made for each member of your audience. You can mention each recipient by name, refer to his address, and incorporate special messages in selected letters. In addition, you can send your letter either to your entire audience or to selected segments.

In this section, you'll learn the basics of creating and printing envelopes, form letters, and mailing labels. In addition, you'll find out how to define the information about yourself (your name, initials, and mailing address) that Word uses in documents.

What You Will Find in This Section

Create and Print an Envelope

Although mass mailers often use mailing labels to address form letters, envelopes provide a more personal touch—especially for letters to individuals. To create and print an envelope using Word, open the **Tools** command and choose the **Envelopes and Labels** command. If a letter is the current document, Word will identify the name and address of the recipient and automatically add that information to the envelope.

In the Envelopes and Labels dialog box, you can click a button to access the Envelope Options dialog box in which you can select envelope size and fonts for both return and delivery addresses, and specify the placement of each address on the envelope. You also can specify printing options, such as the position of an envelope being fed into the printer, whether you feed face down or face up, and the method by which you feed depending on the printer that you are currently using. Word evaluates the default printer and specifies the printing options (which you can override, if necessary).

> If you have filled in the **Mailing Address** box in the Options dialog box for the User Info category, that information will automatically be your return address for envelopes. For information about the Options dialog box for User Info, see "Change User Information" on page 288.

If you plan on reusing this document, it's a good idea to click the **Add to Document** button to insert the envelope at the top of your document. Then when you print the document, the envelope is already available for printing. Just open the **File** menu and select **Print**; click the **Print** button on the Standard toolbar; or press **Ctrl+P**. Place the envelope in the printer, and your printer processes the envelope and then prints the document.

Begin Guided Tour   Create and Print an Envelope

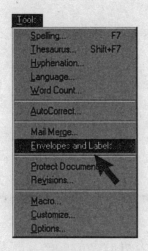

1 With a letter or another document on-screen, open the **Tools** menu and select the **Envelopes and Labels**.

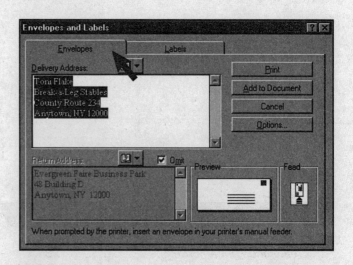

2 Click the **Envelopes** tab to display the Envelopes and Labels dialog box for the Envelopes category.

Guided Tour   Create and Print an Envelope

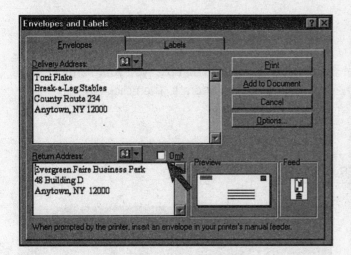

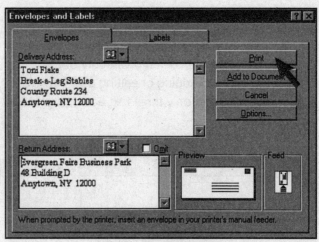

3 If you want to print your return address on the envelope, make sure to clear the **Omit** check box.

If the name and address in the **Delivery Address** text box is not the name and address on the letter, close the dialog box, select that information in the letter, and reopen the dialog box. The proper name and address should now appear in the **Delivery Address** text box.

4 Click the **Print** button. Insert the envelope in your printer using the diagram in the **Feed** box in the Envelopes and Labels dialog box.

If you have any questions about printing an envelope, refer to your printer's manual.

Change User Information

When printing envelopes and compiling summary information for documents, Word uses the information in the User Info category of the Options dialog box. Adding or editing user information involves filling in only three text boxes, so it's quick and easy.

To change your user information, open the **Tools** menu, and select **Options**. Then click the **User Info** tab of the Options dialog box. Type your name, initials, and mailing address. Then click **OK**.

Begin Guided Tour Change User Information

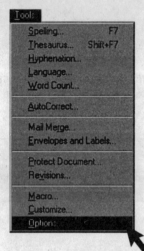

1 With an open document on-screen (otherwise, the **Tools** menu is not available), open the **Tools** menu, and select the **Options** command. Word opens the most recently used Options dialog box.

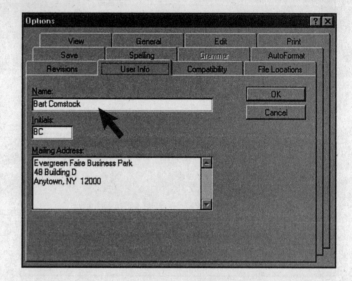

3 Fill in the **Name**, **Initials**, and **Mailing Address** text boxes. Then click **OK**.

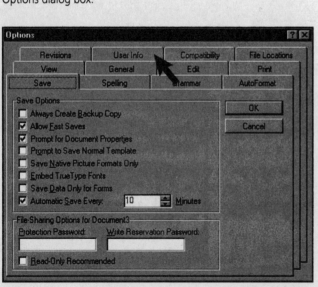

2 Click the **User Info** tab.

Create and Print a Form Letter

The basic components of a form letter are a main document and a data source file. Once you have opened these documents, you must merge them. The merging process actually creates a form letter. The *main document* includes all the text that you plan to send to your audience as a whole but omits the information unique to each individual: name, address, special messages, and so on. You can create a form letter using a brand-new or existing main document. For information about starting or opening a main document, see "Open a Document" on page 79 or "Create a New Document" on page 46. The first step in a mail merge is opening or creating the main document.

The *data source file* contains the unique information about each recipient. A data source file, which is actually a simple database, is a table that includes names, addresses, and information that might not even make its way into your letter, but might trigger selection or a special message. The data source file is made up of one record for each individual to whom you will send a letter. Identifying the data source file is the second step in a mail merge.

The first record in a data source file is the *header record*, containing all the *merge fields*, or field labels, which identify the fields and indicate the location of each field in the main document. Examples of merge fields are FirstName, LastName, and City. Word lists some of the most common from which you can choose but allows you to identify your own merge fields. The remaining records in the data source file contain the actual information about each individual.

After identifying the main document and the data source file, you can start the process of attaching the two documents. Word provides the Mail Merge Helper, which guides you through the process step by step. When you open the **Tools** menu and select **Mail Merge**, Word displays the Mail Merge Helper dialog box, which points out by the dimmed or undimmed state of the buttons exactly what your next step is before you can merge the two documents. The first step in the Mail Merge Helper dialog box is to create and/or edit the main document. Then, you'll create or open a data source and optionally add, delete, or modify records. Finally, you'll merge the two documents and specify the records to be merged, whether blank lines print, and how records are sorted.

Word provides a unique toolbar for the Mail Merge Helper. (For some toolbar buttons to be active, there must be an active data source file.) The toolbar buttons are:

Insert Merge Field   Word opens a list of merge fields (such as field names) from which you can select for inclusion in your letter.

Insert Word Field   Word opens a list of Word fields and functions from which you can select for inclusion in your letter.

View Merged Data   Switches between viewing merge fields and viewing actual data in the main document. If the button does not look pressed in, you can see the merge fields. Otherwise, you see the contents of the field (that is, the actual name, address, and so on).

First Record   Displays the first record in the data source file.

Previous Record   Displays the previous record in the data source file.

Go to Record   Type the number of the data source file record that you want to display.

Next Record   Displays the next record in the data source file.

Last Record   Displays the last record in the data source file.

 Mail Merge Helper   Displays the Mail Merge Helper dialog box so that you can edit or merge either the main document or the data source file.

 Check for Errors   Checks for errors in a mail merge.

 Merge to New Document   Creates a new document in which the results of the mail merge are placed. This document, which uses the mail merge defaults, shows the fields rather than the data and no longer displays the Mail Merge toolbar.

 Merge to Printer   Creates a merge document, which uses the mail merge defaults, and opens the Print dialog box from which you can print the mail merge document.

 Mail Merge   Combines the main document and the data source file to produce form letters, mailing labels, envelopes, or catalogs. When you click this button, Word displays the Merge dialog box in which you can change the defaults. The document consists of a group of sections, one for each selected record.

 Find Record   Opens the Find in Field dialog box in order to search for a search string in a particular field in the data source file.

 Edit Data Source   Opens the Data Form dialog box so that you can edit, delete, or add a record to the data source file.

Begin Guided Tour   Start a Main Document

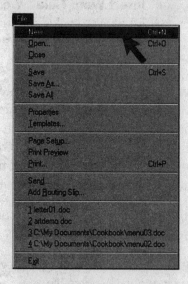

1 Start a new file by opening the **File** menu and selecting the **New** command, clicking on the **New** button, or pressing **Ctrl+N**. (Or you can open the **File** menu and select the **Open** command, click the **Open** button, or press **Ctrl+O** to open an existing document.)

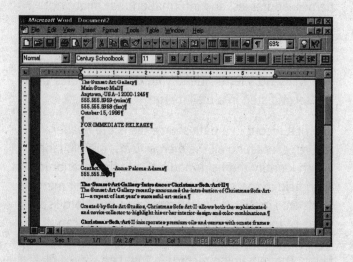

2 Type the body of the letter, omitting the unique name and address information.

Guided Tour   Start a Main Document

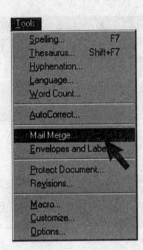

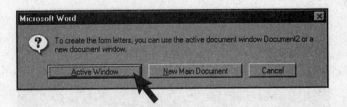

5 Click **Active Window**. (If you hadn't already created a main document, you would have clicked **New Main Document**.) Word returns you to the Mail Merge Helper.

3 Open the **Tools** menu and select the **Mail Merge** command. Word opens the Mail Merge Helper.

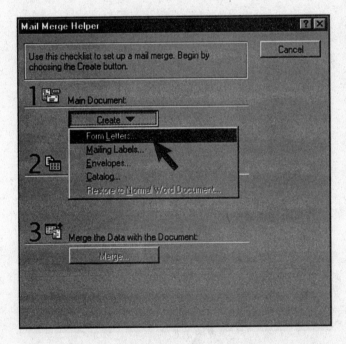

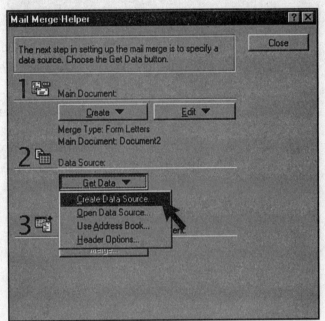

6 Click **Get Data**. Select **Create Data Source**. (If you already created a data file, you would choose **Open Data Source**.)

(continues)

4 Click **Create**, the only button that is available. Select **Form Letters**. A dialog box appears that asks what you want to use as the main document.

Guided Tour   Start a Main Document

(continued)

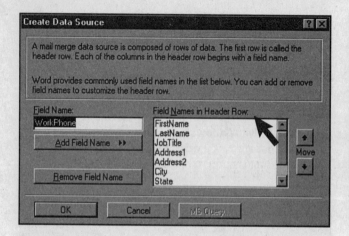

7 In the **Field Names in Header Row** list box, click a field name to be removed from the data source file, clicking on **Remove Field Name** after you select. Repeat to remove all the excess field names.

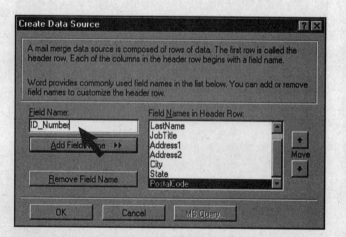

8 To add a new field name, type it in the **Field Name** text box, and click **Add Field Name**. If the name is invalid (for example, it includes spaces or characters other than the underscore, letters, and numbers, or does not start with a letter), the **Add Field Name** button is dimmed. Repeat as needed.

Although you can change the order of the field names by clicking on the Move buttons, there is no need. You can place the field names in the main document in any order that you want.

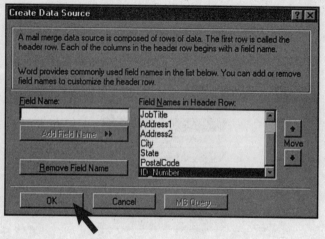

9 Click **OK**. Word opens the Save As dialog box.

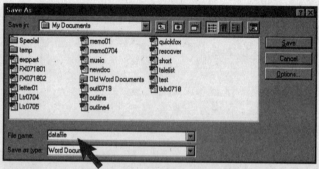

10 Type a data source file name in the **File name** text box. Click the **Save** button. Word displays an information box.

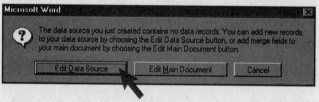

11 Click the **Edit Data Source** button. Word opens the Data Form dialog box.

Guided Tour Start a Main Document

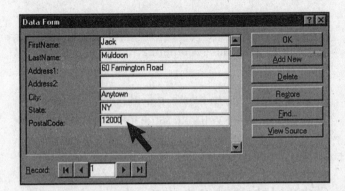

12 Type information in the field text boxes for this record. Click **Add New**.

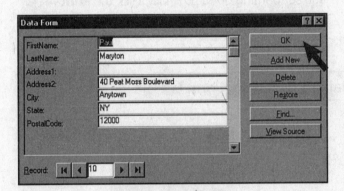

13 Continue to add records. Click **OK** to signal the end of data entry.

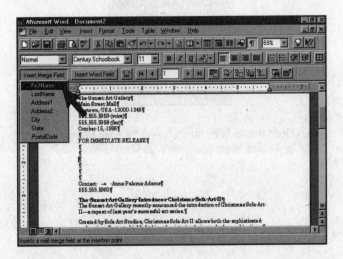

14 In the main document, click at the location in which you will insert the first merge field. Click the **Insert Merge Field** button on the Mail Merge toolbar, and select the first field to be added to the main document.

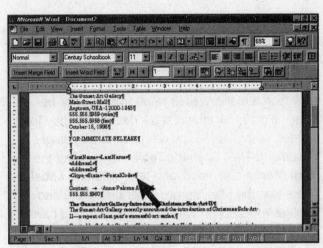

15 Repeat step 14 until the document contains all the desired merge fields. You can start new lines by pressing **Enter**, and you can insert spaces, words, and punctuation as you are inserting merge fields.

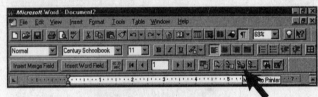

16 Click the **Merge to Printer** button. Word displays the standard Print dialog box. Click **OK** to merge and print the letters.

Create and Print Mailing Labels

There are two types of Word mailing labels: those that result from a mail merge and sheets of labels containing identical information.

Mail merge mailing labels result from the link between a main document and a data source file. To create mailing labels, you can open a new, empty document. Then open the **Tools** menu, select the **Mail Merge** command, and select **Mailing Labels**. (Note that the Mail Merge Helper dialog box also enables you to open a new document, if you haven't opened one before starting the mail merge.) Then select a new or existing data source file. Next, you select a label and specify whether your printer is a dot-matrix or laser. At this point, you create a label by

inserting merge fields and formatting them. To finish, you merge the main document and the data source file.

Word enables you to create individual mailing labels or sheets of labels with the same information (such as return address labels or even business cards). To produce mailing labels this way, open the **Tools** menu and select the **Envelopes and Labels** command. Click the **Labels** tab at the top of the Envelopes and Labels dialog box. Then select the label, specify whether your return address is added to the label, and set printing options. Finally, click the **Print** button.

Begin Guided Tour   Create and Print Mailing Labels for Form Letters

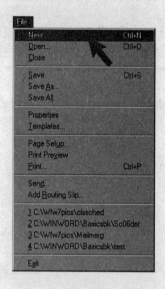

1 Start a new file by opening the **File** menu and selecting the **New** command, clicking on the **New** button, or pressing **Ctrl+N**. (Or you can wait until you start the Mail Merge Helper and create a new document there.

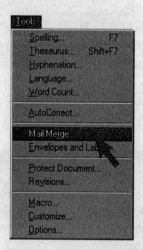

2 Open the **Tools** menu and select the **Mail Merge** command. Word opens the Mail Merge Helper.

Guided Tour   Create and Print Mailing Labels for Form Letters

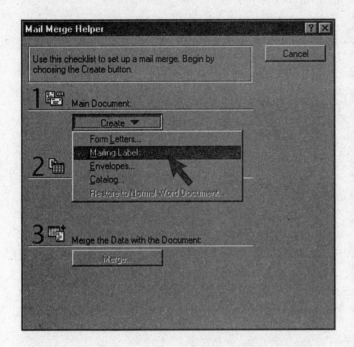

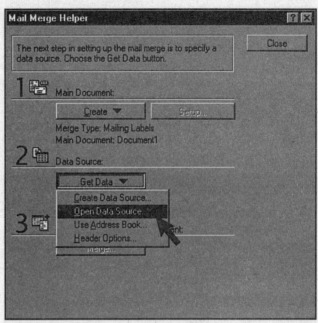

3 Click **Create**, the only button that is available. Select **Mailing Labels**.

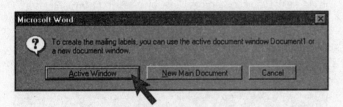

4 Click **Active Window**. (If you hadn't created a main document, you would have clicked **New Main Document**.) Word returns you to the Mail Merge Helper.

5 Click **Get Data**. Select **Open Data Source**, to use an existing data source file (or **Create Data Source**, to create a new data source file). Windows opens the Open Data Source dialog box.

To find out how to create a data source file, see "Create and Print a Form Letter" on page 289.

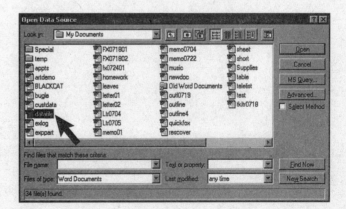

6 Double-click the data source file. Word returns to the Mail Merge Helper and then prompts you to set up your main document.

(continues)

Guided Tour Create and Print Mailing Labels for Form Letters *(continued)*

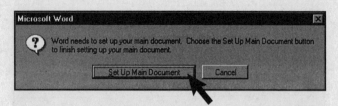

7 Click **Set Up Main Document**. Word opens the Label Options dialog box.

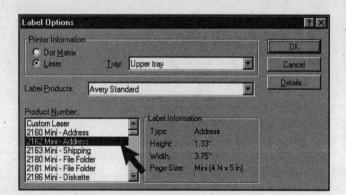

8 Click an option button to select the type of printer on which you are printing the labels. From the **Label Products** drop-down list, select a label brand. In the **Product Number** list box, select a label number, looking at the information in the Label Information box. Click **OK**. Word opens the Create Labels dialog box.

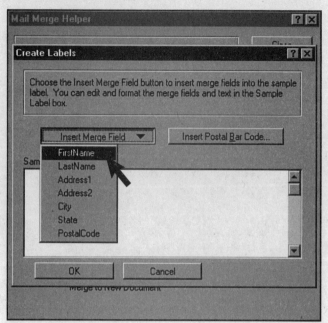

9 Click **Insert Merge Field** and choose a merge field to be inserted in the main document. Select the merge fields in the order in which you want them to appear on the label. As you insert fields, you can start new lines by pressing **Enter**, and insert spaces, punctuation, and text.

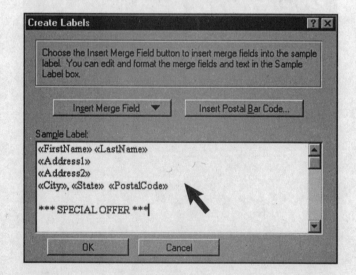

10 Repeat step 9 until the document contains all the desired merge fields. Click **OK**. Word returns to the Mail Merge Helper.

Guided Tour Create and Print Mailing Labels for Form Letters

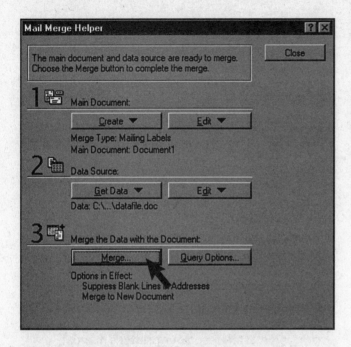

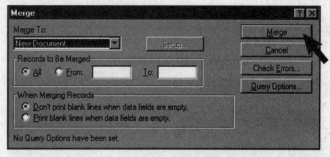

12 Click the **Merge** button. Word merges the data into the labels. After checking to see that the labels are accurate, open the **File** menu and select **Print**, press **Ctrl+P**, or click the **Print** button on the Standard toolbar.

11 Click the **Merge** button. Word displays the Merge dialog box, in which you can select the records to be merged (either All, the default, or a range of records) and indicate whether you want blank lines printed (leaving a blank line on the label) or not (there are no blank lines on the label).

Begin Guided Tour Create and Print Copies of the Same Mailing Label

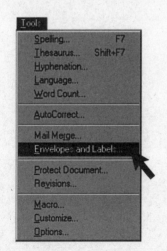

1 Insert a sheet of labels in your printer. Then open the **Tools** menu and select **Envelopes and Labels**.

(continues)

Guided Tour Create and Print Copies of the Same Mailing Label *(continued)*

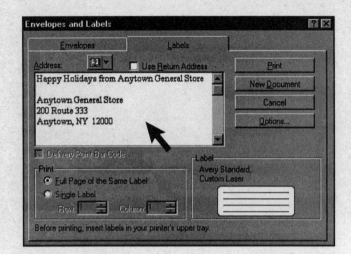

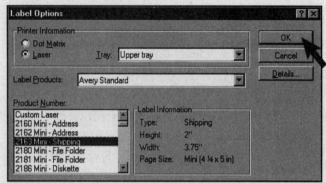

2 In the Envelopes and Labels dialog box, click the **Labels** tab, if needed. Type lines of text in the **Address** box. Click the **Full Page of the Same Label** option button. Click the **Options** button.

3 Select the type of printer, the label manufacturer, and the label number. Then click **OK** to return to the Labels tab of the Envelopes and Labels dialog box. Click **Print**.

Every printer deals with labels in its own way. For help in loading printer stock and other printing matters, see your printer's manual.

HOW TO...

Automate Work with a Macro

Macros are the means by which you can record command and keystroke sequences that you use often. To run a macro after you have recorded it, simply select one command or press a key combination. Word then executes all the commands or keystrokes that you recorded, saving you time and effort.

In this section, you'll learn how to record, run, edit, and delete macros.

What You Will Find in This Section

Record a Macro

Word provides two ways of creating macros: using the macro recorder and using the macro language. Since the macro recorder is easier to learn and to use, this section will focus only on the macro recorder. For information about using Word's WordBasic macro language, see the Word for Windows 95 manual and the Help facility.

When you turn on the macro recorder, it accumulates each command or keystroke as you enter it. After you have recorded a sequence, you can repeat the series of commands and keystrokes by running the macro. Note that the macro recorder does not record mouse movements—just their results.

> If you make a recording mistake, open the **Edit** menu and choose the **Undo** command, press **Ctrl+Z**, or click the **Undo** button on the Standard toolbar. Word will erase the mistake and will not record the undo process.

To start recording, either double-click the **REC** indicator in the status bar, or open the **Tools** menu and select the **Macro** command. Then select **Record**. When Word displays the Record Macro dialog box, you can either accept the name in the Record Macro Name box or type a name. When naming a macro, it's best to relate a macro name to the actions that you're recording. For example, if you're recording a series of actions that turn on the Ruler, you could call the macro **RulerOn**. In addition, Word does not allow you to use spaces, commas, or periods in macro names. After typing the macro name, type a description in the **Description** box—especially if you plan on recording and using many macros.

If you know that you will use this macro often, you can specify a key combination for running the macro, or you can assign a macro to a toolbar button. Just click the **Keyboard** or **Toolbars** button, respectively, in the Record Macro dialog box. When Word displays the Customize dialog box, move the insertion point to the **Press New Shortcut Key** text box, and press the desired key combination.

Word assigns many key combinations to its functions, so there is a limited combination of keys available to you; don't assign shortcut keys to every macro you create. If the key combination is already assigned, Word displays the command or macro with which it is associated. Otherwise, **(unassigned)** appears. You are more likely to find an unassigned shortcut key by pressing both **Ctrl** and **Shift**. When you have successfully pressed a shortcut key, click **Assign** and then **Close**.

Once you have named a macro and optionally assigned a key combination, Word "undims" REC in the status bar, displays the Macro Recorder toolbar, and adds an "audio tape" tail to the mouse pointer. This indicates that the macro recorder is turned on and will record every action or command that you use. To turn off the macro recorder, click the leftmost box on the Macro Recorder box; to switch between pausing and resuming recording, click the rightmost box. You also can stop recording by double-clicking on the **REC** indicator.

By default, Word saves the macro in the Normal template. However, you can copy a macro to another template. Perhaps, you'd like to keep all related templates together to distribute them to others in your workgroup by just giving them a copy of the template file, to organize your macros, to keep certain macros with a template with which they are designed to work, or to keep the Normal template free from a long list of macros.

To copy a macro to another template, click the **Organizer** key in the Macro dialog box. On the left side of the **Macros** section of the Organizer dialog box, select the template in which the macro to be copied is stored. If the template is not open, click the **Close File** button to close the current template; then click the **Open File** button and select the desired template from the Open dialog box.

If you need to open the template to which you want to copy the macro, click the **Close File** button and

the **Open File** button on the right side of the dialog box, and select the desired template from the Open dialog box. Then select one or more macros to be copied. (To select adjacent macros, click on the top macro in the range, press and hold down the **Shift** key, and then click on the bottom macro in the range.) To select noncontiguous macros, click the first macro to be chosen, press and hold down the **Ctrl** key, and then click all other macros to be chosen. Finally, click the **Copy** button and click **Close**.

Begin Guided Tour   Record a Macro

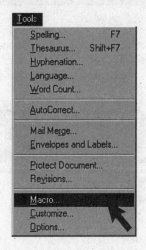

1 With a document that you want to edit on-screen, open the **Tools** menu and select the **Macro** command. Word displays the Macro dialog box.

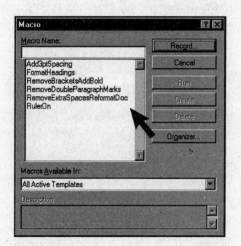

2 Click the **Record** button. Word displays the Record Macro dialog box.

(continues)

Guided Tour   Record a Macro   *(continued)*

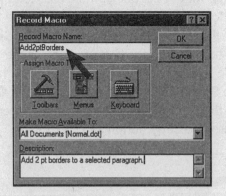

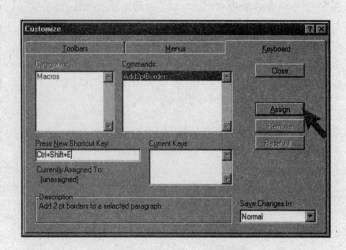

3 In the **Record Macro Name** text box, type a macro name. In the **Description** text box, type a description.

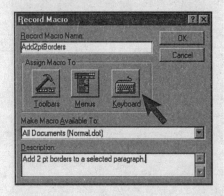

4 To define a shortcut key, click the **Keyboard** button. Word opens the Customize dialog box.

6 Click **Assign** to assign the key combination. Then click **Close**. Word returns to the document window and "undims" REC in the Status bar, displays the Macro Recorder toolbar, and adds an "audio tape" tail to the mouse pointer.

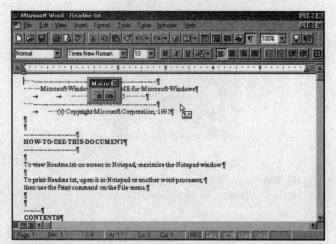

7 Perform commands or press keys that you want recorded. The macro recorder accumulates the actions as you perform them. To stop recording, either double-click the **REC** indicator, or click the **Stop** button on the Macro Recorder toolbar.

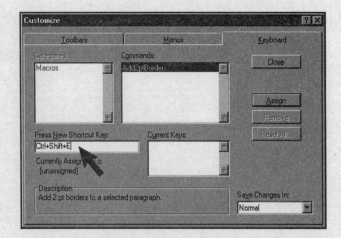

5 Click in the **Press New Shortcut Key** text box, and press the desired key combination. If the key combination is not assigned, Word displays **(unassigned)**.

Run a Macro

To run a macro, you have two choices:

- Press the assigned shortcut key.

- Open the **Tools** menu and choose the **Macro** command. In the Macro dialog box, select the macro name and select **Run**; or press **Enter** or double-click the macro name.

To find out how to assign macros to a toolbar, see "Customize an Existing Word Toolbar" on page 312 and "Create Your Own Word Toolbar" on page 317. To find out how to assign macros to a toolbar, see "Create a New Menu" on page 329 and "Customize Word Menus" on page 324.

Begin Guided Tour   Run a Macro

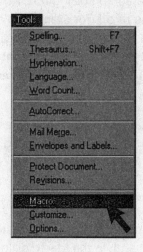

1 Open the **Tools** menu and choose the **Macro** command. The Macro dialog box appears.

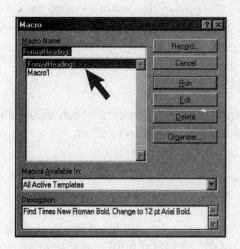

2 Double-click the name of the macro you want to run. The Macro dialog box closes and Word runs the macro.

Edit a Macro

There are two ways to edit a macro that doesn't work or that you want to modify: record it again or edit its programming statements. To rerecord a macro, follow the steps in "Record a Macro" on page 300. When Word asks you if you want to replace the existing macro, click the **Yes** button and continue recording.

Although it may be daunting when you first look at a macro's programming statements, they are relatively easy to interpret. Most statements are *neutral*; that is, they show the current document formats (for example, if you are formatting a paragraph, the statements show all the paragraph settings: indents, line spacing, and so on) and also show the settings changed by this macro.

Macro programming statements, which always end with a paragraph mark, can be short:

```
Sub MAIN
ViewRuler
End Sub
```

which tells the program that this is the start **(Sub MAIN)** and the end **(End Sub)** of a *subroutine*, a block of related programming statements that are outside the main Word program. **ViewRuler**, which is the only processing statement in the macro, tells Word to turn on the Ruler.

Or programming statements can be long (and, as a result, look quite complicated):

```
Sub MAIN
Bold
FormatParagraph .LeftIndent = "0" + Chr$(34),
    .RightIndent = + Chr$(34),
.Before = "2 pt", .After = "8 pt",
    .LineSpacingRule = 0,
.LineSpacing = "", .Alignment = 0,
    .WidowControl = 1, .KeepWithNext = .0,
.KeepTogether = 0, .PageBreak = 0, .NoLineNum
    = 0, .DontHypen = 0,
```

```
.Tab = "0", .FirstIndent = "0" + Chr$(34)
FontSize 12
End Sub
```

Sub MAIN identifies the beginning of the subroutine. **Bold** applies boldface to the selection. The paragraph starting with **FormatParagraph** names all the paragraph formatting values (for example, **.LeftIndent** is the Left text/option box, **.Before** is the Before text/option box, and **.WidowControl** is the Window/Orphan Control check box, and so on), which you can find in the Paragraph dialog box. Note that **0** indicates a setting of off (for example, a cleared check box) and **1** indicates an on setting. The **FontSize 12** statement changes the font size of the selection to 12, and **End Sub** identifies the end of the subroutine.

The main advantage of using subroutines is that programmers don't have to keep writing the same statements over and over. Instead, they can write them once and then call them from the main program whenever they are needed.

To edit a macro, open the **Tools** menu and choose the **Macro** command. In the Macro dialog box, select the macro name and select **Edit.** Then carefully edit the macro as you would any document.

When you edit a macro, Word adds the Macro toolbar above the work area. Using the toolbar buttons, you can run the macro, trace its steps, and make corrections. Macro toolbar buttons are:

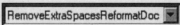

Active Macro
Names the macro that you are currently editing.

Record Opens the Record Macro dialog box so that you can record a new macro without interrupting your editing. When you finish recording, you return to the macro editing window.

Record Next Command   Turns on the macro recorder so that you can record additional commands. Either click the **Record Next Command** button or double-click the **REC** indicator in the status bar to stop recording.

Start   Starts the macro that you are editing so that you can correct a problem associated with a particular statement.

Trace   Selects the statement currently running.

Continue   Continues running the macro.

Stop   Stops running the macro.

Step   Runs the macro one statement at a time. Click this button whenever you want to run the next statement.

Step Subs   Runs the macro one sub (usually one statement) at a time. Click this button whenever you want to run the next sub.

Show Variables   Displays variables, if the current macro uses variables.

Add/Remove REM   Inserts a **REM** in front of the statement in which the insertion point is located. REM (remark) in front of a statement prevents the statement from being processed. If you are trying to find the source of a problem in a macro, sometimes turning off statements, one at a time, can point to the invalid statement.

Macro   Opens the Macro dialog box so you can select a macro for Word to run, delete, or edit; or you can record a new macro.

Dialog Editor   Opens the Dialog Editor window so you can add new elements (buttons, text, boxes, or pictures) to the macro, or edit the existing elements.

To learn more about macros, look at your Word for Windows manual and the Word Help facility.

Begin Guided Tour   Edit a Macro

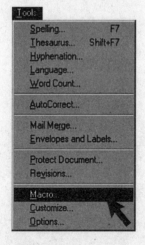

1 Open the **Tools** menu and choose the **Macro** command.

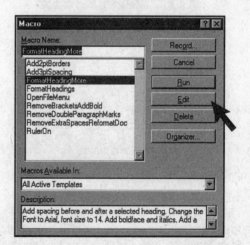

2 In the Macro dialog box, select the macro to be edited, and click the **Edit** button.

(continues)

Guided Tour   Edit a Macro   *(continued)*

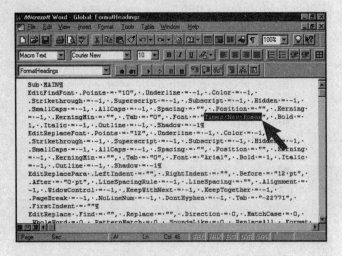

3 Edit the macro's statements. In the example, the Format Paragraph statement indicates the condition of the Paragraph dialog box. The **0**s and **1**s show whether dialog box options are cleared or turned off (**0**s), or checked or turned on (**1**s). The **Chr$(34)** inserts a double quotation mark. The following statements change the font to **Arial**, font size to **14**, and apply **boldface** and **italics** to the selection. The next statements turn on the **Borders** toolbar and "clicks" the **Top Border** button.

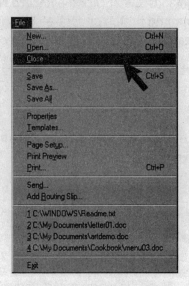

5 Open the **File** menu and choose the **Close** command.

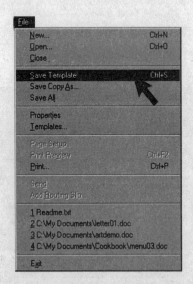

4 To save the edited macro, open the **File** menu and select **Save Template**, press **Ctrl+S**, or click the **Save** toolbar button. Click **Yes** to save the changes.

Delete a Macro

Once you have decided that a macro is no longer useful, delete it. Then you can recover the use of its assigned key combination and some disk space.

To delete a macro, open the **Tools** menu and choose the **Macro** command. In the Macro dialog box, select the macro name and select **Delete.**

Begin Guided Tour   Delete a Macro

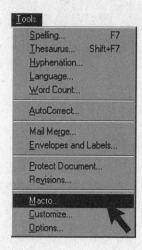

1 Open the **Tools** menu and choose the **Macro** command.

2 In the Macro dialog box, select the macro you want to delete, and click the **Delete** button. Word displays a message box.

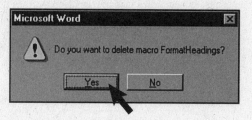

3 Click **Yes** to verify the deletion. Word removes the macro name from the Macro dialog box.

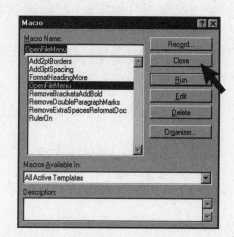

4 Click the **Close** button to close the dialog box.

PART 2

Do It Yourself

The previous part of this book described the basics of using Word for Windows 95. But simply learning how to use a tool isn't enough. You also need to learn how to actually build things.

With a word processor, the "things" that you build are documents. The contents of your documents are, of course, up to you. But in this part, you'll learn to set the stage to quickly and artfully create a wide variety of documents, such as faxes, newsletters, and flyers. You'll also learn how to customize your Word for Windows environment to make you more efficient as you create your documents.

What You Will Find in This Part

DO IT YOURSELF
Customize Your Workspace

When it comes to furniture, comfort is important. It's the same with your word processor. Chances are, you'll be spending a lot of time using Word for Windows to create documents that are important to your life.

So, like furniture, why not make Word for Windows 95 comfortable? Fortunately, you can customize Word so that it works precisely the way you want it to. Specifically, you can customize toolbars, keystroke combinations, and menus. In this section, you'll learn how.

What You Will Find in This Section

Customize an Existing Word Toolbar

In the old days before Windows, nobody envisioned toolbars with buttons on which you click to accomplish basic tasks. In those days, you did everything by typing memorized commands or by going through often unpredictable menus. Today, most of us can't live without toolbars. Clicking on a single toolbar button often replaces several easily forgotten commands from those "old days." And it speeds up procedures you do regularly, such as saving your document.

By default, Word for Windows displays the Standard toolbar and the Formatting toolbar. The Standard toolbar contains buttons for basic functions such as saving and opening files, cutting and pasting, spell checking, and undoing previous actions. The Formatting toolbar is where you can quickly set text and paragraph attributes such as styles, fonts, and sizes. You also can set attributes like boldface or italic.

In addition, Word for Windows has several other toolbars. Those toolbars are for tasks such as creating forms; adding borders and drawings; using Word as a database; and for displaying tips and tricks for using Word.

As with all default settings, the Word for Windows default toolbars strike a happy medium. Most people will be satisfied with most of the buttons most of the time. However, nobody is likely to be satisfied with all of Word's toolbar buttons all the time.

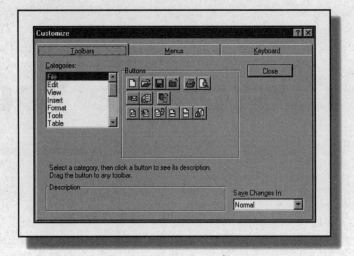

To customize Word to suit your individual needs, you can add buttons, remove buttons, or move them to other locations on Word's toolbars. For example, if you send many letters, you can put the Envelope button on the Standard toolbar. Or if you sort table entries or lists, add the Ascending Sort or Descending Sort button. Word provides buttons for many purposes, such as automating electronic mail; finding text or formats; inserting a sound file or a check box; formatting with line spacing, drop caps, subscript, superscript, and small caps; and more. This project teaches you how to tailor Word's toolbars to fit your specific needs.

Begin Do It Yourself Remove a Toolbar Button

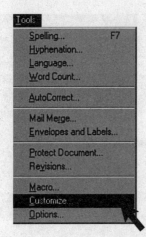

1 Open the **Tools** menu and select the **Customize** command.

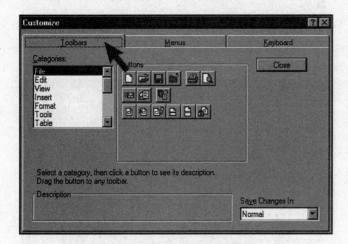

2 This displays the Customize dialog box. Click on the **Toolbars** tab, if it is not already selected.

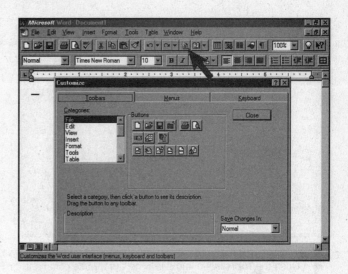

3 Position your mouse cursor over a toolbar button in your toolbar. For example, position it over the AutoFormat button in the Standard toolbar.

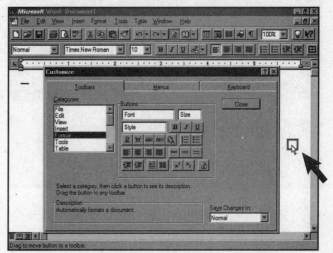

4 Hold down the left mouse button and drag the button to the work area, which is where you create your documents. Click the **Close** button of the Customize dialog box.

Begin Do It Yourself Add a Toolbar Button

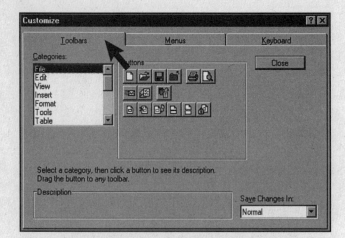

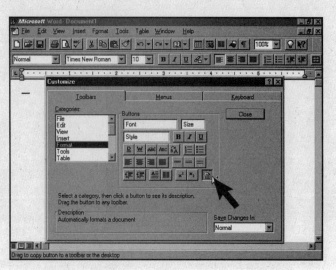

1 Open the **Tools** menu and select the **Customize** command to view the Customize dialog box. Click the **Toolbars** tab.

3 The Buttons window displays the buttons in the category you selected. Position your mouse cursor over the button you want to add (the AutoFormat button in the example) and hold down the left mouse button.

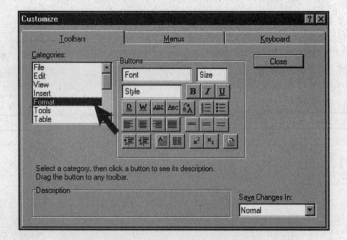

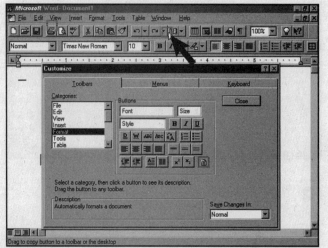

2 Select the category that contains the button you want to add from the **Categories** list. As an example, let's put the AutoFormat button back in the toolbar. In the Categories window, select **Format**.

4 With the left button still pressed, drag the button to the toolbar. Move the pointer to the place on the toolbar where you want the button to go. For example, position it to the left of the Insert Address button. Release the mouse button. Click the **Close** button of the Customize dialog box. The button you chose is now on the toolbar.

Begin Do It Yourself   Rearrange Toolbar Buttons

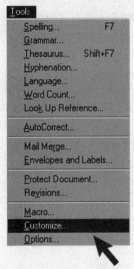

1 Open the **Tools** menu and select the **Customize** command.

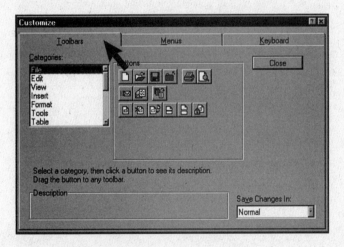

2 Click the **Toolbars** tab.

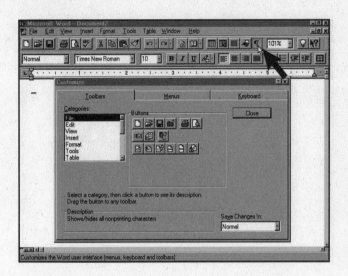

3 Click your left mouse button on the button you want to move.

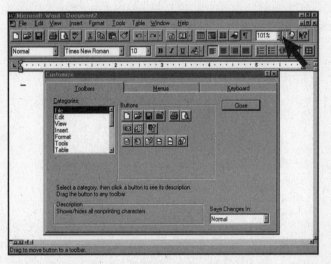

4 Drag the button to the new location.

(continues)

Do It Yourself Rearrange Toolbar Buttons

(continued)

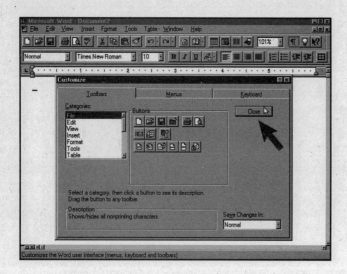

5 Release the mouse button to drop the button in its new location. Click the **Close** button to finish.

Create Your Own Word Toolbar

Word for Windows 95 standard toolbars are useful but, by definition, they are happy mediums. that is, they provide most of the functions most users need most frequently.

But everybody works differently. Perhaps, for example, you commonly use a function that isn't included in the toolbar. You can easily create your own toolbars that you can add to the top of Word for Windows. Those new toolbars can either replace the default toolbars or you can use them along with those standard toolbars.

In this way, you can customize your Word for Windows environment to work precisely the way you work. In this project, you'll learn how to make your own toolbar. While the example used in this project will create only a simple toolbar, you will learn the skills needed to create even the most complex toolbars. When you finish, your most commonly used functions will be only a mouse click away.

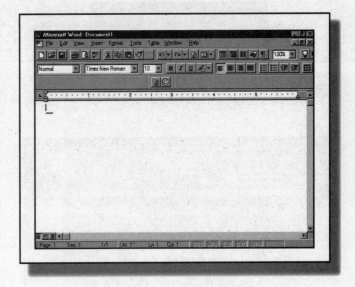

Begin Do It Yourself Create Your Own Toolbar

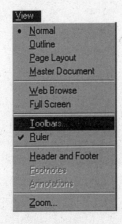

1 Open the **View** menu and select the **Toolbars** command.

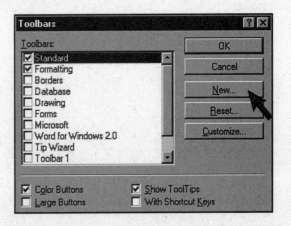

2 In the Toolbars dialog box, click the **New** button.

(continues)

Do It Yourself Create Your Own Toolbar *(continued)*

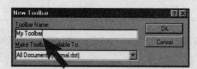

3 Type a toolbar name such as **My Toolbar** in the **Toolbar Name** text box, and click the **OK** button

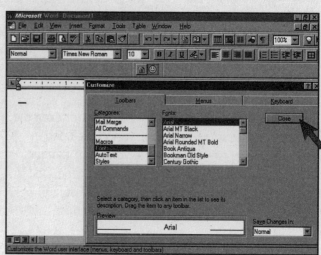

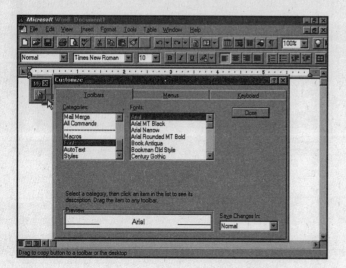

5 When you finish adding all the buttons you want, drag the new toolbar to the toolbar area above the Word work area and click the **Close** button in the Customize dialog box. You can manipulate your new toolbar as you would any other toolbar.

4 An empty toolbar and the Customize dialog box appear. Follow the steps in the previous "Add a Button" project or the steps in the next project, "Create a Button," to add buttons such as the AutoFormat button and the button for the Arial font to your toolbar.

Begin Do It Yourself Create a Button

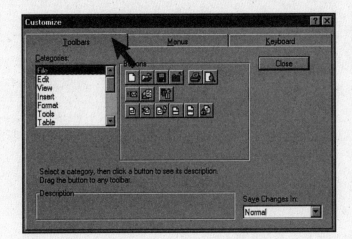

1 Open the **Tools** menu and select the **Customize** command; click the **Toolbars** tab. The Customize dialog box appears.

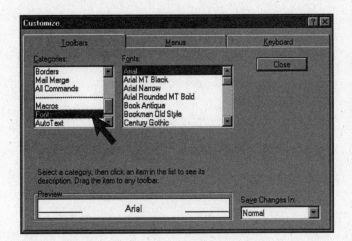

2 Select a category from the bottom of the **Categories** list box. For example, select Fonts to add a button for changing to a specific font. Notice that now, instead of being called Buttons, the list box to the right is called **Fonts**.

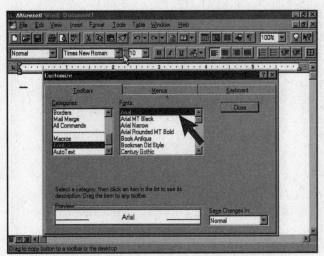

3 Position the mouse cursor over the item in the right hand list box that you want to create a button for, such as the Arial font, and hold down the left mouse button. Drag your mouse to where you want the button to appear and release the mouse button.

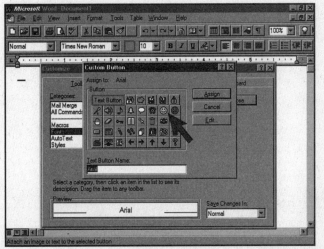

4 A blank button appears in the toolbar and the Custom Button dialog box appears on-screen. Click an icon in the Custom Button dialog box, such as the smiley face button. Alternatively, click the **Text Button** text box and type a name, such as *Arial*. This gives the button a text label instead of an icon. Then click **Assign**.

(continues)

Do It Yourself Create a Button *(continued)*

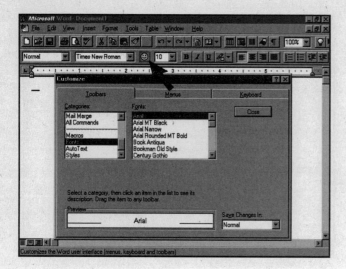

5 The new toolbar button changes to whatever you selected and the Custom Button dialog disappears. You return to the Customize dialog box. Click **Close**.

Change Keystroke Combinations

Many people find that using toolbar buttons is the simplest way to accomplish tasks in Word for Windows 95. Others prefer using the menus; while others find that using shortcut keys is fastest.

Keystroke combinations (or shortcut keys) are simply two or more keys you press to accomplish a specific task. As with most Windows applications, Word for Windows uses shortcut keys to accomplish specific tasks in addition to menu options and toolbar buttons. You can accomplish almost any task by pressing key combinations instead of using the toolbar or the menus.

Initially, many of these combinations are built into the Normal template. For example, by default, to save your current document you press **Ctrl+S**. To copy something to the Windows Clipboard, you press **Ctrl+C**. Other commonly used shortcut keys are **Ctrl+X** to cut an item, **Ctrl+V** to paste an item, and **Ctrl+N** to create a new document.

Although Word's Normal template has many shortcut keys built in, you can delete any of them and create your own. Again, the idea is to make Word work in the way that is most comfortable to you. If you don't like saving a document with Ctrl+S, you can change that combination to something else.

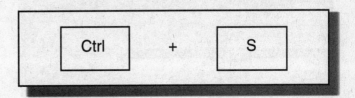

Why bother changing key combinations? One common reason is that you might have learned—and become used to—different shortcut keys when using other applications. For example, most Windows applications use Ctrl+S for saving documents. But what if you are accustomed to an old DOS application that used Ctrl+V? Rather than learn a new shortcut key, it may be easier to change Word so you can use the combination you already know.

Another reason to change shortcut keys is that you simply have a hard time remembering the default. Or, perhaps you created a macro to automate a complex task (refer to "Record a Macro" on page 300 if you don't know how to create macros). You may want to assign a keystroke to that macro to quickly execute it.

In this project, you'll learn how to customize Word to fit your needs by deleting existing shortcut keys and creating new ones.

Begin Do It Yourself   Delete a Keystroke Combination

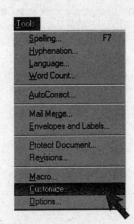

1 Open the **Tools** menu and select the **Customize** command. The Customize dialog box appears.

(continues)

Do It Yourself Delete a Keystroke Combination *(continued)*

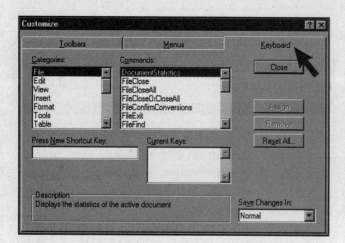

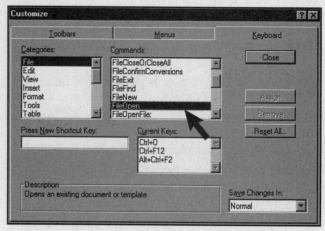

2 Click the **Keyboard** tab.

4 Click the task in the **Commands** window that corresponds to the keystroke you want to delete. For example, click **FileOpen**. The shortcut keys assigned to this task appear in the Current Keys list box.

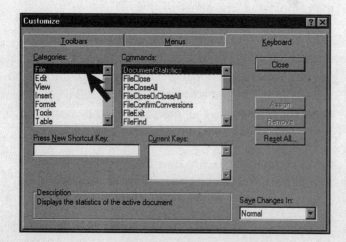

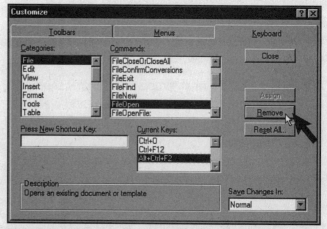

3 Select the category of tasks that corresponds to the keystroke you want to delete from the categories list box. For example, click **File**. All the file related tasks appear in the Commands list box.

5 Click the combination in the **Current Keys** list box that you want to delete. For example, click **Alt+Ctrl+F2**. Then click the **Remove** button. That shortcut key no longer appears in the Current Keys list box. Click the **Close** button to exit the Customize dialog box.

Begin Do It Yourself Add a Keystroke Combination

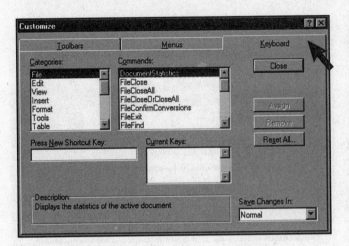

1 Open the **Tools** menu and select the **Customize** command. In the Customize dialog box, click the **Keyboard** tab.

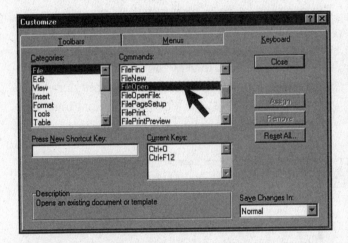

2 In the **Categories** list box, select the category that contains the task you want to assign a shortcut key. For example, select **File**. Then select the task you want, such as **File Open**, from the **Commands** window.

You must include a so-called *control key*, such as Ctrl, Alt, or Shift in any shortcut keys you create. However, those keys alone can't comprise shortcut keys. You must also include "regular" keys such as letters and numbers.

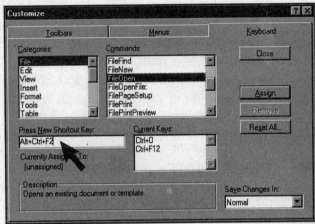

3 Click in the **Press New Shortcut Key** text box. Then press the keys you want to use as the shortcut key. For example, press **Alt**, **Ctrl** and **F2** at the same time. The combination appears in the **Current keys** list box.

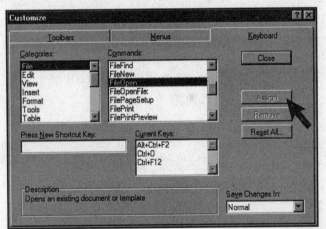

4 Click the **Assign** button. If your current template is *not* Normal and you want to affix the new keystroke to that template, select it in the **Save Changes In** drop-down list. Click the **Close** button to exit the Customize dialog box.

If the shortcut key you choose is already in use by another function, Word tells you that fact below the **Press New Shortcut Key** text box. You can still assign that keystroke to the function of your choice, but it will no longer be available to the previous function.

Customize Word Menus

Keystroke combinations are fast and clicking on toolbar buttons is convenient. But there are many more commands in Word for Windows than can fit in a toolbar. Nor can most people remember all the shortcut keys for all of Word's commands. That's why you go into the menus for those tasks.

Word's default menus are well organized and consistent. This means that even if you don't remember precisely where in the menu structure a command is, you still can usually figure it out. For example, all file-related tasks, such as saving a file, are, quite logically, in the File menu. Want to add or fine-tune a table to your document? What could be more obvious than the Table menu?

However, like any aspect of a software program, some elements of menu organization may work for you and some may not. Word for Windows 95 provides the tools for you to create your own custom menu structure so that the program works precisely the way you want. In this project, we'll learn how to delete and rearrange menus.

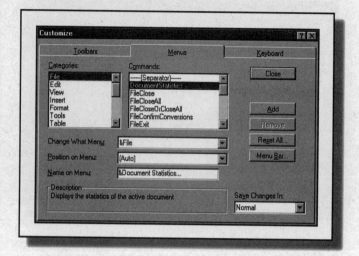

You'll also learn how to change menu *shortcut keys*. These are the letters in menus that are underlined. These enable you to use your keyboard instead of your mouse for accessing the contents of menus. For example, by default, to view the File menu, you could press **Alt+F**. Within that menu, to save your document, you could press the letter **S**. Note that the **S** in Save is underlined.

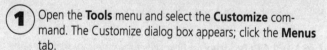

Begin Do It Yourself Change a Shortcut Key

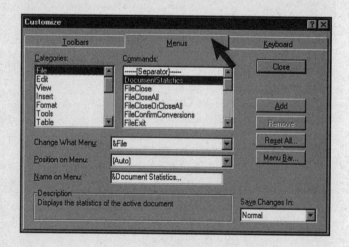

1 Open the **Tools** menu and select the **Customize** command. The Customize dialog box appears; click the **Menus** tab.

Do It Yourself Change a Shortcut Key

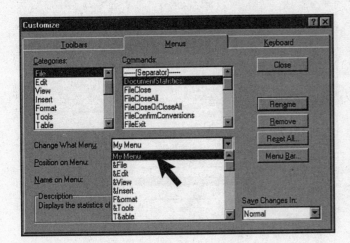

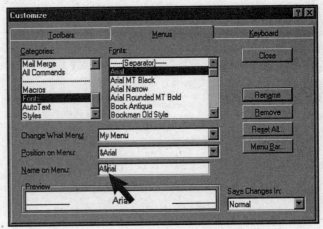

2 In the **Change What Menu** drop-down list, select the name for your menu, such as **My Menu**.

4 In the **Name on Menu** text box, notice it is written as **&Arial**. The next letter after the ampersand is the shortcut key as it appears in the menu. Position your cursor in the **Name on Menu** text box. Delete the ampersand (**&**) before the **A** and type an ampersand before the **R**.

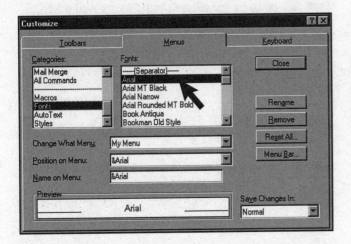

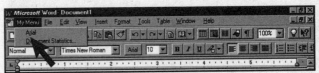

5 Click the **Rename** button; then click the **Close** button. Check your sample menu. The shortcut key is now **r**.

3 In the **Categories** list box, select **Fonts**. In the **Fonts** list box, select a font such as **Arial**.

Begin Do It Yourself   Move a Menu Item

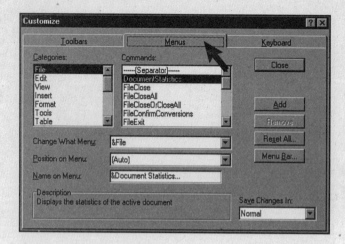

1 Open the **Tools** menu and select the **Customize** command. Click the **Menus** tab.

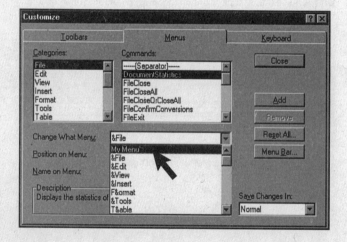

2 In the **Change What Menu** drop-down list, select the name of the menu that contains the item you want to move. For example, select **My Menu**.

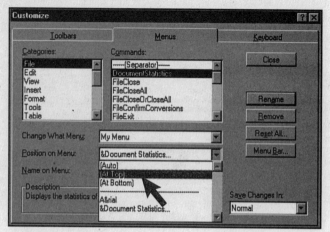

3 In the **Categories** list box, click **File** and in the **Commands** list box select a command—in this example, we'll select **Document Statistics**. Click the down arrow for the **Position in Menu** drop-down list and select **At Top**. Click the **Add** button. This adds an identical menu item to the top of My Menu. Click **Close** to exit the Customize dialog box.

Begin Do It Yourself Remove a Menu Item

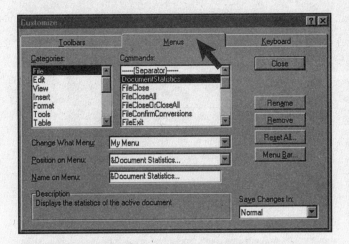

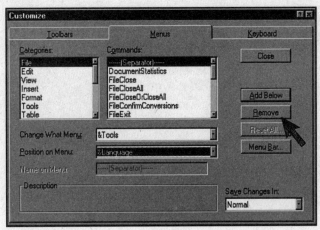

1 Open the **Tools** menu and select the **Customize** command. Click the **Menus** tab.

3 Click the **Remove** button to remove the menu selection. Then click the **Close** button to exit the Customize dialog box.

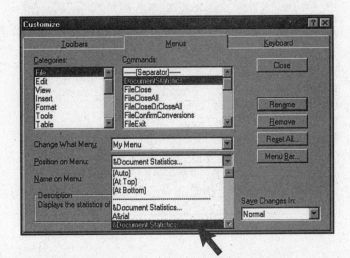

2 In the **Change What Menu** drop-down list, select the menu from which you want to remove an item. In the **Position in Menu** drop-down, select the item you want to remove.

Begin Do It Yourself Remove a Menu

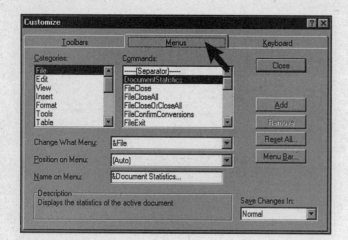

1 Open the **Tools** menu and select the **Customize** command. Click the **Menus** tab.

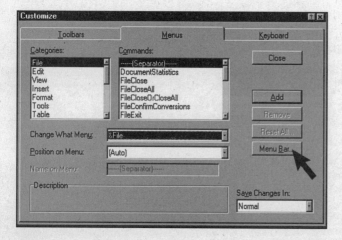

2 Click the **Menu Bar** button.

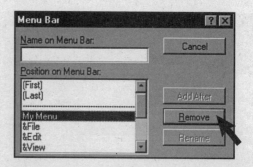

3 Highlight the menu you want to get rid of in the **Position on Menu Bar** list box. Then click the **Remove** button.

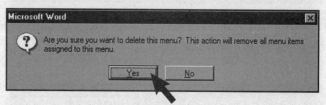

4 In the message box asking you to confirm that you want to remove the menu item, click **Yes**. Then click the **Cancel** button in the Menu Bar box to return to the Customize dialog box. Click the **Close** button to finish the task.

A fast way to reestablish Word's default menu system is to click the **Reset All** button in the Customize dialog box.

Create a New Menu

When creating Word for Windows 95, Microsoft obviously refused to subscribe to the one-size-fits-all theory of software development. At the core of this program, you can bend and shape it to make it work the way you do.

In previous projects, you learned how to do tasks such as changing shortcut keys and toolbars to fit how you work. But, arguably, the most common way of getting things done in Word for Windows is to access functions in the menus.

Not surprisingly, then, you can change Word's menus to virtually anything you want. You can add new main menu headings and, within existing menus, you can add and delete commands. You also can change the order in which the menu commands appear.

Why bother? One reason may be that you are used to the menu structure in another application. Another may be that, for whatever reasons, Word's menu structure simply doesn't fit for the way you work.

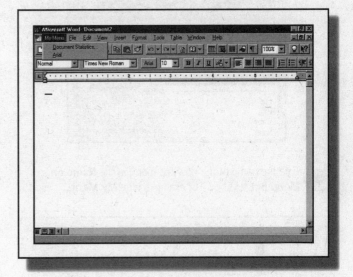

Whatever the reason, this project will teach you to change existing menus and create your own. This is yet another way in which you can tailor Word for Windows 95 to work precisely the way you do.

Begin Do It Yourself   Create a New Menu on the Menu Bar

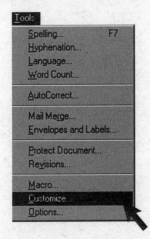

1 Open the **Tools** menu and select the **Customize** command.

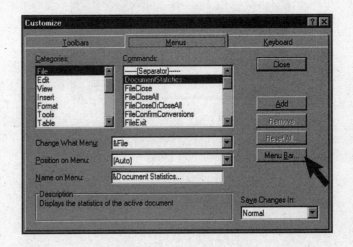

2 Click the **Menus** tab to display the options for altering menus. Then click the **Menu Bar** button; the Menu Bar dialog box appears.

(continues)

Do It Yourself Create a New Menu on the Menu Bar *(continued)*

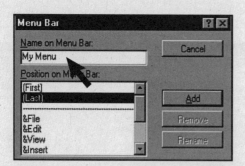

3 Type the name of the new top menu in the **Name on Menu Bar** text box. For example, type **My Menu.**

Notice that in the default menus, all commands have a letter underlined. These are shortcut keys; you can press those keys on your keyboard rather than using your mouse to click on the command. Shortcut keys aren't used in this project for the sake of simplicity. To add a shortcut key, however, place an ampersand (&) before the key you want as the shortcut in the **Name on Menu** text box.

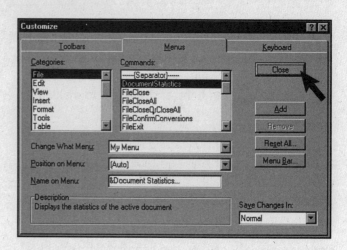

5 In the Customize dialog box, click the **Close** button.

6 Your new menu appears in the toolbar. Note that it won't open until you add menu commands.

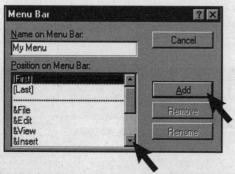

4 Click the down arrow for the Position on Menu Bar drop-down-list. Select a location for your new menu and click the **Add** button. Then click **Close.**

Begin Do It Yourself Add a Menu Item to Your New Menu

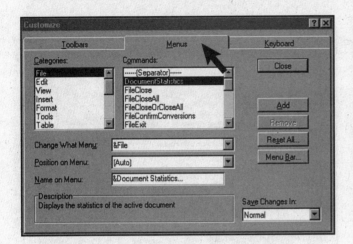

1 Open the **Tools** menu and select the **Customize** command. On the Customize dialog box, click the **Menus** tab.

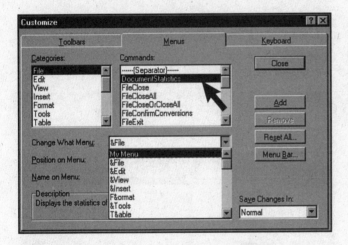

2 Click the down arrow of the **Change What Menu** drop-down list. Select the menu you created in the last part of this project—our example was **My Menu**.

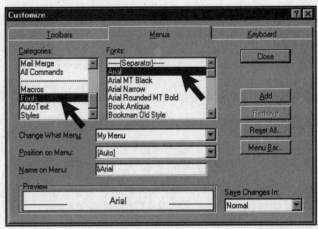

3 In the **Categories** window, click **Fonts**. In the **Fonts** window, select a font; in this example, we'll use **Arial**. Click **Add**.

4 Repeat the process in this section to add another item to My Menu. When you finish adding items, click **Close** to exit the Customize dialog box. If you want, follow this example: In the Customize dialog box, select **Files** in the **Categories** list box and **Document Statistics** in the Commands list box.

Change Your Default Directory

It's only natural to want to be organized. Socks go in one drawer, shirts in another—that sort of thing. The same is true with the documents you create. For easier retrieval and a greater sense of order, you want your program files, such as those needed to run Word, in one folder and your documents in another.

This brief project sets the default folder in which Word for Windows 95 will save new documents. This default folder will be the one that appears in the dialog box when you click the **Open** icon or select **File Open**. First, we'll create a new folder. Then, we'll set Word for Windows so that the new folder is the default for saving your documents.

Of course, you can create as many folders as you want for your documents and select any one of them as your default document folder. But we'll keep it simple in this project and only create one new folder.

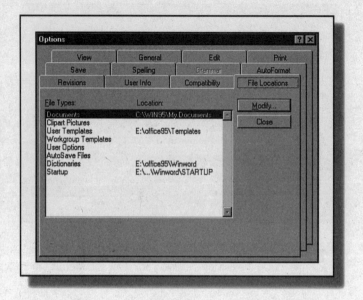

Begin Do It Yourself   Create a New Folder

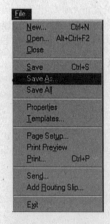

1 Select the **File** menu and the **Save As** command. This displays the Save As dialog box. We won't actually save a document, but rather use this dialog to create a new folder.

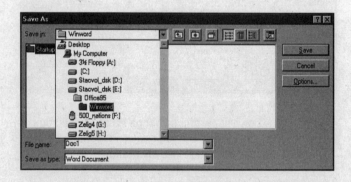

2 Click the down arrow of the **Save in** drop-down list. Select the folder *below* which you want to create the new folder. In this case, select the **Winword** folder that was created during installation. This is the folder in which your Word program files are stored.

Do It Yourself   Create a New Folder

If you use Microsoft Office, Winword will be a subfolder of MSOffice. If you don't use Microsoft Office, the Winword folder probably will be a subfolder to your main drive's folder, such as C:\WINWORD.

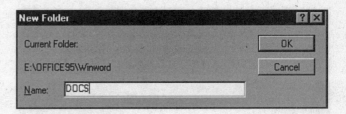

4 The New Folder dialog appears. Type the name of your new folder—for example, Personal Documents—in the **Name** text box. Click **OK** to return to the Save As dialog box.

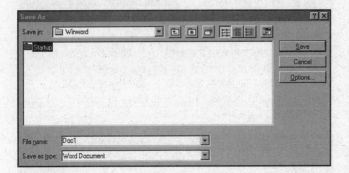

3 Click the **Create New Folder** button, which is the third button from the left at the top of the dialog box.

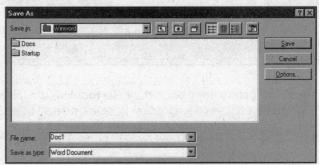

5 Notice that a new folder named **Personal Documents** now appears in the main window of the Save As dialog box. Click **Cancel** to finish.

Begin Do It Yourself   Make the New Folder Your Default

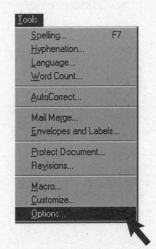

1 Open the **Tools** menu and select the **Options** command.

(continues)

Do It Yourself Make the New Folder Your Default

(continued)

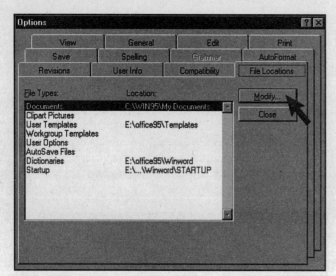

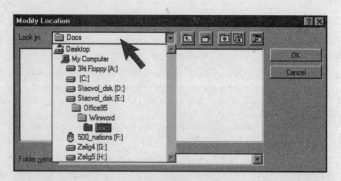

4 If you aren't sure of the path, click the down arrow of the **Look in** drop-down list. Locate your drive in the list and then the WINWORD folder and DOCS subfolder. Click **OK** to return to the Options dialog box. Click **Close** to finish.

2 In the Options dialog box, click the **File Locations** tab. This is where you set default locations for several different types of files, including your documents. In the **File Types** window, click **Documents**. Then click the **Modify** button. The Modify Location dialog box appears.

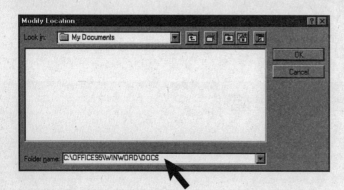

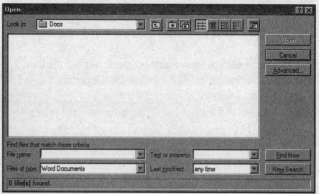

5 Click the **Open** button in the Standard toolbar or select **File Open**. The default directory should now be DOCS.

3 Type the path of the folder you created in the **Folder name** text box. Suppose that you created a DOCS folder as shown in the example in the preceding set of steps. If WINWORD is installed on your C:\ folder, that path would be C:\WINWORD\DOCS. If Microsoft Office is on your C:\ drive, type **C:\MSOffice\Winword\Personal Documents**.

DO IT YOURSELF

Customize Document Appearance

Let's face it: appearance is important. The appearance of your documents conveys a lot to those who read them.

For example, if you put a border around text and give it a gray background, it tells readers that this is important information. Some type fonts convey a more formal feeling while others make your document seem more casual. In this section, you'll learn how to customize the appearance of your document so that it more truly reflects what you want to say.

Change the Default Font and Font Size

When you start a new document, you also affix a *template* to it. Word templates can contain text, images, macros, and information about the on-screen display, such as the Zoom level. If you don't designate a specific template, Word for Windows automatically uses the Normal template.

Within templates are styles. Each style contains specific text formatting information that you apply to your documents. The default style within a template, confusingly, also is Normal. Text in the Normal style in the Normal template is, by default, ten-point Times New Roman type.

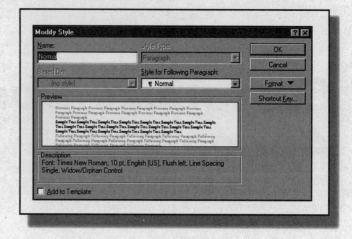

Times New Roman is a perfectly fine type font. And ten-point type is a nice and commonly used type size. But maybe those choices don't suit you. Bigger type would be easier to see, for example. Or maybe you prefer the appearance of another type font. With Word, you need never settle for the defaults, as you'll learn in this project.

Several projects in this part of the book create both styles and templates for specific uses, such as letterhead and fax cover sheets. But this is our first project, so let's start simple. To show that you aren't stuck with the defaults, you'll make some simple changes to the Normal style to change the standard font and size.

Making a Backup of the Normal Template

Because changes we'll make to the Normal template will have an impact on new documents you create, let's first create a copy. That way, you can easily restore the original Normal template if the changes we make in this project don't suit you.

This simple task will take just a moment. We'll accomplish it from the Windows Explorer.

1. In the Windows taskbar, click on the **Start** button. Then select **Programs** and the **Windows Explorer**. This displays the Explorer window.

2. In the "All Folders" window on the left side, select the drive and folder containing your templates. If you are a Microsoft Office user, that will be in the Templates subfolder of the MSOffice folder. If you bought Word for Windows separately, that will be in the *???* folder/ subfolder.

3. Once you are viewing the folder, click once on the document called **Normal**.

4. With the Normal template document highlighted, select **Edit Copy**. Then select **Edit Paste**.

A new document called **Copy of Normal** appears in the folder. That is your backup copy of your original Normal template. No matter how much you change your Normal template, you can always return to the original. If you want to revert to the original template, simply delete or rename the Normal template. Then change the name of the copy to **Normal**.

Begin Do It Yourself Change the Default Font and Size

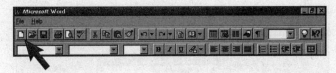

1 Start a new document that uses the Normal template by clicking on the new document icon in the toolbar.

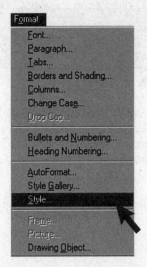

2 Open the **Format** menu and select the **Style** command.

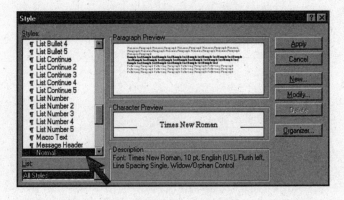

3 This displays the Style dialog box. Make sure that Normal is highlighted in the **Styles** window. Then click on the **Modify** button.

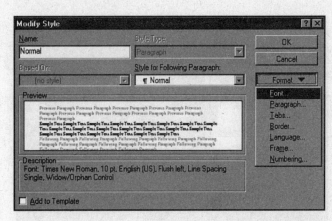

4 The Modify Style dialog box appears on-screen. Click the **Format** button; then select the **Font** command from the list that appears.

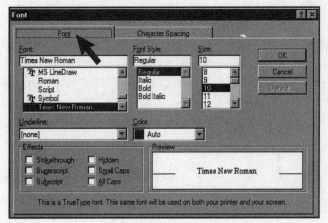

5 In the Font dialog box, click on the **Font** tab.

(continues)

Do It Yourself Change the Default Font and Size *(continued)*

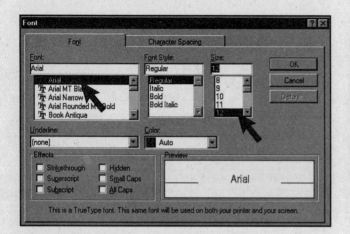

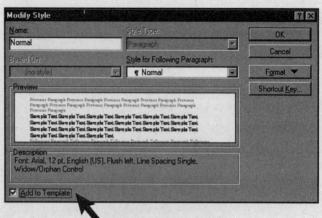

6 In the Font list box, select a font other than Times New Roman, such as Arial. In the **Size** window, select another font size, such as 12. Click the **OK** button to close the Font dialog box.

7 Back in the Modify Style dialog box, make the changes permanent by clicking the **Add to Template** check box in the bottom left corner. A check mark should appear. Click the **OK** button to finish. Click **Apply** to close the Style dialog box.

Create Styles

If you find yourself frequently switching to a different font than the default, you can speed up the process by creating a character style. This is a style that you can apply only to selected text. By contrast, a paragraph style such as Normal applies to an entire paragraph.

When would you use a character style? Say you are writing a newsletter and you want to put the name of your organization in a special type font. Or you are creating an invitation and you want to mix up fonts to give the invitation a varied appearance.

Anytime you mix up fonts within a paragraph, character styles can speed up your job. This project will teach you how to create a paragraph style.

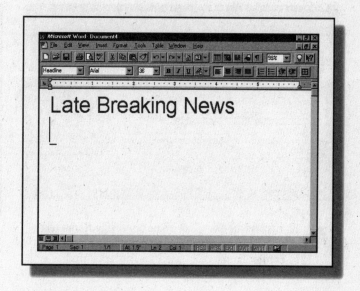

Begin Do It Yourself   Create a New Paragraph Style

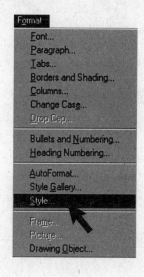

1 Start a new document. Then open the **Format** menu and select the **Style** command.

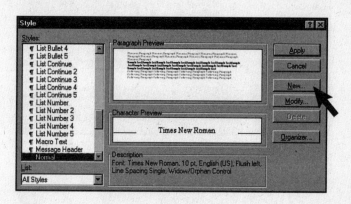

2 In the Style dialog box, click the **New** button.

(continues)

Do It Yourself Create a New Paragraph Style *(continued)*

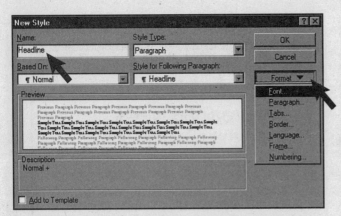

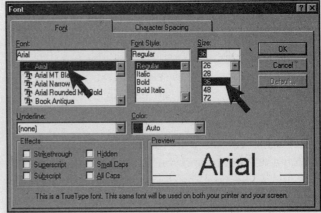

3 This displays the New Style dialog box. In the **Name** text box, type a name for your style, such as **Headline**. Click the **Format** button; then select the Font command.

5 In the **Font** window, select a font such as Arial. In the **Size** window, select a size such as 36.

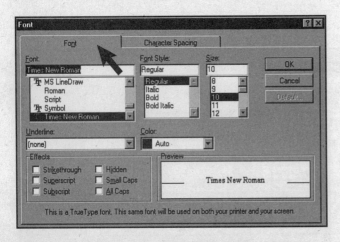

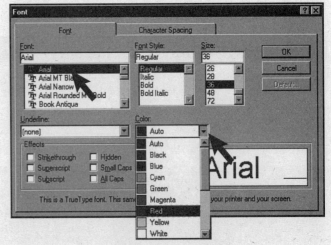

4 In the Font dialog box, click on the **Font** tab.

6 In the **Color** drop-down list, select a color other than black, such as red. Click **OK**.

Do It Yourself   Create a New Paragraph Style

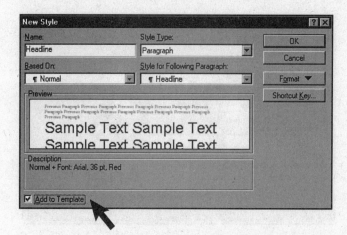

7 This returns you to the Modify Style dialog box. To make the changes permanent, click on the **Add to Template** check box in the bottom left corner. A check mark should appear. Click **OK** to finish, then click **Apply** to leave the Style dialog box.

Begin Do It Yourself   Create a Character Style

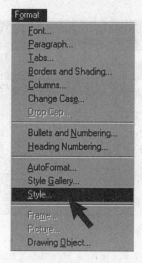

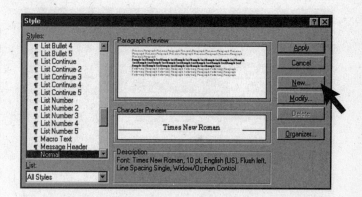

1 Start a new document. Open the **Format** menu and select the **Style** command.

2 The Style dialog box appears, which lists all available paragraph and character styles. Click the **New** button.

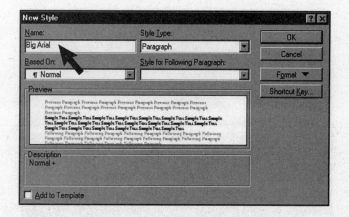

3 In the New Style dialog box, type a name for your style, such as Big Arial, in the **Name** text box.

(continues)

Do It Yourself   Create a Character Style

(continued)

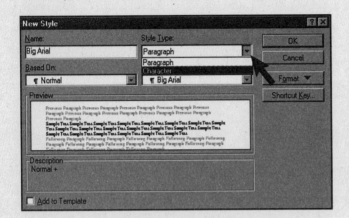

4 Click on the down arrow for the **Style Type** drop-down list. Select **character**, which tells Word you are creating a character style, not a paragraph style.

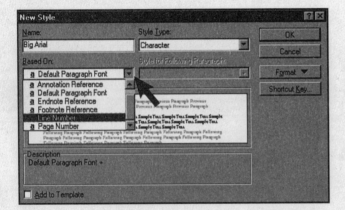

5 Select another character style on which to base your new style in the **Based On** drop-down list. This selects another style to serve as a starting point for your new style.

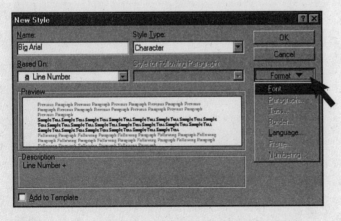

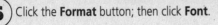

6 Click the **Format** button; then click **Font**.

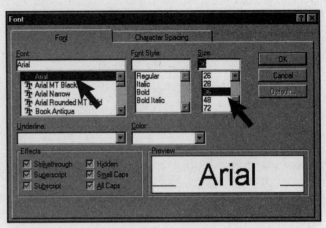

7 The Font dialog box appears. Click on a font name, such as Arial, in the **Font** list box. Click on a size, such as 36, in the **Size** window. Click **OK**.

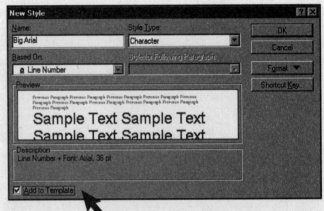

8 You will return to the New Style dialog box. Click the **Add To Template** check box in the lower left corner. A check mark should appear. Click **OK**. Click the **Apply** button to exit the Style dialog box.

Begin Do It Yourself Apply a Character Style

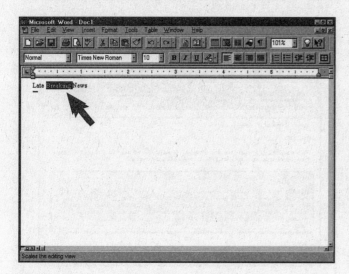

1 Highlight the characters or words to which you want to apply the character style.

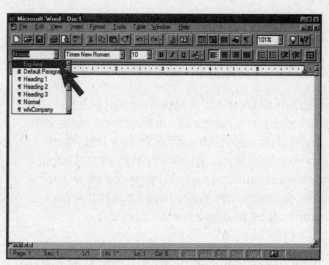

3 Select the character style you want. Character styles have an underlined <u>a</u> to the left of the style name.

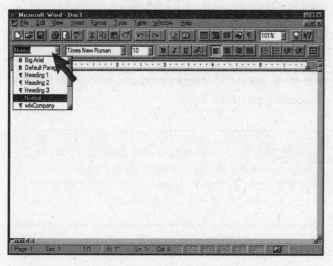

2 Click the down arrow of the Style dialog box in the Formatting toolbar.

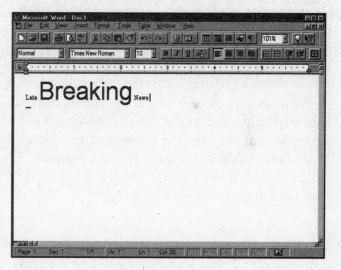

4 Word applies the character style to the selected text.

Add Borders and Shading to Text

In this project, you will learn to add borders that surround paragraphs and to add background shading to paragraphs.

This not only varies the appearance of your documents, but it is particularly useful for giving readers visual clues about what is particularly important. For example, if you are writing a document about a procedure and one part of the procedure is particularly dangerous, you might want to set that paragraph off by placing a border around it.

Shading paragraphs is another way to emphasize them and set them off from other text. Note that shading is different than coloring. Shading is a percentage of gray. A five-percent shading would add just a bit of gray to the background while a 95-percent shading would be much darker. You also can select foreground patterns for the shading from the shading drop-down list. You'll learn how to add color foreground patterns later in this project.

In this project, you'll learn how to add both borders and shading. As with all methods of enhancing the appearance of documents, it is easy to overdo it when you add borders around paragraphs. One important tip is to only add borders and shading to paragraphs that need to stand out from the others.

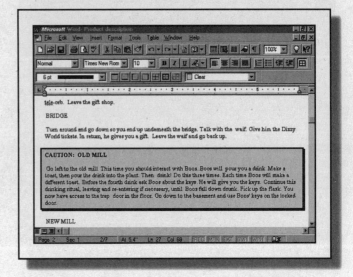

Another tip is to work in Page Layout mode so you can better see the effect of adding borders and shading to paragraphs. To switch to this mode, in which the page appears on-screen just as it will when you print, open the **View** menu and select the **Page Layout** command.

Note that you can't add borders or shading to words or sentences within a paragraph. The procedures in this project only enable you to add borders and shading to entire paragraphs.

Begin Do It Yourself   Add a Border Around a Paragraph

1 Click the **Borders** button in the Standard toolbar. This causes the Borders toolbar to appear.

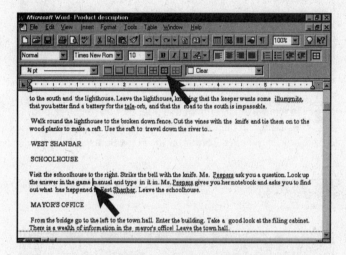

2 Position your mouse cursor anywhere in the paragraph to which you want to add a border. To place a border entirely around the paragraph, click the **Outside Border** button on the Borders toolbar.

The other formatting toolbar buttons enable you to place borders only on the top, bottom, left, and right sides of the paragraph. The **Inside Border** button is for adding borders to cells in tables. Read "Create a Table" on page 202 to learn how to add tables.

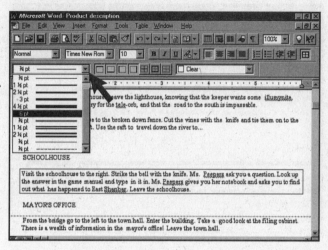

3 To change the thickness or style of the line, click on the down arrow of the **Line Style** drop-down list. Click on the thickness or line style you want. Click on the **Outside Border** button of the Borders toolbar.

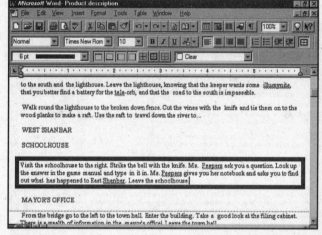

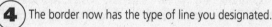

4 The border now has the type of line you designated.

Begin Do It Yourself   Remove a Border

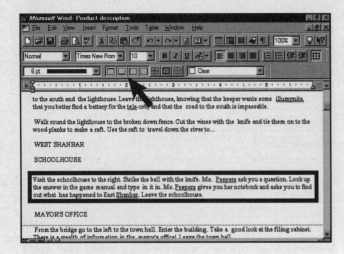

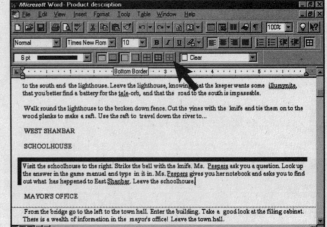

1 Position your cursor anywhere in the bordered paragraph. Notice that the buttons for the top, bottom, left, and right borders appear depressed in the toolbar.

2 To remove a border from one side, click on its corresponding button in the toolbar. You can remove all borders at once by clicking the **No Border** button in the Borders toolbar.

Begin Do It Yourself   Add Shading to a Paragraph

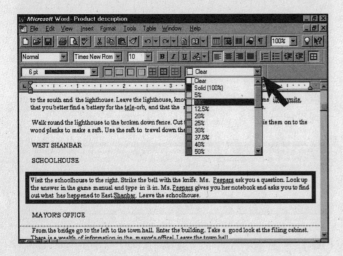

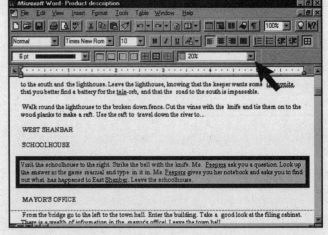

1 Position your cursor anywhere in the paragraph to which you want to add shading. Click the down arrow of the shading drop-down list on the Borders toolbar and select the amount of shading you want.

2 Word applies the shading you chose to the paragraph. To remove the shading, click the down arrow of the shading drop-down list on the Borders toolbar and select **Clear**.

You may need to experiment a bit with shading to find precisely the correct setting, because some settings can make type difficult to read. You can correct this problem by changing the shading and also by changing to a larger type.

Begin Do It Yourself Fine Tune Borders

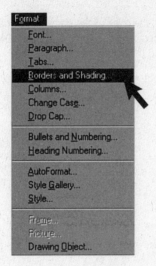

1 Place the mouse cursor anyplace in the paragraph around which you want the border. Then open the **Format** menu and select the **Borders and Shading** command.

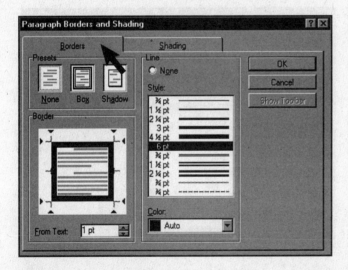

2 Click the **Borders** tab.

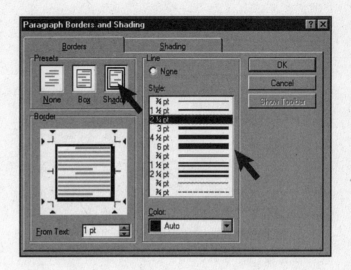

3 To add a shadowed border, click the **Shadow** button. Select a line thickness or style for the shadowed border in the **Style** window.

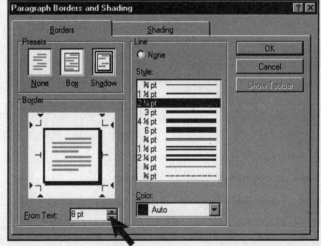

4 To specify a specific distance you want the border to be away from text, pick a number in the **From Text** rotary box. The default distance is one point—for this project, experiment with, say, an eight-point distance.

Points are a traditional way of measuring type; they actually are $1/72$nd of an inch. The default type size in the Normal template is 10 points. You may need to experiment with measuring in this way.

(continues)

Do It Yourself Fine-Tune Borders *(continued)*

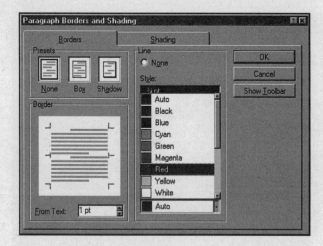

5 To change the color of the border, click the **Color** down arrow. Select a color from the list. Click **OK** when you finish fine-tuning the border.

Begin Do It Yourself Fine-Tune Shading

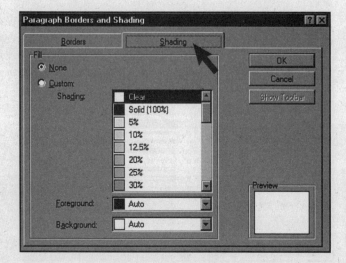

1 Place the cursor anywhere in the paragraph to which you want to apply shading. Then open the **Format** menu and select the **Borders and Shading** command. Click the **Shading** tab.

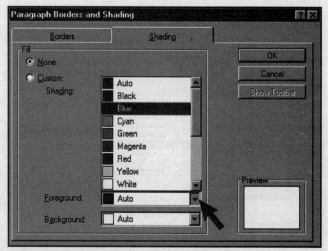

2 Click the down arrow on the **Foreground** drop-down list. From the list, select a color for the foreground of the shading. You can think of foreground color as the color of the shading pattern.

Do It Yourself   Fine-Tune Shading

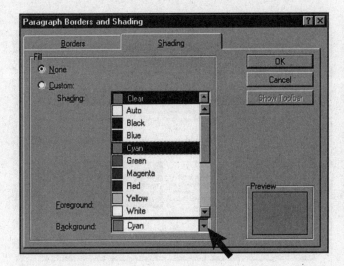

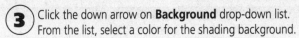

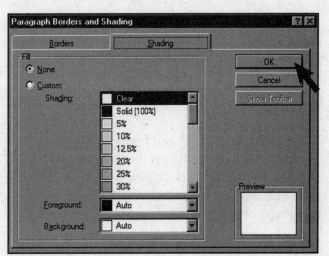

3 Click the down arrow on **Background** drop-down list. From the list, select a color for the shading background.

4 Click **OK** to apply the shading to the paragraph.

Add a Text Frame

You learned in the previous project how to spiff up your documents by adding shading and borders to paragraphs. This project teaches you how to add a specialized type of appearance enhancer: *text frames*.

You've undoubtedly seen text frames many times. For example, text frames are used for so-called pull-out quotes in magazine articles. These are quotes from the article that are important enough to appear in larger type outside the main article.

Another example is commonly found in newsletters. This would be a list of articles in the newsletter, typically found on the first page. In fact, the newsletter heading itself, which includes the newsletter's name, often is in a text frame.

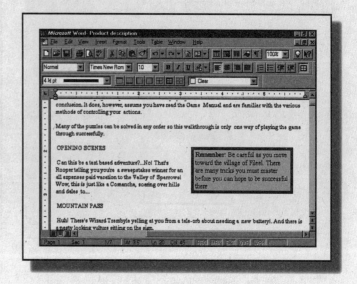

Text frames are a staple of professional designers and layout artists. They provide a lot of flexibility for improving the appearance of documents that you will show to others. You can use them to make your documents more readable and appear more professional.

Best of all, in Word for Window 95, creating and embellishing text frames is a simple task. You will learn how to add a simple text frame and how to move it to different locations in your document. You'll also learn how to resize it and add shading and borders.

To add and modify text frames, you must be in Word's Page Layout view. This is a view in which on-screen appearance is the same as the final printed product. If you aren't in Page Layout view, open the **View** menu; then select the **Page Layout** command.

To do this project, you need to create a sample document that is at least a page long. This is the document in which you will add a frame. As a precaution, don't use a file that is important—we will be changing it in this project and you might forget to change it back.

Begin Do It Yourself   Add a Text Frame

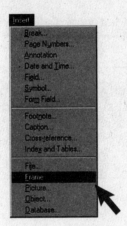

1 With your sample document loaded and Word in Page Layout view, open the **Insert** menu and select the **Frame** command.

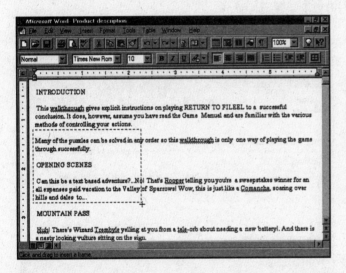

2 The normal Word cursor turns into a cross-hair cursor. Position the cross-hair cursor at the top left corner of where you want the text frame located. Hold down the left mouse button and drag the mouse down and to the right. A dotted box appears outlining the frame.

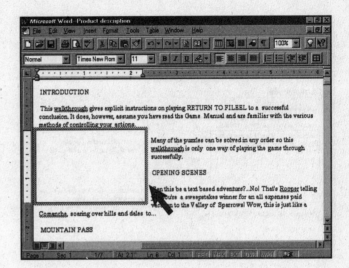

3 Release the left mouse button. A frame with a cross-hatched border appears in your document. A text cursor is inside.

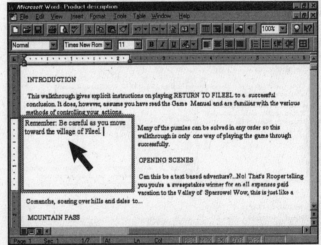

4 Type some text in the box. Don't worry about filling the box with text; you'll learn shortly how to match the box's size to fit the text.

(continues)

Do It Yourself Add a Text Frame

(continued)

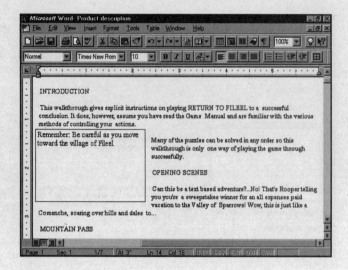

5 Deselect the text box by clicking your mouse anywhere outside of the box.

You can modify, add, or delete text from the text frame at any time. Simply click anywhere inside the box and type; edit and change appearance of the text as you would with any other text in Word.

Begin Do It Yourself Change the Text Frame's Location

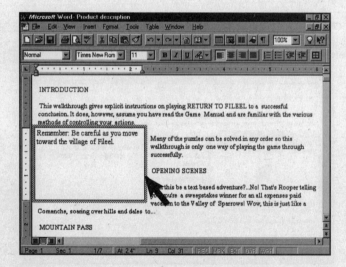

1 Position your mouse cursor over the border of the frame. The cursor turns into a combination of an arrow and a cross-hair cursor.

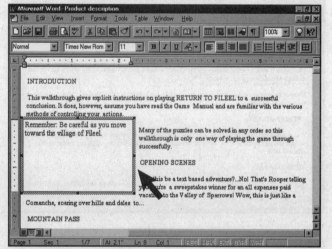

2 Click the left mouse button. The cross-hatch border appears, as do eight small black boxes along the border. These boxes are called *handles*.

Do It Yourself   Change the Text Frame's Location

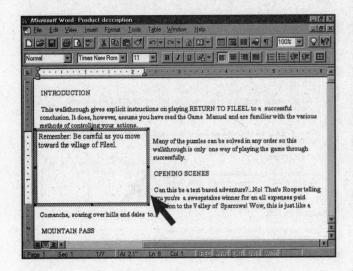

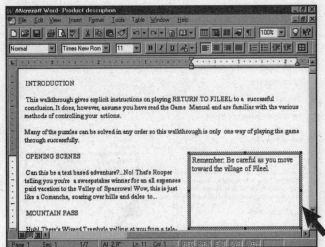

3 Position the mouse cursor over the border of the frame until the combination arrow/cross-hair cursor appears. Don't position the mouse cursor over a handle.

5 Release the left mouse button.

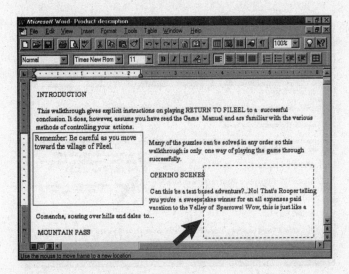

4 Hold down the left mouse button and drag the frame to the new location.

Begin Do It Yourself Change the Text Frame's Size

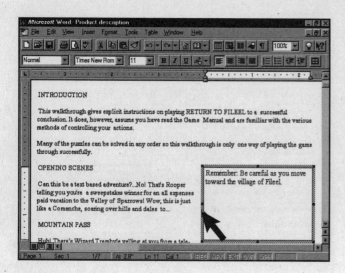

1 Position the mouse cursor over the border of the frame. When the cursor turns into a combination of an arrow and a cross-hair cursor, click the left mouse button.

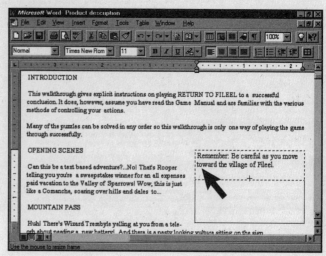

3 With the left mouse button pressed, drag the mouse in one of the directions pointed to by the two-headed arrow. One direction makes the frame larger, the other smaller.

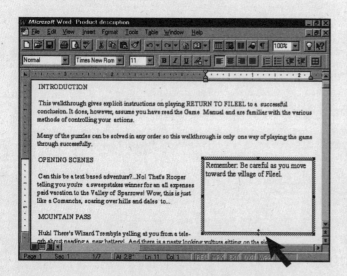

2 Position the mouse cursor over a handle so that it turns into a two-headed arrow. Press the left mouse button.

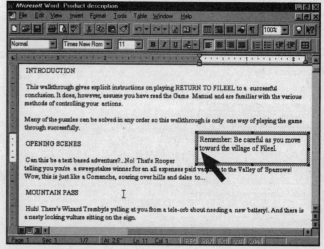

4 Release the left mouse button.

The two-headed arrow tells you the directions in which you resize the frame. For example, a two-headed arrow facing up and down means you can only move the top and bottom borders of the frame. A diagonal two-headed arrow, which appears when you position the mouse cursor over the handles in the corner, means you can resize the box in all directions.

Begin Do It Yourself   Modify Borders and Shading

1 In the formatting toolbar, click on the **Borders** button to display the Borders toolbar.

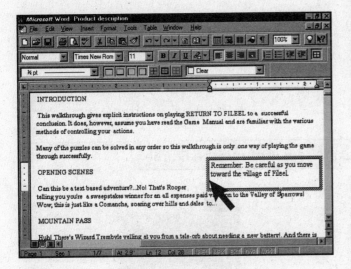

2 Select the frame by clicking anywhere on it.

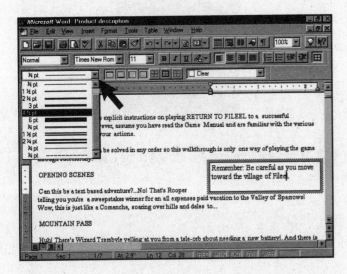

3 Click on the down arrow of the **Line Style** drop-down box of the Borders toolbar. This displays different line styles; click on one of them.

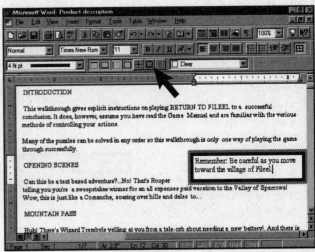

4 Click on the **Outside Border** button in the Borders toolbar to apply the new border style to the frame.

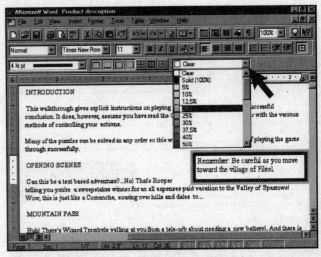

5 With the frame highlighted, click the down arrow of the **Shading** drop-down list in the Borders toolbar. This displays shading options.

(continues)

Do It Yourself   Modify Borders and Shading

(continued)

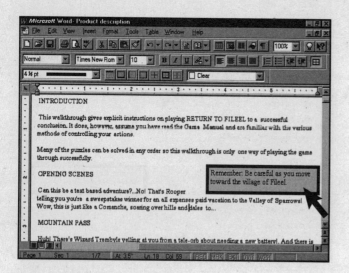

6 Select a shading option from the list; Word applies it immediately to the frame.

Begin Do It Yourself   Determine How Text Wraps Around the Frame

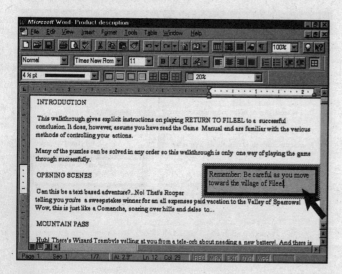

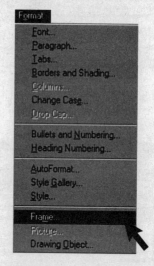

1 Select the frame by clicking anywhere on it.

2 Open the **Format** menu and select the **Frame** command.

Do It Yourself   Determine How Text Wraps Around the Frame

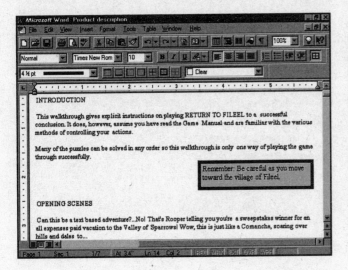

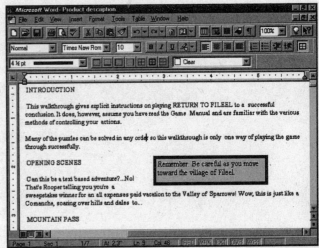

3 The Frame dialog box appears. If you don't want text to wrap around the frame, click on **None**. The result looks like the preceding figure.

4 If you want text to wrap around the frame, click on **Around**. The result looks like the preceding figure. With either choice, click **OK** to finish.

To remove a frame, simply select it by clicking on its borders so that the cross-hatched frame border appears. Then press the **Delete** key. Remember that deleting the frame also deletes the text within it. If you want to save the text, select the **Remove Frame** command from the Frame dialog box.

DO IT YOURSELF

Add Elements to Documents

Previous chapters in the section focused on customizing Word for Windows to work the way you do and improving the appearance of your documents. These are important things to learn, but they are just the beginning of untapping the power in Word.

This chapter focuses on powerful ways to add information to your Word documents. You'll learn how to create, save, and reuse boilerplate text that you must frequently insert into documents. You'll also learn how to use information stored in database and spreadsheet files in your word documents.

Quickly Add Boilerplate Text

Often, we type the same thing, in the same way, over and over again. Before word processing, there were few shortcuts: You typed and typed and typed. However, a good computer program can automate your repetitive tasks so you don't spend so much time typing. Word for Windows 95 provides two powerful tools to quickly add standardized text, sometimes called *boilerplates*, to your documents. These tools are *AutoCorrect* and *AutoText*.

Here are some boilerplate examples you can easily add to documents with just a few keystrokes:

- Letter closings, such as "Very Truly Yours."
- Frequently used legal language.
- Corporate slogans and statements of purpose.
- Various headings, such as a letterhead or fax heading, that go at the top of documents.

The possibilities are endless. If you've been using Word for awhile, you can probably quickly think of text that you type regularly. Any such text is a candidate for AutoCorrect and AutoText. You also can use AutoCorrect and AutoText to insert a graphic image. To do that, simply follow the procedures in this project but substitute the image for text. Commonly used graphic images that you would want to quickly insert may include a digital image of your signature or a corporate logo.

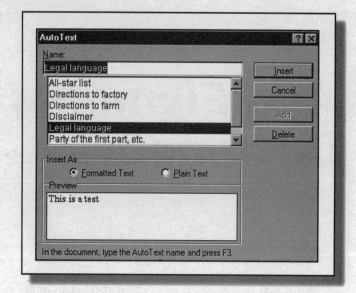

> Here's another application of AutoText that might be useful. If you need to delete text from your document but think you may need to reinsert it later, first save it as an AutoText entry. Then delete the text from your document.

In this project, you'll learn how to add boilerplate text using both AutoCorrect and AutoText. Keep in mind that for longer and less frequently inserted chunks of boilerplate, you're better off using AutoText. That's because, eventually, adding too much boilerplate to AutoCorrect will slow it down. You should also delete old AutoText entries for two reasons. First, if there are a lot of obsolete entries in the Name list box, it can be difficult to find the precise entry you want to add. Second, AutoText entries are stored as part of your Normal template. If you have a lot of entries, it will make Word load more slowly.

Finally, we'll review how to quickly insert a boiler-plate using a keystroke combination. This part of the project describes the fastest way to speed adding of AutoText entries to your documents. This method—assigning keystrokes to AutoText entries—approximates the way that AutoCorrect works and it summarizes "Change Keystroke Combinations" on page 321. You also can assign AutoText entries to menus and toolbar buttons. To do that, first read this part of the project; then read "Change Your Own Word Toolbar" on page 317 or "Customize Word Menus" on page 324.

Begin Do It Yourself   Add Boilerplate Text to AutoCorrect

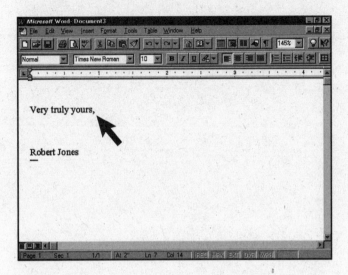

1 In an empty document, type your boilerplate text. For this example, you could, on one line, type **Very truly yours,** press the **Enter** key four times, and type your name.

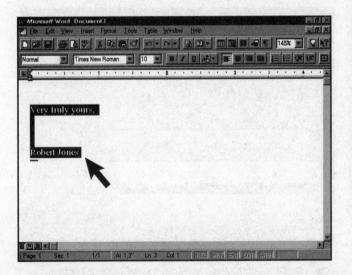

2 Select the entire text, in this case, the letter ending. Do this by dragging your mouse over the entire selection.

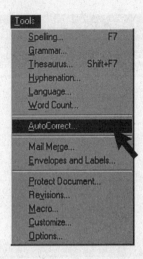

3 Open the **Tools** menu and select the **AutoCorrect** command.

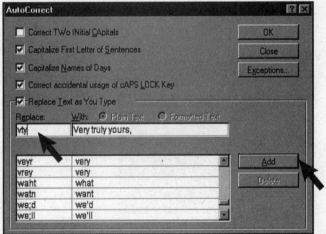

4 In the AutoCorrect window, type an abbreviation for your boilerplate text in the **Replace** text box. For example, type **vty**. The text you selected should appear in the **With** text box. Click the **Add** button; then click the **OK** button.

When adding the two letters that represent the phrase or name, be careful that you don't use letters that comprise short words or other abbreviations. For example, if you want to quickly insert your name and it is Isaac Smith, don't use **is**. If you do, when you type the word **is** as part of the sentence, your name will appear.

(continues)

Do It Yourself Add Boilerplate Text to AutoCorrect

(continued)

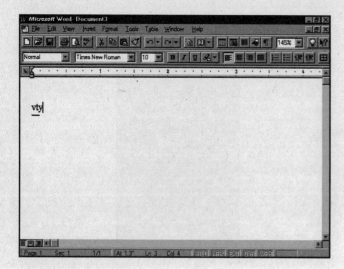

5 To insert your boilerplate text, type the abbreviation you entered for it in the Replace text box and press the **Spacebar**. For example, type **vty** and press **Spacebar** to insert the letter ending in the document.

Begin Do It Yourself Delete an AutoCorrect Entry

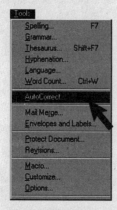

1 Open the **Tools** menu and select the **AutoCorrect** command to display the AutoCorrect window.

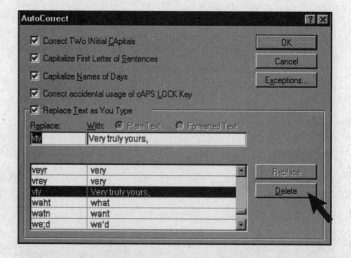

2 In the list window showing all the AutoCorrect entries, highlight the entry you want to delete and click the **Delete** button. Click **OK** to close the AutoCorrect window.

Begin Do It Yourself Create An AutoText Entry

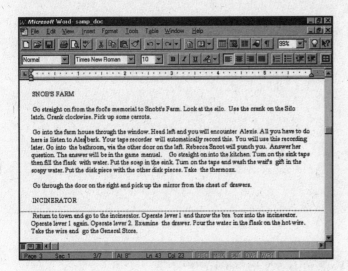

1 Open a document containing the boilerplate or create it in a new document.

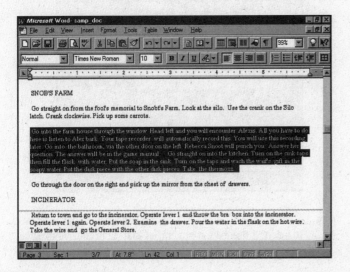

2 Position the mouse cursor before the first word of text. Hold down the left mouse button and drag your mouse to the end of the text. Release the mouse button to highlight the text.

3 Open the **Edit** menu; then select the **AutoText** command.

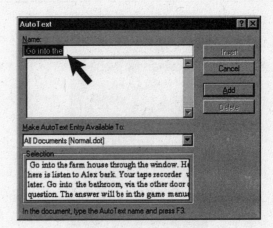

4 In the AutoText dialog box, the text you selected should appear in the preview Window. In the **Name** text box, the first few characters of the text should appear. Type a descriptive name for your text in this box. The name can be as long as 31 characters.

(continues)

Do It Yourself Create An AutoText Entry

(continued)

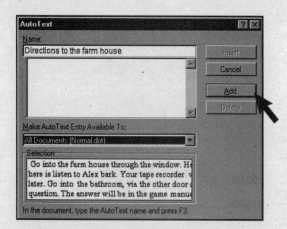

5 In the **Make AutoText Available To** drop-down list, select the template in which this entry will be available. Choosing the default—Normal—makes it available in all documents. If you are using a different template, you can select it in the drop-down list. Click **Add** to finish.

Begin Do It Yourself Insert an AutoText Entry in Your Document

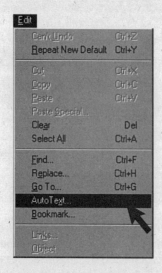

1 Open the **Edit** menu and select the AutoText command. The AutoText dialog box appears.

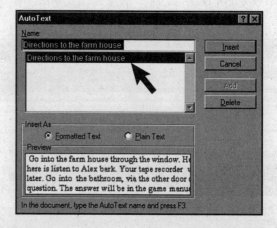

2 In the **Name** window, click on the AutoText entry you want to insert. If there are more entries than fit in the Window, use the scroll bar to view the additional entries.

Here's a shortcut for inserting AutoText. If you remember the name of your entry, type it in your document. Then Press the **F3** key and Word automatically inserts the entry in your document.

Do It Yourself Insert an AutoText Entry in Your Document

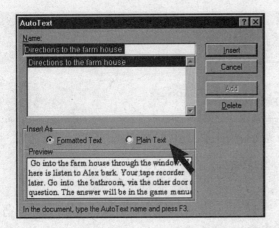 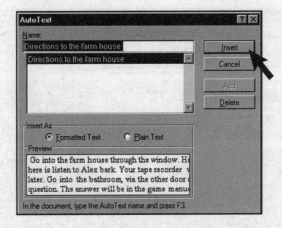

3 In the **Insert As** area of the dialog box, click the **Formatted Text** radio button to insert the text with the same formatting as when you saved it. Click **Plain Text** to insert the text without formatting.

4 Click the **Insert** button to insert the AutoText entry in your document.

Begin Do It Yourself Assign an AutoText Entry to a Keystroke Combination

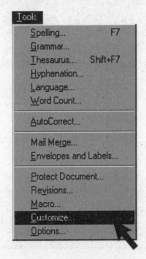 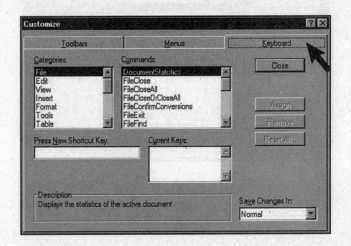

1 Open on the **Tools** menu and select the **Customize** command.

2 In the Customize dialog box, click the **Keyboard** tab.

(continues)

Do It Yourself Assign an AutoText Entry to a Keystroke Combination

(continued)

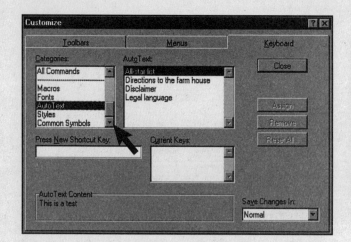

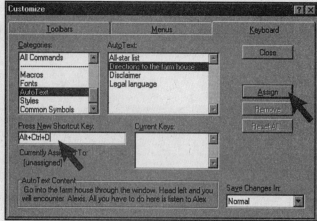

3 Select **AutoText** in the **Categories** list box—you'll probably need to use the scroll bars to find this entry.

5 Click the **Press New Shortcut Key** text box and press the keystrokes you want for launching that specific AutoText entry. Then click the **Assign** button.

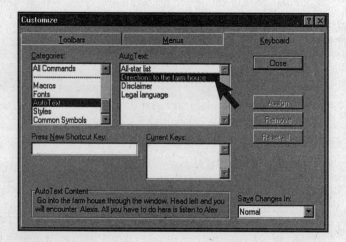

Here are a couple of quick tips about this process. First, note that the Currently Assigned to section of the dialog box tells you whether the shortcut key already is assigned. If so, it tells you what it is assigned to. Also, make sure that the template in the Save Changes In drop-down list is the same one to which you saved the AutoText entry.

4 In the **AutoText** list box, click on the entry to which you want to assign a keystroke combination.

The Press New Shortcut Key text box records keystroke combinations, not specific text. Simply press the key combination and it appears in the text box. Don't type out the characters for the combination.

Do It Yourself Assign an AutoText Entry to a Keystroke Combination

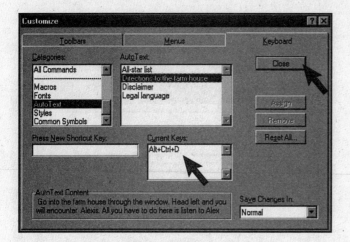

6 The key combination appears in the Current Keys window. Click the **Close** button to finish.

Begin Do It Yourself Delete an AutoText Entry

1 Open the **Edit** menu and select the **AutoText** command. The AutoText dialog box appears.

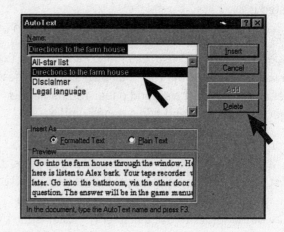

2 In the **Name** window, click the AutoText entry you want to delete. Then click the **Delete** button; Word eliminates your entry.

Add a Header and Footer

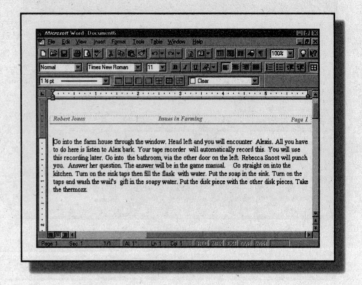

You've created a beautiful, multipage document, such as a long letter to a friend. As your friend is reading the letter, it falls from her hands, with pages spreading everywhere. Let's see...does this page go before that page?

Headers and footers are spaces at the top and bottom of each page that can contain extra information about the document. Obviously, headers and footers can contain the page number, but they also can contain information.

In longer documents, the header or footer can contain a chapter number or title. For documents that you will distribute, the header or footer is a good place to put your name so readers can see who created it.

There are few rules about which to use when—headers or footers. One of the few conventions is that you use a header at the top of all pages of a business letter starting with the second page. You name the subject of the letter and add a page number.

Beyond that, it is entirely your preference which you use. If you are writing for an organization, perhaps it has style standards that specify which to use. However, if such standards don't exist, the best way to figure out whether to use a header or footer is to experiment. The procedures for adding headers and footers are identical. You'll learn how to add those elements in this project.

You'll also learn how to start a header or footer on a page other than the first page of a document. This procedure is helpful if you have several pages of "front matter" such as a title page and a table of contents. When that's the case, you may want to start page numbering on the first page of the main part of the document, not in the front matter.

Tables make it simpler to add headers and footers that include several bits of information such as your name, a title, a page number, and a chapter number. They make it much easier to format and arrange the information. For more about adding tables, read "Create a Table" on page 202.

Begin Do It Yourself   Add a Page Number

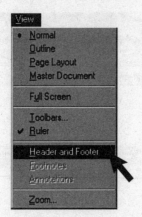

1 Open the **View** menu and select the **Header and Footer** command.

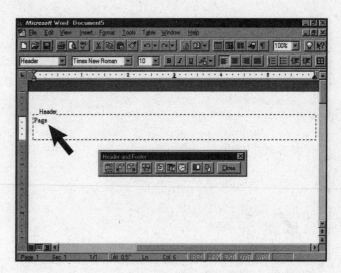

3 In the header (or footer) box, type any text you want to appear in the header or footer in addition to the page number. For example, type **Page**.

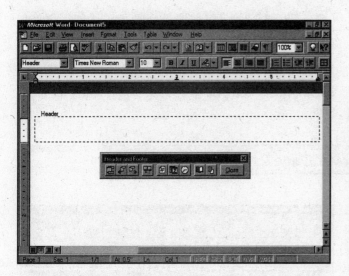

2 The Header and Footer button bar appears and you see the header area of the current page. This is the area at the top of the page. If you prefer a footer, click the leftmost button: the **Switch Between Header and Footer** button.

Word displays the number of your current page in the header box, automatically numbering all pages in the proper sequence.

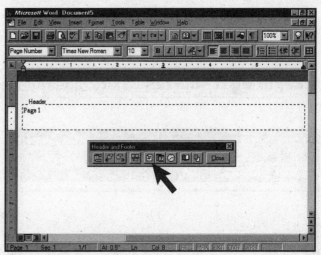

4 Position the insertion point where you want the page number to appear. Then click the **Page Numbers** button in the Header and Footer button bar. This inserts the current page number. Click the **Close** button.

(continues)

Do It Yourself Add a Page Number

(continued)

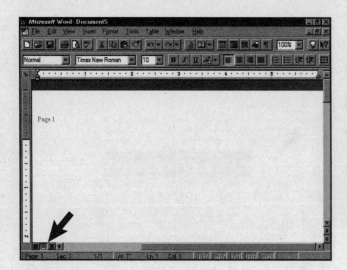

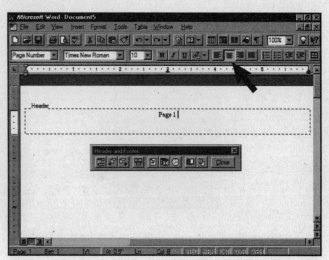

5 Notice that the header now appears in your document when viewed in Page Layout mode. It doesn't appear in Normal mode, but it will appear properly when you print from that mode.

6 You can format the header or footer as you would any text. For example, to center it, place the cursor anywhere in the header text and click the **Center** button in the Formatting toolbar. Other common formatting includes changing fonts (see "Change Fonts and Font Sizes" on page 182) or putting borders around the header or footer (see "Add Borders and Shading to Text" on page 344).

Begin Do It Yourself Start Page Numbers on Page 2

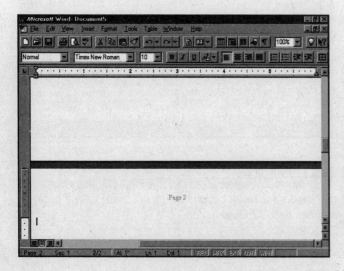

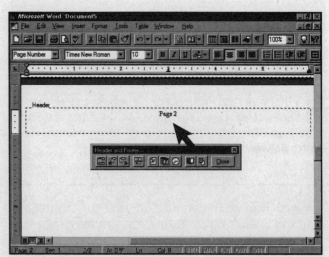

1 To start the header or footer on the second page, position your cursor anywhere after the first page.

2 Open the Header and Footer button bar by opening the **View** menu and selecting the **Header and Footer** command.

Do It Yourself   Start Page Numbers on Page 2

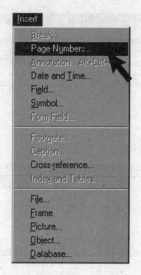

4 In the Page Numbers dialog box, click the **Show Page Number on First Page** check box so that a check mark does *not* appear. Click the **OK** button. The page number now appears only on the second and subsequent pages.

3 Open the **Insert** menu and select the **Page Numbers** command.

Begin Do It Yourself   Start Headers and Footers on Other Pages

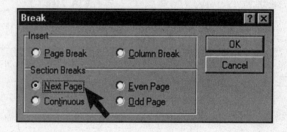

2 In the Break dialog box, click the **Next Page** button to start a new section on the next page. A section break—in the form of a double dotted line—appears on-screen when you view the document in Normal mode.

(continues)

1 Position your cursor precisely at the end of the part of your document in which you *don't* want the header or footer to appear. Open the **Insert** menu and select the **Break** command.

Do It Yourself Start Headers and Footers on Other Pages

(continued)

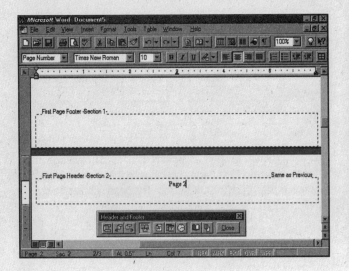

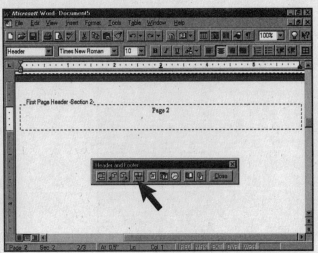

3 Place your cursor after the section break. Then open the Header or Footer toolbar by opening the **View** menu and selecting the **Header and Footer** command. If you haven't already created the header or footer, do so now.

4 Click the **Same as Previous** button in the Header and Footer toolbar. The words **Same As Previous** disappear from the upper right corner of the header or footer box. The header or footer now appear only on pages after the section break.

Begin Do It Yourself Add a Table

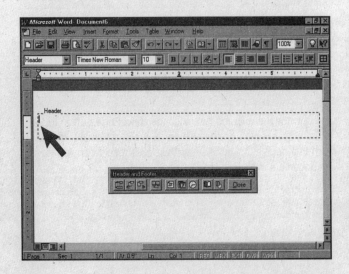

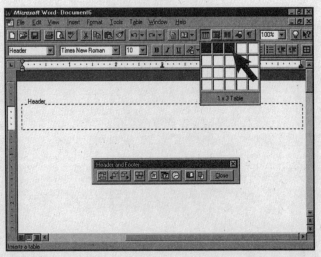

1 Begin a new header or footer by opening the **View** menu and selecting the **Header and Footer** command. Position your cursor within the header or footer.

2 In the Standard toolbar, click the **Table** icon and hold down the left mouse button. In the table selection window that appears, select a table that is one row by three columns. Release the mouse button. This inserts the table in your header or footer.

Do It Yourself Add a Table

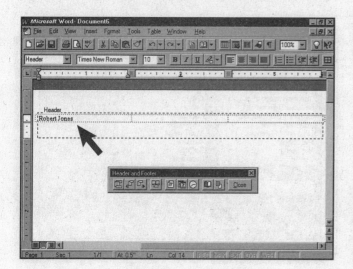

3 Position the mouse cursor in the left-most cell and click the left mouse button. Type your name.

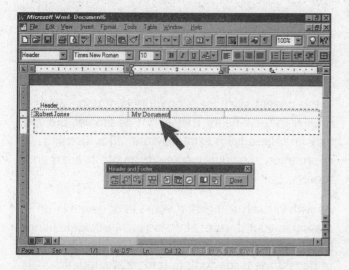

4 Press the **Tab** key once so that the cursor is in the middle cell. Then type a name for your document. For this exercise, it may be as simple as **My Document**.

5 Select the title by dragging your mouse over it. Then click the **Center** button in the Formatting toolbar. This centers the title within the cell.

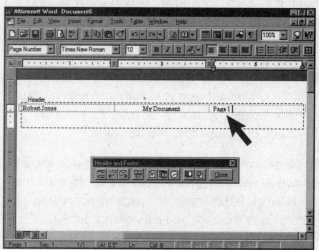

6 Press the **Tab** key once more. This positions the cursor in the right-most cell. Add a page number, as discussed previously in this project.

7 Highlight the page number and click the **Align Right** button in the Formatting toolbar. This positions the page number on the right margin of your document. Click the **Close** button of the Header and Footer button bar to finish.

Add a Field

Most of the documents we create in Word for Windows 95 are relatively simple affairs that consist of words, sentences, and paragraphs. You've already learned how to add power and increase your speed with tools such as macros that automate repetitive tasks and AutoCorrect to quickly insert a boilerplate.

But there's even more power lurking under Word's hood. Word also can think and automate the inclusion of certain types of information. This automated information comes in the form of *fields*. If you followed the project on adding a header or a footer, without knowing it, you've already inserted one type of field: a page number. Other common types of fields add the date, time, and file name.

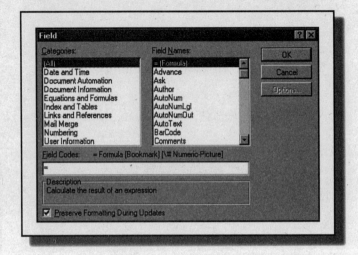

To people with a technical background, fields also are known as *variables*. That's because the information in fields varies. For example, the page number varies according to the page you are viewing. Similarly, the date varies according to what day it is. When you insert a field, Word automatically takes care of displaying the variable information. You don't have to bother changing it to match new conditions.

Fields can be simple, such as the date or page number; we'll focus on simple fields in this project. But they also can be complex. For example, there are fields that read certain information in your document. If that information meets a certain condition, the field initiates an action that you designate.

For example, say you are writing letters to collect on an overdue payment from a client. One of these complex fields examines whether, in a different portion of your letter, the payment is more than 60

days late. If it is that late, the field automatically inserts a boilerplate, such as text that threatens legal action. If payment is less than 60 days late, Word can automatically insert text that has a friendlier tone. A mail merge letter (see "Create and Print a Form Letter" on page 289) might use these complex fields.

In this project, we'll focus on more common—and simpler to use—fields. They might be simpler, but you may find these fields extremely useful for inserting information into your documents or into headers and footers.

As with virtually all fields, if you add or delete information in your document, fields such as PageRef and NumPages will change to reflect the different amount of pages. The fields don't automatically update themselves unless you save the file, print it, or exit Word and return. As a result, you sometimes must manually update the fields. You learn to do that in this project.

Begin Do It Yourself Add the Date

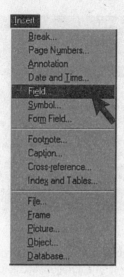

1 Open the **Insert** menu and select the **Field** command. The Field dialog box appears.

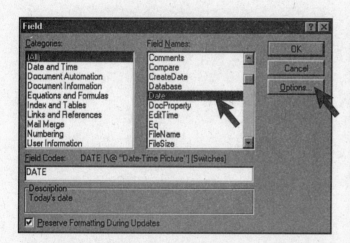

2 In the **Categories** window, select **All**. In the **Field Names** window, scroll down until you find **Date**. Click it to highlight it; then click the **Options** button.

> The Date field always displays and prints the current date. A similar, and often useful field, is the CreateDate field. This displays the date in which you first created your document.

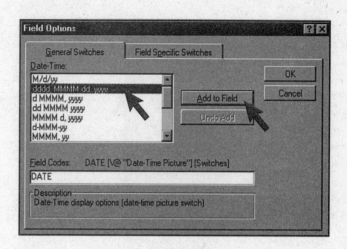

3 Click the **General Switches** tab. In the **Date-Time** list box, select the format you want for the date. This determines how the date appears in your document. Click the **Add to Field** button and then click **OK**.

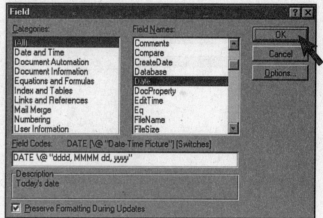

4 In the Field dialog box, click **OK** to insert the date field.

Begin Do It Yourself   Another Way to Add the Date and Time

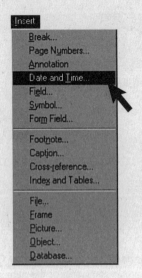

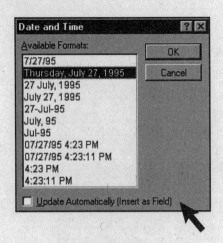

3 Click the **Update Automatically** check box if you want the date or time to automatically change to reflect the current date and time. Otherwise, Word inserts the current date and time and it won't change. When you finish, click **OK**.

1 Open the **Insert** menu and select the **Date and Time** command. The Date and Time dialog box appears.

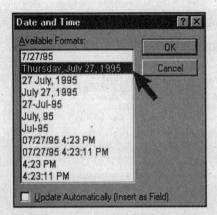

2 In the **Available Formats** window, click the format you want in your document.

Begin Do It Yourself   Insert the Number of Pages

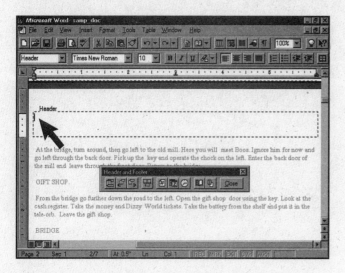

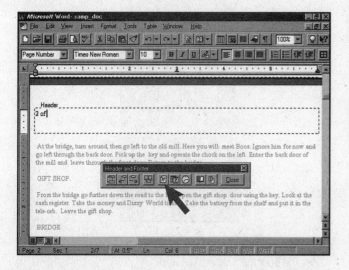

1 Open a multipage document. Within the document, open an existing header or footer or create a new one. Do either by opening the **View** menu and selecting the **Header and Footer** command. Read "Add a Header and Footer" on page 368 to learn more.

2 In the Header or Footer toolbar, add the page number by clicking on the fifth button from the left. Then position the cursor after the page number. Press the **Spacebar** and type the word **of**. Press the **Spacebar** again.

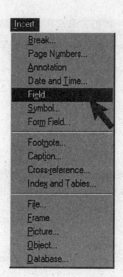

3 Open the **Insert** menu and select **Field**. The Field dialog box appears.

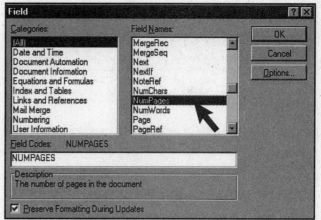

4 In the **Categories** window, select **All**. In the **Field Names** window, select **NumPages**. Click **OK** to finish.

(continues)

Do It Yourself Insert the Number of Pages

(continued)

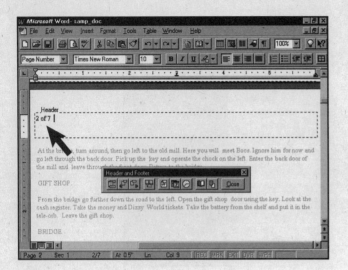

5 The header or footer now includes both the current page number and the total number of pages, such as **2 of 7**.

Begin Do It Yourself Insert a Page Reference

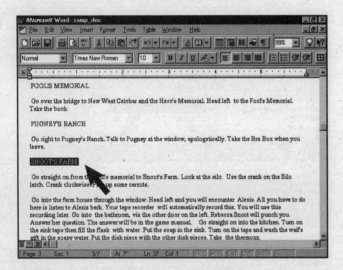

1 Load a multipage document. Highlight the text that you will want to reference later in the document.

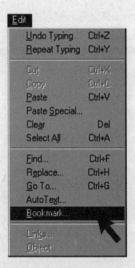

2 Open the **Edit** menu and select the **Bookmark** command. The Bookmark dialog box appears.

Do It Yourself Insert a Page Reference

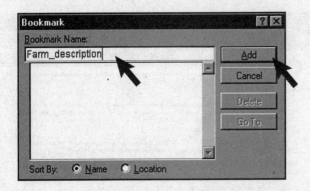

3 In the **Bookmark Name** text box, type a descriptive name for that part of your document; there can be no spaces in the name. Click the **Add** button.

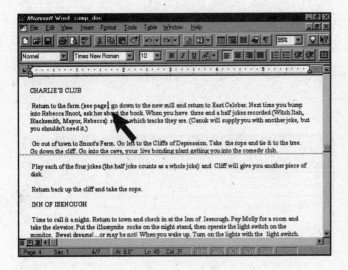

4 Now move to another section of the document. Type a sentence referring to the information in the first part, then, in parentheses, type **see page** and press the **Spacebar**.

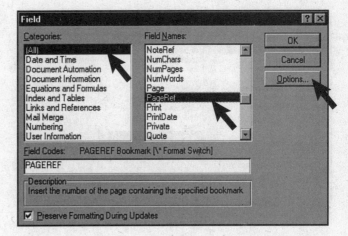

5 Open the Field dialog box by selecting the **Insert** menu and the **Field** command. Highlight **All** in the **Categories** window and **PageRef** in the **Field Names** window. Click the **Options** button.

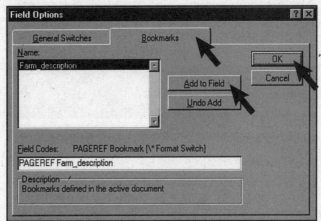

6 In the Field Options dialog box, click the **Bookmarks** tab. Highlight the name of your bookmark in the **Name** window. Click the **Add to Field** button; then click **OK** to return to the Field dialog box.

(continues)

Do It Yourself   Insert a Page Reference

(continued)

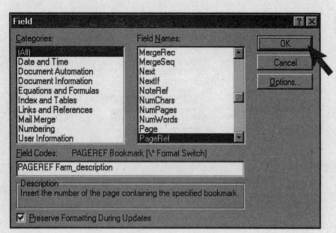

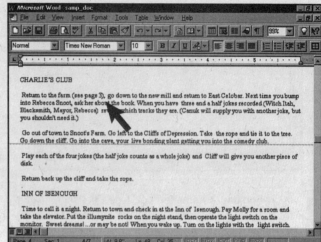

7 Click **OK** to insert the page reference into your document.

8 Your document now has the page reference, such as **see page 3**.

Begin Do It Yourself   Update a Field

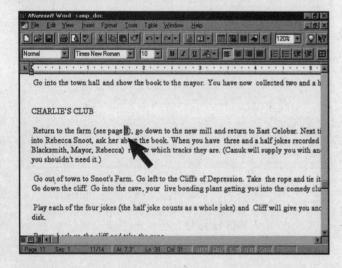

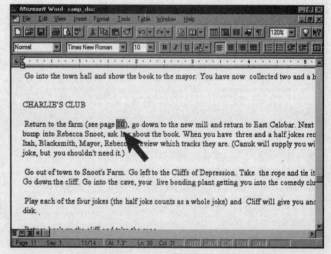

1 Add or delete some pages from your document. Then click a field so the cursor is either in the middle of it or right next to it. In this example, the cursor is next to the NumPages field.

2 Press the **F9** key. Word updates the field to reflect the new page for your reference.

Add an Address Book Entry

This project assumes that you installed Microsoft Exchange as part of your Windows 95 installation. If you didn't do so, the instructions in this project won't make sense. To install exchange, use the Windows 95 setup program.

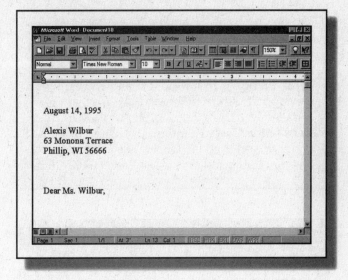

Whether you are writing a letter to a favorite aunt or doing some business-related work at home, there are many times when you need to insert a person's address into a document you are writing.

In the old days, you had to find your paper address book and copy the address into your document. More recently, you could start up a computerized address book, find the information you want, copy it to the Windows Clipboard, and then paste it into your document. Word for Windows 95, however, provides an even easier way to insert addresses. It includes a direct link to the Exchange address book.

Exchange is a built-in part of Windows 95. It is a centralized place for sending e-mail and fax messages and for receiving them. A key part of Exchange is its address book, to which Word for Windows 95 has a direct link. This link makes it easy to use the Exchange address book for inserting names into your

documents. Exchange is a deep communications product that enables you to use Word to create fax and e-mail messages. Learn more about Exchange in your Windows 95 users manual. And if you haven't used Exchange yet, this chapter provides a good introduction to one of its core components.

This project focuses only on adding addresses to the address book and inserting them into your documents. This will save you a lot of time and trouble when you address letters, faxes, and e-mail messages.

Begin Do It Yourself Add an Address

The precise steps for adding an address may vary according to the precise nature of how you installed Windows 95. For example, if you use Schedule+, you would need to include your log-in name for that product. Similarly, screens may appear differently based on whether you installed Microsoft Fax and Microsoft Mail. The steps in this part assume that you are not on a network and that you do not use Schedule+ but that you installed the Mail and Fax options.

1 Click the **Insert Address** button in the Standard toolbar.

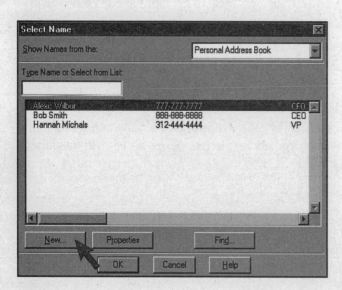

2 In the Select Name dialog box, click the **New** button.

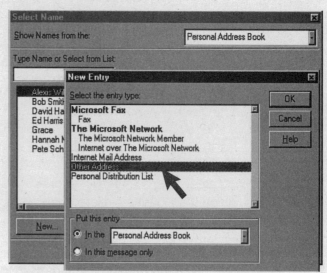

3 In the **Select the entry type** window, click **Other Address**.

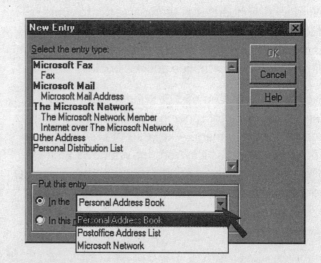

4 In the **In the** drop-down list, select **Personal Address Book**. Click **OK**.

Do It Yourself Add an Address

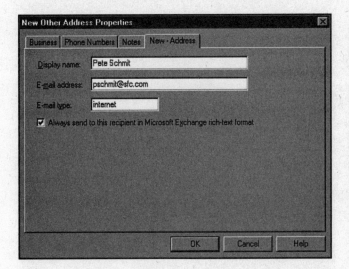

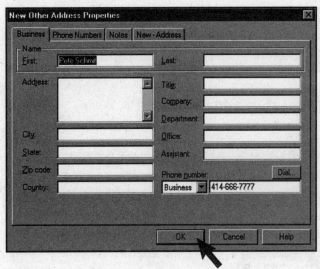

5 The New Other Address Properties dialog box appears. You will see the New-Address tab. In the **Display name** text box, type in the person's name. Press **Tab** to move to other text boxes to type in that information.

Exchange requires that you add an electronic mail address in this dialog box. What if the individual doesn't have an e-mail address or you don't know it? Simply place some characters like **xxx** in the appropriate spaces.

7 Click the **Business** tab. Again, type in any appropriate information, such as the person's address, title, and company. Click **OK** to finish. The new name is now part of the address book.

For inserting names into your documents, you need only add an address to each person's record. However, in other contexts, you can use the address book to send faxes and electronic mail, and to dial the phone for you. As a result, you may want to fill in all the information you can about each person.

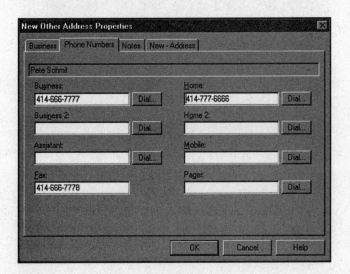

6 Click the **Phone Numbers** tab. Add phone numbers here.

Begin Do It Yourself   Insert An Address

1 Click the **Insert Address** icon in the Standard toolbar.

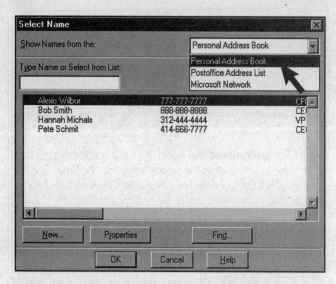

2 In the **Select Name** dialog box, select **Personal Address Book** in the **Show Names from the** drop-down list.

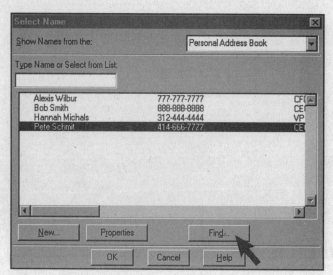

3 Either scroll through the list to find the name you want or click the **Find** button.

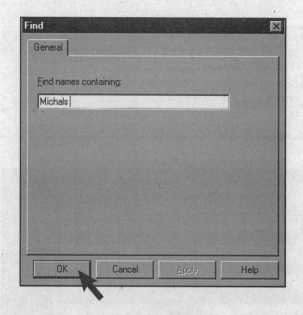

4 In the Find dialog box, type all or a part of the person's name you are looking for. Click **OK** to launch the search.

Do It Yourself Insert An Address

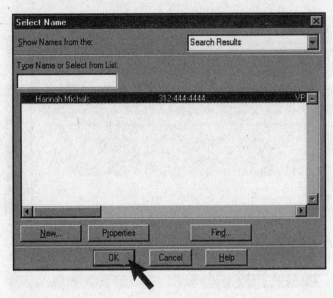

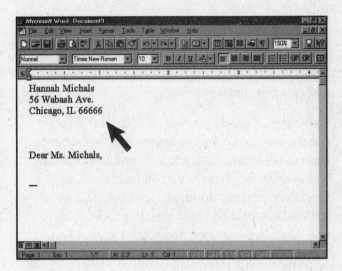

5 The people with names matching your search appear in the name window of the Select Name dialog box. Click the name you want to highlight it. Then click **OK**.

6 The name and address appear in your document.

To quickly insert an address you've recently used, click the down arrow of the **Insert Address** icon located on the Standard toolbar. A list of the most recently inserted names appears. Click the name you want to insert. The name and address appear in your document.

Import Database Information

In the last project, you learned how to add a name to your document from the Exchange address book. This relatively simple operation enables you to add only one name at a time.

Sometimes, though, you will need to add larger numbers of names and addresses and the Exchange address book can't help you with that task. Typically, you would keep those names and addresses (or virtually any other information) in a database or spreadsheet. You also may keep it in tables in separate Word files—you learned about tables in Part 1.

Adding database information such as names and addresses to Word documents is relatively simple. Plus, Word gives you control over precisely what information you add from the database. Word inserts the information into a table in your new document. Besides letting you control what information you add, Word also lets you determine how the table will look.

Once the information is in Word, you can do many things with it. You may want to make it part of your document. For example, for your softball team's newsletter, you can import a list of team members. Or you can use the information to print labels or envelopes.

This project teaches you the ins and outs of importing database information into a Word document. It assumes that you already have a database. If not, create a small one for demonstration purposes before you read on. The simplest way to do this is to create a simple Word table and save it in a file named

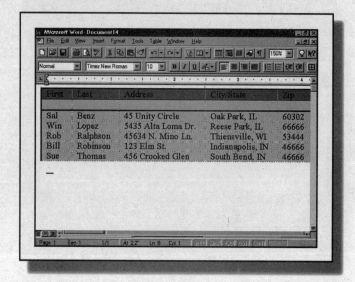

DATABASE. Create enough columns for last name, first name, address, city, state and ZIP code—in database parlance, these columns are called *fields*. Add enough rows to add three or four names.

Names and addresses aren't the only type of database information you can use, of course. Say, for example, you are a button collector and you keep a database of your collection. When corresponding with other collectors, you can insert database information about buttons into your Word documents. The possibilities for using database information are endless.

The first set of steps in this task tells you how to quickly insert all the information in your database into your document. To be more particular about the information you add, read the last three sets of steps.

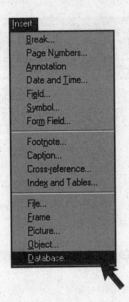

1 After starting a new Word document, open the **Insert** menu and select the **Database** command.

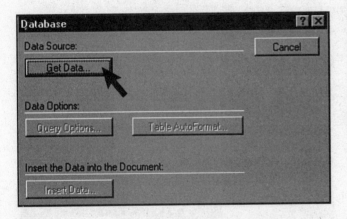

2 The Database dialog box appears. Click the **Get Data** button.

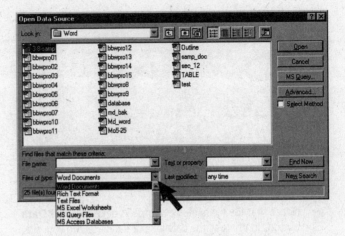

3 In the Open Data Source dialog box, select the type of file you are opening in the **Files of type** drop-down list. In our example, we will open a Word document.

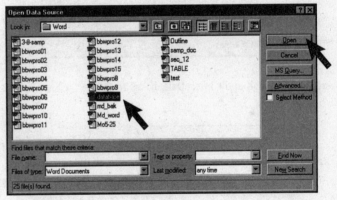

4 Select the folder containing the database file in the **Look in** drop-down list and the file in the file list window. Click the **Open** button.

(continues)

Do It Yourself Select the Database

(continued)

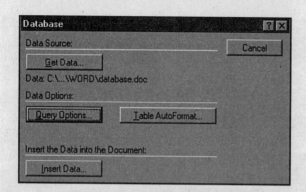

5 Notice that the file name now appears below the **Get Data** button. To insert all the data in your database into your file, click the **Insert Data** button.

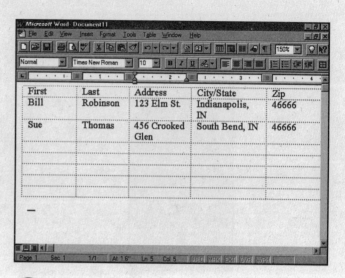

7 Word inserts the data into a table in your document.

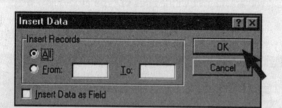

6 Click **OK** in the Insert Data dialog box.

Begin Do It Yourself Determine the Specific Information to Include

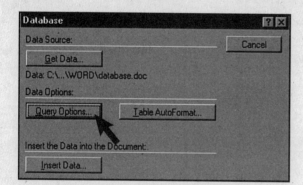

1 Start a new document by clicking the **New** button in the Standard dialog box. Open the **Insert** menu and select the **Database** command. Select your data source as you learned in the previous part. Click the **Query Options** button.

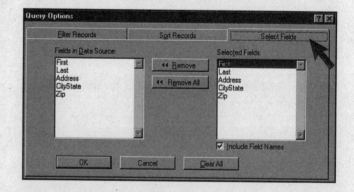

2 Click the **Select Fields** tab. All the fields in your database appear in the Selected Fields Window.

Do It Yourself   Determine the Specific Information to Include

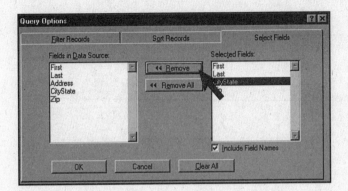

3 If you don't want the information in a field in your document, highlight it in the **Selected Fields** window. Then click the **Remove** button.

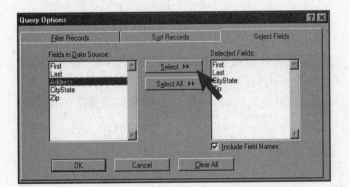

4 To add a field back, highlight it in the **Fields in Data Source** window and click **Select**. To include field names at the top of the table in your Word document, click the **Include Field Names** check box so a check appears. Click **OK**.

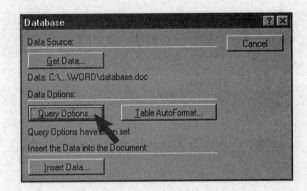

5 In the Database dialog box, click the **Insert Data** button.

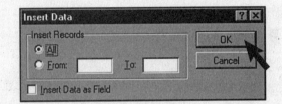

6 In the Insert Data dialog box, make sure the **All** radio button is activated. Do that by clicking on it so a dot appears in the middle. Click **OK** to insert your data.

Begin Do It Yourself   Insert Specific Records

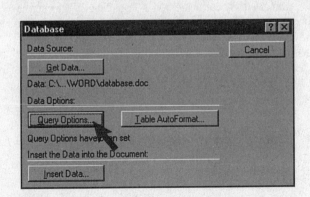

1 Open the **Insert** menu and select the **Database** command. Select your data source as you learned in the previous part. Click the **Query Options** button.

(continues)

Do It Yourself Insert Specific Records

(continued)

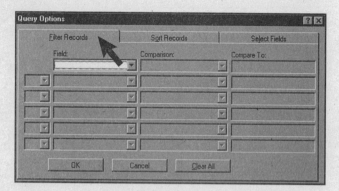

2 Click the **Filter Records** tab.

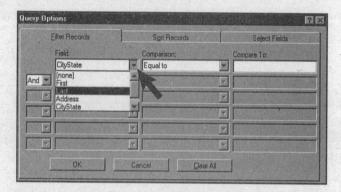

3 Click the top-most **Field** drop-down list. The names of the fields in the database, such as **Last** and **Address** appear. Select the field from which you want to choose specific records.

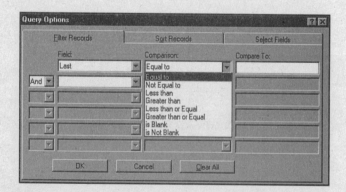

4 In the **Comparison** drop-down list, select **Equal to**. This is the default, so you shouldn't have to change it.

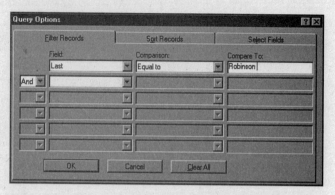

5 In the **Compare To** drop-down list, select the condition that must be met before Word will insert the specific record in your document. For example, if the Last Name field is equal to Robinson, Word only inserts the records of people who have that last name. Click **OK**. Click **Insert Data** in the Database dialog box.

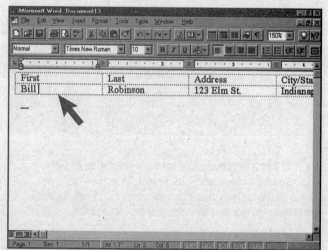

6 Word inserts the records you chose in the document. This is an extremely useful method of inserting only the information you want. For example, if you want a list of people who live in a specific state or who are a certain age, you can use the Filter Records dialog box to specify that.

Begin Do It Yourself   Sort the Information

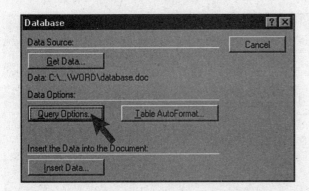

1 Open the **Insert** menu and select the **Database** command. Select your data source as you learned in the previous part. Click the **Query Options** button.

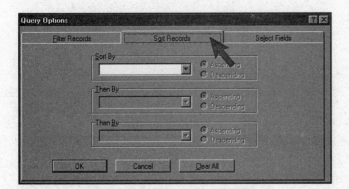

2 Click the **Sort Records** tab.

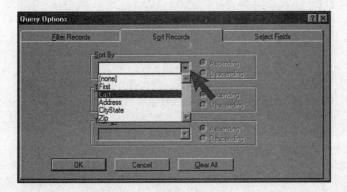

3 Click the down-arrow in the **Sort By** area of the dialog box. Select the field on which you want to sort. For example, you could pick the field containing last names. Click **Ascending** to sort in A–Z order or **Descending** to sort in Z–A order.

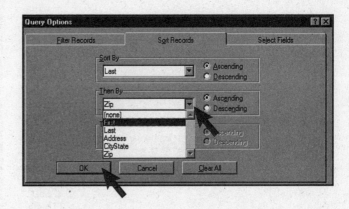

4 In the **Then By** drop-down list, optionally select a secondary field on which to sort. If, for example, you have ten people named Smith, this selection tells Word to sort those last names on the basis of first names. Click **OK**.

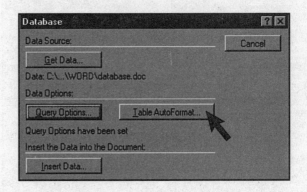

5 In the Database dialog box, click the **Insert Data** button.

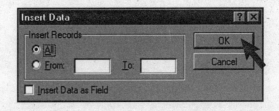

6 In the Insert Data dialog box, make sure the **All** radio button is activated. Do that by clicking on it so a dot appears in the middle. Click **OK** to insert your data.

Begin Do It Yourself   Automatically Format the Table

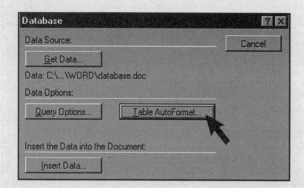

1 Open the **Insert** menu and select the **Database** command. The Database dialog box appears. Select your data source as you learned in the previous part. Click the **Table AutoFormat** button.

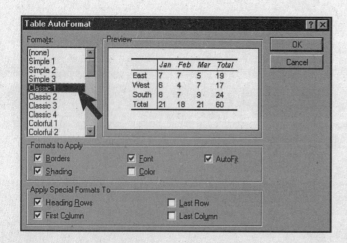

2 In the **Formats** window, click a format name. See a sample of the formatted table in the Preview window. Select the format you like.

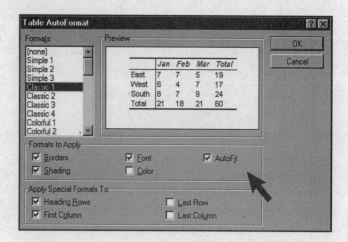

3 In the **Formats to Apply** area of the dialog box, check the specific types of formatting you want to apply. For example, if you check **Borders**, Word will apply the borders as shown in the Preview window.

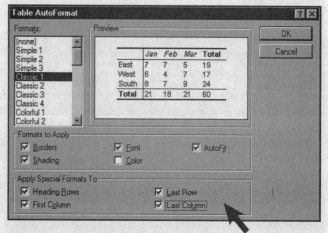

4 In the **Apply Special Formats To** area, select parts of the table in which you want Word to apply special formats. For example, selecting **Last Row** applies special formatting to that part of the table.

Do It Yourself   Automatically Format the Table

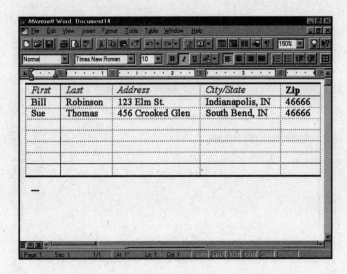

5 Click **OK**. When you insert the data into your document, the table containing the data will be formatted as you specified.

Import Spreadsheet Information

You previously learned how to import database information directly into a Word for Windows 95 table. Typically, this information consists of names and addresses. It also can include lists of virtually any other type of information. In this project, you'll learn how to import spreadsheet information into a Word file.

Spreadsheet information and database information often are similar, but often they are not. One important difference is that you use different programs for creating spreadsheet information than for database information. Microsoft Excel is a popular spreadsheet program and Microsoft Access is a popular database program. You use different programs because the basic nature of the information is different. Spreadsheet information can contain textual information such as names and addresses, but they typically are number-oriented. Typical spreadsheet applications, for example, would be statistical information about the members of your softball team or sales results for all sales personnel in an office. Database information, as discussed in the last project, can contain numbers, but it typically is more list-like and text-oriented. A typical database application is a list of contacts and their addresses and phone numbers.

Because of these differences, spreadsheet programs have more algebraic and statistical tools for analyzing rows and columns of information. Database programs focus more on the capability to sort and sift information, such as tools for finding only the specific records you want.

The process of importing spreadsheet information to a Word document is similar to the procedures described in the previous projects. In this project, you'll learn how to import spreadsheet data.

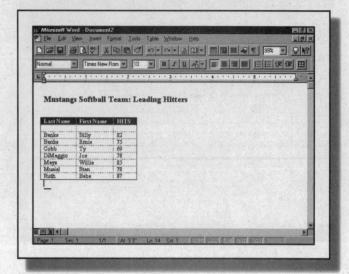

Before you can import spreadsheet information into a Word document, you must give Word the capability to read files created by spreadsheet programs. You add that capability with the installation program that comes with Word for Windows or with Microsoft Office 95. Read "Install Word for Windows 95" on page 4 to learn more about that installation process. In addition, you must have installed an up-to-date version of a spreadsheet program, such as Microsoft Excel 7.0 for Windows 95.

You don't need a spreadsheet program to create simple spreadsheets in your Word documents. Simply create a table and use formulas to perform simple arithmetic. To learn more about tables and formulas, read "Create a Table" on page 202 and "Calculate Numbers in a Table" on page 234.

Begin Do It Yourself Import a Spreadsheet

1 Start a new Word document. Then open the **Insert** menu and select the **Database** command.

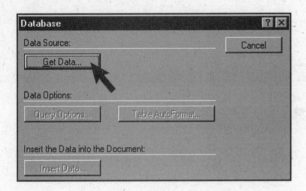

2 In the Database dialog box, click the **Get Data** button.

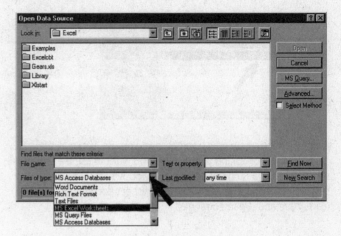

3 The Open Data Source dialog box appears. Select the type of file you are opening in the **Files of type** drop-down list. In this example, you open an Excel spreadsheet.

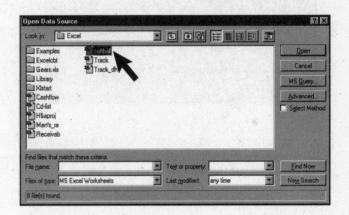

4 Select the folder containing the spreadsheet file in the **Look in** drop-down list. Select the specific file in the file list window. Click the **Open** button.

(continues)

Do It Yourself Import a Spreadsheet

(continued)

5 Depending on which spreadsheet you use, you may see a dialog box asking you whether you want to use the entire spreadsheet or a range of cells you previously named. Make a selection and click **OK** (read your spreadsheet documentation to learn more about named ranges).

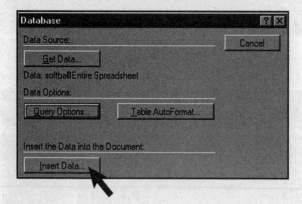

6 The file name now appears below the Get Data button. To insert all the information in your spreadsheet into your file, click the **Insert Data** button.

7 In the Insert Data dialog box, select the **All option** button. Then click **OK**.

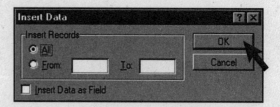

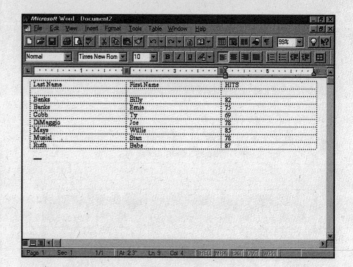

8 Word inserts the spreadsheet information into a table in your document.

Begin Do It Yourself Determine Specific Information to Insert

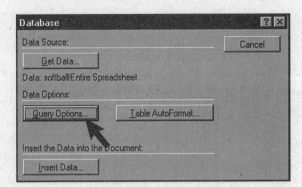

1 Open the **Insert** menu and select the **Database** command; then select your data source as you learned in the preceding set of steps. In the Database dialog box, click the **Query Options** button.

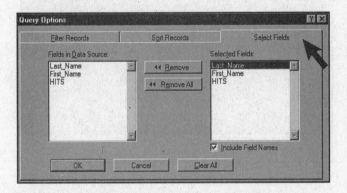

2 In the Query Options dialog box, click the **Select Fields** tab. All the fields in your spreadsheet appear in the **Selected Fields** window.

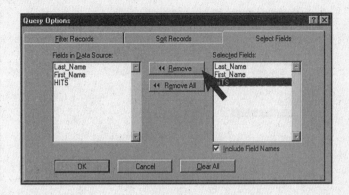

3 If you don't want to import a field into your document, highlight it in the **Selected Fields** window. Click the **Remove** button.

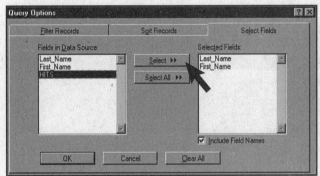

4 To add a field back to the list of fields you are importing, highlight it in the **Fields in Data Source** window and click **Select**. Click **OK** to finish.

Field is a database term that, when describing a spreadsheet refers to the contents of a column. If the column has a discrete heading, such as **Name** or **Address**, those names appear in the **Selected Fields** window. If columns aren't discretely named, you will see coded names in this dialog box; one example of such a name is **M_1**. These names don't provide clues about the contents of the column. If that is the case, you may want to import the entire spreadsheet and delete the columns you don't want.

Begin Do It Yourself Insert Specific Records

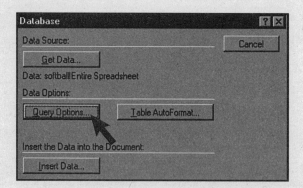

1 Open the **Insert** menu and select the **Database** command; then select your data source as you learned in the first set of steps in this project. In the Database dialog box, click the **Query Options** button.

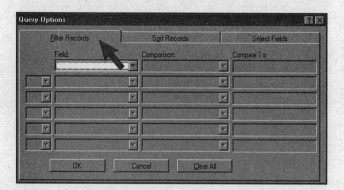

2 In the Query Options dialog box, click the **Filter Records** tab.

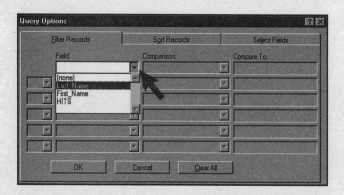

3 Click the top-most **Field** drop-down list. The names of the fields in the database, such as Last_Name and HITS appear. Select the field that determines which records you want.

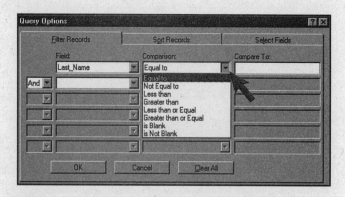

4 In the Comparison drop-down list, select **Equal to**.

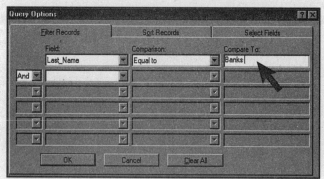

5 In the **Compare To** drop-down list, select the condition that must be met before Word will insert a specific record. For example, if the Last Name field is equal to Banks, Word only inserts the names of people with that last name. Click **OK**; then click **Insert Data** in the Database dialog box. Click **OK** again.

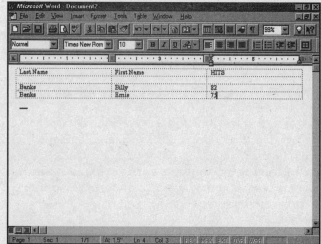

6 Word inserts the records you chose in the document.

Begin Do It Yourself   Sort the Information

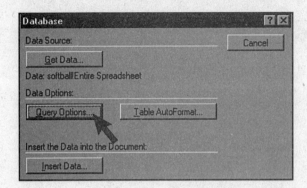

1 Open the **Insert** menu and select the **Database** command; select a data source as you learned in the first set of steps in this project. In the Database dialog box, click the **Query Options** button.

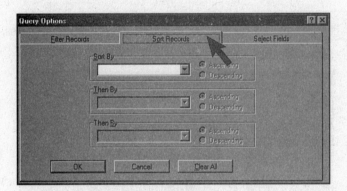

2 Click the **Sort Records** tab.

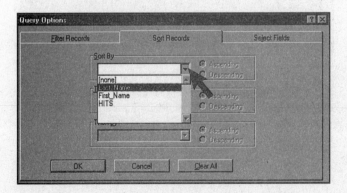

3 Click the down-arrow in the **Sort By** section of the dialog box. Select the field on which you want to sort. For example, you could pick the field containing last names. Click **Ascending** to sort in A–Z order or **Descending** to sort in Z–A order.

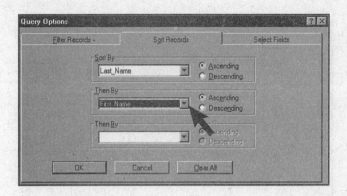

4 In the **Then By** drop-down list, optionally choose a secondary field on which to sort. If, for example, you have 30 people named Banks, you can instruct Word to sort those last names on the basis of first names. Click **OK**.

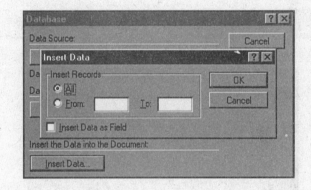

5 Click **Insert Data** in the Database dialog box.

(continues)

Do It Yourself Sort the Information

(continued)

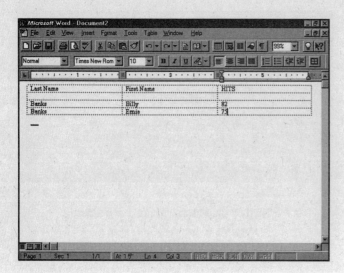

6 Word inserts the information in your document sorted in precisely the order you want.

Begin Do It Yourself Automatically Format the Table

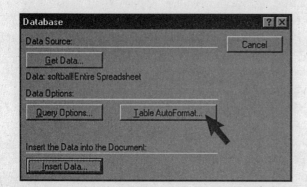

1 Open the **Insert** menu and select the **Database** command. Select a data source as described in the first set of steps in this project. In the Database window, click the **Table AutoFormat** button.

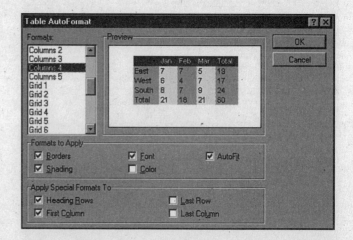

2 In the **Formats** window, click a format name. See a sample of the formatted table with that option in the Preview window. Click different format names until you find one you like.

Do It Yourself   Automatically Format the Table

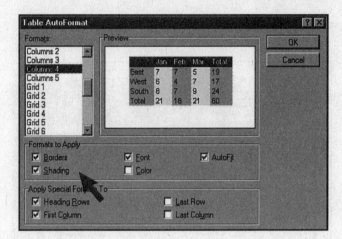

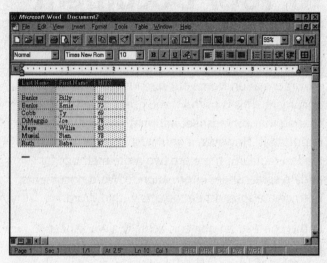

3 In the **Formats to Apply** area, click the specific types of formatting you want to apply. For example, if you check **Shading**, Word applies the shading shown in the Preview window. You can deselect a type of formatting by removing the check.

5 Click **OK**. When you insert the data into your document, the table containing the data will be formatted as you specified.

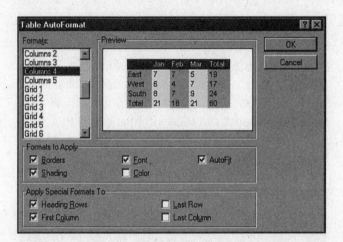

4 In the **Apply Special Formats To** area, select sections of your table to which you want to apply special formats. For example, selecting **First Column** applies special formatting to that part of the table.

Add a Spreadsheet Object to Your Document

The previous project described how to import information from your spreadsheet into a Word document. This is useful if you don't have to regularly change that spreadsheet information after you've imported it. However, if you must change the information regularly, there are two more methods for adding spreadsheet information to Word documents. Both create spreadsheet *objects* within Word.

In this context, an object is actually a worksheet created by your spreadsheet program that you place directly within your Word document. However, you can access all the power of your spreadsheet program without leaving Word. You'll learn how in this project.

In one method described in this project, you drag information from a spreadsheet and drop it into Word. You then can access your spreadsheet's capabilities from within Word to manipulate the information. In the other, similar method, you add a new spreadsheet object within Word and then add the data you want. These methods not only let you add spreadsheet information to Word documents, but also provide the full power of your spreadsheet program. This, in turn, enables you to include more sophisticated spreadsheet information in your document than you can with simple *importing*, as described in the last project. If, for example, you have a statistical bent, you can use all your spreadsheet's statistical power from within Word.

When would you use these *spreadsheet objects*? For the most simple of spreadsheets, say a brief list of people and phone numbers, it's simpler to create a table. If the spreadsheet information is more sophisticated but you aren't going to change it, use the importing procedures described in the last project.

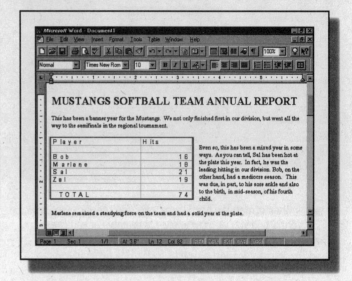

However, you may want to create spreadsheet objects if the information you want to add is changeable or requires powerful math or statistical functions. For example, you may want to use spreadsheet objects when you create a document about your softball team that includes statistical information. With a spreadsheet object, it is easy to update things like batting averages after every game.

The procedures described in this project require that you have sufficient random-access memory (RAM)—at least 8MB is necessary to perform these tasks. You also must use a spreadsheet program that can handle these tasks; specifically, it must be OLE 2-compliant. Most spreadsheet programs sold in the last year meet this requirement, but read your program's documentation to make sure.

Begin Do It Yourself   Drag-and-Drop an Existing Spreadsheet

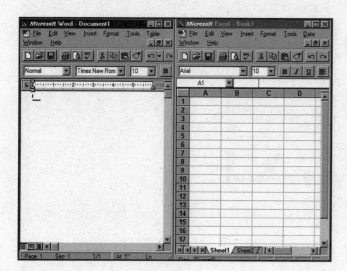

1 Open both your spreadsheet program and Word. This example uses Microsoft Excel for Windows 95.

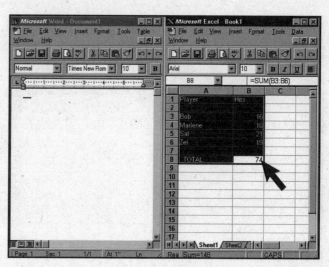

3 Highlight the section of the worksheet you want to transfer to your Word document.

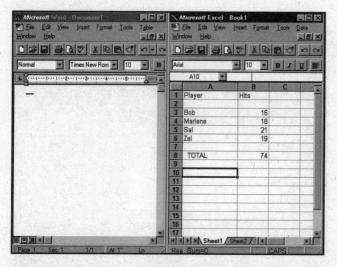

2 Either load an existing worksheet or create one.

4 Position your mouse cursor over the edge of the high-lighted area so that it becomes a solid arrow. Hold down the left mouse button and the **Ctrl** key and drag the information to your Word document.

(continues)

Do It Yourself Drag-and-Drop an Existing Spreadsheet *(continued)*

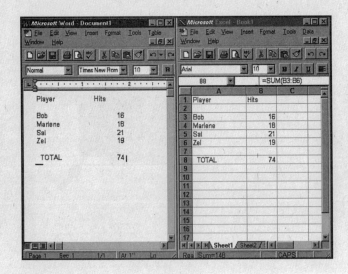

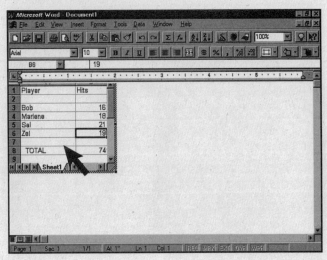

5 Release the left mouse button. The information is now part of your Word document.

6 To edit the spreadsheet within Word using the spreadsheet program's capabilities, double-click anywhere on the spreadsheet.

Begin Do It Yourself Add a New Spreadsheet Object

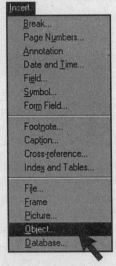

1 Open the **Insert** menu and select the **Object** command.

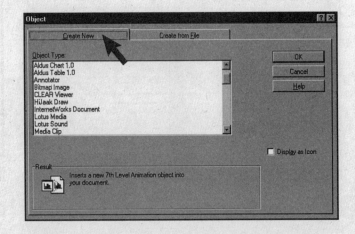

2 In the Object dialog box, click the **Create New** tab.

Do It Yourself Add a New Spreadsheet Object

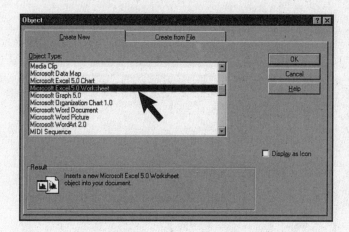

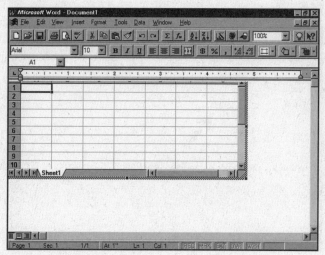

3 In the **Object Type** window, select your spreadsheet. In our example, the object type is Microsoft Excel Worksheet. Click **OK**.

4 A new spreadsheet appears in your Word document. Word's menus and toolbars change to those of your spreadsheet program.

Begin Do It Yourself Edit and Format a Spreadsheet Object

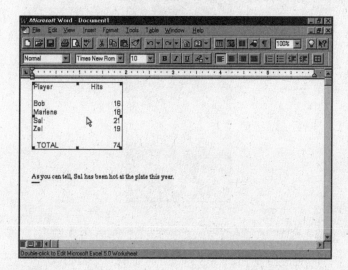

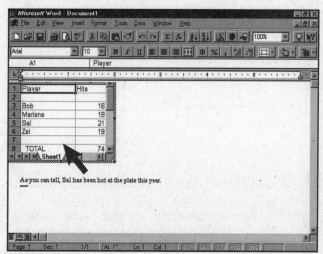

1 Position the mouse cursor over the spreadsheet object.

2 Double-click the left mouse button. The toolbars and menus change to those of your spreadsheet program. Edit your spreadsheet as if you were using that program.

(continues)

Do It Yourself Edit and Format a Spreadsheet Object *(continued)*

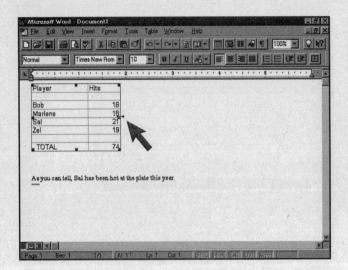

3 To change the size of the spreadsheet object, click it. Then position the mouse cursor over a handle, which appears as a small black box.

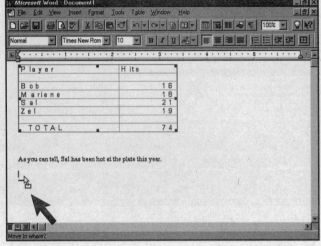

5 To move the spreadsheet, click it. Position the cursor over the spreadsheet and drag it to its new location. Release the left mouse button.

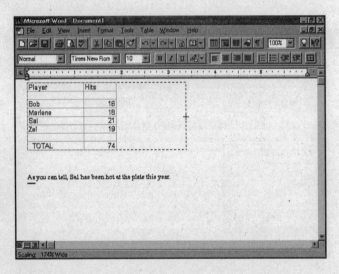

4 When the mouse cursor turns into a two-headed cursor, hold down the left mouse button and drag your mouse to make the spreadsheet larger or smaller.

6 To control how text flows around the spreadsheet, click it once. Open the **Insert** menu and select the **Frame** command. This places a frame around the spreadsheet.

Do It Yourself   Edit and Format a Spreadsheet Object

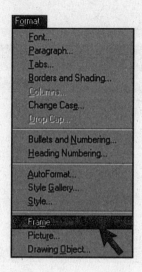

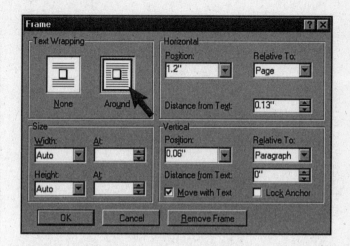

7 Click the spreadsheet and select the **Format** menu and the **Frame** command.

8 In the Frame dialog box, select **Around** if you want text to flow around the spreadsheet. Select **None** if you want text to appear only above and below the spreadsheet. Click **OK** to close the Frame dialog box.

Add a Graphic Object

In "How to Add Graphics to a Document," you learned how to add graphic images to your documents; these images can really dress up a document. Sometimes, you may want to create images from scratch or edit existing images in the program you created them in. With Word for Windows 95, you can accomplish those tasks directly from within the program. You do that by creating so-called *objects*. In computer-speak, you *embed* an object created by another program within your Word document.

Objects really are a way to use another program, such as a drawing program, without ever leaving Word. When you activate an object by double-clicking on it, the menus, toolbar, and capabilities of the other program—in this case, a drawing program—become available to you from within Word. Ordinarily, an image you add in this way looks like an integral part of your Word document. However, you then can edit the image with all the power given to you by the other program.

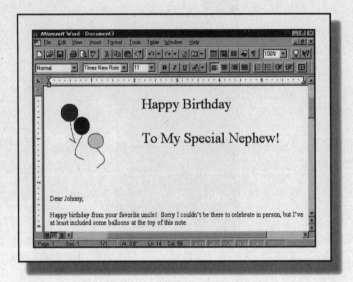

The techie term for this process is called *Object Linking and Embedding*, or *OLE* for short. Word for Windows 95 supports the most recent standard for OLE, called OLE 2.0. In order for this process to work, the other program, such as the drawing program, also must support OLE 2.0. You can find out whether it does by reading that program's documentation.

Why is embedding objects useful? Say you want to create a simple company logo for a document. Embedding an object is an easy way to accomplish that task. Or say you want to use an existing image but want to change some aspect of it, such as colors. Embedding that image in Word as an object makes that task simple.

In this project, you'll learn how to embed Microsoft Paint objects into Word documents. Paint comes with Windows 95, so it should already be on your hard drive. However, you can use any drawing or paint program that supports OLE 2. (Note, though, that you won't learn how to use Paint. To do that, read your Windows 95 user documentation.)

Begin Do It Yourself Create a New Image

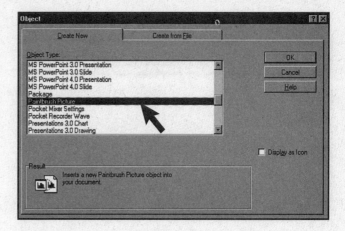

3 Scroll down in the **Object Type** window until you highlight **Paintbrush Picture**. Click **OK**.

1 Position your cursor where you want the image to appear in your document. Open the **Insert** menu and select the **Object** command.

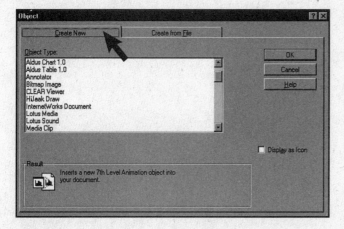

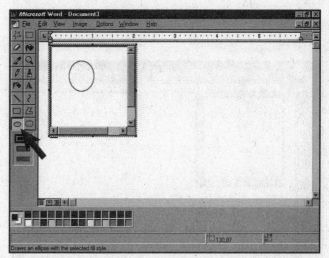

2 In the Object dialog box, click the **Create New** tab.

4 The menus and toolbars change to those of Microsoft Paint, even though you still are in Word. For practice, click the circle icon in the toolbar. Position the crosshair cursor over the work area and hold down the left mouse button and drag your mouse. Release the mouse button to finish the circle.

(continues)

Do It Yourself Create a New Image *(continued)*

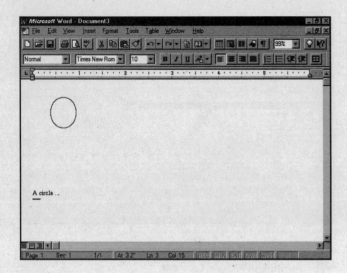

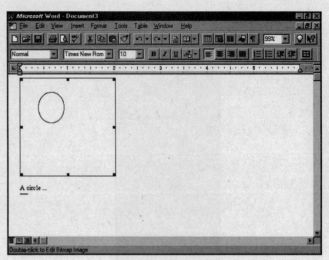

5 Click outside of the drawing work area. Your Word menus and toolbars return and the image is part of your document.

7 To remove the object, click it once so a border appears around it. Press the **Delete** key on your keyboard.

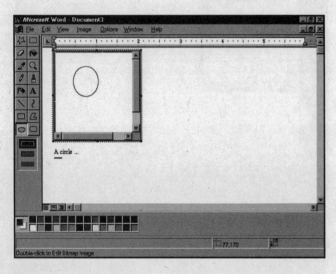

6 To edit the image file, double-click it. Microsoft Paint's menus and toolbars replace those of Word's.

Begin Do It Yourself   Add An Existing Image

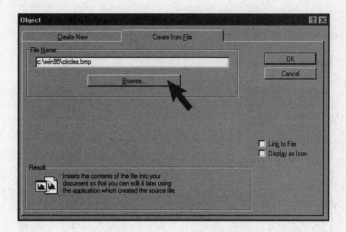

1 Determine where you want the image in your document and place the cursor there. Open the **Insert** menu and select the **Object** command.

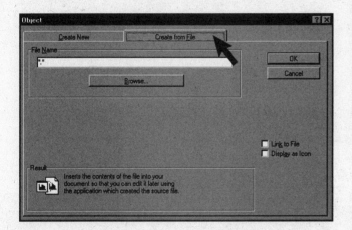

2 In the Object dialog box, click the **Create from File** tab.

3 In the **File Name** text box, type the location and name of the image file you want to insert. If you're not sure of the name or location of the image file, click the **Browse** button.

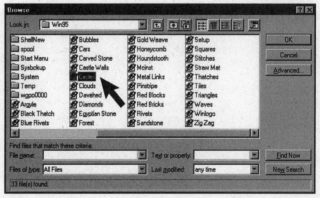

4 In the Browse dialog box, use the **Look in** drop-down list and window to find the folder and the file you want to insert. For this example, in the WIN95 folder (yours may be called WINDOWS), click **Circles**; then click **OK**. This inserts the selected file name in the Object dialog box. Click **OK** to insert the image in your document.

(continues)

Do It Yourself Add An Existing Image

(continued)

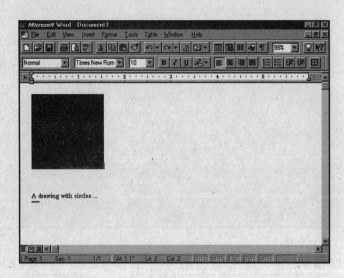

5 To edit the image, double-click it.

DO IT YOURSELF

Present Yourself to the World

When all is said and done, word processing is about presenting yourself to the world. You write letters and memos, send faxes, and create flyers and advertisements. For many users, these are among the most typical uses of Word for Windows.

In this section, you'll learn how to speed along the process of creating these and other types of documents. Specifically, you'll learn how to create templates that greatly speed the process of writing letters, résumés, fax cover sheets, memos, and even newsletters and press releases.

What You Will Find in This Section

Create Your Own Letterhead

It has been said that the more things change, the more they stay the same. In one way, that's true about word processors such as Word for Windows 95. Even though Word has all kinds of modern high-tech aids to make you more efficient, one of its most common uses is for creating old-fashioned letters.

You write letters to your friends, to your family, and for business. Even though letters are an old-fashioned method of communicating, it only makes sense that you would use the high-tech power of your computer—and Word for Windows 95—to create them.

In the old days, you would preprint letterhead stationery, roll a sheet of that stationery into your typewriter, and write your letter. These days, however, you can use different font types and sizes and Word's other capabilities to create a letterhead template. Then, whenever you start a letter, you can use that template.

Templates can include formatting for fonts and font sizes, and any text you care to include. When you start a document, you select a template on which to base it (if you don't select a specific template, Word automatically uses a template called **Normal**).

In this project, you'll create a simple letterhead template with your name, address, phone number, and the date. It also will include the salutation and the closing. When you use this template, all you have to do is type your message and not worry about all the other extraneous issues.

True, Word for Windows 95 does include several letter templates. It even includes a wizard that walks you through the process of creating letters. However, neither the templates nor the letter wizard automatically provide personalized letterhead for your letter. Rather, each time you start the provided templates or wizard, you still must enter your own personal information, such as your address. After you create this template, you never have to add that information again.

Pierre Schmit
12345 Alta Loma Circle
New Luxembourg, WI 55555
(414) 444-6666

Saturday, October 14, 1995

Dear Joe,

Thank you so much for your hospitality and help during my recent time of distress. Usually, I am hesitant to mix my work life and my personal life, but you proved that a colleague can also be a great comfort and help.

My regards to Hannah and the kids. Once again, thank you for all that you've done.

Regards,

Pete Schmit

Begin Do It Yourself Add Basic Information

1 Open the **File** menu and select the **New** command.

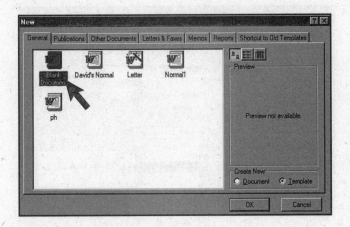

2 In the New dialog box, click the **General** tab. Then click the **Template** radio button. Click **Blank Document** icon and click **OK**.

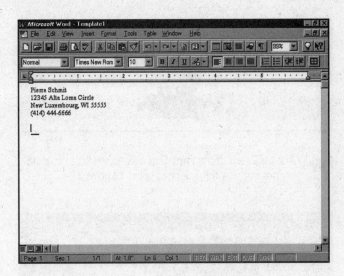

3 Word creates a new blank template that is identical to the Normal template. At the top of the document, type, on separate lines, your name and address. On another line, type your city, state, and ZIP code. On the fourth line, type your phone number, including area code; press **Enter** four times.

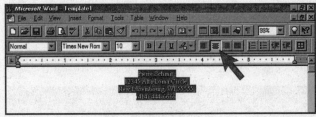

4 Select all the information by dragging your mouse over it. Click the **Center Justify** button in the Formatting toolbar.

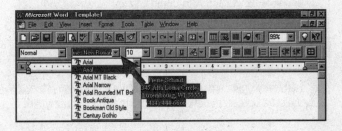

5 Click the **Font** drop-down list of the Formatting toolbar to change the font, if you want. For this example, use **Arial**.

(continues)

Do It Yourself Add Basic Information   *(continued)*

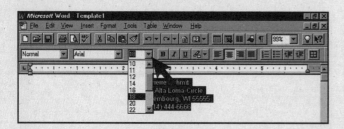

6 Click the arrow of the **Font Size** drop-down list to change the font size. For this example, select **18** point type.

7 Place the cursor at the end of the line containing the phone number. Click the **Borders** button on the Formatting toolbar to make the Borders toolbar appear.

8 Click the down arrow of the **Line Style** drop-down list to select a border for beneath the information you just typed.

9 Click the **Bottom Border** button in the Borders toolbar. A border appears beneath the letterhead heading. Return the cursor to the bottom of the page, which should be four lines below the border.

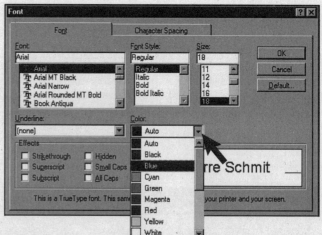

10 Optionally, to spice things up, select the entire heading, open the **Format** menu and select the **Font** command. In the **Color** drop-down list, select a color for your heading.

Do It Yourself Add Basic Information

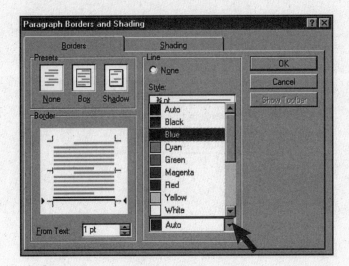

11 Similarly, with the cursor in the last line of the heading, select **Paragraph Borders and Shading**. Click the **Borders** tab and select a color from the **Color** drop-down list. Then click **OK**. Your letterhead heading is now the color you selected.

> Adding colors makes the on-screen appearance more attractive but won't make much difference in printing on a black and white printer. However, if you have a color printer, adding colors to your letterhead enlivens your letters.

Begin Do It Yourself Add the Date

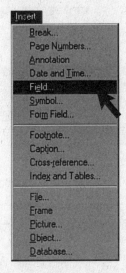

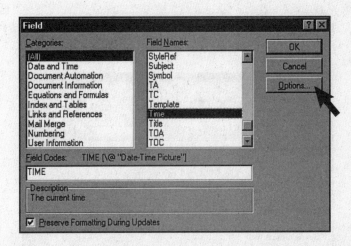

1 With the cursor four lines below the border, open the **Insert** menu and select the **Field** command. The Field dialog box opens.

2 In the **Field Names** window, scroll down until you highlight **Time**. Click the **Options** button.

(continues)

Do It Yourself Add the Date *(continued)*

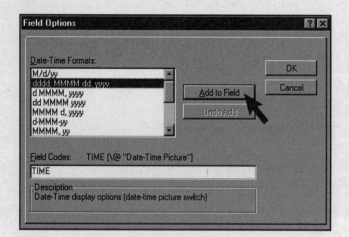

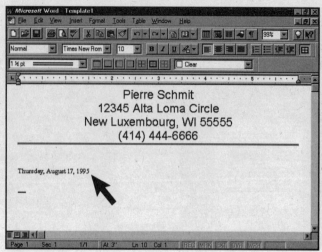

3 In the Field Options dialog box, scroll down the list of date formats until you find one you like. With that format highlighted, click the **Add to Field** button. Click **OK**.

4 In the Field dialog box, click **OK** to place the date in your letter template.

Begin Do It Yourself Add a Heading and Closing

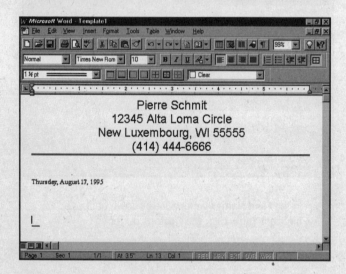

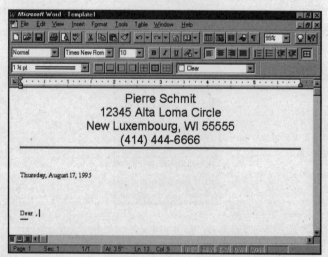

1 Place the cursor after the date; then press the **Enter** key five times.

2 Type **Dear** and press **Spacebar** twice; type a comma. Press the **Enter** key five more times.

Do It Yourself   Add a Heading and Closing

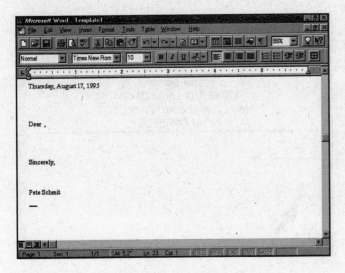

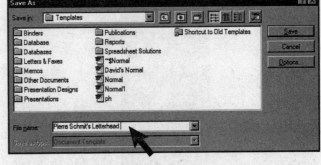

5 In the Save As dialog box, type a name for your template in the **File name** text box. Click **Save**. Then, close the template by opening the **File** menu and the **Exit** command.

3 Type **Sincerely** and a comma; press the **Enter** key four times. Type your name.

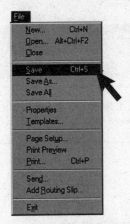

4 Open the **File** menu and select the **Save** command.

Begin Do It Yourself Use Your Letterhead

1 Open the **File** and select the **New** Command.

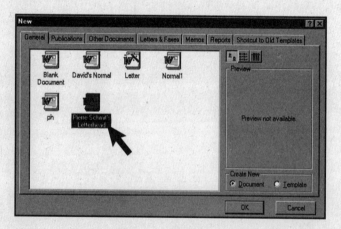

2 In the New dialog box, click the icon for the template you just created and click **OK**.

3 In the document, move the cursor so it is one space to the right of the word **Dear**. Type in the name of the person to whom you are writing.

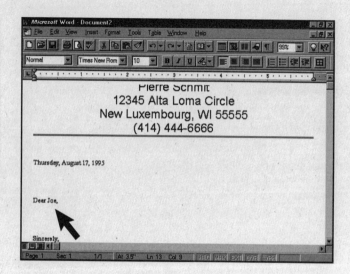

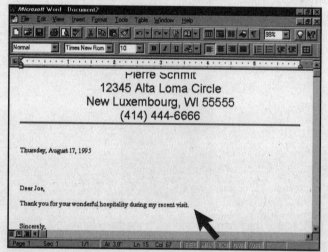

4 Use your arrow keys to move down two lines and start typing your letter. Remember to periodically save your work.

Create a Personal Note Pad

In the last project, we created a letterhead template. That sort of template is appropriate for sending formal letters to people you don't know, such as correspondence with a business. However, most of us also jot notes to friends, relatives, and acquaintances. These are hardly formal documents, which is why it isn't appropriate to use a formal letterhead.

In those cases, something akin to a note card or a jotting pad is more appropriate. That's what you'll create in this project. Specifically, you'll create a template on which you can base your notes and other informal correspondence.

Of course, note cards and other personal note pads should reflect your personality. By definition, though, the personal note template we're creating may not do that. As a result, you can use this project as a learning experience; then revise it to more accurately reflect your personality.

For example, we'll use simple clip art to embellish the note pad a bit. But you could have a photograph of yourself developed using a process called Kodak Photo CD. This creates computerized images of your photos that you can insert into your note template (learn more about it from your photo processor). Or more simply, you can select fonts and font sizes that you like. When you finish, you can jot off that note to Aunt Joan or Uncle Bob on appropriate stationery.

This template is a good opportunity to take advantage of a color printer. Simply use the Font dialog box (which you access by opening the **Format** menu and selecting the **Font** command) to change the color of highlighted text. This means you could, for example, print your name and address in red ink.

Begin Do It Yourself Create the Grid

1 Open the **File** menu and select the **New** command.

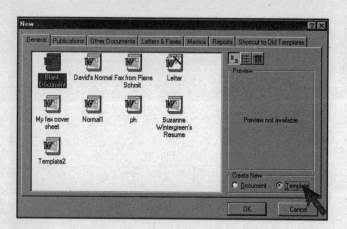

2 Click the **Template** radio button in the New dialog box. Click **OK**.

3 In the Standard toolbar, click the **Insert Table** button.

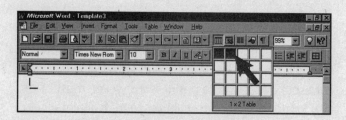

4 Click the second square from the left in the top row.

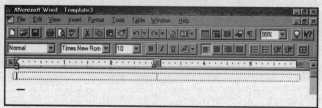

5 This creates a one row, two column table and places it at the top of your document template.

Begin Do It Yourself   Add an Image

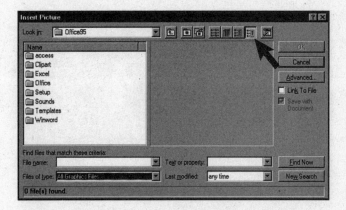

1 Position the cursor in the left cell; then open the **Insert** menu and select the **Picture** command.

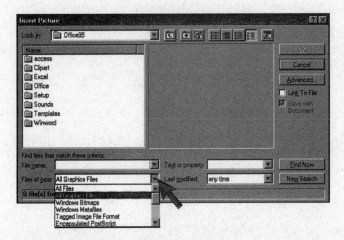

2 Click the down arrow of the **Files of type** drop-down list in the Insert Picture dialog box. From the list, select **All Graphic Files** if it isn't already selected (it is the default).

3 If it already isn't done, click the **Preview** button to view images before you insert them. (This is the default for this dialog box, and you'll only need to do this if you previously changed this setting.)

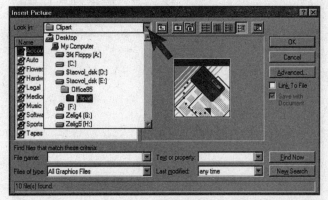

4 Click the down arrow of the **Look in** drop-down list to find the location of the images. CLIP art is in the **Clipart** folder, either below the **\MSOFFICE**, **\OFFICE95,** or **\WINWORD** folders, depending on your specific installation.

(continues)

Do It Yourself Add an Image

(continued)

5 Click each image and preview it in the right window. Click **OK** when you find the image you want.

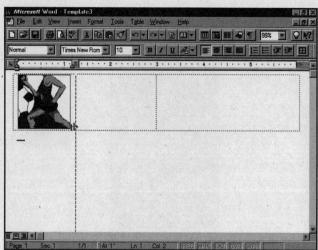

7 Hold down the left mouse button. Drag the mouse to the left so the left cell is slightly wider than the image, then release the mouse button.

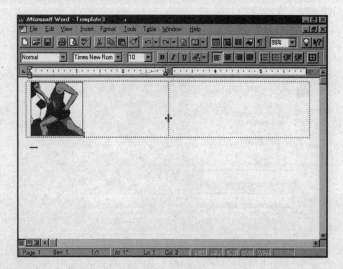

6 Word inserts the image into the template. Position the mouse cursor above the vertical line separating the cells. The cursor should turn into a two-headed cursor.

Begin Do It Yourself Add Information at the Top

1 Position the insertion point in the right cell of the table. Click the down arrow of the **Font Size** drop-down list. From the list, select **9**.

4 Click the down arrow of the **Font** drop-down list and select another font. In this example, we'll use **Arial**.

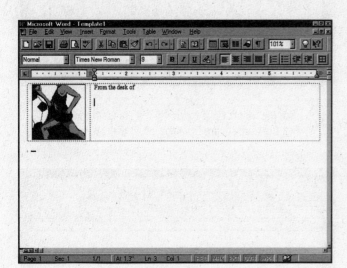

2 Type **From the desk of...** and press the **Enter** key twice.

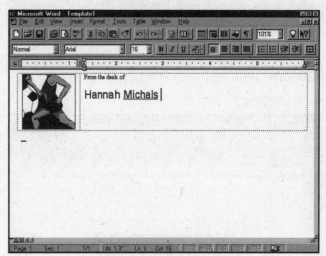

5 Type your name.

3 Click the down arrow in the **Font Size** drop-down list and select **16**.

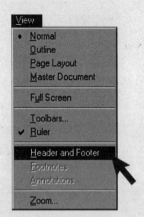

Begin Do It Yourself Add Additional Information

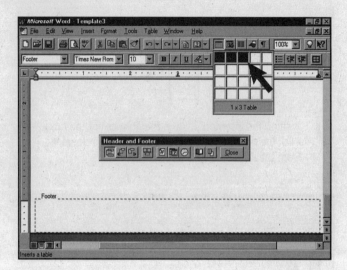

1 Open the **View** menu and select the **Header and Footer** command.

3 Click the **Insert** table button in the Standard toolbar, and click the third square from the left in the top row.

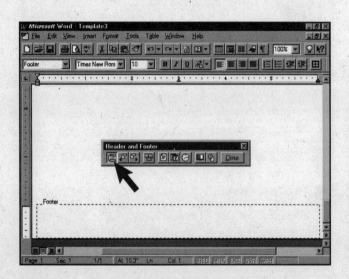

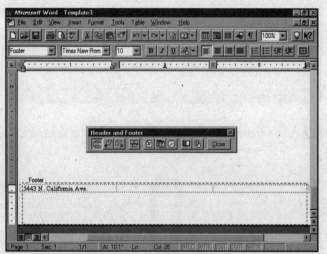

2 In the Header and Footer button bar, click the left most button to switch to the footer.

4 Position the cursor in the left cell and type your street address. Press the **Tab** key to move to the middle cell.

Do It Yourself Add Additional Information

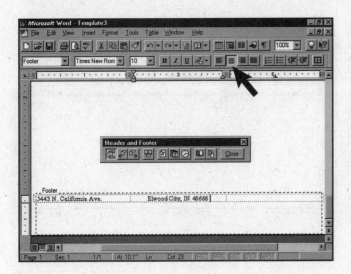

5 Type your city, state, and ZIP code. Click the **Center** button in the Formatting toolbar; press **Tab** to move to the next cell.

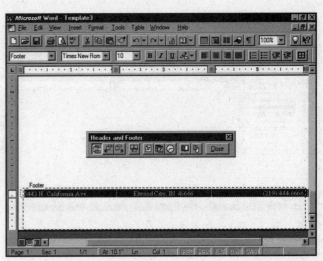

7 Position the mouse cursor to the left of the first cell so it becomes a right-facing arrow. Click the left mouse button to highlight all cells.

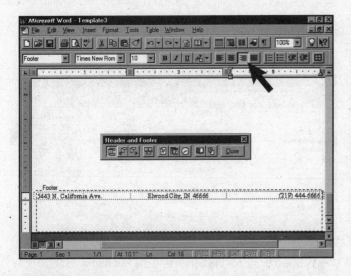

6 Type your area code and telephone number. Click the **Right Alignment** button in the Formatting toolbar.

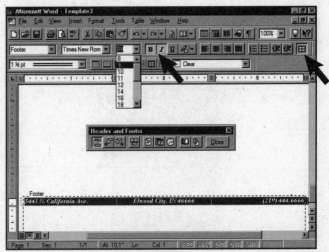

8 Click the down arrow of the **Font Size** drop-down list in the Formatting toolbar. Select **9**. Click the **Italic**, **Bold**, and **Borders** buttons.

(continues)

Do It Yourself Add Additional Information

(continued)

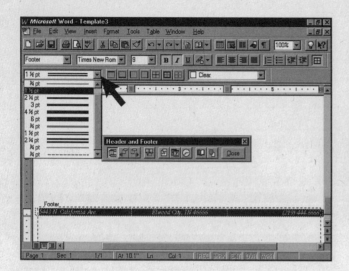

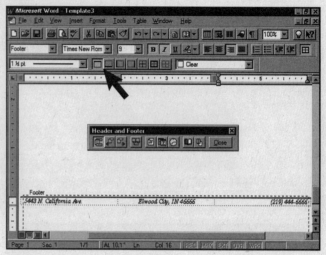

9 With the entire table still highlighted, in the Borders toolbar, click the down arrow of the **Line Types** drop-down list. Select a line type you like.

10 Click the **Top Border** button in the Borders toolbar. Click the **Close** button in the Header and Footer toolbar.

Begin Do It Yourself Save and Use Your Note Pad

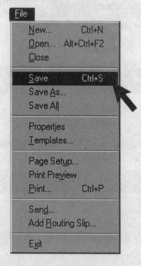

1 Open the **File** menu and select the **Save** command.

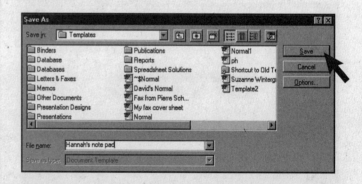

2 Type a name for the template in the **File name** text box. Click **Save**. Open the **File** menu and select the **Exit** command to exit the template.

Do It Yourself Save and Use Your Note Pad

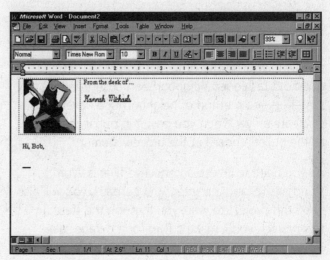

3 To use the template, select the **File** menu and the **New** command.

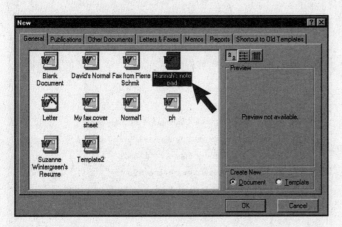

4 In the New dialog box, click the icon for the template you created. Click **OK.**

5 Position your cursor underneath the header information and begin your note.

Create a Flyer

Your cat is missing. Or perhaps you're having a garage sale. When you need to reach out to people in your neighborhood, it's time to do some good old-fashioned neighborhood advertising. A time-honored method of neighborhood advertising is to create a flyer. Then you post it in public places such as the bulletin board at the grocery store.

All you need to create an effective flyer is Word for Windows 95 and a printer. And perhaps, you will also need this project to walk you through the steps. In this project, you'll make a flyer for a garage sale. However, the principles are the same for other flyers, such as one in which you ask help for finding a lost cat or try to sell your car.

This is a good learning project because it is a bit trickier to create an effective flyer than you would think. That's because a good flyer must stand out from the crowd. Anybody who's ever seen a jam-packed grocery store bulletin board knows that.

A good flyer should have a graphic image to make it eye catching. Also, the fonts must be large enough to be clearly seen and read in public places. Finally, you'll use bullets to set off important points that you want to make.

It is easiest to accomplish this project if you use Page Layout view. This is the on-screen view that shows how an item will look when it is printed. To access Page Layout view, open the **View** menu and select the **Page Layout** command.

BIG GARAGE SALE

Five families in the 1700 block of Rutledge Street are offering their wares for sale at a large garage sale. From treasures to trash, this sale is packed with interesting and valuable merchandise. Among the offerings are:

- Two bicycles
- A stove
- A men's tuxedo
- A motor boat
- Three bowling balls

WHO: Five families living in the 1700 block of Rutledge Street

WHAT: A huge garage sale featuring all types of quality material

WHEN: 9 a.m. to 5 p.m., Friday, Saturday and Sunday

WHY: Our attics, basements and garages or overflowing!

For more information, call Susan at 456-7890 or Louisa at 457-9876

Begin Do It Yourself Add the Headline

1 Start a new document by clicking the **New** button in the Standard toolbar.

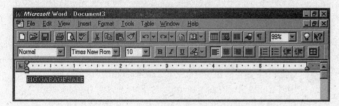

2 With the cursor at the top of the document, type (all in uppercase letters) **BIG GARAGE SALE** and press **Enter** twice.

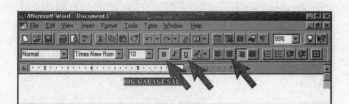

3 Highlight the words **BIG GARAGE SALE**. Then click the **Bold**, **Center,** and **Underline** buttons in the Formatting toolbar.

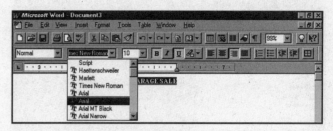

4 With the words still highlighted, click the down arrow of the **Font** drop-down list. Select **Arial**.

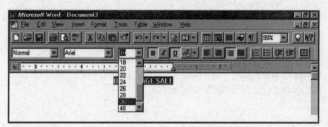

5 Click the down arrow of the **Font Size** drop-down list. Select **36**.

Begin Do It Yourself Add an Image

1 Position the cursor beneath the headline. Open the **Insert** menu and select the **Picture** command.

(continues)

Do It Yourself   Add an Image   *(continued)*

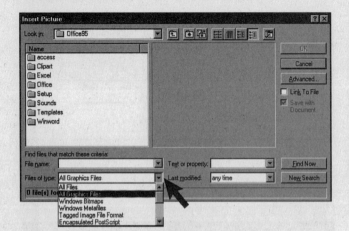

2 Click the down arrow of the **Files of type** drop-down list in the Insert Picture dialog box. From the list, select **All Graphic Files**. This is the default setting so you won't have to do this unless you previously changed it.

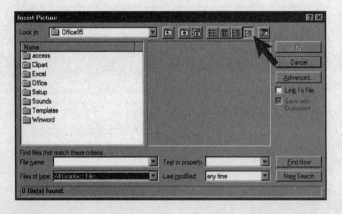

3 Click the **Preview** button to view images before you insert them. This is the default; you'll only have to do this step if you previously used another setting.

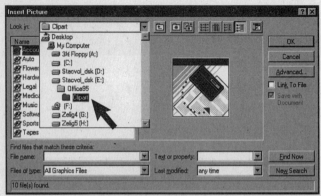

4 Click the down arrow of the **Look in** drop-down list to find the location of the images. For clipart, that location would be the **Clipart** folder, either below the **\MSOFFICE** or **\WINWORD** folders, depending on your specific installation.

5 Click the **Auto** (as in automobile) clipart file and click **OK**.

Do It Yourself Add an Image

6 Word inserts the image into the flyer. Click on the image so a border appears around it. Eight small boxes, called *handles*, appear around the border.

8 Hold down the left mouse button and drag the mouse down and to the right until the image is about twice as large as it was originally.

7 Position the mouse cursor over the handle in the lower right corner; it turns into a two-headed cursor with the arrows facing diagonally.

9 Release the mouse button to finish resizing the picture.

(continues)

Do It Yourself   Add an Image

(continued)

10 With the image still selected so the border and handles appear, open the **Insert** menu and select the **Frame** command. Click **Yes** when a dialog box asks if you should switch to Page Layout view.

Begin Do It Yourself   Add Text

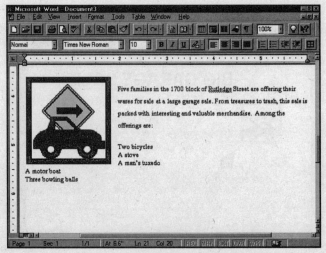

1 Position the cursor to the right of the image and type descriptive text about the garage sale. Conclude this first part by typing **Among the offerings are:**. Press **Enter** twice.

2 Type short lines describing items being sold, such as **Two bicycles** and **Men's tuxedo**. Add between four and ten of these items, pressing **Enter** once after typing each item.

Do It Yourself   Add Text

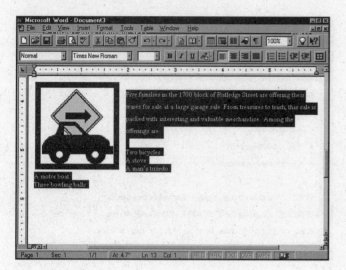

3 Highlight all the text below the main headline.

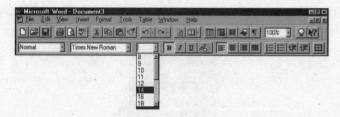

4 Click the down arrow of the **Font Size** dialog box and select **14**. Click the **Bold** button in the Formatting toolbar.

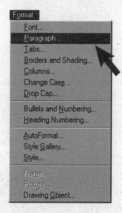

5 Open the **Format** menu and select the **Paragraph** command.

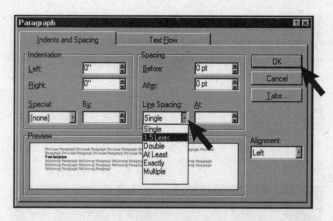

6 Click the **Indents and Spacing** tab in the Paragraph dialog box. Click the down arrow of the **Line Spacing** drop-down list and select **1.5 Lines**. Click **OK**.

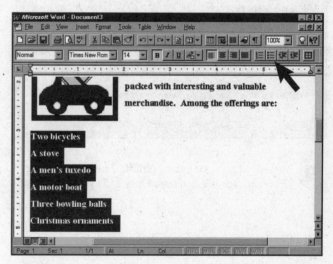

7 Highlight the list of items for sale. Click the **Bullets** button in the Formatting toolbar.

(continues)

Do It Yourself Add Text *(continued)*

8 Position the cursor after the last bulleted line, at the bottom of the page. Click the **Bold** button in the Formatting toolbar.

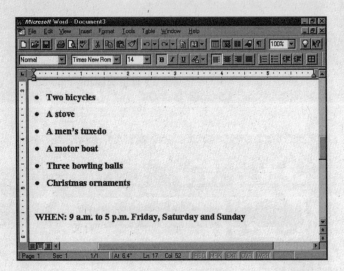

9 Type, all in uppercase letters, **WHEN:**. Type times and days for your garage sale and press **Enter** twice when you finish.

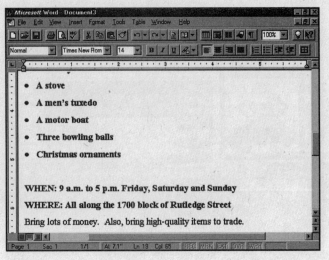

10 Type all in capital letters, **WHERE:**. Add information about the location of the garage sale and press **Enter**. Add any other information you want.

11 Open the **File** menu and select the **Save** command. Type a name for the flyer in the **File name** text box. Click **Save**.

Create a Résumé Template

Job hunting, it has been said, is a full-time job in its own right. It takes hard work and persistence to find the job you want. And the more professional-looking your résumé, the better your chances of landing that job.

Besides using a professional-looking résumé, it makes sense to change your résumé each time you apply for a job to more precisely reflect the position. That way, you can emphasize your strong points as they pertain to a specific job.

Use Word for Windows 95—and this project—to create a template for an effective résumé. Once created, you can change your résumé as needed. The résumé you will create in this project includes all the basic information that a résumé should contain.

This project also provides good practice at using some of Word's basic features such as tables and character formatting. However, we won't get too fancy with this résumé; it's up to you to add your own flourishes and formatting touches. That's because there is no such thing as one size fitting all when it comes to résumés. Yours must fit you as well as your best business suit. So feel free to make any formatting changes—such as changing fonts—to the examples in this project.

Remember, too, that Word comes with some prebuilt templates for creating résumés. These templates (which you can access by opening the **File** menu and selecting the **New** command) are good, but they aren't as automated as the template you'll create in this project. Still, check them out; they may fill the bill for you or, at the very least, give you some ideas about how you want to format your own résumé.

Suzanne Wintergreen
45678 Northport Road
Oak Brook, IL 66666
(708) 555-5555

Objective   To use and expand my background and skills in the area of manufacturing and materials management.

Experience   **Manufacturing Manager; Acme Manufacturing Title; Iowa City, IA; 1992 to present**
In charge of manufacturing for this Fortune 500 corporation. Supervised 30 people. Productivity increased by 25 percent since assuming this position.

Assistant Manager; Acme Manufacturing; Iowa City, IA; 1990 to 1992
Assisted the manager in overseeing manufacturing. Also had primary responsibility for inventory and receiving.

Manufacturing team member; Acme Manufacturing; Iowa City, IA; 1988-1990
Member of the manufacturing team. Worked in all manufacturing positions from initial material collection to final packaging and shipping. Cited as "employee of the month" twice.

Dormitory residence assistant; University of Iowa; Iowa City, IA; 1987-1988
Supervised the activities of 52 dormitory residents. Enforced university rules and suggested corrective action when rules were violated. Cited as "most popular residence assistant" for the second semester.

Education   M.A. Business, 1988, from University of Iowa, Iowa, Iowa City, IA.

B.A. Business Administration, 1986 from University of Wisconsin, 1986. Was graduated with honors.

Interests   Hiking, bicycling, 19th Century American fiction

References available upon request

Begin Do It Yourself Add Header Information

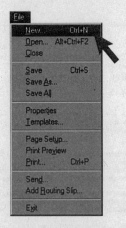

1 Begin a new template by opening the **File** menu and selecting the **New** command.

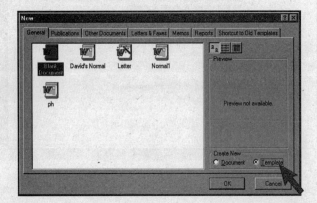

2 In the New dialog box, click the **Template** radio button. Then click **OK**.

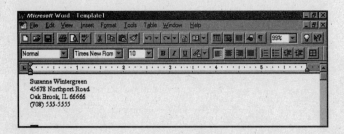

3 At the top of the new, empty template, type your name and press **Enter**. Type your address and press **Enter** again. Type your city, state and ZIP code, and press **Enter**. Then type your telephone number on the last line and press **Enter** twice.

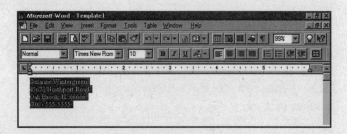

4 Highlight all the information you just typed. Do that by positioning your cursor before the first letter of your name and dragging the mouse to the end.

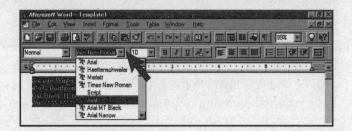

5 Click the down-arrow of the **Font** drop-down in the Formatting toolbar. Use the scroll bars to find the **Arial** font. Click it.

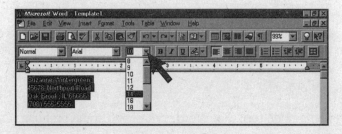

6 Click the down-arrow of the **Font Size** drop-down list of the Formatting toolbar. Click **14**.

7 Click the **Italic** button in the Formatting toolbar.

Do It Yourself Add Header Information

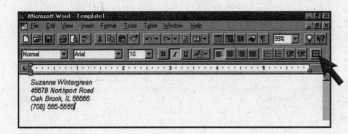

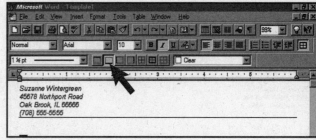

8 Position the mouse cursor anywhere in the line with your phone number. Click the **Borders** button in the Formatting toolbar.

10 Click the **Bottom Border** button in the Borders toolbar.

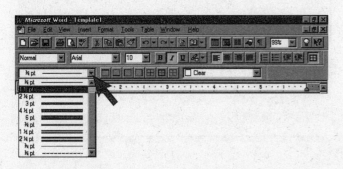

9 Click the down-arrow of the **Line Style** drop-down list, and select the type of line you want under your header information.

Begin Do It Yourself Create the Grid

1 Position the cursor at the bottom of the page. Click the **Insert Table** button in the Standard toolbar.

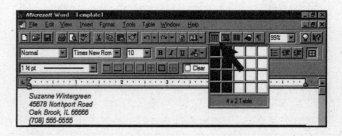

2 Click the square in the **Add Table** box that is four rows down and two columns to the right. This inserts a table in your document.

(continues)

Do It Yourself   Create the Grid

(continued)

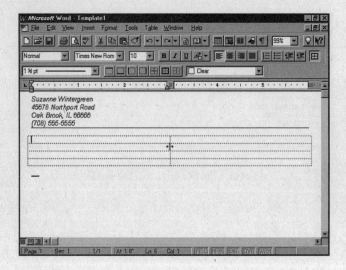

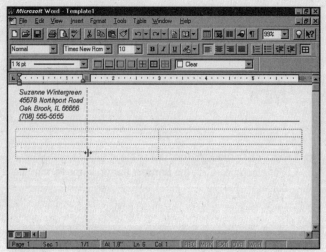

3 Position your cursor over the vertical line dividing the rows in the table. When the cursor turns into a two-headed arrow, hold down the left mouse button.

4 Drag your mouse to the left to make the left column roughly half its original width. Release the left mouse button.

Begin Do It Yourself   Add Main Headings

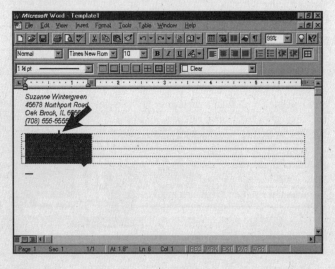

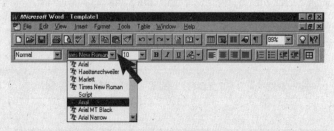

2 Click the down arrow of the **Fonts** drop-down list in the Formatting toolbar. For this example, select **Arial**.

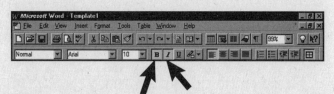

1 Position your mouse cursor just above the top of the left column. When it turns into a solid black down-arrow, click the left mouse button to highlight the entire column.

3 Click both the **Bold** and **Italic** buttons in the Formatting toolbar.

Do It Yourself Add Main Headings

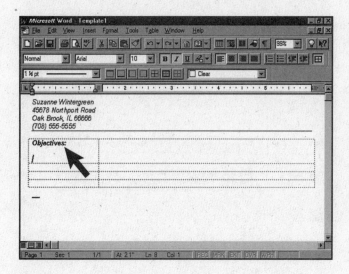

4 Click the top left-most table cell and type **Objectives:**. Press **Enter** twice.

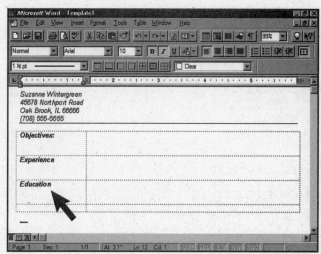

6 Click the next cell below and type **Education**. Press **Enter** twice.

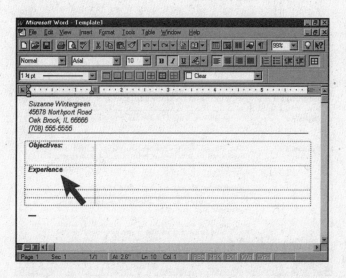

5 Click the next cell below and type **Experience**. Press **Enter** twice.

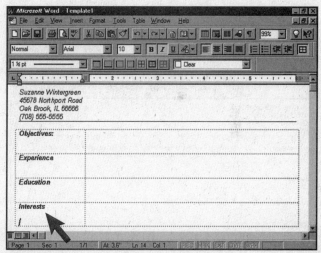

7 Click the bottom left-most cell and type **Interests**. Press **Enter** twice.

Begin Do It Yourself Add Information

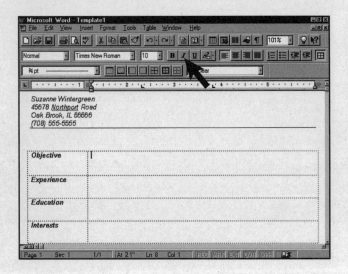

1 Position the cursor in the top right-most cell. Click the **Italic** button in the Formatting toolbar. Then type your objective in applying for this particular position.

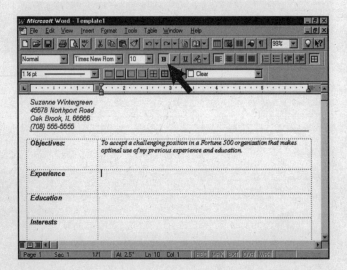

2 Position your cursor in the cell below. Click the **Bold** button in the Formatting toolbar. Type your position title, company, city and state, and the dates of employment of your most recent position. Type a semicolon between each of those types of information.

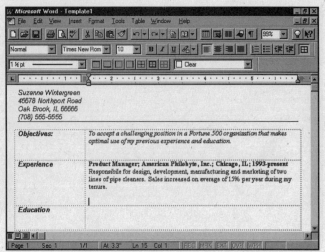

3 Click the **Bold** button again and press **Enter**. Type descriptive information about the position. When you finish, press **Enter** twice.

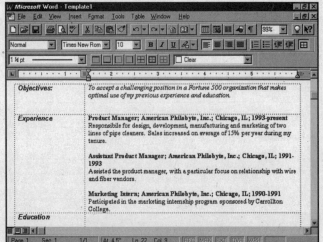

4 Repeat the process for as many positions as you want to include. Press **Enter** twice after your last position.

Here are a couple of basic résumé-writing tips. Keep the descriptions extremely concise and start with verbs. Don't say, "In this position, I supervised five people." Rather, simply say, "Supervised five people..." plus any other descriptive information that's appropriate.

Do It Yourself   Add Information

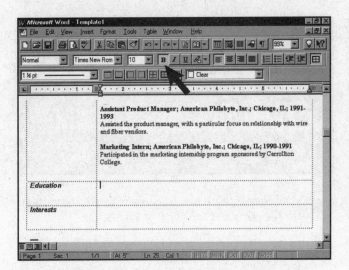

5 Position the cursor in the next cell down. Click the **Bold** button in the Formatting toolbar. Then type the name of your most recent educational institution, the institution's city and state, and the years you attended. Place a semicolon between each type of information. Click the **Bold** button again and press **Enter** once.

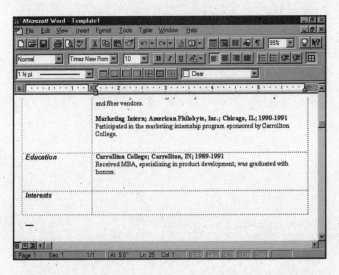

6 Type additional information about your time at that institution, including degrees, major courses of study, and points of distinction. When you finish, press **Enter** twice.

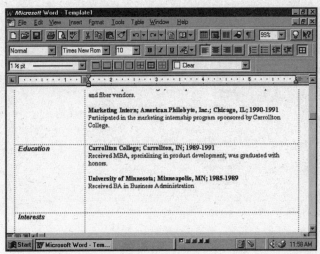

7 Repeat the process for the institutions you want to include. After the last entry, press **Enter** twice.

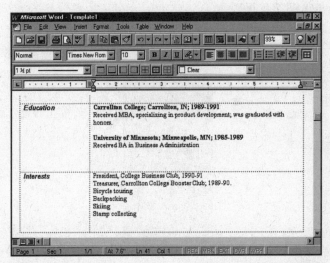

8 Position the cursor in the next cell down. Briefly type your interests, such as hobbies and clubs to which you belong, on separate lines. Press **Enter** to move to the next line and press it twice when you finish.

Begin Do It Yourself Finish the Résumé

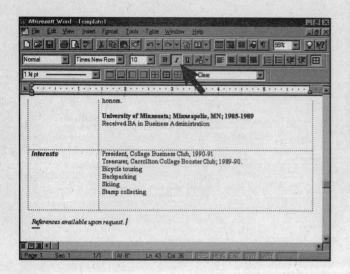

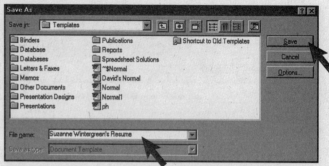

3 In the Save As dialog box, type a name for your template in the **File name** text box. Click the **Save** button.

1 Position your cursor below the table containing your objective, experience, education, and interests. Click the **Italic** button in the Formatting toolbar. Type **References available upon request.**

At this point, you can exit your résumé template. However, before you do, proofread it, spell check it, and make any changes to formatting and content that you want. Also, if the résumé is longer than one page, add a header to the second (and subsequent) pages. Check out the How To section of this book for instructions on how to do these things.

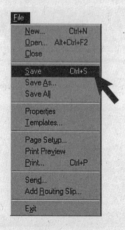

2 Open the **File** menu and select the **Save** command.

Begin Do It Yourself   Use the Résumé Template

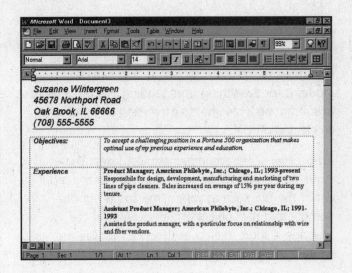

1 Open the **File** menu and select the **New** command.

3 A new document starts based on the template you created in this project. Alter the résumé as appropriate.

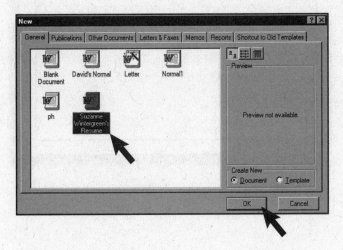

2 In the New dialog box, click the icon for the résumé template you created. Click **OK**.

Personalize Your Fax Cover Sheet

These days, fax modems are pretty much standard equipment with PCs. That is one reason why faxing has become so ubiquitous. You can use fax modems for everything from sending in a pizza order to submitting a résumé, to expressing an opinion to an elected official.

A fax cover sheet accompanies most faxes. These cover sheets provide basic information for the recipient of the fax, such as your name and telephone number and the subject of the fax. Also, if the message is short, the cover sheet can convey the entire message.

Most cover sheets are pretty mundane affairs that provide space for basic information such as your name and the date. But why not create your own custom fax cover sheets? These sheets can express a bit about your personality. After all, there's no reason why communications in the modern age needs to be dreary. So let's create a template for a custom fax cover sheet. When you're done, you can start your fax by starting a new Word document and basing it on this template.

As with the other projects in this section, this sheet both will be useful to you and should spur your imagination about how to create additional custom fax cover sheets. Although Word comes with several templates for faxes, they aren't automated as the one you'll create here. Rather, they are more oriented toward typical business situations—hardly the place in which it's appropriate to display some personality.

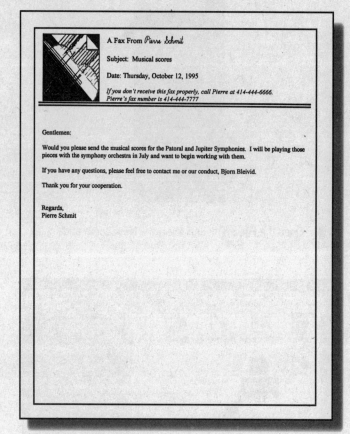

A Fax From *Pierre Schmit*

Subject: Musical scores

Date: Thursday, October 12, 1995

If you don't receive this fax properly, call Pierre at 414-444-6666.
Pierre's fax number is 414-444-7777

Gentlemen:

Would you please send the musical scores for the Patoral and Jupiter Symphonies. I will be playing those pieces with the symphony orchestra in July and want to begin working with them.

If you have any questions, please feel free to contact me or our conduct, Bjorn Bleivid.

Thank you for your cooperation.

Regards,
Pierre Schmit

Begin Do It Yourself   Create the Grid

1 Open the **File** menu and select the **New** command.

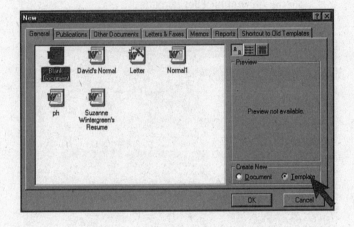

2 In the New dialog box, click the **Template** radio button. Then click **OK**.

3 Click the **Insert Table** button in the Standard toolbar.

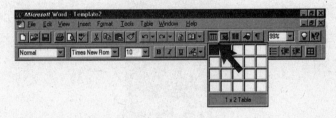

4 Click the second square from the left in the top row. This creates a one row, two column table at the top of your document template.

Begin Do It Yourself Add an Image

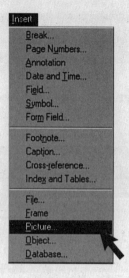

1 Position the cursor in the left cell. Open the **Insert** menu and select the **Picture** command.

In this example, we'll insert some simple clip art that comes with Word for Windows 95. You can, of course, insert any graphic image you want. You might, for example, insert a photo of yourself your photo processor developed digitally using the Kodak Photo CD format. Remember, though, that photos and other high-detail images don't transmit clearly via fax.

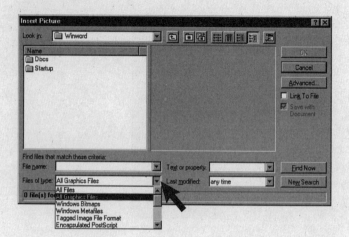

2 In the Insert Picture dialog box, click the down arrow of the **Files of type** drop-down list. If it isn't already selected, choose **All Graphic Files** from the list.

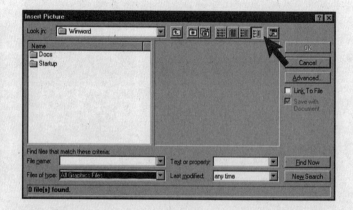

3 Click the **Preview** button to view images before you insert them. Preview is the default setting; you'll only need this step if you previously used another setting for this dialog box.

Do It Yourself Add an Image

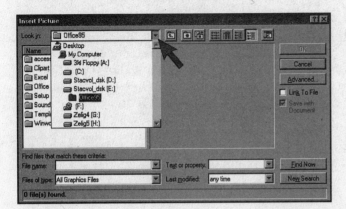

4 Use the **Look in** drop-down list to find the location of the images. For clip art, that location would be the **Clipart** folder, either below the **\MSOFFICE** or **\WINWORD** folders, depending on your specific installation.

6 Position the mouse cursor above the vertical line separating the cells. The cursor should turn into a two-headed cursor.

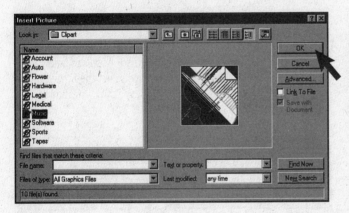

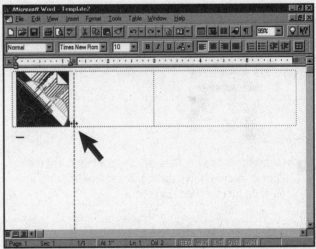

5 Click on each image and preview it in the right window. When you find the image you want, click **OK**. This inserts the image into the template.

7 Hold down the left mouse button, and drag the mouse to the left until the left cell is just a bit wider than the image. Release the mouse button.

Begin Do It Yourself   Add Information at the Top

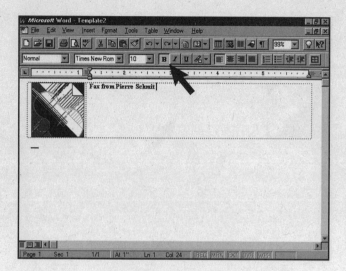

1 Position the cursor in the right cell of the table. Click the **Bold** button in the Formatting toolbar. Type **Fax from** and then your name. Press **Enter** twice.

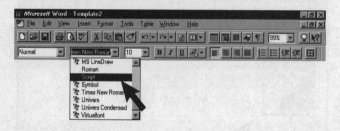

2 Highlight your name. Then click the down arrow of the **Font** drop-down list in the Formatting toolbar. Select a different font than the current one.

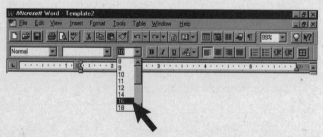

3 Highlight the entire line. Then click the down-arrow of the **Font Size** drop-down list. Select a larger-than-normal font size. A 16-point size is good for a fax heading.

The font with your name may need to be different than that for the words **Fax From**. That's because font sizes don't always match when using multiple fonts. For example, we sometimes use a font called Script, which appears smaller than a similarly sized Times New Roman. As a result, you must increase the size of the Script font to a higher point size than you would when using Times New Roman.

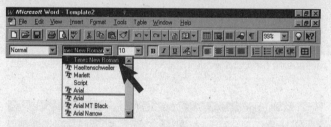

4 Use the arrow keys to move the cursor two lines below the first. In the **Font** drop-down list, select the font you normally use—by default, this is Times New Roman. You need only take this step if you just used another font.

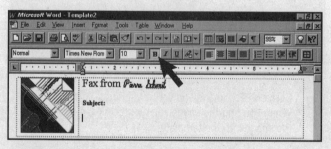

5 Click the **Bold** button of the Formatting toolbar and type **Subject:**. Press **Enter** twice.

Do It Yourself Add Information at the Top

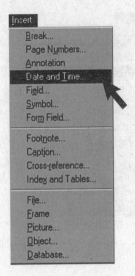

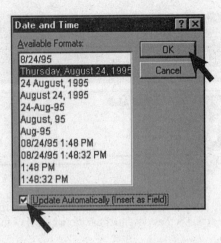

6 Open the **Insert** menu and select the **Date and Time** command.

7 Find a date format you like in the **Available Formats** window of the Date and Time dialog box. Click the **Update Automatically (Insert as Field)** check box so a check appears. Click **OK**. Word inserts the date.

Begin Do It Yourself Finish the Cover Sheet

1 Place the cursor anywhere in the cell, and click the **Borders** button in the Formatting toolbar.

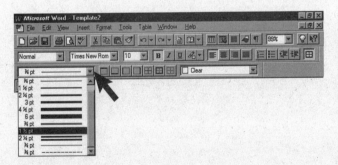

2 Click the down arrow of the **Line Style** drop-down list. Select a line style you like.

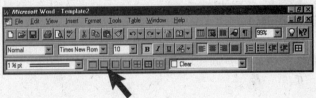

3 Click the **Bottom Border** button in the Borders toolbar. This inserts a border below the right cell.

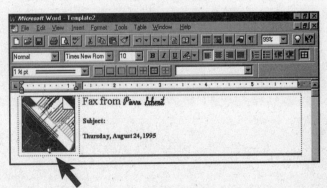

4 Click the image so a border with eight small square boxes, called handles, appears. Position the mouse cursor over the middle handle on the bottom border so the cursor turns into a two-headed cursor.

(continues)

Do It Yourself Finish the Cover Sheet

(continued)

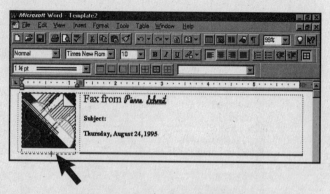

5 Hold down the left mouse button, and drag the mouse so the image comes close to the bottom border of the right cell.

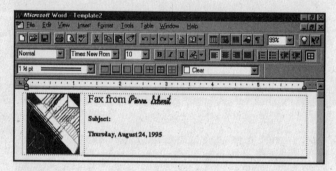

6 Release the mouse button to finish resizing the image.

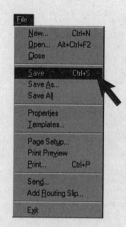

7 Open the **File** menu and select the **Save** command.

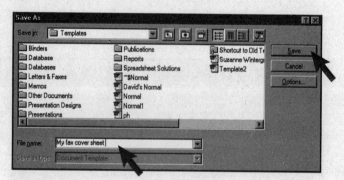

8 Type a name for the template in the **File name** text box. Click **Save**. Then open the **File** menu and select the **Exit** command to close the template.

Begin Do It Yourself Use the Cover Sheet

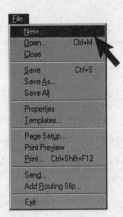

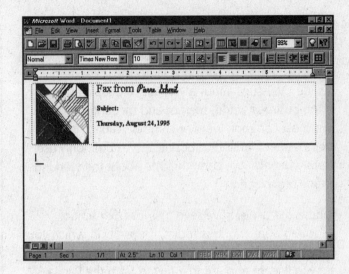

1 Open the **File** menu and select the **New** command.

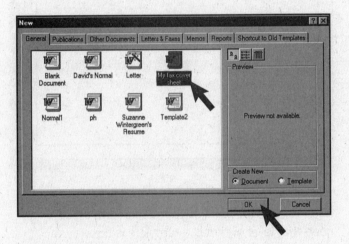

3 Position your cursor underneath the header information and begin your fax.

2 In the New dialog box, click the icon for the fax cover page you created. Click **OK**.

Write a Memo

Sure, some people find memoranda—memos for short—to be cold, but they also are useful. That's because memos can be concise, to the point, and outline the issues about a very specific topic. In fact, in the business world, memos and meetings are the two most common ways of communicating. But memos aren't limited to business; we commonly use them whenever we communicate about the workings of any organization.

Parents, certainly, have seen memos from school principals about various topics. If the city in which you live changes the day it picks up your trash, chances are you'll learn about it in a memo from the Sanitation Department. You may need to use Word to write memos at work about job-related issues or in behalf of organizations to which you donate your time. Also, memos are useful when you must communicate with business or governmental entities about a very specific issue.

Word comes with several templates with which you can create memos. They are generally useful, but they aren't particularly personalized. In this project, you can create a simple, but more personalized, memo form. And, instead of creating it as a template on which you can base your memos, we'll create it as an AutoCorrect entry.

As an AutoCorrect entry, creating a memo is particularly fast and easy. You simply start a new document, type a couple of letters, and Word automatically inserts your memo heading. You could, of course, create your personalized memo heading as a template—using templates is, overall, more powerful. You can, for example, use templates to set specific type

fonts for specific parts of your document. If you need that level of detail, a template is the way to go. However, using AutoCorrect is faster and works almost as well. It's the perfect way to create a template for those times when you don't need anything fancy but need to get the job done quickly. You also can make AutoCorrect entries out of similar types of pages. For example, you can create an AutoCorrect heading for fax headings rather than using templates.

MEMO

TO: Hannah Michals

FROM: Al Greene

SUBJECT: Property Tax Assessments

October 12, 1995

In regard to the most recent notification of property tax assessments, I wish to express my displeasure at the way the city handled the matter.

I'm particularly disturbed by the fact that assessments rose, in our area, by an average of twenty-five percent, nearly twice the average increases city-wide. However, we had no indication of the magnitude of the assessments until we received our notice from the city.

In the future, it would be appreciated if the city were more aware that these types of increases are a financial burden for many taxpayers. It always helps to plan for such burdens, so earlier notification would be greatly appreciated.

Begin Do It Yourself   Add Heading Information

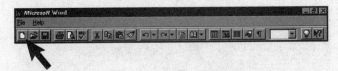

1) Start a new document by clicking the **New** button in the Standard toolbar.

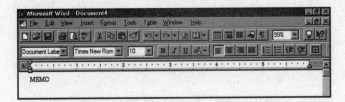

2) At the top of the new document, type, in all uppercase letters, the word **MEMO**. Press **Enter** twice.

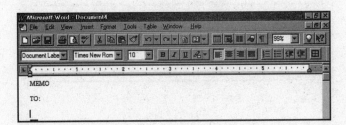

3) Type the word **TO:**, press **Tab** three times, and then press **Enter** twice.

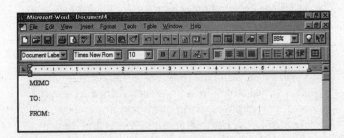

4) Type the word **FROM:**, press **Tab** three times, type your name, and press **Enter** twice.

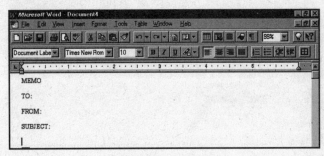

5) Type the word **SUBJECT:**, press **Tab** twice, and press **Enter** twice.

6) Open the **Insert** menu and select the **Date and Time** command.

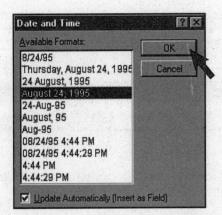

7) Select a date format you like. Check the **Update Automatically (Insert as Field)** check box. Click **OK**. Press **Enter** twice.

Begin Do It Yourself   Format the Memo Heading

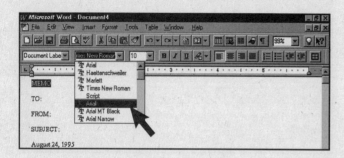

1 Highlight the Word **MEMO**. Then click the down arrow of the **Font** drop-down list in the Formatting toolbar. Select a font other than the default, which is Times New Roman.

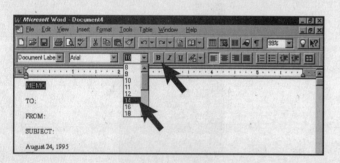

2 Click the down arrow of the **Font Size** drop-down list. Select **14**. Click the **Bold** button in the Formatting toolbar.

3 Select the word **TO:**; then click the **Bold** button in the Formatting toolbar. Do the same with **FROM:** and **SUBJECT:**.

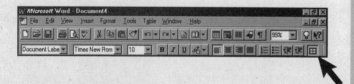

4 Position your cursor after the date, and click the **Borders** button on the Formatting toolbar.

5 Click the down-arrow in the Line Style drop-down list, and click a type of line you like.

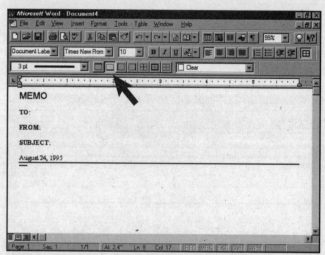

6 Click the **Bottom Border** button in the Borders toolbar to add a line below the date.

As always, the formatting in this example is just a suggestion. You are free to format as you want. For example, one common approach would place a border around the entire heading and shade the background (you can do this bit of formatting by opening the **Format** menu and selecting the **Borders and Shading** command).

Begin Do It Yourself Save the Heading with AutoCorrect

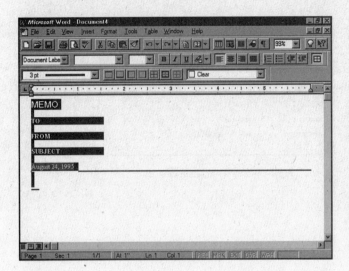

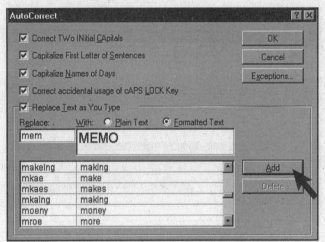

1 Highlight the entire document by pressing **Ctrl+A**.

3 In the **Replace** text box, type two or three letters to represent the heading. Click the **Formatted Text** radio button to make sure it's active. Click the **Add** button to add the text to the AutoCorrect list.

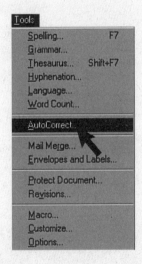

Be cautious when selecting the letters to represent the memo heading. Specifically, don't use letters that are used for other words or abbreviations, such as the word "memo." That's why, in this example, we use the letters "mem."

2 Open the **Tools** menu and select the **AutoCorrect** command.

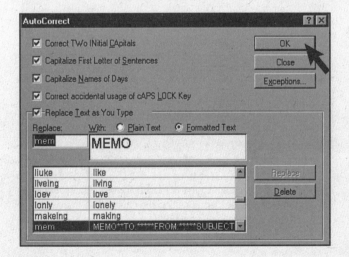

 Click **OK**.

Begin Do It Yourself Use the Memo Heading

1 Start a new document by clicking the **New** button in the Standard toolbar.

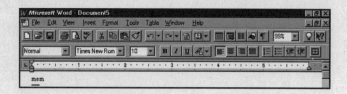

2 With the cursor at the top of the document, type the letters you selected to represent the memo heading and press the **Spacebar**. In this example, the letters were **mem**. Word displays the memo heading.

After typing mem you need to type a space or hit Enter before Word will display the memo heading. If you use mem: as the text, Word will replace the text as soon as you type the colon, or any other punctuation you use.

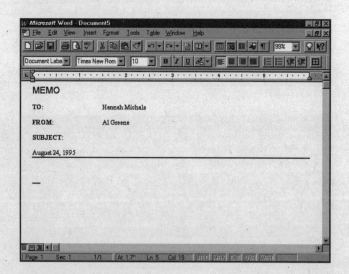

3 Position the cursor to the right of the word **TO:**. Type the name of the recipient. Position the cursor after the word **FROM:** and type your name.

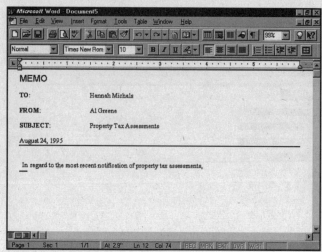

4 Position the cursor to the right of the word **SUBJECT:**. Type the subject of the memo. Position the cursor below the line and begin typing your memo.

Create a Template for a Family Newsletter

A newsletter is a document just like any other: to create one, you set margins and formats as you would for any document. Then add elements such as the title, articles, and a table of contents.

Newsletters have *nameplates*, which hold the title, version, and date information about the particular issue. In addition, you can insert graphics such as a company logo, your motto, and other information. Although this project does not include a graphical nameplate, you can use Microsoft WordArt to convert text to graphics and then manipulate it in almost any way you can imagine.

The newsletter you will create uses a header to hold the nameplate, so you can utilize a three-column format without adding a section break. Within each of the three columns is a headline and article that is a placeholder for your actual text. When you are ready to create an issue of your newsletter, just open this template and type over the headline and each paragraph. To open a template, which is simply a Word document, open the **File** menu and choose **Open**, press **Ctrl+O**, or click the **Open** button on the Standard toolbar. In the Open dialog box, double-click the document icon. Then save the file under a new, unique name by opening the **File** menu and selecting **Save As**. In the Save As dialog box, type a name in the **File name** text box, and click the **Save** button. This process creates a copy of the original document, preserving the integrity of the original document.

Many newsletters include a small table of contents on the first page. In this project, you will add a frame in which you type an "editable" table of contents. Use the same principles to insert frames in which you insert illustrations.

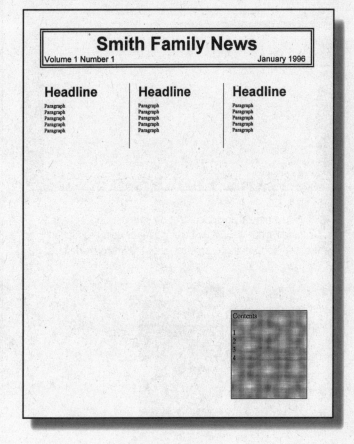

If your newsletter goes beyond a single page, you can insert the page number in the header (see "Add a Header and Footer" on page 368) as well as a small title of the publication.

You don't have to create a newsletter from scratch. Word provides both a Newsletter template from which you can apply styles and a Newsletter Wizard, which leads you through the creation process.

Begin Do It Yourself Specify Margins and Document Formats for a New Document

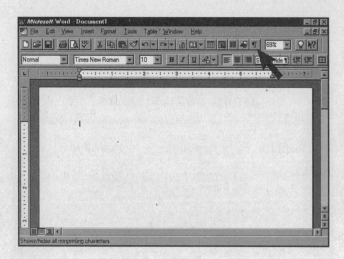

1 With a new, blank document on your desktop, change to Page Layout view, if you aren't already doing so. (If you want to see nonprinting characters, click the **Show/Hide** button.)

2 Open the **File** menu and select the **Page Setup** command.

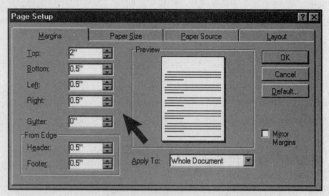

3 Click the **Margins** tab, if needed. Set **Top** to **2.0"**. Set **Bottom**, **Left**, and **Right** to **0.5"**. Click the **Layout** tab.

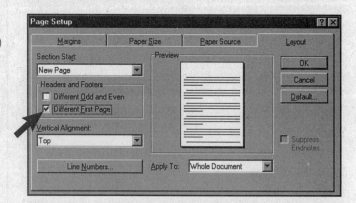

4 Click the **Different First Page** check box. Click **OK**.

If you want to see the width of a document on your computer screen, open the **View** menu and select the **Zoom** command. Then click the **Page Width** option button and click **OK**. Or you can open the **Zoom Control** box and select **Page Width**.

Begin Do It Yourself Insert a Nameplate

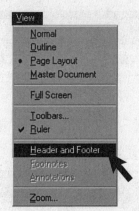

1 Open the **View** menu and choose **Header and Footer**.

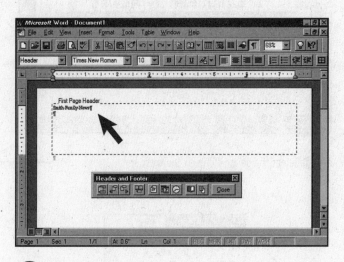

2 Type **Smith Family News** in the header. Press **Enter**.

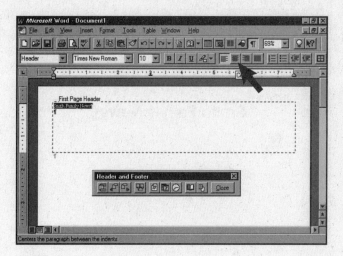

3 Select the first line of the header. Then click the **Center** button.

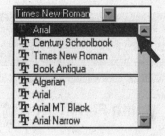

4 From the **Font** drop-down list, select **Arial**.

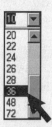

5 From the **Font Size** drop-down list, select **36**.

6 Click the **Bold** button.

(continues)

Do It Yourself Insert a Nameplate *(continued)*

7 Move the mouse pointer to the left of the paragraph mark on the second line of the header.

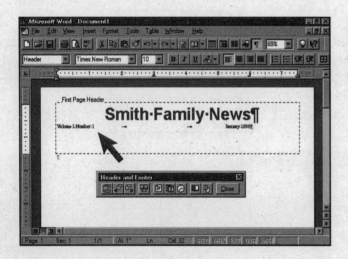

8 Type **Volume 1 Number 1**. Press **Tab** twice. Type **January 1996**.

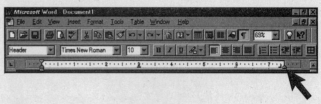

9 Drag the right-aligned tab stop to the right margin.

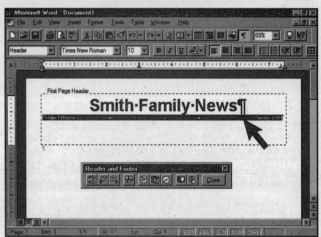

10 Select the second line of the header.

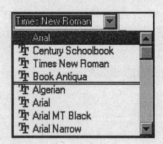

11 From the **Font** drop-down list, select **Arial**.

Do It Yourself   Insert a Nameplate

12 From the **Font Size** drop-down list, select **16**.

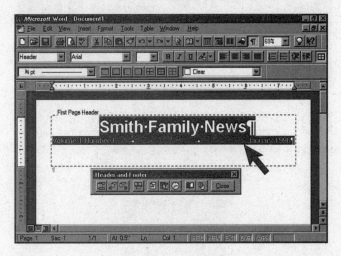

13 Click the **Borders** button if the Borders toolbar is not on your computer screen. Then select both lines of the header.

> Remember that if the Header and Footer toolbar hides part of a header or footer, you can just move the mouse pointer to the title bar, press and hold down the left mouse button and drag it out of the way.

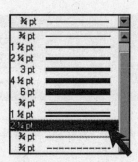

14 From the **Line Style** drop-down list, select the **2 1/4 pt** double line.

15 Click the **Outside Border** button.

16 Click the **Close** button on the Header and Footer toolbar.

Begin Do It Yourself Use a Three-Column Format

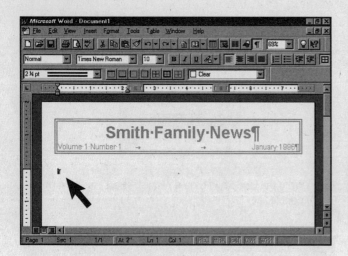

1 If the insertion point is not next to the paragraph mark below the header, click there.

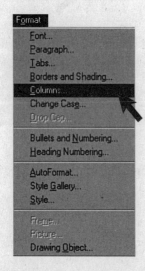

2 Open the **Format** menu and select the **Columns** command.

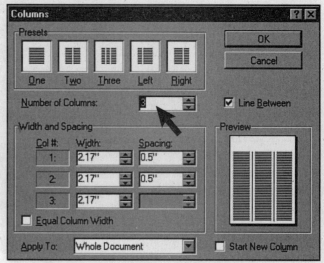

3 In the **Number of Columns** text/options box, type or select **3**. Or you can click on **Three** in the Presets group. Check the **Line Between** check box. Click **OK**.

4 Press **Enter**. Open the **Insert** menu and choose the **Break** command.

Do It Yourself   Use a Three-Column Format

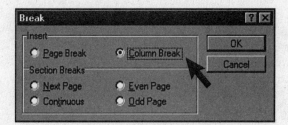 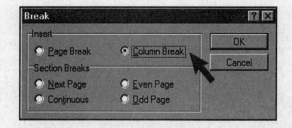

5 Click the **Column Break** option button. Click **OK**.

6 Press **Enter**. Open the **Insert** menu and choose the **Break** command. Click the **Column Break** option button. Click **OK**.

Begin Do It Yourself   Insert Placeholder Headlines and Articles

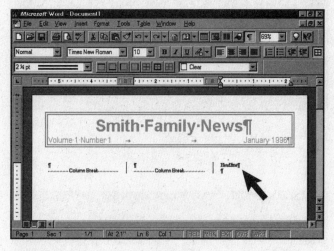 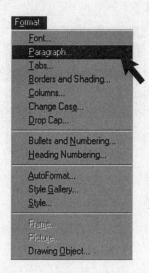

1 Type **Headline**. Press **Enter**.

2 Select **Headline**. Then open the **Format** menu and select **Paragraph**.

(continues)

Do It Yourself Insert Placeholder Headlines and Articles *(continued)*

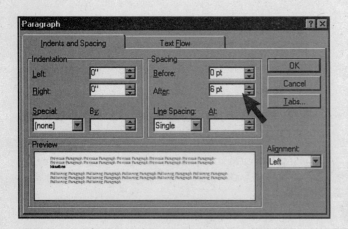

When changing the font, font size, and font style, rather than selecting from the Formatting toolbar, another choice is to open the **Format** menu, choose the **Font** command, and select options from the Font dialog box.

3 Click the **Indent and Spacing** tab of the Paragraph dialog box, if necessary. Set **After** to **6 pt**. Click **OK**.

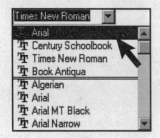

4 Select **Arial** from the **Font** drop-down list.

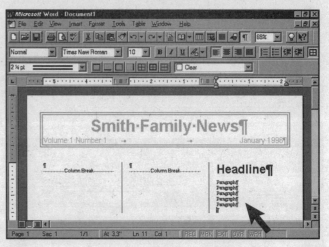

7 Click to the left of the paragraph mark under the headline. Type **Paragraph** and press **Enter** five times.

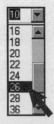

5 Select **26** from the **Font Size** drop-down list.

8 Select all the text and paragraph marks including the headline. Then click the **Copy** button.

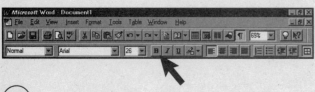

6 Click the **Bold** button.

Do It Yourself Insert Placeholder Headlines and Articles

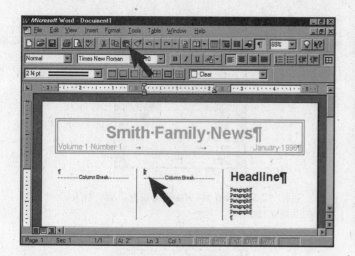

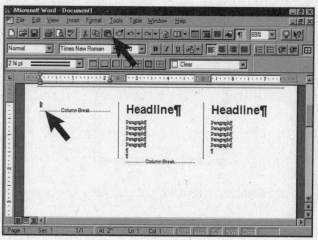

9 Click to the left of the paragraph marker above the middle column's column break marker. Then click the **Paste** button.

10 Click to the left of the paragraph marker above the leftmost column's column break marker. Click the **Paste** button.

Begin Do It Yourself Create the Table of Contents Frame

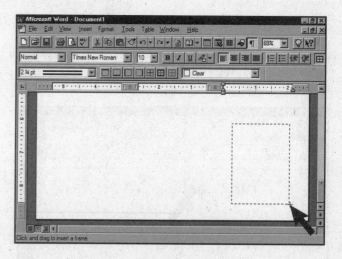

1 Scroll down to the bottom of the page. Open the **Insert** menu and choose the **Frame** command. Word changes the mouse pointer to crosshairs.

2 Using the Ruler as a guide, drag the mouse pointer diagonally from top left to bottom right to make a frame the width of the far right column.

(continues)

Do It Yourself Create the Table of Contents Frame

(continued)

3 If the mouse pointer is not next to the paragraph marker within the frame, click the left mouse button there.

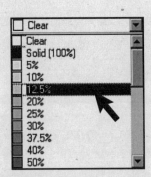

6 Select **12.5%** from the **Shading** drop-down list in the Borders toolbar.

4 Type **Contents**. Press **Enter** two times. Type **1**. Press **Enter**. Type **2**. Press **Enter**. Type **3**. Press **Enter**. Type **4**.

7 Select **Contents**. Click the **Bold** button.

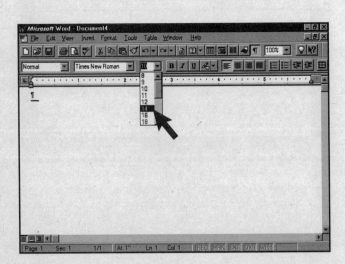

5 Select the contents of the frame. Then select **14** from the **Font** Size drop-down list.

Make a Greeting Card

When you want to send a message, use this greeting card project. Decorate the front of the card with a picture—either clip art, an imported file, or your own special design. Add a message to the card and you're ready to send it. This project uses a table as a four-cell template. Then it's foolproof to insert the art and the message in the proper cells.

After specifying margins and adding the table, the next step is to add art. For help, see "Insert Pictures and Clip Art" on page 247 and "Draw a Picture with Microsoft Drawing Tools" on page 274.

Use Microsoft WordArt to add text to the card and then turn it upside down to allow for folding. Microsoft WordArt enables you to change your font and font size as well as manipulate text as though it's a graphic.

Begin Do It Yourself Set Page Dimensions for a New Document

① With a new, blank document on your desktop, you can switch to Page Layout view in order to see the document as it will print. (If you want to see nonprinting characters, click the **Show/Hide** button.)

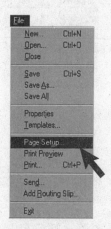

② Open the **File** menu and choose **Page Setup**.

(continues)

Do It Yourself Set Page Dimensions for a New Document *(continued)*

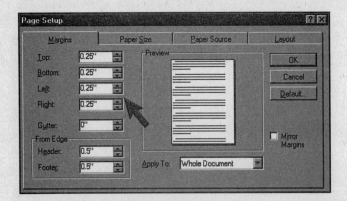

3 Click the **Margins** tab, if needed. Set **Top**, **Bottom**, **Left**, and **Right** to **0.25"**. Click **OK**.

Begin Do It Yourself Insert and Adjust a Table as a Template

1 Click the **Insert Table** button.

2 Select a 2 x 2 table.

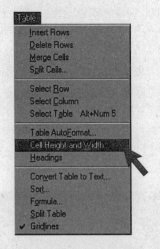

3 Press **Ctrl+5** to select the entire table. Then open the **Table** menu and choose **Cell Height and Width**.

Do It Yourself   Insert and Adjust a Table as a Template

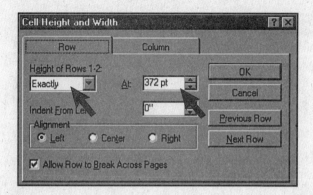

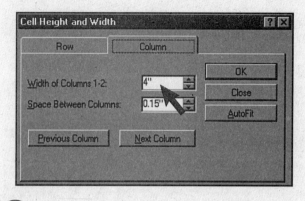

4 Click the **Row** tab, if needed. Set **Height of Rows 1-2** to **Exactly**. Set **At** to **372 pt**. Then click the **Column** tab.

5 Set **Width of Columns 1-2** to **4"**. Then click **OK**.

Begin Do It Yourself   Add Art to the Card

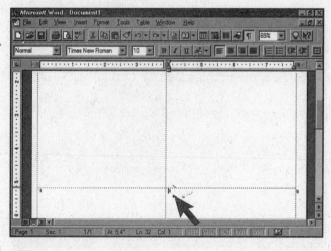

1 Click in the lower right cell.

2 Open the **Insert** menu and select the **Picture** command.

(continues)

Do It Yourself Add Art to the Card *(continued)*

3 Click the **Up One Level** button twice.

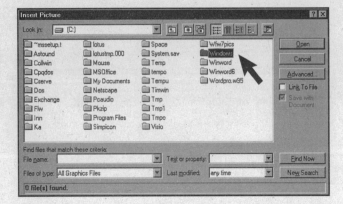

4 Double-click the **Windows** folder icon.

If you want to see a preview of a picture that you intend to insert in a document before actually inserting it, click on the **Preview** button (the second button from the right at the top of the Insert Picture dialog box).

5 Double-click the **Clouds** icon.

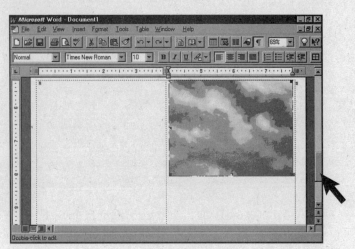

6 Move the scroll box down the vertical scroll bar to display the picture at the top of the work area. Then click in the picture to make it active.

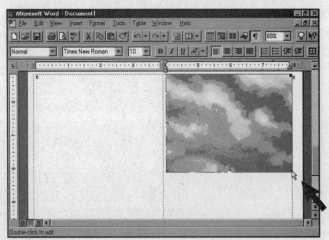

7 Moving the mouse pointer to the bottom right handle, drag the picture's border toward the right margin. Then release the mouse button. (This is not absolutely necessary for a picture as wide as Clouds; however, consider increasing the size of a smaller picture or at least centering it in its cell by clicking on the **Center** button on the Formatting toolbar.)

Using a corner handle enables you to keep the picture in proportion. If you use a handle in the middle of a border, you'll stretch the picture in one direction.

Begin Do It Yourself   Add Art to the Card

(continued)

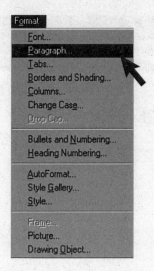

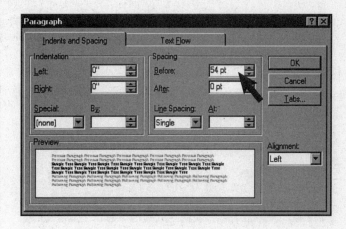

9 To insert white space before the picture, set **Before** to **54 pt**. Then click **OK**.

8 Open the **Format** menu and choose **Paragraph**.

Begin Do It Yourself   Add WordArt Text to the Card

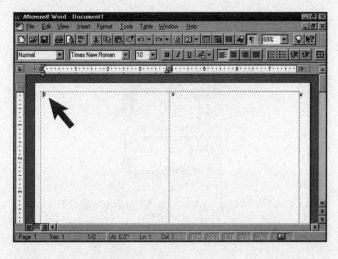

1 Using the vertical scroll bar, move to the top of the page. Then click in the top left cell.

2 Open the **Insert** menu and select the **Object** command.

(continues)

Do It Yourself Add WordArt Text to the Card *(continued)*

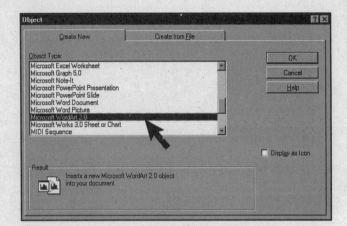

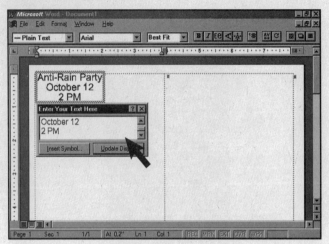

3 In the **Create New** section of the Object dialog box, double-click **Microsoft WordArt 2.0**.

4 In the Enter Your Text Here box, type **Anti-Rain Party**, and press **Enter**. Type **October 12**, and press **Enter**. Type **2 PM**. Then click **Update Display**.

Begin Do It Yourself Edit and Rotate the Word Art

1 Click the **Special Effects** button on the WordArt toolbar.

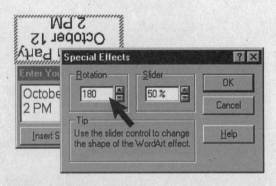

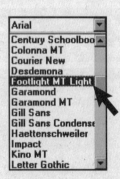

3 From the **Font** drop-down list, select **Footlight MT Light**.

2 In the Special Effects dialog box, set **Rotation** to **180**. (Notice that the graphic changes as you change **Rotation**.) Click **OK**.

Do It Yourself Edit and Rotate the Word Art

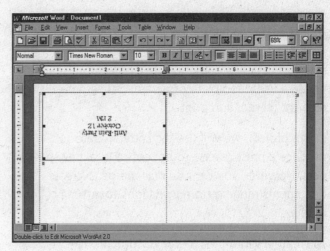

4 From the **Font** size drop-down list, select **16**. Then click away from the graphic and the dialog box to close WordArt.

6 Click and press down the left mouse button. Then drag the border toward the right side of the cell. Then release the mouse button.

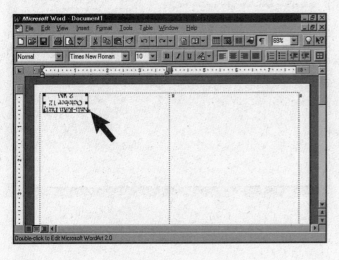

5 Move the mouse pointer to the bottom handle on the right border of the graphic.

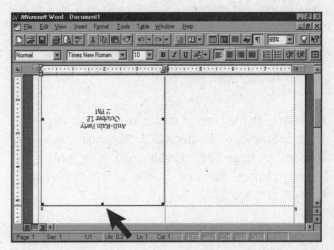

7 Move the mouse pointer to the center handle of the bottom border of the picture. Then press and hold down the left mouse button and drag down to the bottom of the cell.

8 After saving and printing the card, fold the paper along the border between the two rows (so the picture is on one side of the paper and the greeting is on the flip side). Fold again along the border between the columns.

Create a Press Release

Mail merge letters are a quick way to send business or personnel correspondence to many recipients at once. Either create a letter from scratch or use a Word template or wizard; define data records; merge, and print.

In this project, we will use the Letter Wizard to produce a press release to be sent to local newspapers. However, you can use mail merge to create documents ranging from invitations to résumé cover letters.

To create a Word mail merge document:

1. Create a letter with everything but specific recipient information.

2. Create a data file containing only recipient information.

3. Merge the data file into the letter.

4. Print the letter.

For help with mail merge topics, see "Create and Print an Envelope" on page 286, "Change User Information" on page 288, "Create and Print a Form Letter" on page 289, and "Create and Print Mailing Labels" on page 294.

The Sunset Art Gallery
Main Street Mall
Anytown, USA 12000-1245
555.555.5959 (voice)
555.555.5958 (fax)
October 15, 1996

FOR IMMEDIATE RELEASE

Sallyanne Elven
Reporter
Penny Paper
11 Ritz Building
Birmington, NY 12100

Contact: Anna Paloma Adams
555.555.5960

The Sunset Art Gallery Introduces Christmas Sofa Art II
The Sunset Art Gallery recently announced the introduction of Christmas Sofa Art II—a repeat of last year's successful art series.

Created by Sofa Art Studios, Christmas Sofa Art II allows both the sophisticated and novice collector to highlight his or her interior design and color combinations.

Christmas Sofa Art II incorporates premium oils and canvas with ornate frames for all decors. Real artists produce these works of art—just in time for the holidays.

Christmas Sofa Art II has a suggested list price range of $49.99 to $349.99; it can be purchased directly from The Sunset Art Gallery or through clothesline arts shows at the Civic Park on November 5 and 12.

The Sunset Art Gallery has been selling quality arts and crafts for homes and businesses for more than seven years. Founded in 1988, The Sunset Art Gallery has consistently provided high quality arts and crafts at the lowest prices. Other annual art series include the Easter Bunny Children's Art Show two Saturdays before Easter and the Back to School Poster Happening every Saturday in August.

—30—

Begin Do It Yourself Create and Edit a New Document Using the Letter Wizard

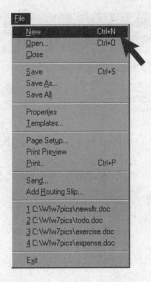

1 Open the **File** menu and select the **New** command to open the New dialog box.

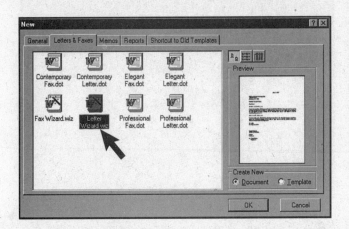

2 In the New dialog box, click the **Letters & Faxes** tab, and double-click **Letter Wizard**.

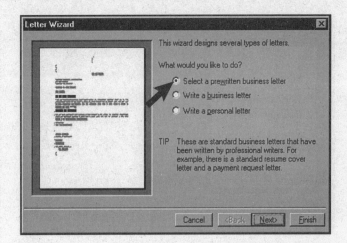

3 Click **Select a Prewritten Business Letter**. Click **Next**. The next Letter Wizard dialog box appears.

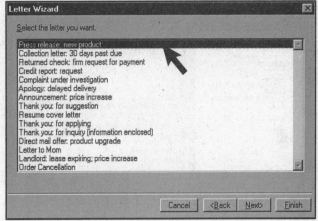

4 Select **Press release: new product**. Click **Next**. The next Letter Wizard dialog box appears.

(continues)

Do It Yourself Create and Edit a New Document Using the Letter Wizard

(continued)

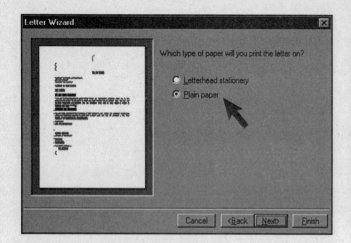

5 Click **Plain paper**. Click **Next**. The next Letter Wizard dialog box appears.

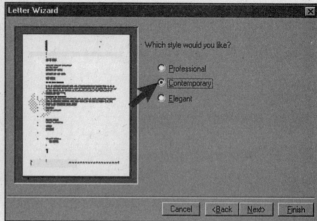

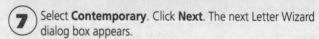

7 Select **Contemporary**. Click **Next**. The next Letter Wizard dialog box appears.

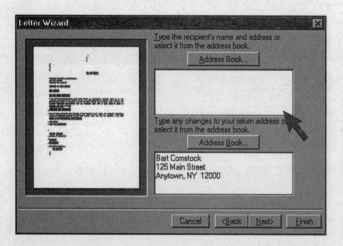

6 Remove the recipient's name and address from the upper text box. Click **Next**. The next Letter Wizard dialog box appears.

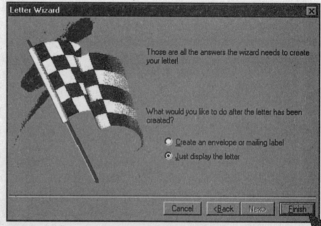

8 Click **Finish**. Word creates and displays the form letter.

Do It Yourself Create and Edit a New Document Using the Letter Wizard

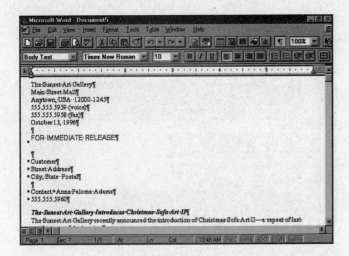

9 Fill in the letter. For the moment, ignore the recipient's name and address.

Begin Do It Yourself Define the Letter as a Form Letter

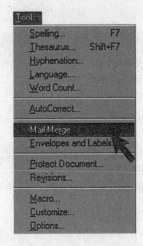

1 Open the **Tools** menu and select the **Mail Merge** command.

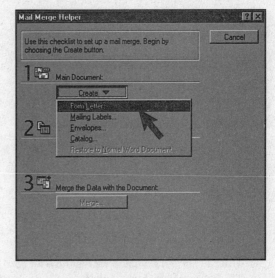

2 In the Mail Merge Helper dialog box, click **Create**. Select **Form Letters**.

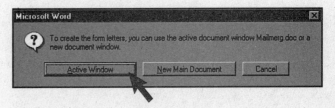

3 Click **Active Window** in the dialog box that appears. You are returned to the Mail Merge Helper dialog box.

Begin Do It Yourself   Create a Data File

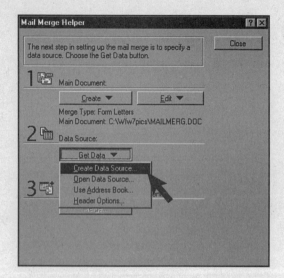

1 In the Mail Merge Helper dialog box, click **Get Data**. Select **Create Data Source**.

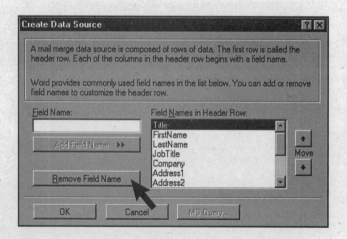

2 Click **Title** in the **Field Names in Header Row** list box. Click the **Remove Field Name** button.

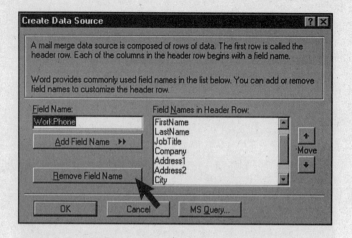

3 Click **Country** in the **Field Names in Header Row** list box. Click **Remove Field Name**. Click **HomePhone** in the **Field Names in Header Row** list box. Click **Remove Field Name**. Click **WorkPhone** in the **Field Names in Header Row** list box. Click **Remove Field Name**. Click **OK**.

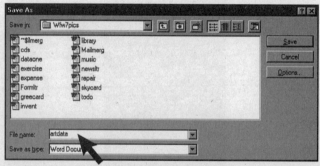

4 In the Save As dialog box that appears, type a data source file name in the **File name** text box. Click **Save**.

Begin Do It Yourself   Add Records to the Data File

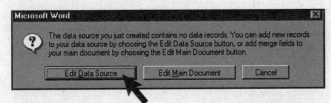

1 In the dialog box that appears, click the **Edit Data Source** button.

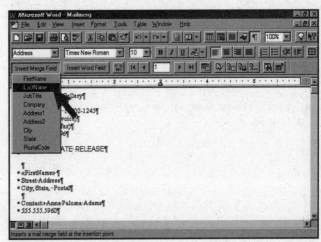

3 Continue to add records by following the instruction in step 2. Click **OK** to signal the end of data entry.

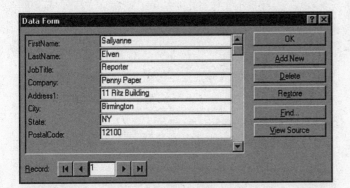

2 In the Data Form that appears, type information in the field text boxes for a record. Click **Add New**.

Begin Do It Yourself   Merge Recipient Data into the Letter and Print

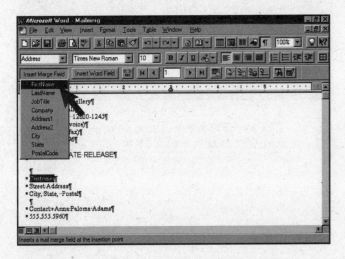

1 In the press release, double-click the word **Customer** to select it. Click the **Insert Merge Field** button on the Mail Merge toolbar, and select **FirstName**. Word replaces Customer with **FirstName**.

2 Press the **Spacebar**. Click the **Insert Merge Field** button. Select **LastName**. Press **Enter**.

(continues)

Do It Yourself   Merge Recipient Data into the Letter and Print   *(continued)*

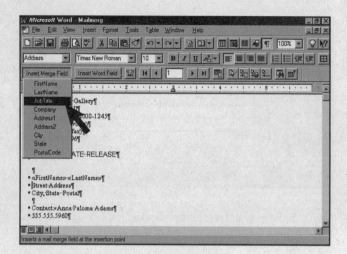

3 Click the **Insert Merge Field** button. Select **JobTitle**. Press **Enter**.

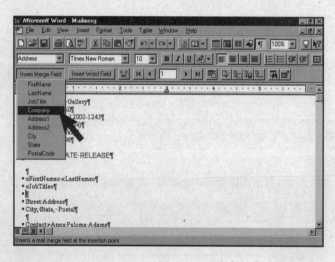

4 Click the **Insert Merge Field** button. Select **Company**. Press **Enter**.

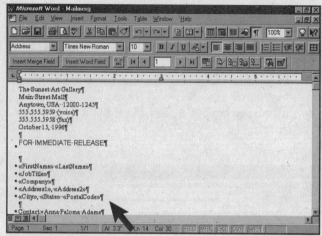

5 On the next two lines, add the Address1, Address2, City, State, and PostalCode (ZIP) fields, adding a comma after Address1 and City and two spaces after State.

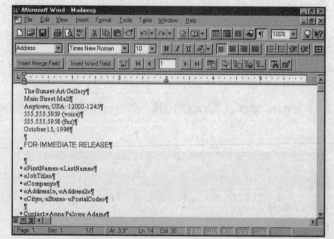

6 Click the **Merge to Printer** button. Word displays the standard Print dialog box. Click **OK** to merge and print the letters. (If you haven't already saved the letter, do so.)

PART 3

Quick Fixes...

f you turned to this section, you're probably having a problem. But don't get frustrated—that's what the Quick Fixes are all about. 101 of the most common problems are organized along with their solutions to make solving your problem a snap.

Here you will find a handy quick-finder table to help you locate the solution that you need. The table divides into categories with the problems listed alphabetically under each category. Just scan through the table until you find a problem that looks like yours; then turn to the indicated Quick-Fix number to find the solution. If you are having trouble finding your problem, try looking in the Miscellaneous category.

What You Will Find in This Part

101 QUICK FIXES

Questions and Answers

Quick-Finder Table

Editing Problems

Field Problems

Problem	Quick Fix	Page
Word **beeps when trying to change field**	47	510
Can't **change field**	47	510
Field does not display correct result	45	509
Field is locked	45	509
{INDEX} displays instead of my index	48	510
Index does not display correctly	48	510
Field doesn't work after **manual insert**	46	509
Can't **update field**	45	509

File Problems

Problem	Quick Fix	Page
Converter wasn't installed with Word	76	522
Accidentally **deleted file**	74	521
File is not converted properly	76	522
Can't **find file in Open dialog box**	75	521
Can't **find Wizard when opening new document**	77	522
Can't **read a Macintosh disk**	81	524
Read-only message when saving	78	523
Document **saved to wrong folder**	79	523
Need to **unprotect document**	78	523
Weird characters in document	76	522
Wizard was not installed with Word	77	522
Can't open **Word for Macintosh document**	81	524
Write-protect error when saving to floppy	80	524

Formatting Problems

Problem	Quick Fix	Page
Another style changed when I changed another	44	509
Word puts **big gaps between words**	37	506
Can't select **blank line** after paragraph	39	507
Columns are all equal width	35	505
Need to change the **default font**	41	508
Font keeps changing to default	41	508
Can't change **font or formatting**	42	508
Fonts all look the same	42	508

Need to automatically **hyphenate** my document	37	506
Justified text doesn't look right	37	506
Last page only has a few lines	38	506
Newspaper-style columns won't display	34	505
Can't move **number**	40	507
Can't select **number**	40	507
Text is automatically converted to **numbered list**	36	505
Can't stop **numbering**	36	505
Numbers appear after pressing Enter	36	505
Need to **Shrink-to-Fit** my document	38	506
Need to change the **spacing between paragraphs**	39	507
Style is based on another style	44	509
Word **underlines instead of bolding or italicizing**	42	508
Can't change **width of second column**	35	505
Text won't **wrap around object**	43	508

Installation Problems

Problem	Quick Fix	Page
Setup **can't write to floppy disk**	2	492
Installation **didn't complete successfully**	3	492
Disk Write Failure error message	2	492
Installation disks have been used before	1	492
Insufficient disk space	4	492

Macro Problems

Problem	Quick Fix	Page
Need to **add steps to a macro**	51	511
Need to **delete a step from a macro**	50	510
Need to **edit a macro**	50	510
Can't **find macro**	52	511
Cannot use **mouse** when recording a macro	49	510
Need to **record a new step in an existing macro**	51	511
Recorded macro not available after restarting	52	511
Saved my macro to the wrong template	52	511
Can't **select text when recording a macro**	49	510
Stopped recording macro before finished	51	511

Mail Merge Problems

Problem	Quick Fix	Page
Blank lines when merging data	57	513
Need to **change envelope size**	56	513
Need to **convert Mail Merge document to normal**	53	512
Need to **convert my data source to normal**	54	512
Data doesn't line up correctly on envelope	56	513
Data source turned into main document	54	512
Need to turn off **display of empty merge fields**	57	513
Word thinks **document is a Mail Merge document**	53	512
Empty fields are printed in Mail Merge	57	513
Word can't **find data source**	53	512
Funny characters are printed instead of data	55	512
Word thinks **main document is data source**	54	512
Merge fields are printed instead data	55	512

Menu and Toolbar Problems

Problem	Quick Fix	Page
All I see on the screen is my document	12	497
Buttons in my toolbar are in a box	13	497
Someone **changed my menu**	15	498
Someone **changed my toolbar**	14	497
Document in **Full screen** mode	12	497
Menus no longer have the commands I need	15	498
I want to **reset the menu**	15	498
I want to **reset the toolbar**	14	497
Toolbar icons difficult to see	16	498
Toolbar is missing	13	497
Toolbar is no longer under the menu bar	13	497
Toolbar no longer has the buttons I need	14	497
Can't find the **toolbars**	12	497

Miscellaneous Problems

Problem	Quick Fix	Page
Add Routing Slip option is not available	101	531
AutoSave takes too long	94	529
Unwanted **captions are inserted with object**	99	531
Captions are only added with certain objects	99	531

Problems with Proofing Tools

System Problems

Problem	Quick Fix	Page
Disk performance is decreasing	11	496
Double-click speed is too fast	9	495
Double-clicking doesn't work	9	495
Hard drive is **fragmented**	11	496
Insufficient memory	5	493
Keys on my keyboard **stick**	7	494
Left-handed mouse needs to be right-handed	10	495
Letters I type appear more than once	7	494
Mouse pointer moves too fast	8	495
Mouse right button does not work properly	10	495
Repeat rate is set too high	7	494
Screen redraws too slowly	6	494
Can't **select** anything **with my mouse**	8	495
Takes **too long to open files**	11	496

Table Problems

Problem	Quick Fix	Page
Can only **add one line in row**	29	503
Can only change the **column width** of one cell	28	502
Document is shifted after table move	31	503
Table won't **fit in the margins**	33	504
Text won't **fit in the table**	30	503
Can't **insert column**	29	503
Insert Columns not in Table menu	29	503
Need to change **row height**	30	503
Row is split across pages	32	504
Can't see document after **table** move	31	503
Table did not adjust after changing margin	33	504

Installation Problems

1: When I try to install Word, Setup tells me that the disks have already been used to install Word.

When you first install Word, Setup copies your name and company information to the first installation disk. You will get this message whenever you try to install word again even if you did not complete the installation the first time. So, if you are only completing the first installation, or you have another legal reason to install the software again, just click **OK** to continue with the installation.

2: During Setup I got an error message that said Setup needs to modify a file on my floppy disk.

This error occurs when you write-protect the first installation disk. Many people will automatically write-protect the disks as soon as they get them to prevent accidentally overwriting them. In this case, it can get you into trouble. Fortunately, the fix is easy. Just remove the disk and move the write-protect tab to the opposite position. Reinsert the disk and click **OK**. Installation will continue normally.

3: I got an error message that said installation did not complete successfully.

Make sure that you don't have any applications open when you start the Setup program. Any other application that is running can interfere with the installation (especially virus checking software). Restart your computer, close any applications that opened on startup, and run the Setup program again.

4: I got part way through installation and Word told me that I didn't have enough disk space.

Word can take up a lot of disk space. The typical installation needs 16 MB of disk space, the compact installation needs 6 MB, and the custom installation can take up to 33 MB. There are a few different options you can take at this point. You can click the **Exit Setup** button and try to free up some disk space. Remove files that you no longer need or move them to another drive, and run Setup again. Another choice is to not install all of the Word components. Follow these steps to change the setup options:

1. From the Setup dialog box, click the **Change Options** button.

2. Click the **Compact** button to install only the bare minimum to run Word. Skip the remaining steps and continue with setup. If you would rather choose which options to install, click the **Custom** button.

3. Remove the check marks from the options you don't need right now (for example, the grammar checker). Remember, you can always add or remove options after you have installed Word. You can also highlight an option and click the **Change Option** button to remove the check marks from individual components of an option.

4. Continue to remove the check marks from options until the required disk space is less than the available disk space (you can see the totals at the bottom of the dialog box). Click the **Continue** button to finish the installation.

5. A message box will tell you when the installation is complete. Click **OK** to finish.

System Problems

5: I keep getting insufficient memory messages when I try to open an application.

Windows 95 does a much better job of managing memory, but it does have its limits. More than likely, the real problem is that you are running out of disk space. Since Windows 95 can swap memory from RAM and put it on your hard drive, when it runs out of memory, there probably isn't enough room on the drive to swap the memory to. Adding more memory to your system would help, and it would speed up your system, but memory is expensive.

The easiest way to solve your problem is to free up disk space. Back up files that you don't use very often and delete them from your system. You can also empty the Recycle Bin (make sure you don't need to recover any files before you do this).

If you aren't able to free up enough disk space, you may want to use DriveSpace. DriveSpace is a program that comes with Windows 95 that allows you to compress the data on your hard drive, effectively giving you more drive space. Since Windows has to decompress files before they can run, the penalty is that DriveSpace may slow down performance slightly. Follow these steps to compress your drive with DriveSpace:

1. From the **Start** menu, point to **Programs**, **Accessories**, and **System Tools**; then click **DriveSpace**.

> If the DriveSpace option is not available in the System Tools folder, it probably wasn't installed in your Windows 95 installation. Use Windows 95 Help for instructions on installing DriveSpace.

2. In the DriveSpace dialog box, click the drive that you want to compress and choose **Compress** from the **Drive** menu.

3. The Compress a Drive dialog box will open showing you the details of the compression. Click **Start** to begin compressing the drive.

4. DriveSpace will ask if you're sure you want to compress the drive. Click the **Compress Now** button to begin compression.

Since DriveSpace uses your hard drive exclusively, you won't be able to use your computer until it finishes compressing. Depending on your system, it may take several hours.

6: It takes too long for the screen to update when I page through my document.

If you are working in a form or a document with inserted objects or graphics, it may take awhile for the screen to update. To make the updates faster, you can change to Normal view. Just click the **Normal View** button in the lower left corner next to the horizontal scroll bar (or choose **Normal** from the **View** menu). In Normal view, graphics and objects will not appear on the screen correctly, but if you are just adding text, it won't matter. When you want to see how things will actually print, or you want to change the layout, switch back to Page Layout view by clicking the **Page Layout View** button (or choosing **Page Layout** from the **View** menu).

7: When I hold down a key too long, the key repeats too many times.

When you hold down a key for a little while, it's supposed to repeat at a certain rate. That rate is the *repeat rate*; the speed at which the letters shoot across your screen. Sometime, it can get out of control when it is set too fast. Another problem could be in the *repeat delay*; the amount of time you have to hold down a key before it starts to repeat. If the delay is set too short, it's easy to accidentally have a string of letters across the screen before you even know what's happening. You can change the repeat rate or repeat delay by following these steps:

1. From the **Start** menu, point to **Settings** and click **Control Panel**.

2. Double-click the **Keyboard** icon.

3. In the Keyboard Properties dialog box, click the **Speed** tab.

4. In the **Repeat delay** and **Repeat rate** sections there are sliding scales. Move the sliders in the desired directions. Move the repeat delay slider to the left to increase the delay. Move the repeat rate slider to the left to slow down the repeat rate.

5. Click in the box labeled **Click here and hold down a key to test repeat rate** to check your settings. Hold down a key and see what happens. If the repeat rate or repeat delay are still not working correctly, repeat steps 4 and 5 until you are comfortable with the results.

6. Click **OK**.

8: My mouse pointer is out of control.

When your mouse pointer speed is set too fast, it can be very difficult to control. It can make it almost impossible to select text or click a menu because it seems like you're chasing that mouse pointer all over the screen. Follow these steps to change the pointer speed:

1. From the **Start** menu, point to **Settings** and click **Control Panel**.

2. Double-click the **Mouse** icon.

3. In the Mouse Properties dialog box, click the **Motion** tab.

4. In the **Pointer speed** section, there is a sliding scale. Move the slider to the left to slow down the speed of the pointer, or to the right to speed it up.

5. After you move the slider, click the **Apply** button.

6. Try moving the mouse across the screen. Repeat steps 3 and 4 until you are comfortable with the speed you have selected.

7. Click **OK** to close the dialog box.

9: I can't quite get the hang of double-clicking.

Double-clicking is definitely an acquired skill. It does take some time to get used to. Fortunately, Windows 95 decreases the number of situations where you need to double-click something to make it work, but there are still some times when you need to double-click. One thing you can do to make it easier is to change the double-click speed in your mouse properties. Follow these steps to change the mouse properties:

1. From the **Start** menu, point to **Settings** and click **Control Panel**.

2. Double-click the **Mouse** icon.

3. In the Mouse Properties dialog box, click the **Buttons** tab.

4. In the **Double-click speed** section, there is a sliding scale. Move the slider to the left to increase the amount of time allowed between clicks. Move it to the right to decrease the time.

5. Double-click in the **Test area** to test the results. Repeat step 4 until you are comfortable with the results.

6. Click **OK**.

10: My mouse is set left-handed, but I need it to be right-handed.

It can be annoying if your mouse has been set up left-handed and you use the mouse with your right hand. You will find yourself always clicking the wrong button and getting unexpected results. Changing the mouse to left-handed really only changes the primary button.

The primary button should be the one under your index finger. Follow these steps to change the mouse button orientation to right-handed:

1. From the **Start** menu, highlight **Settings** and click **Control Panel**.

2. Double-click the **Mouse** icon.

3. In the Mouse properties dialog box, click the **Buttons** tab and click the radio button next to **Right-handed**.

4. Click **OK** and your mouse will be set up right-handed.

11: Word takes too long to open files.

When it seems to take longer to open files than it used to, it's probably time to do a little maintenance on your hard drive (put away your screwdriver, this won't involve taking anything apart).

Data on your hard drive is stored in *sectors*. A sector is a fixed block of space that holds the data. When files are first written to the disk, they will be in continuous sectors. After you make changes to files, the next sector may no longer be available, so part of your file is stored in another sector that may be far away from the rest of the file. When this happens, the disk is *fragmented*. Windows does a fine job of keeping track of all the pieces to the file, but after awhile it can slow down performance. So, you should really defragment your disk on a regular basis to keep fragmentation to a minimum. Follow these steps to run the Disk Defragmenter program:

1. From the **Start** menu, point to **Programs**, **Accessories**, and **System Tools**; click **Disk Defragmenter**.

2. The Select Drive dialog box appears asking which drive you want to defragment. Click the desired drive and click **OK**.

3. The Disk Defragmenter dialog box will open showing you how much of the drive is fragmented. Click the **Start** button to begin defragmenting. Depending on the speed of your system, and how much of the disk was fragmented, it may take a couple of hours to defragment the disk. You can continue working in other applications while the Disk Defragmenter is running, but the performance will be slower.

4. When the Defragmenter finishes, it will ask if you want to defragment another drive. Click **Yes** if you have another drive to defragment.

Menu and Toolbar Problems

12: All I see on the screen is my document. There are no toolbars or menus.

You are in *full screen* mode. Full screen mode maximizes the amount of your document that can be seen on the screen at one time. This mode is great for proofreading. You can edit the document as you normally would. You can even use the menus if you remember the shortcut keys to open them (for example, **ALT+F** to open the File menu). When you are ready to bring the normal Word screen back, click the **Full Screen** button located at the bottom right corner of the screen (or press the **Esc** key). If you ever want to try full screen mode again, select **Full Screen** from the **View** menu.

13: The Standard toolbar is no longer under the menu bar. All the buttons are in a box in the middle of the screen.

Your toolbar has been transformed into a *toolbox*. A toolbox serves the same function as a toolbar, but you can move the box anywhere on the screen you prefer. Some people like the functionality of a toolbox better than a toolbar. You can transform any toolbar into a toolbox by double-clicking on an empty space in the toolbar. If you prefer the buttons to be on a toolbar, simply double-click the title bar of the toolbox, or drag the toolbox to the desired toolbar location. It will change back into a toolbar and be located under the menu bar where you would expect it to be. If the Standard toolbar is not on the screen, and there isn't a toolbox either, follow these steps:

1. Select **Toolbars** from the **View** menu.

2. In the **Toolbars** section of the Toolbars dialog box, check the **Standard** check box.

3. Click **OK**.

14: Someone changed my toolbar. Now I don't have the buttons I need.

It can be very aggravating when someone changes the toolbars on your computer. After you've finally gotten used to the old toolbar, someone rudely changed it. Or maybe you were trying to customize the toolbar yourself, but are unhappy with the results. Follow these steps to reset the toolbar to the default configuration:

1. Select **Toolbars** from the **View** menu.

2. In the Toolbars dialog box highlight the toolbar you want to change in the **Toolbars** section.

3. Click the **Reset** button.

4. The Reset Toolbar dialog box opens asking you for what documents you want to change the toolbar. Click **OK** to change the toolbar for all documents.

5. Click **OK** to close the dialog box. Your toolbar will be as good as new.

15: Someone changed my menu. Now the commands I need aren't there.

In the previous question someone messed up your toolbar. Now they've fouled up your menus, too. You just can't trust anyone these days. Maybe you can't even blame someone else. Maybe you were trying to customize the ultimate menu, and now you can't live with the results. Whatever happened to the menu, Word makes it easy to repair. Just follow these steps:

1. Choose **Customize** from the **Tools** menu.

2. In the Customize dialog box, click the **Menus** tab.

3. Click the **Reset All** button.

4. A message box opens asking if you're sure you want to reset your menus. Click **Yes** and your menus will return to their original configuration.

5. Click the **Close** button to close the dialog box.

16: I can barely see the toolbar icons on my laptop computer.

If your laptop has a monochrome screen, the buttons can be difficult to see because they were meant to be displayed in color. These icons look great on a color screen, but they are practically unreadable on a black-and-white screen. To make the buttons easier to see, follow these steps:

1. Choose **Toolbars** from the **View** menu.

2. At the bottom of the Toolbars dialog box, remove the check mark from the **Color Buttons** check box.

3. Click **OK**.

The other problem with a laptop is the screen is small. Even if your buttons are properly displayed without color, they may still be too small to easily see. Fortunately, you can make the buttons larger, however, you won't have as many buttons available on the toolbar. Follow these steps to change the size of the buttons:

1. Choose **Toolbars** from the **View** menu.

2. At the bottom of the Toolbars dialog box, check the **Large Buttons** check box.

3. Click **OK**.

Editing Problems

17: I moved to a different page in the document to add text, but it showed up where I was before.

When you page through your document it is important to move the insertion point (the flashing bold vertical line) to the desired location before you add text. Even though you may be looking at another paragraph. Word will insert the text wherever the insertion bar happens to be. The way to move the insertion point is to move the mouse pointer to the desired location and click the left mouse button.

Insertion point——| I———Mouse pointer

18: When I try to insert text, it types over the text that is already there.

You have accidentally hit the Insert key on your keyboard. The Insert key toggles *overtype* mode, which allows you to type over existing text in your document. When you are in overtype mode, a bold **OVR** appears in the status bar. To get out of overtype mode, press the **Insert** key again or double-click the **OVR** in the status bar.

If Word always starts in overtype mode, follow these steps to change the default:

1. Choose **Options** from the **Tools** menu.

2. Click the **Edit** tab in the Options dialog box, and remove the check mark from the check box next to **Overtype Mode**.

3. Click **OK**. The next time you start Word, it will not be in overtype mode.

19: I am trying to edit a document my coworker gave me, but it is protected from revisions.

When a document is protected from revisions, you cannot change existing text in the document. Instead, Word will add the text in a different color and put a line through text that you delete, as shown in the following figure. When your coworker gets the document back, they can review the corrections you made and then incorporate them into the document.

This is the original ~~text.~~ This is the revised text|

If you want to unprotect the document, follow these steps:

1. Open the document and choose **Unprotect Document** from the **Tools** menu.

2. If the **Unprotect Document** dialog box pops up asking you for a password, you will have to get it from your coworker.

3. Type in the password and click **OK** to close the dialog box. The document will now be unprotected.

20: There is a revision bar in my document, but the revision isn't shown on the screen.

The revisions have been made in hidden text, field codes, or annotations. You can double-click the annotation mark to see the revisions in the annotation. To see the revisions in field codes and hidden text, follow these steps:

1. From the **Tools** menu, choose **Options**.

2. In the Options dialog box, click the **View** tab.

3. In the **Show** section, check the **Field Codes** check box.

4. In the **Nonprinting Characters** section, check the **Hidden Text** check box.

5. Click **OK**.

21: I accidentally deleted some text. Is there any way to get it back?

We have all been victims of these little accidents. Luckily, Word has the *Undo* command. Undo will bring back those little editing blunders with the click of a button. If you need to recover some text you deleted, click the **Undo** button on the toolbar (or choose **Undo** from the **Edit** menu). If you deleted the text a little while ago, keep clicking the **Undo** button until the deleted text returns. Remember that anything you did after you deleted the text will be un-done also. You could also click on the down arrow next to the **Undo** button on the toolbar to drop down a list of actions to undo. Click on the desired action in the list to undo it.

22: After I selected a block of text, I accidentally got the drag-and-drop pointer.

When you select text and then click in the selection and move the mouse pointer, the drag-and-drop cursor will appear.

Drag-and-drop is a convenient way of moving text without having to use the **Cut** and **Paste** commands. If you really don't want the drag-and-drop cursor, move the cursor back into the selection and click the left mouse button (or press the **Esc** key). This will clear the selection. If you don't like the drag-and-drop feature, follow these steps to turn it off:

1. Choose **Options** from the **Tools** menu.

2. In the Options dialog box, click the **Edit** tab.

3. Remove the check mark from the **Drag-and-Drop Text Editing** check box.

4. Click **OK**.

23: When I try to move a drawing object, the object just gets bigger instead of moving.

When you move an object, it is important that you not click a *sizing handle*. Sizing handles are the little squares that surround the object. When you click-and-drag on a sizing handle, the object will grow or shrink depending on where you drag it. To move the object, click an area of the object that is not a sizing handle, and drag the object to its new location.

24: I can't delete an annotation mark.

Annotation marks are special characters, so they can't be deleted by simply pressing the Backspace or Delete keys. To delete an annotation mark, you must select it first. Now, press the Delete key, and the annotation mark will be erased.

25: When I insert an annotation, the wrong initials are used in the annotation mark.

If someone else's initials are entered when you make an annotation, they will get credit for all your work (and it could give you an identity crisis). This problem occurs when the User Info stored in Word is incorrect. Follow these steps to change the User Info:

1. From the **Tools** menu, choose **Options**.

2. In the Options dialog box, click the **User Info** tab.

3. Enter your initials in the **Initials** box. You will probably want to correct your name in the **Name** box and your address in the **Mailing Address** box (Word uses the address entered here as the default return address when you print envelopes).

4. Click **OK**.

All new annotations that you make will have the correct initials in the annotation marks. If you want to change the annotation marks that had the incorrect initials, you will have to delete the previous annotations and reenter them.

26: My ruler is in inches, but I would rather work in centimeters.

The units on the ruler can display in inches, centimeters, points, or picas. To change the measurement units, follow these steps:

1. Choose **Options** from the **Tools** menu.

2. In the Options dialog box, click the **General** tab.

3. Click the desired measurement units from the drop-down list in the **Measurement Units** box.

4. Click **OK**.

27: Word won't let me edit a subdocument.

If you are working on a network and another user has the same subdocument or the master document open, you won't be able to edit the subdocument. Wait until the other person finishes and try again. Another possibility is that the subdocument is locked. Follow these steps to unlock the subdocument:

1. Open the master document.

2. Click the **Outline View** button to switch to Outline view.

3. If there is a padlock displayed next to the subdocument, it is locked. Click the **Lock Document** button on the Master Document toolbar to unlock the subdocument.

Table Problems

28: When I changed the column width, it only changed in one row.

When you change the width of a column, it only affects the rows that are selected. If you want to change the width of the entire column, select the column and then change the column width. To select the column, move the mouse pointer to the top of the column until it turns into a down-pointing arrow, and click the left mouse button.

29: I want to insert a column in my table, but Insert Columns doesn't appear in the Table menu.

For the **Insert Columns** or **Insert Rows** commands to appear on the **Table** menu, you must have an entire column or row selected in your table. Otherwise, only the **Insert Cells** command will be available. To remedy the situation, select the column to the left of where you want to insert a column, or the row above where you want to insert a row, and click the **Table** menu. The appropriate command will be available. Another way is to select a cell and choose **Insert Cells** from the **Table** menu. When the Insert Cells dialog box opens, click **Insert Entire Column** or **Insert Entire Row**, and click **OK**.

30: My text won't fit in the table.

The best way to fix this problem is to set the height of the table rows to automatic. In automatic mode, the row height will expand when you type in more data than will fit on one line. Follow these steps to change the row height:

1. Select the row(s) of your table that you want to change. To select the entire table, click anywhere in the table, and press **Alt+5** on the numeric keypad (make sure that Num Lock is off).

2. Choose **Cell Height and Width** from the **Table** menu.

3. Click the **Row** tab in the Cell Height and Width dialog box (see the following figure).

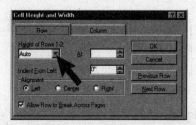

4. Select **Auto** from the drop-down list in the **Height of Row** box.

5. Click **OK**.

31: I can't see much of my document after I move a table.

Sometimes, when you move a table, it shifts the view point of the document past the left or right margins. This shows a column of blank space to the left or right of your text. To display the document correctly, click to the right of the horizontal scroll box then move it all the way to the left.

◄▐▌▐► ── Horizontal scroll box

32: Half of the text in a row is on one page, and the other half is on the next page.

It is usually not desirable to have your rows split between pages, but that is the default setting. If you would like to keep the contents of your row together on one page, follow these steps:

1. Click anywhere in the table.

2. Choose **Cell Height and Width** from the **Table** menu.

3. In the Cell Height and Width dialog box, click the **Row** tab.

4. Remove the check mark from the **Allow Row to Break Across Pages** check box.

5. Click **OK**.

33: When I changed the margins in my document, the width of my table did not change to match the margins.

Changing the margins will not affect the width of your existing tables. If you want to keep your table within the new margins, you will have to manually adjust the table width. Follow these steps to change the table width:

1. Select the entire table by clicking anywhere in the table, and pressing **Alt+5** on the numeric keypad (make sure that Num Lock is off).

2. Move the mouse pointer to the left edge of the table until it turns into a bar with an arrow on each side (see the following figure).

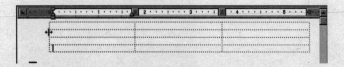

3. Drag the edge of the table until it fits in the left margin.

4. Repeat steps 2 and 3 for the right edge of the table.

Formatting Problems

34: Only one column displays on the screen, but it should have two.

To display more than one column on the screen, you have to be in Page Layout view. You are currently in Normal view. Normal view is best for editing because Word runs faster in Normal view. The columns will print correctly even though they do not appear on-screen. To see the columns as they will print, choose **Page Layout** from the **View** menu (or click the **Page Layout View** button).

35: I want to change the width of one of my columns, but I can only change the first column.

Your columns are set to equal width. In this mode, all of the columns and spacing are adjusted to equal whatever you set in column one. To turn this option off, follow these steps:

1. Choose **Columns** from the **Tools** menu.

2. In the **Width and Spacing** section of the **Columns** dialog box, remove the check mark from the **Equal Column Width** check box.

3. Set the spacing of each column in the **Width and Spacing** section.

4. Click **OK** when you finish.

36: I'm finished with my numbered list, but Word keeps adding numbers when I press Enter.

Word will automatically add a number to the next line after you start a numbered list. This is quite convenient because you don't have to click the Numbering button on every line. If you need a blank line after the numbered line, hold down the **Shift** key and press **Enter**. Now, press **Enter** again, and Word will start the next line with the next number. When you finish with the list, press **Enter** to move to the next line. Click the **Numbering** button to remove the number.

Numbering button

37: There are big gaps between some of the words when I use justified alignment.

The only way Word can justify your text is to add space between words to stretch out the lines to the right margin. If you want to avoid large gaps between the words you must use hyphenation. The easiest way to hyphenate is to let Word do it for you automatically. Follow these steps to turn on automatic hyphenation:

1. Choose **Hyphenation** from the **Tools** menu.

2. In the Hyphenation dialog box, check the **Automatically Hyphenate Document** check box.

3. Click **OK** to close the dialog box. Word will go through your document and hyphenate words at the appropriate places.

If you would like more control over your hyphenation, Word can hyphenate in manual mode. Click the **Manual** button in the Hyphenate dialog box and Word will go through your document one line at a time and suggest words to hyphenate. The suggested word will appear in the Manual Hyphenation dialog box (see the following figure). If the word can be hyphenated in more than one place, it will have a hyphen at all possibilities. Click the desired hyphen. Click **Yes** to hyphenate the word, **No** to not hyphenate the word, or **Cancel** to quit manual hyphenation.

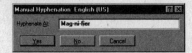

38: I have a two-page document with only one line on the second page. Can't I get it to fit on one page?

There are several ways you can make the last line fit on the first page, but the easiest is to use the **Shrink to Fit** option. Shrink to Fit does just what it sounds like; it shrinks the text to fit on the first page. This option also works on a document with more than two pages, the text is just shrunk to the next to the last page. Follow these steps to use Shrink to Fit:

1. Choose **Print Preview** from the **File** menu.

2. Click the **Shrink to Fit** button in the toolbar (see the following figure). This will compress the lines on the previous page to allow all the lines to fit.

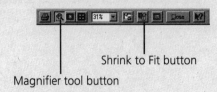

Shrink to Fit button

Magnifier tool button

3. Use the **Magnifier** tool to make sure you are happy with the appearance of the shrunken lines. If you're not, select **Undo** from the **Edit** menu to return your document to regular size.

39: Word won't let me delete the blank line at the end of my paragraphs.

If you like to have a blank line separating your paragraphs, Word makes it easy by allowing you to set the spacing before or after the paragraphs. If you decide you don't like the blank line, you can reset the spacing. Follow these steps to change the spacing:

1. Highlight the paragraph(s) for which you want to change the spacing.

2. Choose **Paragraph** from the **Format** menu.

3. In the Paragraph dialog box, click the **Indents and Spacing** tab (see the following figure).

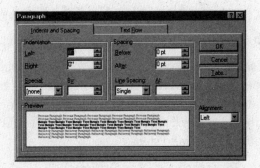

4. In the **Spacing** section, you can either add space before or after the paragraph using the **Before** or **After** boxes. The spacing is given in point size. If you're using a 10-point font, 5 points would be half a line, 10 points would be a whole line. To eliminate the spacing, set these values to zero.

5. Click **OK**.

40: When I tried to move one item in a numbered list, the text moved but the number didn't.

To move the number along with the text, you have to include the paragraph mark with the selection. To be sure that you have selected the paragraph mark, click the **Show/Hide** button on the toolbar to make the paragraph marks visible. Select the paragraph mark along with your text, and the number or bullet will move with the text.

41: After I changed the font, it keeps changing back to the default.

Word will revert back to whatever font is default for the template you used to create your document. One way to change the font throughout your document is to wait until you have typed the whole document and then select it by pressing **Ctrl+A**. Now change the font. If you always want this font to be used in this template, follow these steps to change the default font:

1. Choose **Font** from the **Format** menu.

2. In the Font dialog box, click the **Font** tab.

3. Choose the desired font and click the **Default** button. A message box will open asking if you are sure you want to change the default font. Remember, this will change the default font in all documents you have created using this template. If you are sure you want to change the default font, click **Yes**.

42: When I change the font or formatting, nothing happens.

If the new font did not display correctly, Word is probably in draft mode. Word runs the fastest in draft mode, but none of the formatting appears. All of the fonts will look the same also. If you bold or italicize the text, it will show up on the screen underlined. The document will still print correctly, but you will have a hard time seeing what your document will look like. To turn off draft mode, follow these steps:

1. From the **Tools** menu, choose **Options**.

2. In the Options dialog box, click the **View** tab.

3. In the **Show** section, remove the check mark from the **Draft Font** check box.

4. Click **OK**.

43: I can't get text to wrap around an embedded object.

To get text to wrap around an object, you must enclose the object in a frame. A frame is simply an invisible box that encloses your object. Follow these steps to enclose your object in a frame:

1. Click the object to select it.

2. Choose **Frame** from the **Insert** menu. If you're not in Page Layout view, Word will ask you if you want to switch to Page Layout view. Click **Yes** because you cannot see the frame and formatting in one of the other views.

Word inserts the frame around the object. If the text still doesn't wrap around the object, follow these steps to change the format of the frame:

1. Click the object to select it.
2. Choose **Frame** from the **Format** menu.
3. In the **Text Wrapping** section of the Frame dialog box, click **Around**.
4. Click **OK**.

44: When I changed the font in one of my styles, the font changed in another style, too.

If you change the font in a base style, the font will change in all styles that are based on that style. A *base style* is a style in which other styles are dependent. If you want to make a style independent (it won't change when you change another style), follow these steps:

1. From the **Format** menu, choose **Style**.
2. In the **Styles** box, click the style you want to make independent.
3. Click the **Modify** button.
4. In the Modify Style dialog box, choose **(no style)** from the drop-down list in the **Based On** box.
5. Click **OK** and **Close**. The style will no longer be dependent on another style.

Field Problems

45: A field in my document does not display the correct result.

Your field needs to be updated. Click the field and press **F9** to update it. If the field did not update, it may be locked. Press **Ctrl+Shift+F11** to unlock the field, and press **F9** again to update it.

46: I inserted a field using the bracket {} characters, but the field doesn't work.

When you are creating a field, you cannot type in the bracket {} characters from the keyboard. To let Word know that you are creating a field, press **Ctrl+F9** to insert empty field brackets. If the brackets do not appear, press **Alt+F9** to turn on the display of field codes. Now type the desired field between the brackets.

47: When I try to change my field, Word just beeps at me.

Don't you hate it when your computer beeps at you for no apparent reason. Wouldn't it be nice if it just told you what was wrong? You may be in overtype mode. Word is just beeping at you to keep you from overwriting the field brackets. Press the **Insert** key to turn overtype mode off. Another possibility is that the field is locked. Press **Ctrl+Shift+F11** to unlock the field.

48: I created an index, but {INDEX} appears on the screen instead of the index.

If you see **{INDEX}** instead of your index, or **{TOC}** instead of your table of contents, Word is displaying the field codes. *Field codes* are the underlying codes that make up your indexes and table of contents. To display the index or table of contents instead of the field codes, follow these steps:

1. From the **Tools** menu, choose **Options**.

2. In the Options dialog box, click the **View** tab.

3. In the **Show** section, remove the check mark from the **Field Codes** check box.

4. Click **OK**. The index or table of contents will appear properly.

Macro Problems

49: I can't select text when I'm recording a macro.

You can use your mouse to select menu commands or click toolbars, but you can't perform any mouse functions in the document while you are recording your macro. If you need to select text, hold down the **Shift** key and use the arrow keys on the keyboard to select the desired text. You will also have to use the arrow keys to move the selection bar throughout the document. See "Select Text" on page 92 for more information on selecting text and navigating with the keyboard.

50: I made some mistakes when I recorded a macro. Now the mistakes are repeated every time I run the macro.

It's easy to make some mistakes while you're recording a macro (especially if it is a fairly long macro). There are two things you can do here. You can either record the macro again (not recommended if the macro is long) or you can edit the macro. Follow these steps to edit the macro:

1. Choose **Macro** from the **Tools** menu.

2. In the Macro dialog box, click the macro that you need to change and click the **Edit** button.

3. Edit the mistakes from the macro. See "Edit a Macro" on page 304 for more information on editing macros.

4. When you finish editing the macro, choose **Close** from the **File** menu. Word will ask you if you want to save the changes to the macro. Click the **Yes** button.

51: I stopped recording the macro before I was finished. Do I have to record it all over again?

Fortunately, Word doesn't make you waste all the time you spent recording your macro. If you accidentally stopped recording before you were finished, or you just want to add some commands to the macro, it's easy to record them, but you can only record one command at a time. Follow these steps to add commands to a macro:

1. From the **Tools** menu, choose **Macro**.

2. In the Macro dialog box, select the name of the macro you want to add to from the list under **Macro Name** and click the **Edit** button.

3. Position the insertion point where you want to add the new command.

4. Choose your document from the **Window** menu to switch back to your document.

5. Position the insertion point where you want to begin recording the next step of the macro.

6. From the Macro toolbar, click the **Record Next Command** button.

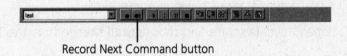

Record Next Command button

52: The macro I recorded is not available after I restarted Word.

You spent all that time recording your macro, and now you can't use it. Either you forgot to save the macro before you closed Word, or you saved it to a different template. To make sure that you save the macro, choose **Save All** from the **File** menu after you record it. Word will ask you if you want to save changes to the template; click **Yes**. If you saved the macro to a different template, open a document that is based on that template. The macro should be available. Remember in the future to save your macros to the NORMAL template. Macros saved in the NORMAL template will be available for all documents.

Mail Merge Problems

53: When I open my document, Word tells me it can't find the data source.

You will get this error message when you open a mail merge document, and Word cannot find the file that contains data for the merge. In the error message dialog box there will be three buttons, **Find Data Source**, **Options**, and **Cancel**. If you have moved the document that contains the data, click the **Find Data Source** button. The Open Data Source dialog box will open to help you locate the file.

If you are finished with the mail merge and would like to restore the document to a normal Word document, instead of clicking the Find Data Source button, follow these steps:

1. Click the **Options** button.

2. In the Options dialog box, click the **Remove All Merge Info** button. Your document will open as a normal Word document.

54: When I try to open the main document, Word tells me that the data source is a main document.

You have accidentally turned your data source into a main document. Word cannot use a main document as a data source, that's why you got the error message. You probably had the data source open in the active window when you started mail merge. To remove main document status from your data source, follow these steps:

1. Open the data source and choose **Mail Merge** from the **Tools** menu.

2. In step 1 of the Mail Merge Helper dialog box, click the **Create** button.

3. Choose **Restore to Normal Word Document** from the drop-down list.

4. Word will warn you that the file will no longer be a main document. Click **Yes** to continue.

5. Click the **Close** button. Your main document will now open normally.

55: When I print my mail merge document, the merge fields are printed instead of the data.

Word is set up to print field codes. You need to change the options to prevent the field codes from printing. Follow these steps:

1. From the **Tools** menu, choose **Options**.

2. In the Options dialog box, click the **Print** tab.

3. In the **Include with Document** section, remove the check mark from the **Field Codes** check box.

4. Click **OK**.

5. From the main document, click the **Merge to Printer** button on the Mail Merge toolbar to print the document.

Merge to Printer button

56: I changed the size of my envelopes. Now the mail merge does not print correctly.

Word is not smart enough to know when you change the size of your envelopes, so you have to let it know. You may also have to change the settings if you change printers. Follow these steps to change the settings for your envelopes:

1. Choose **Envelopes and Labels** from the **Tools** menu.

2. In the Envelope Options dialog box, choose the correct size envelope from the drop-down list in the **Envelope Size** box.

3. Click **OK**.

57: When I merge my data, there are blank lines between some of the data.

Usually, you would not want blank lines to show up in names or addresses if the field was empty. These extra fields make room for long addresses, but you don't need them to be printed if they're empty. Follow these steps to turn off display of the blank lines:

1. Open the main document and click the **Mail Merge** button on the Mail Merge toolbar.

Mail merge button

2. In the Merge dialog box, click the radio button next to **Don't print blank lines when data fields are empty**.

3. Click the **Merge** button to continue with the mail merge.

Problems with Proofing Tools

58: Some of the words in my document are underlined with wavy lines.

These wavy lines indicate a misspelled word. Word automatically checks the spelling of your document in the background as you work. If you click the word with the right mouse button, a list of suggested corrections will appear. Click one of the suggestions to correct the word. Or you can click **Add** to add the word to the custom dictionary, or click **Ignore All** to ignore this word throughout the document. If you find the automatic spell checking distracting, you can turn it off. Follow these steps:

1. Choose **Options** from the **Tools** menu.

2. In the Options dialog box, click the **Spelling** tab.

3. In the Automatic Spell Checking area, Remove the check mark from the **Automatic Spell Checking** check box.

4. Click **OK**.

If you want Word to check spelling in the background, but you don't want to see the red, wavy lines, check the **Hide Spelling Errors in Current Document** check box in step 3. When you are ready to see your mistakes, simply remove the check mark from the check box.

59: Word changes my text after I type it.

You are witnessing the results of *AutoCorrect*. AutoCorrect is a feature in Word that senses when you incorrectly spell a word and changes the word to the correct spelling. You can also add common mistakes to the list of words to be corrected. Follow these steps to edit which mistakes are automatically corrected:

1. Select **AutoCorrect** from the **Tools** menu.

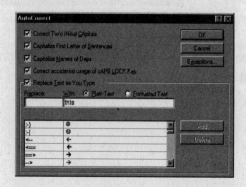

2. Enter the misspelled word in the **Replace** box.

3. Enter the correct spelling of the word in the **With** box.

4. Click the radio button next to **Formatted Text** if you want the replaced word to be formatted as it is in the **With** box.

5. Click the **Add** button to include it in your list.

6. Repeat steps 2 through 5 for any other words you want to add.

7. When you finish making changes, click **OK** to close the dialog box.

> If you don't like the AutoCorrect feature at all, you can turn it off by clearing the **Replace Text as You Type** check box in the AutoCorrect dialog box.

60: During spell check, I tried to add a word to the custom dictionary but the Add button was not available.

The **Add** option is not available because Word doesn't know where your *custom dictionary* is. The custom dictionary is a file that Word stores the words in when you add them to the dictionary. Follow these steps to let Word know where the custom dictionary is:

1. Choose **Options** from the **Tools** menu.

2. In the Options dialog box, click the **Spelling** tab and click the **Custom Dictionaries** button.

3. Check the **CUSTOM.DIC** check box in the **Custom Dictionaries** box.

4. Click **OK**; then click **OK** again to close the dialog boxes. The next time you use the spelling checker, the Add option will be available.

61: I added a word to the custom dictionary, but Word still thinks it is misspelled.

You may have added the word to a custom dictionary that is not open. Word allows you to have more than one custom dictionary. This is useful if you want to use one custom dictionary for certain types of documents, and a different custom dictionary for other documents. You can tell which custom dictionaries are open by choosing **Spelling** from the **Tools** menu and dropping down the list in the **Add Words To** box. If your custom dictionary is not listed, you need to open it. Follow these steps:

1. From the Spelling dialog box, click the **Options** button.

2. In the Options dialog box, click the **Custom Dictionaries** button.

3. In the Custom Dictionaries dialog box, check the check box next to the desired custom dictionary. If the custom dictionary is not listed, click the **Add** button and search for the dictionary.

4. Click **OK**; then click **OK** again to bring you back to the Spelling dialog box. Word will search all open custom dictionaries when it spell checks your document. Be sure to select the appropriate custom dictionary in the **Add Words To** box so Word will store added words in the dictionary that you want them in.

62: I have measurements in my document, and Word thinks they're all misspelled.

It can be very time consuming to click **Ignore** or **Add** to get through a long document with a lot of measurements in it. Fortunately, Word gives you a way to ignore all the words with numbers in them. Follow these steps to change the option:

1. From the **Tools** menu, choose **Options**.

2. In the Options dialog box, click the **Spelling** tab.

3. In the **Ignore** section, check the **Words with Numbers** check box.

4. Click **OK**.

63: I accidentally added a misspelled word to the custom dictionary.

This can be a dangerous problem because every time you misspell the word again, Word will think it's spelled correctly. To prevent this from happening, you need to edit your custom dictionary to delete the incorrectly spelled word. You can edit the dictionary as a Word document. Follow these steps to open your custom dictionary:

1. Choose **Options** from the **Tools** menu.

2. Click the **Spelling** tab in the Options dialog box, and click the **Custom Dictionaries** button.

3. In the Custom Dictionaries dialog box, click the check box next to the name of your custom dictionary (it is usually called CUSTOM.DIC) to check it. Click the **Edit** button.

4. A message box will open telling you that Word will disable automatic spell checking when you edit the dictionary. Click **OK** to continue.

5. Your custom dictionary will open in Word. You will see a single column of words. Scroll through the dictionary until you find the word that you incorrectly added to the list. Highlight the word and type in the correct spelling (or press the **Delete** key to erase it). If there are other words that you do not want in the dictionary, go ahead and delete them, too.

6. When you finish editing the dictionary, choose **Close** from the **File** menu. Word will ask you if you want to save the changes. Click **OK** to save the dictionary. Word will tell you that the document contains formatting that cannot be saved in text format. Click the **Yes** button. Word will then tell you that your dictionary is a Text Only document. Click the **Text Only** button to save the dictionary in Text Only format.

7. Since automatic spell checking was disabled automatically in step 4, you will need to manually turn it back on. Choose **Options** from the **Tools** menu. Click the **Spelling** tab, and check the check box next to **Automatic Spell Checking**. Click **OK** to close the Options dialog box.

64: I've looked up several meanings in the Thesaurus, and I can't remember what the original word was.

Click the drop-down list in the **Looked Up** section of the Thesaurus dialog box. The word you started with is always at the top of the list.

65: When I ran the grammar checker, it didn't find any errors.

You probably have exceptional grammar skills. Or maybe, your document do not have any punctuation. If you have a list of phrases that do not have periods or other ending punctuation marks, Word will not perform a grammar check. Another possibility is that the document was formatted with no proofing. Follow these steps to check:

1. Highlight the document.

2. Choose **Language** from the **Tools** menu.

3. If **(no proofing)** is selected in the Language dialog box, select the desired language (for example, **English (US)**). If you want this language to be the default for your document, click the **Default** button.

4. Click **OK** and run the grammar checker again. It should find any grammar errors in the document.

66: When I use the grammar checker, it stops on spelling errors.

By default, the grammar checker will check the spelling of the document while it is checking the grammar. This saves you time because you don't have to use two steps to check the spelling and the grammar. If you normally check the spelling before you run the grammar checker, or Word has checked the spelling in the background, it will waste your time to have to go through the spelling check again. Follow these steps to turn off spell checking during grammar checking:

1. From the **Tools** menu, choose **Options**.

2. In the Options dialog box, click the **Grammar** tab.

3. Remove the check mark from the **Check Spelling** check box and click **OK**.

67: When I tried to use one of the proofing tools, Word told me it wasn't installed.

Not all of the proofing tools are installed in a typical installation. You will have to manually install the proofing tools that you need. Follow these steps:

1. From the **Start** menu, point to **Settings** and click **Control Panel**.

2. Double-click the **Add/Remove Programs** icon.

3. In the Add/Remove Programs Properties dialog box, click **Microsoft Word 7.0** and click the **Add/Remove** button.

4. Click the **Add/Remove** button in the Setup dialog box.

5. In the **Options** box, click **Proofing Tools** and click the **Change Option** button.

6. Check the desired check boxes in the **Options** box and click **OK**.

7. Click the **Continue** button.

8. When setup is finished, click **OK**.

Object Linking and Embedding Problems

68: When I double-click a linked object, I get an error message telling me it cannot edit.

Whenever you double-click a linked object, the *source* application should open to edit the object (the source application is the one that created the object). If the source application doesn't open when you double-click the object, check the following:

- If the source application is open, close any open dialog boxes.

- Close all other open applications to make sure you have enough memory to open the source application.

- If you are on a network, check that someone else doesn't have the linked object open.

- Make sure that the source application hasn't been removed from your hard drive.

69: I want to edit an embedded object in a document that a coworker gave me, but I don't have the source application on my computer.

The source application is the one that was used to create the embedded object. If you don't have the application on your computer to edit the object, you may be able to convert the file into a format you can edit. Follow these steps to convert the object:

1. Click the object to select it.

2. From the **Edit** menu, point to *file type* **Object** (for example, **Bitmap Image Object**), and click **Convert**.

3. In the Convert dialog box, click the desired format to which to convert the object.

4. Click **OK**.

If you are unable to find a format to convert to, you will have to give the file back to your coworker to edit.

70: When I embedded an object into Word, the object appeared as an icon.

One possibility is that you embedded a sound or video object. They are always embedded as icons. Another possibility is that you had **Display as Icon** checked when you embedded the object. If you have a large object that you don't need to appear all the time in your document, it could be useful to display it as an icon. When you double-click the icon, the source application will open to display the object. If you would rather display the object instead of the icon, follow these steps:

1. Click the icon to select it.

2. From the **Edit** menu, point to *file type* **Object** (for example, **Bitmap Image Object**), and click **Convert.**

3. In the Convert dialog box, Remove the check mark from the **Display as Icon** check box.

4. Click **OK** to close the dialog box. The object will now appear in your worksheet.

71: When I copy data from another application into Word, it doesn't update automatically when I edit it in the other application.

You probably used the Copy and Paste commands to copy the data from the other application. This will not create a *link* between the applications. When an object is linked to Word, it will update automatically when you edit it in the other application. To link your data to Word, follow these steps:

1. Open the document in Word and move the insertion point where you want the data inserted.

2. If you want to insert data from a file that is already created, choose **Object** from the **Insert** menu and click the **Create from File** tab.

3. Enter the name and folder of the file in the **File Name** box (if you don't remember where it is, click the **Browse** button). Be sure to check the **Link to File** check box.

4. Click **OK**. This will establish the link between the two files. Any changes that you make to the data in the other application will be reflected in the Word document.

If you would rather link only part of a file, follow these steps:

1. Select the desired data in the other application and choose **Copy** from the **Edit** menu.

2. Open Word and bring up the document that you want to link the data to. Move the insertion bar to the desired location in your document and choose **Paste Special** from the **Edit** menu.

3. When the Paste Special dialog box appears, choose the desired format from the **As** box and click **Paste Link**.

4. Click **OK**, and the selected data from the other application will be linked to your Word document.

72: The link used to work correctly, but now it doesn't.

Somehow the link between the files has been broken. This could have happened if you re-named the source file or moved it to a different folder. You can try to relink the files by doing the following:

1. Choose **Links** from the **Edit** menu.

2. In the Links dialog box, click the link you are having trouble with in the **Source File** box.

3. Click the **Change Source** button, and choose the name and folder where the linked file is located.

4. Click the **Open** button.

5. Click the **Update Now** button to update the link. If the link is still not updated, you'll have to delete the data from your document and insert it again using the techniques in the previous problem.

73: After I inserted an object, it took up too much room in my document.

If you need to adjust the size of an embedded object, Word makes it easy. Click the object and you will see some sizing handles surrounding the object. Click and drag a sizing handle to change the size. Drag a sizing handle on one of the sides to change the width of the object. Drag a sizing handle on the top or the bottom to change the height of the object. If you drag one of the corner sizing handles, it will change the height and the width.

File Problems

74: I accidentally deleted a file. Is it gone forever?

You're in luck. When Windows 95 deletes a file, it isn't removed from the disk, it's just moved to the Recycle Bin. The Recycle Bin will hold your deleted files for awhile until it gets full and then will permanently delete the oldest files. If you just deleted the file from **My Computer** or **Explorer**, choose **Undo Delete** from the **Edit** menu. If you have already closed My Computer or Explorer, or you have deleted some other files after the one you want to recover, follow these steps:

1. Double-click the **Recycle Bin** icon on the desktop. A window appears.

2. Click the file that you want to recover. You may need to scroll down the list if it has been awhile since you deleted it. You can select multiple files by holding down **Ctrl** as you select files.

3. From the **File** menu, click **Restore**.

4. When you finish restoring files, click the **Close** button. Word restores your files to their original locations.

75: I can't find the file I want to open in the Open dialog box.

You probably saved the file in another folder than the one Word uses for the default. The easiest way to find your file is to use the built-in file finder in the Open dialog box. Follow these steps:

1. From the **File** menu, choose **Open**. The Open dialog box appears (see following figure).

2. If you remember the file name, type it in the **File name** box in the **Open** dialog box. If you don't remember the name, leave it blank.

3. If you want Word to search all of the folders on the drive, click the **Commands and Settings** button and click **Search Subfolders**. Word will search the drive and list all of the Word files that it finds.

4. Click the file you want to open, and click the **Open** button.

76: A coworker gave me a document created in Word for DOS, but when I open it there are a lot of funny characters on the screen.

Word did not convert your Word for DOS file correctly. The Word for DOS converter is not installed by default. You can install this converter along with a bunch of others by following these steps:

1. Close all open applications, including Word.

2. From the **Start** menu, point to **Settings**, and click **Control Panel**.

3. Double-click the **Add/Remove Programs icon** and click the **Install/Uninstall** tab.

4. Click **Microsoft Word** 7.0 from the list of programs, and click the **Add/Remove** button.

5. Click the **Add/Remove** button in the Setup dialog box.

6. In the **Options** box, click **Converters and Filters**, and click the **Change Option** button.

7. In the **Options** box, click **Converters**, and click the **Change Option** button.

8. Check the check box next to **Word for DOS 3.0-6.0 Converter** in the **Options** box and click **OK**.

9. Click **OK** again and click **Continue**.

10. When Setup finishes, click **OK**.

77: The wizard I want is not available when I try to open a new document.

It's not obvious where Word keeps the wizards when you are opening a new document. They do not all appear when you choose **New** from the **File** menu. Try clicking through all the tabs in the New dialog box. Each tab has a different set of templates and wizards.

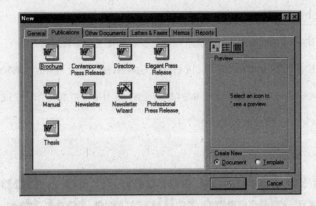

If you still can't find the wizard you are looking for, it may not have been installed when you installed Word. In a typical installation, not all of the wizards are installed. Follow these steps to install more wizards:

1. Close all your open applications.

2. From the **Start** menu, point to **Settings** and click **Control Panel**.

3. Double-click the **Add/Remove Programs** icon.

4. In the Add/Remove Programs Properties dialog box, click **Microsoft Word 7.0**, and click the **Add/Remove** button.

5. Click the **Add/Remove** button in the Setup dialog box.

6. In the **Options** box, click on **Wizards**, **Templates**, and **Letters**, and click the **Change Option** button.

7. Check the check boxes next to the desired templates in the **Options** box, and click the **OK** button.

8. Click the **Continue** button.

9. When Setup is finished, click **OK**.

78: When I try to save my document, I get a message telling me that the file is read-only.

This document was saved with the **Read-Only Recommended** option. Read-only means that you can look at the document, but you won't be able to save any changes that you make to it. If you need to keep the changes, choose **Save As** from the **File** menu and save the document under a different name or in another folder. Another option is to close the document and open it again. When Word asks if you want to open the document as Read-only, click the **No** button. You can now edit the document normally.

79: My documents keep getting saved to the wrong folder.

If you don't change the folder when you originally save a document, Word stores the document in a default folder. If you would rather save the files to a different folder by default, follow these steps:

1. From the **Tools** menu, choose **Options.**

2. In the Options dialog box, click the **File Locations** tab.

3. In the **File Types** box, click **Documents** and click the **Modify** button.

4. Choose the folder you want to use as the default and click **OK.**

5. Click the **Close** button.

80: I tried to save my document to a floppy disk, but got an error message telling me that the device is write-protected.

All floppy disks can be write-protected. When a disk is write-protected, it keeps you or someone else from accidentally deleting or changing files on that disk. It is a good idea to write-protect floppies when you have important data on them. You can unprotect the disk if you want to add data to it. Follow this procedure depending on the size of the floppy disk.

- For a 3 1/2-inch floppy disk, turn the disk to the back side. There is a square piece of plastic in the upper left corner of the disk that you can move to cover or uncover a square hole. If the square hole is visible, the disk is write-protected. If the plastic piece covers the hole, the disk is not write-protected. Use your fingernail or the end of a pen to move the piece of plastic to the desired location.

- For a 5 1/4-inch floppy disk, there is a notch on the right edge of the disk about an inch from the top. To write-protect these disks, get a piece of tape and cover the notch (packages of disks come with pieces of tape for this purpose). To unprotect the disk, simply remove the tape.

81: When I try to open a Word for Macintosh document I have on floppy disk, Word tells me that I don't have access to the folder.

The disk that contains your file is probably formatted for Macintosh. Windows-based computers cannot read Macintosh formatted disks. Take a Windows formatted disk over to your Macintosh and tell it to save the file in MS-DOS format. If you don't have access to a Macintosh, there are some applications on the market that allow you to read Macintosh formatted disks. If you're sure the disk was formatted in MS-DOS format, but you still get the error, you probably have a defective disk. You will have to copy the file again using a different disk.

Printing Problems

82: I can't print because the print option is unavailable.

All these great features in Word are practically useless if you can't print the document. You probably don't have a printer installed in Windows. To install your printer, do the following:

1. From the **Start** menu, point to **Settings** and click **Printers**.

2. Double-click the **Add Printer** icon.

3. The Add Printer Wizard will open to help you add your printer. Choose your printer from the list of **Manufacturers** and **Printers**. If you have a disk from your printer manufacturer, click the **Have Disk** button. After you have chosen your printer, click the **Next** button.

4. Choose the port that you want to use with this printer. Most printers connect to the parallel port (LPT1). Click the **Next** button.

5. Type a name for the printer and click **Yes** if you want to use this printer as the default printer. If this is the only printer you have, this is the obvious choice. Click the **Next** button.

6. Click **Yes** to print a test page and click the **Finish** button. It is a good idea to print the test page to see if your printer will work correctly.

7. A dialog box will appear asking if your test page printed correctly. If it did, click the **Yes** button and you are finished setting up your printer. If it didn't print correctly, click the **No** button. Windows will bring up the Help menu to aid in troubleshooting the problem. Check to make sure the cable is attached to the computer and the printer. Also, make sure that the printer is on, on-line, and loaded with paper.

83: When I try to print my document, my modem starts dialing.

The wrong printer has been selected. Word is trying to fax your document instead of printing it. Follow these steps to change the printer:

1. Choose **Print** from the **File** menu.

2. In the Print dialog box, select your printer from the drop-down list in the **Name** box.

3. Click **OK** to print your document.

84: Word numbers the first page when I print the document.

For most types of documents, you don't want the first page numbered. When you add page numbers to a document, Word numbers the first page by default. Fortunately, there is an easy way to suppress the page number on the first page. Follow these steps:

1. Choose **Page Numbers** from the **Insert** menu.

2. In the Page Numbers dialog box remove the check mark from the **Show Number on First Page** check box.

3. Click **OK** to close the dialog box.

85: A blank page always prints after certain documents print.

While this isn't a huge problem, it can be annoying. After all, you wouldn't want to be caught wasting paper. You probably have some blank lines at the bottom of your document. To look for the blank lines, click the **Show/Hide** button in the toolbar. If you see one or more para- graph marks on blank lines at the end of your document, highlight and delete them. You can see if this fixed your problem by choosing **Print Preview** from the **File** menu and scrolling to the last page to see if it is blank.

Show/Hide button

86: When I print my document, it is in reverse order.

Your printer controls the order that your pages print. It can be time consuming to have to reorder all your pages every time you print a document, so Word has given you a way to fix the problem. Follow these steps to change the print order:

1. From the **Tools** menu choose **Options**.

2. In the Options dialog box, click the **Print** tab.

3. Click the **Reverse Print Order** check box and change it from what it was (remove the check mark if it's checked; check it if it's not).

4. Click **OK**.

87: My table gridlines do not print.

By default, table gridlines don't print. Some tables can be difficult to read without the gridlines, so there is a way to get them to print. To print the gridlines, follow these steps:

1. Select the table (click somewhere in the table, and then press **Alt+5** on the numeric keypad with Num Lock off).

2. Choose the **Borders and Shading** option in the **Format** menu.

3. In the Table Borders and Shading dialog box, click the **Borders** tab.

4. Click **Grid** in the **Presets** box. If you want, you can change the thickness and style of the lines in the **Style** box.

5. Click **OK**.

88: My fonts look great on the screen, but they look terrible when I print my document.

Your printer probably doesn't support the font you have chosen. Check your printer documentation to see what fonts are supported with your printer and use one of those. Another alternative is to use a *TrueType* font. Windows 95 includes some TrueType fonts, and they print well on virtually all printers. If you want to check which TrueType fonts are available, simply drop down the font list on the Formatting toolbar (or choose **Font** from the **Format** menu). The TrueType fonts have double "T"s (**TT**) next to them.

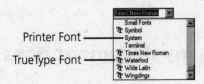

89: When I print a document with embedded graphics or drawing objects, the resolution is too low.

The resolution is how many dots per inch the printer will use to print your graphics. The higher the resolution, the better it looks, but it will also take longer to print. To change the resolution, do the following:

1. Choose **Print** from the **File** menu.

2. In the Print dialog box, click the **Properties** button.

3. Click the **Graphics** tab and drop-down the list in the **Resolution** box. The list shows all of the resolutions supported by your printer. Click the highest one.

4. Click **OK**; then click **OK** again to print your document.

90: The header and footer look fine in Print Preview, but they won't print.

The header and footer are set too close to the edge of the page. Most printers cannot print all the way to the edge, so you need to adjust the location of the header and footer. Check your printer documentation to see how close to the top and bottom of the page the printer can print. Follow these steps to change the header and footer spacing:

1. From the **File** menu, choose **Page Setup**.

2. In the Page Setup dialog box, click the **Margins** tab.

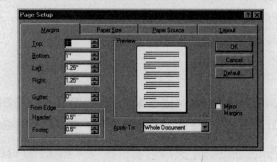

3. In the **From Edge** section, increase the distance in the **Header** and **Footer** boxes to match where your printer can print.

4. Click **OK**.

5. Print your document. If the header and footer still don't print, increase the distances in step three and try again.

91: The date field in my document does not update when it prints.

The date that is printing is the date that was current when you inserted the field in your document. To update the field to the correct date, highlight the field and press **F9**. If you want your fields to be updated automatically when you print, follow these steps:

1. Choose **Options** from the **Tools** menu.

2. In the Options dialog box, click the **Print** tab.

3. Under **Printing Options**, check the **Update Fields** check box.

4. Click **OK**.

92: When I print my document, the embedded drawing object doesn't print.

The option to print the embedded drawing object is turned off. If you just had the drawing in your document for reference, you wouldn't need it to print. Since this obviously isn't the case, follow these steps to turn the option back on:

1. Choose **Options** from the **Tools** menu.

2. In the Options dialog box, click the **Print** tab.

3. In the **Include with Document** section, check the **Drawing Objects** check box.

4. Click **OK**.

Miscellaneous Problems

93: When I first opened Word after installation, I closed the What's New opening screen before I read it.

The What's New screen only appears the first time you open Word. It does have some interesting overviews of the new features. Follow these steps to open it again:

1. Choose **Answer Wizard** from the **Help** menu.

2. In the Help Topics dialog box, type in **what's new** in the first dialog box and click the **Search** button.

3. From the list of topics under **Tell Me About**, select **What's new in ... Microsoft Word 95**.

4. Click the **Display** button to open the What's New screen.

94: I have to keep stopping my work because Word is automatically saving my document.

If you've used computers for awhile, you've probably had an experience where something goes wrong and you end up losing half a day's work. If you've had an experience like that, or know someone who has, you are probably in the habit of frequently saving your files as you work on them. If this is the case, you really don't need the AutoSave feature, and it can be annoying because you have to stop what you are doing every time Word saves your document for you. If, however, you are not in the habit of frequently saving your work, you should leave this option on. It could save you valuable time if you have a power surge. If you are convinced that you don't need AutoSave, follow these steps to turn it off:

1. From the **Tools** menu, choose **Options**.

2. In the Options dialog box, click the **Save** tab.

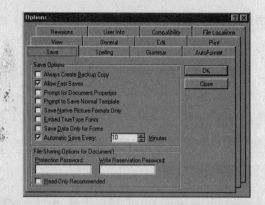

3. Remove the check mark from the **Automatic Save** check box to turn off AutoSave. For a compromise, you can leave AutoSave on and increase the time between saves. Just increase the time next to the **Automatic Save** option.

4. Click **OK** to accept the changes and return to your document.

95: I want to add page numbers to my document, but Page Numbers is unavailable in the Insert menu.

You are in Outline view. You cannot add page numbers in Outline view, so choose Normal or Page Layout view by clicking on the **Normal View** or the **Page Layout View** button in the lower left corner next to the horizontal scroll bar (or choose **Normal** or **Page Layout** from the **View** menu).

96: I just created a cool WordArt image, but now I can't get out of WordArt.

Just click somewhere outside of the WordArt image to get back to your document. To open WordArt again, double-click the WordArt image.

97: The page numbers are not correct in my table of contents.

If you make a lot of changes to your document, it could change the numbering of the pages. You may also need to hide hidden text if you have it displayed. Click the **Show/Hide** button on the Standard toolbar to hide the hidden text. Now, click somewhere in your table of contents and press **F9** to update the table.

98: The vertical scroll bar is not displayed; how can I see the rest of my document?

You could use the arrow keys or the **Page Up** and **Page Down** keys to page though your document, or you could turn the scroll bar back on. In Word, it is possible to turn off either of the scroll bars. Follow these steps to turn them back on:

1. Choose **Options** from the **Tools** menu.

2. In the Options dialog box, click the **View** tab.

3. In the **Window** section, check the **Vertical Scroll Bar** check box (if the horizontal scroll bar is off, you can check the **Horizontal Scroll Bar** check box, too).

4. Click **OK**.

99: When I insert an object, a figure number is added automatically.

AutoCaption is turned on for the object you inserted. This can be a very handy feature if you are writing a report that requires figure numbering. However, if you don't need the figure numbering, it is a waste of time. Follow these steps to turn off AutoCaption:

1. From the **Insert** menu, choose **Caption**.

2. In the Caption dialog box, click the **AutoCaption** button.

3. Remove the check mark from the check boxes next to the objects that you don't want captions for.

4. Click **OK**.

100: I deleted the text of a footnote, but the number is still in the document.

Deleting the footnote text will not remove the reference mark from the document. To remove the reference mark, just highlight the number and press **Delete**. An easier way to delete a footnote is to simply delete the reference mark. The text will be deleted automatically.

101: When I mail my document I want to add a routing slip, but the Add Routing Slip option is not available.

The **Add Routing Slip** option is available from the **File** menu when MS Mail is installed on your computer. This option allows you to mail your Word document to several addressees and attach a routing slip to the document. Unfortunately, Mail is not set up properly on your computer. You probably need to reinstall it. Contact your system administrator for instructions.

PART 4

Handy References

Part 4 provides reference information about Word for Windows 95 toolbars and dialog boxes. Use this part of the book to learn about buttons on commonly used toolbars, options in the dialog boxes that you'll use most often, and Word key combinations.

What You Will Find in This Part

HANDY REFERENCE

I n this part, you'll find everything you need to be able to use Word for Windows 95 without stopping every five minutes to check something in Help. And instead of confusing techno-talk, you'll find easy-to-understand lists, tables, and other handy references such as the basic toolbars, commands in various dialog boxes and what they do, and a table of shortcut keys and key combinations.

Standard Toolbar

Use the Standard toolbar to perform the most-often-used commands, from opening a new document to printing, from cutting, copying, and pasting to opening Microsoft Drawing.

The following list describes the buttons and drop-down lists on the Standard toolbar, presents the equivalent commands and shortcut keys, and refers you to How To's in which you can learn more:

New   Opens a new document. The equivalent shortcut key combination is **Ctrl+N**. The **File New** command opens the New dialog box from which you can open a new document. See "Create a New Document" on page 46.

Open   Opens an existing document. The equivalent command is **File Open**; the shortcut key combination is **Ctrl+O**. See "Open a Document" on page 79.

Save   Saves the current document using its present name and location. The equivalent command is **File Save**; the shortcut key combination is **Ctrl+S**. See "Save a Document" on page 73.

Print   Prints the current document using the present printing defaults. The equivalent command is **File Print** and clicking **OK**; the shortcut key combination is **Ctrl+P** and clicking **OK**. See "Print a Document" on page 69.

Print Preview   Shows the current document as it will print. The equivalent command is **File Print Preview**. See "View Text as It Will Print" on page 67.

Spelling   Checks the spelling of the current document or selection. The equivalent command is **Tools Spelling**; the shortcut key is **F7**. See "Check Your Spelling" on page 118.

Cut   Removes the current selection to the Windows Clipboard. The equivalent command is **Edit Cut**; the shortcut key combination is **Ctrl+X**. See "Move Text" on page 99.

Copy   Copies the current selection to the Windows Clipboard. The equivalent command is **Edit Copy**; the shortcut key combination is **Ctrl+C**. See "Copy Text" on page 103.

Paste   Pastes the current contents of the Windows Clipboard to the place in which the insertion point is located. The equivalent command is **Edit Paste**; the shortcut key combination is **Ctrl+V**. See "Move Text" on page 99 and "Copy Text" on page 103.

Format Painter   Selects the character formats of the current selection and applies them to the next characters selected. There is no equivalent command. See "Add Emphasis to Selected Text" on page 170.

Undo   Click to undo the most recent action, if allowed, or if you click the downward-pointing arrow, opens a drop-down list, from which you can undo one or more most recent actions. The equivalent command is **Edit Undo**; the shortcut key combination is **Ctrl+Z**. See "Undo and Redo Actions" on page 105.

Redo   Repeats the most recent action, if allowed, or if you click the downward-pointing arrow, opens a drop-down list, from which you can repeat one or more most recent actions. The equivalent command is **Edit Redo**; the shortcut key combination is **Ctrl+Y**. See "Undo and Redo Actions" on page 105.

 AutoFormat   Automatically formats the current document using predefined formats. The equivalent command is **Format AutoFormat**. See "Use Automatic Styles (AutoFormat)" on page 194.

 Insert Address   Inserts a name and address into the current document. There is no equivalent command.

 Insert Table   Inserts a table at the current location of the insertion point. The equivalent command is **Table Insert Table**. See "Create a Table" on page 202.

 Insert Microsoft Excel Worksheet   Inserts a Microsoft Excel worksheet at the current location of the insertion point. The equivalent command is **Insert Object**; then select **Microsoft Excel Worksheet**.

 Columns   Defines a multicolumn document or section of the current document. The equivalent command is **Format Columns**. See "Add Multiple Columns to a Document" on page 165.

 Drawing   Starts Word's Microsoft Drawing feature. The equivalent command is **View Toolbars**; then check the **Drawing** check box. See "Start and Exit Microsoft Drawing" on page 273 and "Draw a Picture with Microsoft Drawing Tools" on page 274.

 Show/Hide   Shows or hides all nonprinting symbols in a document. The equivalent command is **Tools Options**; then click on **All** in the **View** category of the Options dialog box, and click **OK**. See "Change View Options" on page 65.

 Zoom Control   Increases or decreases the size of the current document on-screen. Either type a percentage or choose from the drop-down list. The equivalent command is **View Zoom**. See "Magnify or Reduce Your View of a Document" on page 63.

 TipWizard   Displays the TipWizard toolbar. There are two equivalent commands: **Tools Options**, click the **General** tab, and check the **TipWizard Active** check box; **View Toolbars** and check the **Tip Wizard** check box.

 Help   Starts Word's context-sensitive Help facility. The equivalent shortcut is right-clicking an element or clicking the question mark box in a dialog box. See "Get Help in Word" on page 39.

Formatting Toolbar

The Formatting toolbar is the center of commonly used formatting commands, for both paragraphs and characters.

The following list describes the buttons and drop-down lists on the Formatting toolbar, presents the equivalent commands and shortcut keys, and refers you to How To's in which you can learn more:

 **Style**   Applies a style, a predefined set of formats, to one or more selected paragraphs. The equivalent command is **Format Style**.

 **Font**   Chooses a font for selected text. The equivalent command is **Format Font**. See "Change Fonts and Font Sizes" on page 182.

 Font Size   Chooses a point size for selected text. The equivalent command is **Format Font**. Shortcut keys for decreasing and increasing font size one point at a time are Ctrl+[and Ctrl+], respectively. See "Change Fonts and Font Sizes" on page 182.

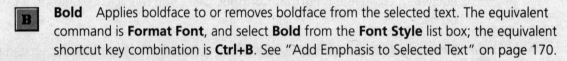 **Bold**   Applies boldface to or removes boldface from the selected text. The equivalent command is **Format Font**, and select **Bold** from the **Font Style** list box; the equivalent shortcut key combination is **Ctrl+B**. See "Add Emphasis to Selected Text" on page 170.

Italic   Italicizes or removes italics from the selected text. The equivalent command is **Format Font**, and select **Italic** from the **Font Style** list box; the equivalent shortcut key combination is **Ctrl+I**. See "Add Emphasis to Selected Text" on page 170.

Underline   Underlines or removes an underline from the selected text. The equivalent command is **Format Font**, and select a type of underline from the **Underline** drop-down list; the equivalent shortcut key combination is **Ctrl+U**. See "Add Emphasis to Selected Text" on page 170.

Highlight   Highlights or removes the highlight from the selected text. Click on the downward-pointing arrow to select a highlight color. There is no equivalent command.

Align Left   Aligns the selected paragraphs against the left margin. The equivalent command is **Format Paragraph**, and select **Left** from the **Alignment** drop-down list; the shortcut key combination is **Ctrl+L**. See "Format Pages and Paragraphs" on page 141.

Center   Centers the selected paragraphs between the left and right margin. The equivalent command is **Format Paragraph**, and select **Centered** from the **Alignment** drop-down list; the shortcut key combination is **Ctrl+E**. See "Format Pages and Paragraphs" on page 141.

Align Right   Aligns the selected paragraphs against the right margin. The equivalent command is **Format Paragraph**, and select **Right** from the **Alignment** drop-down list; the shortcut key combination is **Ctrl+R**. See "Format Pages and Paragraphs" on page 141.

Justify Aligns the selected paragraphs with both the left and right margins. The equivalent command is **Format Paragraph**, and select **Justified** from the **Alignment** drop-down list; the shortcut key combination is **Ctrl+J**. See "Format Pages and Paragraphs" on page 141.

Numbering Creates a numbered list from the selected paragraphs. The equivalent command is **Format Bullets and Numbering**; click on the **Numbered** tab and select a format. See "Create Bulleted and Numbered Lists" on page 190.

Bullets Creates a bulleted list from the selected paragraphs. The equivalent command is **Format Bullets and Numbering**; click on the **Numbered** tab and select a bullet type. See "Create Bulleted and Numbered Lists" on page 190.

Decrease Indent Moves the selected indented paragraphs toward the left margin. The equivalent command is **Format Paragraph**; then decrease the value in the **Left** text/list box. The equivalent shortcut key combination is **Ctrl+Shift+M**. See "Format Pages and Paragraphs" on page 141.

Increase Indent Moves the selected paragraphs away from the right margin. The equivalent command is **Format Paragraph**; then increase the value in the **Left** text/list box. The equivalent shortcut key combination is **Ctrl+M**. See "Format Pages and Paragraphs" on page 141.

Borders Turns on or off the Borders toolbar. The equivalent command is **View Toolbars**; then click on the **Borders** check box. See "Add Lines and Shading" on page 257.

Drawing Toolbar

Use the Drawing toolbar to draw and edit pictures in Word documents. To learn how to use the Drawing toolbar, see "Start and Exit Microsoft Drawing" on page 273, "Draw a Picture with Microsoft Drawing Tools" on page 274, and "Edit a Microsoft Drawing Picture" on page 281.

The following list describes the buttons on the Drawing toolbar:

Line Draws a line in the document window.

Rectangle Draws a rectangle or square in the document window.

Ellipse Draws an ellipse or circle in the document window.

Arc Draws an arc in the document window.

Freeform Draws a freeform object in the document window.

Text Box Draws a box in which you can type text in the document window.

Callout Inserts a callout in the document window.

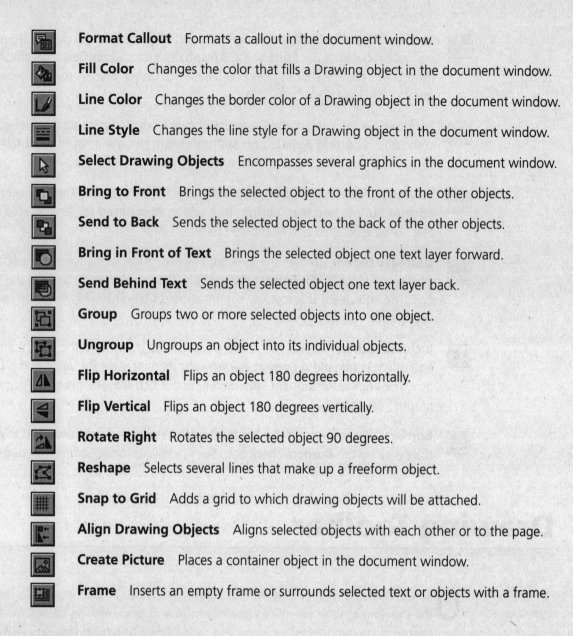

Format Callout   Formats a callout in the document window.

Fill Color   Changes the color that fills a Drawing object in the document window.

Line Color   Changes the border color of a Drawing object in the document window.

Line Style   Changes the line style for a Drawing object in the document window.

Select Drawing Objects   Encompasses several graphics in the document window.

Bring to Front   Brings the selected object to the front of the other objects.

Send to Back   Sends the selected object to the back of the other objects.

Bring in Front of Text   Brings the selected object one text layer forward.

Send Behind Text   Sends the selected object one text layer back.

Group   Groups two or more selected objects into one object.

Ungroup   Ungroups an object into its individual objects.

Flip Horizontal   Flips an object 180 degrees horizontally.

Flip Vertical   Flips an object 180 degrees vertically.

Rotate Right   Rotates the selected object 90 degrees.

Reshape   Selects several lines that make up a freeform object.

Snap to Grid   Adds a grid to which drawing objects will be attached.

Align Drawing Objects   Aligns selected objects with each other or to the page.

Create Picture   Places a container object in the document window.

Frame   Inserts an empty frame or surrounds selected text or objects with a frame.

TipWizard Toolbar

Word uses the TipWizard toolbar to present Tip of the Day information and instructions about working in Word efficiently.

The following list describes the default buttons on the TipWizard toolbar:

TipWizard Box   In this list box, view the current tip. Click on the arrows at the right side of the box to review other tips from this Word session.

Show Me   Reads more about the current tip or the TipWizard.

Header and Footer Toolbar

Use the Header and Footer toolbar to insert and manipulate headers and footers in Word documents. To learn how to use the Header and Footer toolbar, see "Add a Header and Footer" on page 368 and "Insert Page Numbers" on page 150.

The following list describes the buttons on the Header and Footer toolbar:

Switch Between Header and Footer   Jumps between the header and footer.

Show Previous   Jumps to the header or footer in the previous section if there is one.

Show Next   Jumps to the next header or footer in the next section if there is one.

Same As Previous   Changes the current header or footer to the header or footer in the previous section.

Page Numbers   Inserts a page number field in this header or footer.

Date   Inserts a today's date field in this header or footer.

Time   Inserts a current time field in this header or footer.

Page Setup   Opens the Page Setup dialog box in which you can specify headers and footers on the first page, odd pages, or even pages.

Show/Hide Document Text   Hides document text while you are working on headers or footers that overlay your document. An example is a watermark graphic.

Close   Inserts a page number field in this header or footer.

Options Dialog Box—View Tab

Use the Option dialog box for the View tab to change the way you view the Word document window: the characters and elements that you can see. To learn how to use this dialog box, see "Change View Options" on page 65.

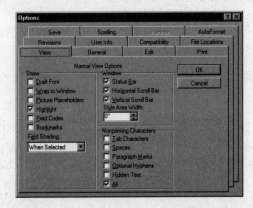
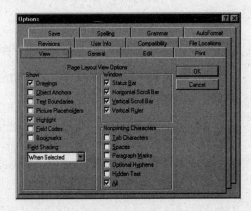

The following list describes the options of the Options dialog box for the View tab and whether you are available for Normal view, Page Layout view, or both:

Drawings   Displays drawings that you have created with the Word drawing tools. This is a Page Layout view option. A checked check box is the default.

Object Anchors   Displays object anchors, which tie an object to a particular paragraph. This is a Page Layout view option. A cleared check box is the default.

Text Boundaries   Mark margins, columns, objects, and frames with dotted borders. This is a Page Layout view option. A cleared check box is the default.

Draft Font   Hides some of the formatting, speeding up changes in the screen display. This is a Normal view option. A cleared check box is the default.

Wrap to Window   Keep most of the text within the document window. This is a Normal view option. A cleared check box is the default.

Picture Placeholders   Temporarily replaces graphics with boxes. This is a Normal view and Page Layout view option. A cleared check box is the default.

Highlight   Shows and prints the highlighted text in a document. This is a Normal view and Page Layout view option. A checked check box is the default.

Field Codes   Displays *field codes*, which represent information (such as today's date or the page number) that is inserted into a document. This is a Normal view and Page Layout view option. A cleared check box is the default.

Bookmarks   Displays *bookmarks*, marking important places in a document to which you can easily return. This is a Normal view and Page Layout view option. A cleared check box is the default.

Field Shading   Selects the shading of fields: Never shaded, Always shaded, or shaded only when you select a field. This is a Normal view and Page Layout view option, when Selected is the default.

Status Bar   Displays the status bar. This is a Normal view and Page Layout view option. A checked check box is the default.

Horizontal Scroll Bar   Displays the horizontal scroll bar. This is a Normal view and Page Layout view option. A checked check box is the default.

Vertical Scroll Bar   Displays the vertical scroll bar. This is a Normal view and Page Layout view option. A checked check box is the default.

Vertical Ruler   Displays the vertical ruler. This is a Page Layout view option. A checked check box is the default.

Style Area Width   Select or type a number from 0 to 3.31" to define the width of an area next to the left margin in which you want to display the names of styles from Word templates. Word templates are beyond the scope of this book. This is a Normal view option. 0" is the default.

Nonprinting Characters Displays nonprinting characters when you click on the **Show/ Hide** button. These options are available when you are in both Normal view and Page Layout view. A checked box for the All option is the default. For all other options, a cleared check box is the default.

- **Tab Characters** Displays tab characters (« . »).

- **Spaces** Displays symbols for spaces (·).

- **Paragraph Marks** Displays paragraph marks (¶).

- **Optional Hyphens** Displays hyphens (–) that indicate the location of a break in a word that runs from the end of one line to the beginning of the next.

- **Hidden Text** Displays all hidden text along with the dotted underline that indicates hidden text.

- **All** Displays all nonprinting characters.

Options Dialog Box—General Category

Use the Option dialog box for the General category to change miscellaneous Word options—from your computer beeping when errors occur to the number of documents displayed at the bottom of the File menu. To learn how to use this dialog box, see "Change General Options" on page 132.

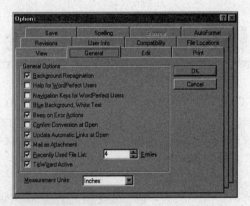

The following list describes the options of the Options dialog box for the General category:

Background Repagination Repaginates, sets the number of lines of text on each page, as you edit a document. A checked check box is the default.

Help for WordPerfect Users Provides Word counterpart commands and keystrokes for those familiar with WordPerfect 5.1 for DOS but not with Word. When you check this check box, the WPH indicator in the status bar is bold. A cleared check box is the default.

Navigation Keys for WordPerfect Users   Converts the functions of the End, Esc, Home, PgDn, and PgUp keys to their WordPerfect functions. A cleared check box is the default.

Blue Background, White Text   Shows white text on a blue background rather than black text on a white background. A cleared check box is the default.

Beep on Error Actions   Word beeps when you make a mistake. A checked check box is the default.

Confirm Conversion at Open   Automatically uses Word's converter to load a document created using another program. A cleared check box is the default.

Update Automatic Links at Open   Automatically updates text and graphics created in and linked to other programs. A checked check box is the default.

Mail as Attachment   Automatically attaches documents to e-mail messages being sent from your computer. A checked check box is the default.

Recently Used File List   Displays at the bottom of the File menu a list of the most recently opened documents. Type the number of entries (from 1 to 9) in the **Entries** text box/option box. A checked check box and 4 **Entries** is the default.

TipWizard Active   Word displays the TipWizard toolbar whenever you are performing an action for which Word has a tip. A checked check box is the default.

Measurement Units   Open this drop-down list box to select the unit of measure (inches, centimeters, points, or picas) for all Word documents. Inches is the default value.

Options Dialog Box—Edit Category

Use the Option dialog box for the Edit category to specify editing options from whether you can drag text from one location and drop it in another location to making insert or overtype the default typing mode. To learn how to use this dialog box, see "Customize Editing Options" on page 135.

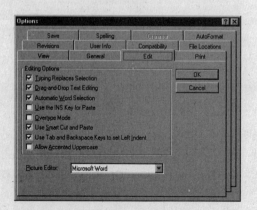

The following list describes the options of the Options dialog box for the Edit category:

Typing Replaces Selection   Word automatically deletes a selection when you start typing. A checked check box is the default.

Drag-and-Drop Text Editing   Enables you to drag selected text and drop it in a new location. A checked check box is the default.

Automatic Word Selection   Enables you to select entire words and a single space following when you click on a word. A checked check box is the default.

Use the INS Key for Paste   Pastes a selection when you press the Ins key. A cleared check box is the default.

Overtype Mode   Replaces a character or space every time you type a character or enter a space. A cleared check box is the default. Note that when revision marks are turned on, Overtype mode is not available.

Use Smart Cut and Paste   Automatically removes excess spaces when you cut a selection and insert enough spaces when you paste a selection. A checked check box is the default.

Use Tab and Backspace Keys to set Left Indent   Sets or removes a left indentation whenever you press the **Tab** or **Backspace** key, respectively. A checked check box is the default.

Allow Accented Uppercase   Enables Word to prompt to insert accent marks for uppercase letters for documents formatted in French. A cleared check box is the default.

Picture Editor   Open the drop-down list to display the picture editor to be used in Word. Microsoft Word is the default.

Options Dialog Box—Print Category

Use the Option dialog box for the Print category to change the way Word prints documents. To learn how to use this dialog box, see "Print a Document" on page 69.

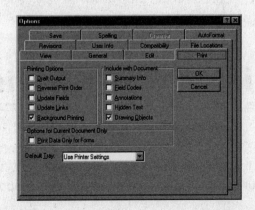

The following list describes the options of the Options dialog box for the Print category:

Draft Output   Prints documents in draft mode, with very little formatting. This can result in faster printing. A cleared check box is the default.

Reverse Print Order   Prints pages from the last to the first. If you need to shuffle printed pages after your printer completes a job, check this check box. A cleared check box is the default.

Update Fields   Updates all the fields (for example, updates a date field to today's date or inserts the correct page number if you have inserted several pages while editing) in documents before printing. A cleared check box is the default.

Update Links   Updates all the objects created in other applications and linked to a document before printing. A cleared check box is the default.

Background Printing   Print while you continue to work in Word; clear to make printing faster but interrupt your work time. A checked check box is the default.

Summary Info   Prints summary information (for example, your name, the document title, and keywords) about documents when you print. A cleared check box is the default.

Field Codes   Prints field codes instead of the results of the codes when printing. A cleared check box is the default.

Annotations   Prints annotations (notes you have inserted in a document) associated with documents after printing a document. A cleared check box is the default.

Hidden Text   Prints text you have hidden as well as the other text in documents. A cleared check box is the default.

Drawing Objects   Displays Microsoft Drawing objects inserted in documents. A checked check box is the default.

Print Data Only for Forms   Prints only the data in an online form (such as an application form or tax form in which you can see the labels, boxes, and lines that show where you type) and does not print the form itself—just for the current document. A cleared check box is the default.

Default Tray   Select from this drop-down list to specify the tray from which you will print. The options in this drop-down list vary depending on the default printer. Use Printer Settings is the default.

Options Dialog Box—Revisions Category

Use the Option dialog box for the Revisions category to specify how you handle revision marks for newly inserted and newly deleted text. If, typically, a group of people work on and edit your documents, revision options are very important.

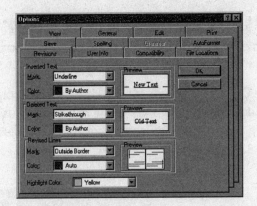

The following list describes the options of the Options dialog box for the Revisions category:

Inserted Text:

- **Mark**   From this drop-down list, select the way that newly inserted text will be marked in your documents.

- **Color**   From this drop-down list, select the color of newly inserted text in your documents. If you select **By Author** (the default), the color changes from computer to computer.

- **Preview**   In this sample box, see the way newly inserted text will look with the selected options.

Deleted Text:

- **Mark**   From this drop-down list, select the way that newly deleted text will be marked in your documents.

- **Color**   From this drop-down list, select the color of newly deleted text in your documents. If you select **By Author** (the default), the color changes from computer to computer.

- **Preview**   In this sample box, see the way newly deleted text will look with the selected options.

Revised Lines:

- **Mark**   From this drop-down list, select the location of vertical revision marks in your documents.

- **Color**   From this drop-down list, select the color of vertical revision marks in your documents.

- **Preview**   In this sample box, see the way vertical revision marks will look with the selected options.

- **Highlight Color**   From this drop-down list, select the color given to text applied using the **Highlight** button on the Formatting toolbar.

Options Dialog Box—User Info Category

Use the Option dialog box for the User Info category to specify how you are identified in Word documents. Word fills in the initial values using the information you provided when you installed the program. To learn more about this dialog box, see "Change User Information" on page 288.

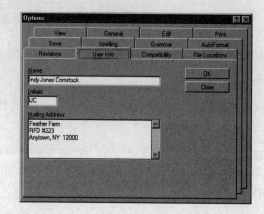

The following list describes the options of the Options dialog box for the User Info category:

Name   Type your name in this text box, or edit the name that the Word installation program automatically inserted here.

Initials   Type your initials in this text box, or edit the initials the Word installation program automatically inserted here.

Mailing Address   Type your return address in this text box, or edit the initials the Word installation program automatically inserted here. Word uses this address in the Envelopes and Labels dialog box.

Options Dialog Box—Compatibility Category

Use the Option dialog box for the Compatibility category to specify formatting for a document that you are converting to Word for Windows 95. You can convert formatting for older versions of Word for Windows, Word for DOS, Word for Mac, WordPerfect, and you can create custom options.

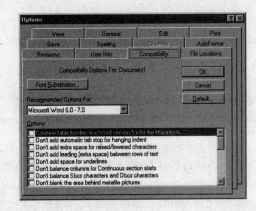

The following list describes the options of the Options dialog box for the Compatibility category:

Font Substitution   Opens a dialog box in which you can select fonts that you will use in place of fonts in the document being converted. When there aren't any fonts that need to be substituted, Word displays an information box stating that all fonts used in this document are available.

Recommended Options For   Open this drop-down list to choose the word processor in which the document was created.

Options   Check or clear these check boxes to customize formatting options for the document. The default condition of these check boxes varies depending on the **Recommended Options For** selection.

Default   Click on this button to specify that the checked or cleared options in the Options box become the default for conversion.

Options Dialog Box—File Locations Category

Use the Option dialog box for the File Locations category to specify the folders in which files and file types are automatically located on your computer when you save or open them.

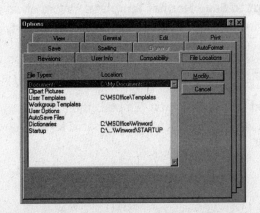

To change from the default folder to one of your own choice, select a file type and click the **Modify** button. In the Modify Location dialog box, click the desired folder and click **OK**.

Options Dialog Box—Save Category

Use the Option dialog box for the Save category to specify how Word documents are saved: whether backup copies are kept, the automatic save feature is turned on, and whether the current document is password-protected. For information about saving documents and using this dialog box, see "Save a Document" on page 73 and "Change Save Options" on page 76.

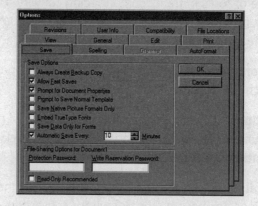

The following list describes the options of the Options dialog box for the Save category:

Always Create Backup Copy   Saves the new version of a document as well as the prior version. A cleared check box is the default.

Allow Fast Saves   Saves only the most recent changes rather than the entire document. A checked check box is the default.

Prompt for Document Properties   Automatically displays a dialog box in which you can type the document title, keywords, and so on, when you first save a document. A cleared check box is the default.

Prompt to Save Normal Template   Word always prompts you to save the Normal template, although you may not have changed styles. A cleared check box is the default.

Save Native Picture Formats Only   Saves imported pictures in the Windows format only rather than in their original formats, too. A cleared check box is the default.

Embed TrueType Fonts   Embeds the fonts that you have used in a document so that others viewing the document can see it as you formatted it. A cleared check box is the default.

Save Data Only for Forms   Saves each form in an online form (a form, such as an application form, in which you enter one record, which is similar to a database record) as one database record. A cleared check box is the default.

Automatic Save   When you check this check box and set a time interval, Word automatically saves the current document every few minutes as you work on it. This means that you'll have a current copy no older than the interval that you defined. A checked check box is the default.

File-Sharing Options for Document *n*   In this group, you can specify a read-only and write-protection password for the current document only. If you check the **Read-Only Recommended** check box, people who open the current document cannot save it under its current name.

Options Dialog Box—Spelling Category

U se the Option dialog box for the Spelling category to fine-tune spelling options: whether automatic spell checking is turned on, whether correctly spelled words are listed when an error is found, and whether certain words are ignored. In addition, you can define custom dictionaries starting in this dialog box. For information about the spell check and this dialog box, see "Check Your Spelling" on page 118, "Use a Custom Dictionary" on page 123, and "Change Spelling and Grammar Options" on page 137.

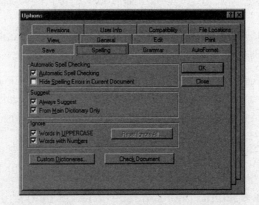

The following list describes the options of the Options dialog box for the Spelling category:

Automatic Spell Checking   Runs the spell checker as you edit a document. A checked check box is the default.

Hide Spelling Errors in Current Document   Hides the jagged red line that marks misspellings or words that are not in the main or active custom dictionaries. A cleared check box is the default.

Always Suggest   The spell checker displays a list of suggested words to replace a word that it identifies as misspelled. A checked check box is the default.

From Main Dictionary Only   Uses the main dictionary only as the source of suggested words; the spell checker does not access custom dictionaries. A cleared check box is the default.

Words in UPPERCASE   The spell checker ignores words in all uppercase letters; these types of words are more likely to be company or product names. A checked check box is the default.

Words with Numbers   The spell checker ignores words containing numbers; these types of words are more likely to be company or product names. A checked check box is the default.

Reset Ignore All   Clears the ignored words accumulated during the current spell check, thereby enabling Word to completely check future documents.

Custom Dictionaries   Opens a dialog box in which you can add, modify, and delete custom dictionaries.

Check Document   Reruns the spell checker for the current document, thereby rechecking your corrections and edits.

Options Dialog Box—Grammar Category

The following list describes the options of the Options dialog box for the Grammar category:

Use Grammar and Style Rules   Specifies the level, from Strictly (all rules) to For Casual Writing and three custom levels at which the grammar checker checks documents. Runs the spell checker as you edit a document. For Business Writing is the default.

Customize Settings   Opens a dialog box in which you can specify rules for grammar and style that the grammar checker applies when checking documents.

Check Spelling   Runs the spell checker before running the grammar checker. A checked check box is the default.

Show Readability Statistics   Displays a variety of statistics on how easy or difficult your document is to read.

Options Dialog Box—AutoFormat Category

Use the Option dialog box for the AutoFormat category to specify automatic formatting options. For information about AutoFormat, see "Use Automatic Styles (AutoFormat)" on page 194 and "Change Automatic Format Options" on page 197.

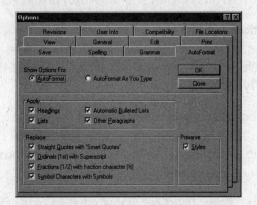

The following list describes the options of the Options dialog box for the AutoFormat category:

AutoFormat   Click this option button to see the options that Word will use when automatically formatting.

AutoFormat As You Type   Click this option button to see the options that Word will use to format when you type.

Headings   AutoFormat automatically formats up to nine levels of headings. A checked check box is the default. This option is available when you select the **AutoFormat** and **AutoFormat As You Type** option.

Lists   AutoFormat automatically formats numbered and bulleted list styles. A checked check box is the default. This option is available when you select the **AutoFormat** option.

Borders   AutoFormat automatically inserts borders as you type. A checked check box is the default. This option is available when you select the **AutoFormat As You Type** option.

Automatic Bulleted Lists   AutoFormat automatically changes list items to bulleted items. A checked check box is the default. This option is available when you select the **AutoFormat** and the **AutoFormat As You Type** options.

Automatic Numbered Lists   AutoFormat automatically changes list items to numbered items. A checked check box is the default. This option is available when you select the **AutoFormat As You Type** option.

Other Paragraphs AutoFormat automatically formats text that isn't headings in several ways: for example, body text. A checked check box is the default. This option is available when you select the **AutoFormat** option.

Straight Quotes with 'Smart Quotes' Automatically replaces straight quotes with typographically correct "curly" quotes. A checked check box is the default. This option is available when you select the **AutoFormat** and the **AutoFormat As You Type** options.

Ordinals with Superscript Automatically replaces ordinals (such as 1st and 2nd) with a superscript st or nd. A checked check box is the default. This option is available when you select the **AutoFormat** and the **AutoFormat As You Type** options.

Fractions with Fraction Character Automatically replaces fractions that you enter by typing separate numbers and characters with fraction symbols. A checked check box is the default. This option is available when you select the **AutoFormat** and the **AutoFormat As You Type** options.

Symbol Characters with Symbols Automatically replaces symbols that you have typed with special characters not on your keyboard. A checked check box is the default. This option is available when you select the **AutoFormat** and the **AutoFormat As You Type** options.

Styles Keeps the styles that you have already applied to the document and only formats text to which you have not applied styles. A checked check box is the default. This option is available when you select the **AutoFormat** option.

Print Dialog Box

Word for Windows 95 provides many printing options. You can print ranges of pages, all odd or even pages, an entire document, related material, or even to a file for later printing.

To print parts of a document, open the **File** menu and select the **Print** command, or press **Ctrl+Shift+F12** or **Ctrl+P**. Word opens a dialog box that offers a variety of options from which you can choose.

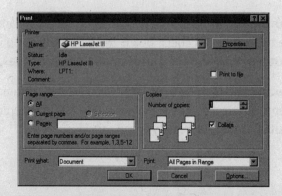

The Print dialog box offers the following options:

Name   Select a printer on which to print the document from this drop-down list. The name of the default printer is shown.

Status   Windows provides current status information about the selected printer.

Type   Windows provides the name of the selected printer and, sometimes, the version number of its *driver*, the software that operates the printer.

Where   Windows provides the name of the LPT or COM port or network connection to which the printer is attached via cables to your computer.

Comment   Windows displays printer information that you typed in the Properties dialog box for your printer.

Properties   Opens the Properties dialog box for the selected printer. In this dialog box, you can specify paper dimensions and graphics, fonts, and device options.

Print to File   Prints the selected file and its formats to a file. When you want to print the stored document, open the MS-DOS window and type **COPY *filename.ext* PRN/B** command, where ***filename.ext*** is the name and extension of the print file.

All   Prints the entire document. This is the default.

Pages   Specifies a range of pages to be printed (such as 1–5,7,9–50).

Selection   Prints the part of the document that you have selected.

Current Page   Prints the page on which the insertion point is located.

Number of Copies   In this text box, type the number of copies to be printed.

Collate   Check this check box to have the printer collate pages; that is, when printing multiple copies, it prints all the pages in one copy before printing the first page of the next copy. If this check box is unchecked, Word prints multiple copies of one page, multiple copies of the next page, and so on.

Print What   From this drop-down list, you can specify the document element to be printed: the document (the default), summary information, annotations, styles, AutoText entries, or key assignments for the document. Document is the default.

Print   You can print the entire document, all odd pages, or all even pages by selecting from this drop-down list.

Options   Click this button to open the Options dialog box—Print category.

Font Dialog Box

Word for Windows 95 provides many character formatting options. You can change the font, font style, and point size of selected text, and you can enhance a selection with effects and color.

To format selected characters, open the **Format** menu and select the **Font** command. Word opens a dialog box that offers a variety of options from which you can choose.

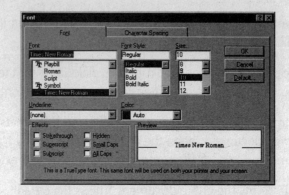

The following list describes the options in the two sections of the Font dialog box:

Default   Click this button to make the current selections in the dialog box the new default for this and all future Word documents.

Font:

- **Font**   Type or select a font in this text box/list box. The fonts appearing in the list box are those installed on your computer.

- **Font Style**   Type or select an enhancement for the selected text in this text box/list box. You can choose from Regular (no enhancement), Italic (italicized characters), Bold (boldface characters), or Bold Italic (italicized, bold characters).

- **Size**   Type or select a point size, font size, in this text box/list box. The sizes appearing in the list box are those applying to the selected font.

- **Underline**   From this drop-down list, select an underline type (none, Single, Words Only, Double, or Dotted) for the selected text.

- **Color**   From this drop-down list, select one of 17 colors. Auto, the default, represents black or the color that you have set in the Windows Control Panel.

- **Strikethrough**   Inserts a horizontal line through the center of the selected text.

- **Superscript**   Raises the selected text above the *baseline*, the imaginary horizontal line on which the body of each character in a line of text rests.

- **Subscript**   Lowers the selected text below the baseline.

- **Hidden**   Hides the selected text and indicates that it is hidden by underlining it with a dotted line.

- **Small Caps**   Changes the selected text to small uppercase.

- **All Caps**   Changes the selected text to standard uppercase.

- **Preview**   View the results of your selected options in this box. This allows you to fine-tune your options before clicking **OK**.

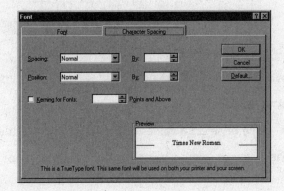

Character Spacing:

- **Spacing**   From this drop-down list, choose the distance between selected characters: Normal (the default), Expanded (more space between the characters), or Condensed (less space between the characters). To adjust the spacing further, type or select a value in the **By** option box. Valid values are from –1584 pt to 1584 pt.

- **Position**   From this drop-down list, choose the measurement of subscript (Lowered) or superscript (Raised) characters below or above the baseline, respectively. Valid values are from 0 to 1638 pt.

- **Kerning for Fonts**   Check this check box to automatically set kerning for characters of a particular point size or greater. In the **Points and Above** option box, select a value from 8 to 72.

- **Preview**   View the results of your selected options in this box. This allows you to fine-tune your options before clicking **OK**.

Paragraph Dialog Box

Word for Windows 95 provides many paragraph formatting options: from indentation and spacing to pagination control.

To format selected paragraphs, open the **Format** menu and select the **Paragraph** command. Word opens a dialog box that offers a variety of options from which you can choose.

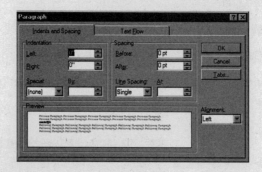

The following list describes the options in the two sections of the Paragraph dialog box:

Indents and Spacing:

- **Left**   Type or select a value for the left margin of the indentation in this text box/list box.

- **Right**   Type or select a value for the right margin of the indentation in this text box/list box.

- **Special**   From this drop-down list, select **First Line** for a first-line indent or **Hanging** for a hanging indent.

- **By**   Type or select the amount of indentation in this text box/list box. See the effect of the value in the **Preview** box.

- **Before**   Type or select the amount of space before the selected paragraphs. See the effect of the value in the **Preview** box.

- **After**   Type or select the amount of space after the selected paragraphs. See the effect of the value in the **Preview** box.

- **Line Spacing**   The measurement between the bottom of one line of text and the bottom of the next line, including the text and the white space between the lines of text. You can select from

  - **Single**, a single space (the default).

  - **1.5 Lines**, 1.5 times Single.

  - **Double**, twice the measurement of Single.

  - **At Least**, a minimum measurement typed into or selected from the **At** option box. (This option adjusts line spacing when it encounters a large character.)

  - **Exactly**, an exact measurement typed into or selected from the **At** option box.

  - **Multiple**, a percentage by which line spacing is increased or decreased.

- **At**   Select or type an exact measurement when you select At Least or Exactly from the Line Spacing drop-down list.

- **Preview**   View the results of your selected options in this box. This allows you to fine-tune your options before clicking **OK**.

- **Alignment**   From this drop-down list, select the paragraph alignment:
  - **Left** (aligned with the left margin and not aligned with the right margin).
  - **Centered** (aligned along the center point of the page).
  - **Right** (aligned with the right margin and not aligned with the left margin).
  - **Justified** (aligned with both the left margin and the right margin.)
- **Tabs**   Click this button to open the Tabs dialog box.

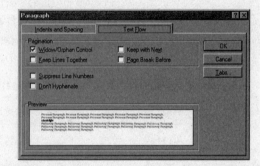

Text Flow:

- **Widow/Orphan Control**   Indicates that Word does not allow the first line of a paragraph to print on the bottom of a page or the last line of a paragraph to print on the top of the next page.

- **Keep Lines Together**   Forces Word to print a paragraph on one page to keep the paragraph together.

- **Keep with Next**   Keeps the current paragraph and the next paragraph together on the same page.

- **Page Break Before**   Inserts a hard page break before the current paragraph.

> Be very careful about selecting the Page Break Before option. If you select several paragraphs, Word will insert a page break in front of each, causing one page per selected paragraph.

- **Suppress Line Numbers**   Causes line numbers in a document with line numbers to be hidden.

- **Don't Hyphenate**   Suppresses automatic hyphenation from selected paragraphs. For this option to be active, automatic hyphenation must be turned on.

- **Tabs**   Opens the Tabs dialog box in which you can set or clear tab stops for the selected text.

- **Preview**   View the results of your selected options in this box. This allows you to fine-tune your options before clicking **OK**.

Word's Default Shortcut Keys and Key Combinations

The following table lists the default Word for Windows shortcut keys and key combinations, arranged by command. With each entry is a brief description.

Word's Default Shortcut Keys and Key Combinations

Command	Key Combination	Description
File Exit	Alt+F4	Exits Word
File New	Ctrl+N	Opens a new document window
File Open	Ctrl+O, Ctrl+F12, Alt+Ctrl+F2	Opens an existing document
File Print	Ctrl+P, Ctrl+Shift+F12	Prints the current document
File Print Preview	Ctrl+F2, Alt+Ctrl+I	Views the current document as it will print
File Save	Ctrl+S, Shift+F12, Alt+Shift+F2	Saves the current document using its current name and location; saves and names a new document
File Save As	F12	Saves the current document using a new name and/or location
Edit AutoText	F3, Alt+Ctrl+V	Enables you to insert often-used text and graphics into the document
n/a	Ctrl+Shift+F3	Inserts the contents of the *Spike*, which accumulates selections so that they can be inserted at one time
Edit Bookmark	Ctrl+Shift+F5	Inserts a bookmark to mark the current location of the insertion mark in a document
Edit Clear	Del	Permanently deletes the selected characters

Command	Key Combination	Description
Edit Copy	Ctrl+C, Ctrl+Ins	Copies the selection to the Clipboard
Edit Cut	Ctrl+X, Shift+Del	Removes the selection from its current location and places it in the Clipboard
Edit Find	Ctrl+F	Searches for a search string or formats
Edit Go To	Ctrl+G, F5	Goes to a page, section, line, or element of the current document
Edit Go To; click on Next	Alt+Ctrl+PgDn	Goes to the next page
Edit Go To; click on Previous	Alt+Ctrl+PgUp	Goes to the previous page
Edit Paste	Ctrl+V, Shift+Ins	Pastes the contents of the Clipboard at the current location of the insertion point
Edit Paste Special	Ctrl+Shift+V	Pastes the contents of the Clipboard as they are formatted
Edit Redo or Repeat	Ctrl+Y, F4, Alt+Enter	Repeats the last action, if allowed
Edit Replace	Ctrl+H	Searches for a search string or formats and optionally replaces with a replace string or formats
Edit Select All	Ctrl+A, Ctrl+Num 5	Selects the entire document
Edit Undo	Ctrl+Z, Alt+Backspace	Reverses the most recent action, if allowed
n/a	Ctrl+3, Ctrl+F11	Locks fields so that they cannot be updated
n/a	Shift+F4, Alt+Ctrl+Y	Searches for the next occurrence of the search string
n/a	Ctrl+F3	Cuts a selection to the Spike
n/a	Ctrl+6, Ctrl+Shift+F9	Unlinks fields that are linked
n/a	Ctrl+4, Ctrl+Shift+F11	Unlocks locked fields
View Normal	Alt+Ctrl+N	Changes to Normal View mode
View Outline	Alt+Ctrl+O	Changes to Outline View mode
View Outline; click Collapse button	Alt+Shift+Num	Collapses the outline by one level

(continues)

Command	Key Combination	Description
View Outline; click Demote button	Alt+Shift+Right	Demotes the selection by one heading level
View Outline; click Expand button	Alt+Shift+Num	Expands the outline by one level
View Outline; click Move Down button	Alt+Shift+Down	Moves the selection below the next heading
View Outline; click Move Up button	Alt+Shift+Up	Moves the selection below the previous heading
View Outline; click Promote button	Alt+Shift+Left	Makes the selection the next higher level of heading
View Outline; click Show First Line Only button	Alt+Shift+L	Displays the first line or all lines of each paragraph
View Outline; click Show All Headings	Alt+Shift+A	Shows all headings in the document
View Outline; click View Outlines: click on Show Heading 2 button	Alt+@	Shows level 1 and level 2 headings
View Outline; click Show Heading 3 button	Alt+#	Shows level 1, 2, and 3 headings
View Outline; click Show Heading 4 button	Alt+$	Shows level 1 to 4 headings
View Outline; click Show Heading 5 button	Alt+%	Shows level 1 to 5 headings
View Outline; click Show Heading 6 button	Alt+^	Shows level 1 to 6 headings

Command	Key Combination	Description
View Outline; click Show Heading 7 button	Alt+&	Shows level 1 to 7 headings
View Outline; click Show Heading 8 button	Alt+*	Shows level 1 to 8 headings
View Outline; click Show Heading 9 button	Alt+(	Shows level 1 to 9 headings
View Page Layout	Alt+Ctrl+P	Changes to Page Layout View mode
Insert Annotation	Alt+Ctrl+A	Inserts an annotation at the insertion point location
Insert Break; select Column Break	Ctrl+Shift+Enter	Inserts a column break at the insertion point location
Insert Break; select Page Break	Ctrl+Enter	Inserts a page break at the current insertion point location
Insert Date and Time; select a date	Alt+Shift+D	Inserts the date at the insertion point location
Insert Date and Time; select a time	Alt+Shift+T	Inserts the time at the insertion point location
Insert Footnote; select Endnote	Alt+Ctrl+E	Inserts an endnote at the end of the document
Insert Footnote; select Footnote	Alt+Ctrl+F	Inserts a footnote at the bottom of the current page
Insert Index and Tables; select Index	Alt+Shift+X	Inserts an index entry
Insert Index and Tables; select Table of Authorities; select Mark Citation	Alt+Shift+I	Inserts a citation in a table of authorities
Insert Index and Tables; select Table of Contents	Alt+Shift+O	Marks a table of contents entry
Insert Page Field	Alt+Shift+P	
Format AutoFormat	Ctrl+K	Automatically formats the selection

(continues)

Command	Key Combination	Description
Format Bullets and Numbering; Bulleted tab; select a bullet	Ctrl+Shift+L	Makes the selected paragraph a bulleted list
Format Change Case	Shift+F3	Cycles through upper- and lowercase combinations for the selected characters
Format Change Case; UPPERCASE	Ctrl+Shift+A	Converts the selection to all uppercase
Format Font	Ctrl+D	Opens the Font dialog box
Format Font	Ctrl+Shift+F	Highlights the Font drop-down list; the next click opens the Font dialog box
Format Font	Ctrl+Shift+P	Highlights the Font Size drop-down list; the next click opens the Font dialog box
Format Font; Bold or Regular	Ctrl+B, Ctrl+Shift+B	Applies or removes boldface from the selection
Format Font; select a higher size	Ctrl+]	Makes the selection one point size larger
Format Font; select a lower size	Ctrl+[	Makes the selection one point size smaller
Format Font; select Double Underline	Ctrl+Shift+D	Applies a double underline to the selected characters
Format Font; select Hidden	Ctrl+Shift+H	Hides the selected text
Format Font; select Italic or Regular	Ctrl+I, Ctrl+Shift+I	Applies or removes italics from the selection
Format Font; select Regular	Ctrl+Shift+N, Alt+Shift+Num 5	Removes formatting from the selection
Format Font; select Small Caps	Ctrl+Shift+K	Changes the case of the selection to small uppercase letters
Format Font; select Subscript	Ctrl+=	Applies subscript to the selection
Format Font; select Superscript	Ctrl++	Applies superscript to the selection
Format Font; select Symbol from the Font list box	Ctrl+Shift+Q;	Applies the Symbol font to the selection

Command	Key Combination	Description
Format Font; select Underline	Ctrl+U, Ctrl+Shift+U	Underlines the selected characters
Format Font; select Words Only	Ctrl+Shift+W	Underlines the selected words (not spaces)
Format Paragraph; add 5 to Left	Ctrl+M	Increases the left indent by 0.5-inch
Format Paragraph; Left	Ctrl+L	Aligns the selected paragraphs with the left margin
Format Paragraph; remove 5 from Left	Ctrl+Shift+M	Decreases the left indent by 0.5-inch
Format Paragraph; Right	Ctrl+R	Aligns the selected paragraphs with the right margin
Format Paragraph; select 1.5	Ctrl+5	Applies one-and-one-half spacing to the selection
Format Paragraph; select Centered	Ctrl+E	Centers the selected paragraphs between the left and right margins
Format Paragraph; select Double	Ctrl+2	Applies double-spacing to the selection
Format Paragraph; select Hanging	Ctrl+T	Applies a hanging indent to each selected paragraph
Format Paragraph; select Justify	Ctrl+J	Aligns the selected paragraphs with the left and right margins
Format Paragraph; select None	Ctrl+Shift+T	Removes a hanging indent from the selected paragraphs
Format Paragraph; select Single	Ctrl+1	Applies single-spacing to the selection
Format Style	Ctrl+Shift+S	Highlights the Style drop-down list; the next click opens the Style dialog box
Tools Spelling	F7	Runs the spell check
Tools Thesaurus	Shift+F7	Runs the thesaurus
Tools Options; check Field Codes in View category	Alt+F9	Views field codes rather than field results in a document
Help Microsoft Word Help Topics	F1	Opens the most recently viewed help window

(continues)

Command	Key Combination	Description
n/a	Shift+F1	Turns on the Help tool
Window; Split	Alt+Ctrl+S	Displays a document in two panes
Window; select a document	Ctrl+F6, Ctrl+Shift+F6	Activates another document window if more than one document is displayed on-screen

Index

G

H

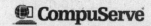

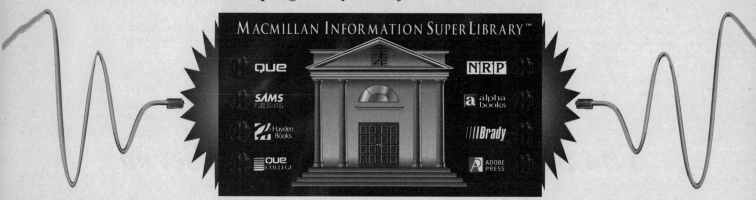

Complete and Return this Card
for a *FREE* Computer Book Catalog

Thank you for purchasing this book! You have purchased a superior computer book written expressly for your needs. To continue to provide the kind of up-to-date, pertinent coverage you've come to expect from us, we need to hear from you. Please take a minute to complete and return this self-addressed, postage-paid form. In return, we'll send you a free catalog of all our computer books on topics ranging from word processing to programming and the internet.

Mr. ☐   Mrs. ☐   Ms. ☐   Dr. ☐

Name (first) ☐☐☐☐☐☐☐☐☐☐☐☐ (M.I.) ☐ (last) ☐☐☐☐☐☐☐☐☐☐☐☐☐☐☐☐

Address ☐☐☐☐☐☐☐☐☐☐☐☐☐☐☐☐☐☐☐☐☐☐☐☐☐☐☐☐☐☐☐

☐☐☐☐☐☐☐☐☐☐☐☐☐☐☐☐☐☐☐☐☐☐☐☐☐☐☐☐☐☐☐

City ☐☐☐☐☐☐☐☐☐☐☐☐☐☐☐☐ State ☐☐ Zip ☐☐☐☐☐ ☐☐☐☐

Phone ☐☐☐ ☐☐☐ ☐☐☐☐ Fax ☐☐☐ ☐☐☐ ☐☐☐☐

Company Name ☐☐☐☐☐☐☐☐☐☐☐☐☐☐☐☐☐☐☐☐☐☐☐☐☐☐☐

E-mail address ☐☐☐☐☐☐☐☐☐☐☐☐☐☐☐☐☐☐☐☐☐☐☐☐☐☐☐

1. Please check at least (3) influencing factors for purchasing this book.

Front or back cover information on book .... ☐
Special approach to the content .... ☐
Completeness of content .... ☐
Author's reputation .... ☐
Publisher's reputation .... ☐
Book cover design or layout .... ☐
Index or table of contents of book .... ☐
Price of book .... ☐
Special effects, graphics, illustrations .... ☐
Other (Please specify): _____ ☐

2. How did you first learn about this book?

Saw in Macmillan Computer Publishing catalog .... ☐
Recommended by store personnel .... ☐
Saw the book on bookshelf at store .... ☐
Recommended by a friend .... ☐
Received advertisement in the mail .... ☐
Saw an advertisement in: _____ ☐
Read book review in: _____ ☐
Other (Please specify): _____ ☐

3. How many computer books have you purchased in the last six months?

This book only .... ☐   3 to 5 books .... ☐
2 books .... ☐   More than 5 .... ☐

4. Where did you purchase this book?

Bookstore .... ☐
Computer Store .... ☐
Consumer Electronics Store .... ☐
Department Store .... ☐
Office Club .... ☐
Warehouse Club .... ☐
Mail Order .... ☐
Direct from Publisher .... ☐
Internet site .... ☐
Other (Please specify): _____ ☐

5. How long have you been using a computer?

☐ Less than 6 months   ☐ 6 months to a year
☐ 1 to 3 years   ☐ More than 3 years

6. What is your level of experience with personal computers and with the subject of this book?

	With PCs	With subject of book
New	☐	☐
Casual	☐	☐
Accomplished	☐	☐
Expert	☐	☐

Source Code ISBN: 0-7897-0460-9

7. Which of the following best describes your job title?

Administrative Assistant .... ☐
Coordinator .... ☐
Manager/Supervisor .... ☐
Director .... ☐
Vice President .... ☐
President/CEO/COO .... ☐
Lawyer/Doctor/Medical Professional .... ☐
Teacher/Educator/Trainer .... ☐
Engineer/Technician .... ☐
Consultant .... ☐
Not employed/Student/Retired .... ☐
Other (Please specify): _____ ☐

8. Which of the following best describes the area of the company your job title falls under?

Accounting .... ☐
Engineering .... ☐
Manufacturing .... ☐
Operations .... ☐
Marketing .... ☐
Sales .... ☐
Other (Please specify): _____ ☐

9. What is your age?

Under 20 .... ☐
21-29 .... ☐
30-39 .... ☐
40-49 .... ☐
50-59 .... ☐
60-over .... ☐

10. Are you:

Male .... ☐
Female .... ☐

11. Which computer publications do you read regularly? (Please list)

_____
_____
_____
_____
_____
_____
_____
_____
_____
_____
_____

Comments: _____
_____
_____

Fold here and scotch-tape to mail.